More Windows® 95 Simplified®

IDG's 3-D Visual™ Series

IDG Books Worldwide, Inc.
An International Data Group Company
Foster City, CA • Indianapolis • Chicago • Southlake, TX

More Windows® 95 Simplified®

Published by
IDG Books Worldwide, Inc.
An International Data Group Company
919 E. Hillsdale Blvd., Suite 400
Foster City, CA 94404

Library of Congress Catalog Card No.: 96-075406

ISBN: 1-56884-689-4

Printed in the United States of America

10 9 8 7

Distributed in the United States by IDG Books Worldwide, Inc.

Distributed by Transworld Publishers Limited in the United Kingdom; by IDG Norge Books for Norway; by IDG Sweden Books for Sweden; by Woodslane Pty. Ltd. for Australia; by Woodslane Enterprises Ltd. for New Zealand; by Longman Singapore Publishers Ltd. for Singapore, Malaysia, Thailand, and Indonesia; by Simron Pty. Ltd. for South Africa; by Toppan Company Ltd. for Japan; by Distribuidora Cuspide for Argentina; by Livraria Cultura for Brazil; by Ediciencia S.A. for Ecuador; by Addison-Wesley Publishing Company for Korea; by Ediciones ZETA S.C.R. Ltda. for Peru; by WS Computer Publishing Corporation, Inc., for the Philippines; by Unalis Corporation for Taiwan; by Contemporanea de Ediciones for Venezuela; by Computer Book & Magazine Store for Puerto Rico; by Express Computer Distributors for the Caribbean and West Indies. Authorized Sales Agent: Anthony Rudkin Associates for the Middle East and North Africa.

For corporate orders, please call maranGraphics at 800-469-6616.
For general information on IDG Books Worldwide's books in the U.S., please call our Consumer Customer Service department at 800-762-2974.
For reseller information, including discounts and premium sales, please call our Reseller Customer Service department at 800-434-3422.
For information on where to purchase IDG Books Worldwide's books outside the U.S., please contact our International Sales department at 415-655-3200 or fax 415-655-3295.
For information on foreign language translations, please contact our Foreign & Subsidiary Rights department at 415-655-3021 or fax 415-655-3281.
For sales inquiries and special prices for bulk quantities, please contact our Sales department at 415-655-3200.
For information on using IDG Books Worldwide's books in the classroom or for ordering examination copies, please contact our Educational Sales department at 800-434-2086 or fax 817-251-8174.
For press review copies, author interviews, or other publicity information, please contact our Public Relations department at 415-655-3000 or fax 415-655-3299.
For authorization to photocopy items for corporate, personal, or educational use, please contact maranGraphics at 800-469-6616.

Trademark Acknowledgments

The animated characters are the copyright of maranGraphics, Inc.

U.S. Corporate Sales
Contact maranGraphics at (800) 469-6616 or Fax (905) 890-9434.

U.S. Trade Sales
Contact IDG Books at (800) 434-3422 or (415) 655-3000.

Welcome to the world of IDG Books Worldwide.

IDG Books Worldwide, Inc., is a subsidiary of International Data Group, the world's largest publisher of computer-related information and the leading global provider of information services on information technology. IDG was founded more than 25 years ago and now employs more than 8,500 people worldwide. IDG publishes more than 270 computer publications in over 75 countries (see listing below). More than 90 million people read one or more IDG publications each month.

Launched in 1990, IDG Books Worldwide is today the #1 publisher of best-selling computer books in the United States. We are proud to have received eight awards from the Computer Press Association in recognition of editorial excellence and three from Computer Currents' First Annual Readers' Choice Awards. Our best-selling ...For Dummies® series has more than 25 million copies in print with translations in 30 languages. IDG Books Worldwide, through a joint venture with IDG's Hi-Tech Beijing, became the first U.S. publisher to publish a computer book in the People's Republic of China. In record time, IDG Books Worldwide has become the first choice for millions of readers around the world who want to learn how to better manage their businesses.

Our mission is simple: Every one of our books is designed to bring extra value and skill-building instructions to the reader. Our books are written by experts who understand and care about our readers. The knowledge base of our editorial staff comes from years of experience in publishing, education, and journalism - experience which we use to produce books for the '90s. In short, we care about books, so we attract the best people. We devote special attention to details such as audience, interior design, use of icons, and illustrations. And because we use an efficient process of authoring, editing, and desktop publishing our books electronically, we can spend more time ensuring superior content and spend less time on the technicalities of making books.

You can count on our commitment to deliver high-quality books at competitive prices on topics you want to read about. At IDG Books Worldwide, we continue in the IDG tradition of delivering quality for more than 25 years. You'll find no better book on a subject than one from IDG Books Worldwide.

John Kilcullen
President and CEO
IDG Books Worldwide, Inc.

IDG Books Worldwide, Inc., is a subsidiary of International Data Group, the world's largest publisher of computer-related information and the leading global provider of information services on information technology. International Data Group publishes over 276 computer publications in over 75 countries. Ninety million people read one or more International Data Group publications each month. International Data Group's publications include: Argentina: Annuario de Informatica, Computerworld Argentina, PC World Argentina; Australia: Australian Macworld, Client/Server Journal, Computer Living, Computerworld, Computerworld 100, Digital News, IT Casebook, Network World, On-line World Australia, PC World, Publishing Essentials, Reseller, WebMaster; Austria: Computerwelt Osterreich, Networks Austria, PC Tip; Belarus: PC World Belarus; Belgium: Data News; Brazil: Annuário de Informática, Computerworld Brazil, Connections, Super Game Power, Macworld, PC Player, PC World Brazil, Publish Brazil, Reseller News; Bulgaria: Computerworld Bulgaria, Networkworld/Bulgaria, PC & MacWorld Bulgaria; Canada: CIO Canada, Client/Server World, ComputerWorld Canada, InfoCanada, Network World Canada; Chile: Computerworld Chile, PC World Chile; Colombia: Computerworld Colombia, PC World Colombia; Costa Rica: PC World Centro America; The Czech and Slovak Republics: Computerworld Czechoslovakia, Elektronika Czechoslovakia, Macworld Czech Republic, PC World Czechoslovakia; Denmark: Communications World, Computerworld Danmark, Macworld Danmark, PC Privat Danmark, PC World Danmark, PC World Danmark Supplements, TECH World; Dominican Republic: PC World Republica Dominicana; Ecuador: PC World Ecuador; Egypt: Computerworld Middle East, PC World Middle East; El Salvador: PC World Centro America; Finland: MikroPC, Tietoverkko, Tietoviikko; France: Distributique, Golden, Hebdo-Distributique, Info PC, Le Guide du Monde Informatique, Le Monde Informatique, Reseaux & Telecoms; Germany: Computer Partner, Computerwoche, Computerwoche Extra, Computerwoche Focus, I/M Information Management, Macwelt, PC Welt; Greece: GamePro, Multimedia World; Guatemala: PC World Centro America; Honduras: PC World Centro America; Hong Kong: Computerworld Hong Kong, PCWorld Hong Kong, Publish in Asia; Hungary: ABCD CD-ROM, Computerworld Szamitastechnika, PC & Mac World Hungary, PC-X Magazine; Iceland: Tolvuheimur/PC World Island; India: Information Systems Computerworld, PC World India, Publish in Asia; Indonesia: InfoKomputer PC World, Komputek Computerworld, Publish in Asia; Ireland: ComputerScope, PC Live!; Israel: People & Computers; Italy: Computerworld Italia, Computerworld Italia Special Editions, Macworld Italia, Networking Italia, PC Shopping, PC World Italia, PC World/Walt Disney; Japan: DTP World, HP Open World Japan, Macworld Japan, Nikkei Personal Computing, Open World Japan, OS/2 World Japan, SunWorld Japan, Windows World Japan; Kenya: East African Computer News; Korea: Hi-Tech Information/Computerworld, Macworld Korea, PC World Korea; Macedonia: PC World Macedonia; Malaysia: Computerworld Malaysia, PC World Malaysia, Publish in Asia; Mexico: Computerworld Mexico, Macworld, PC World Mexico; Myanmar: PC World Myanmar; Netherlands: Computer! Totaal, LAN Magazine, LanWorld Buyers Guide, Macworld, Net Magazine, Totaal! Beurskrant; New Zealand: Absolute Beginner's Guide, Computer Buyer, Computer Industry Directory, Computerworld New Zealand, MTB, Network World, PC World New Zealand; Nicaragua: PC World Centro America; Nigeria: PC World Nigeria; Norway: Computerworld Norge, Computerworld Privat (Datamagasinet), CW Rapport Norge, IDG's KURSGUIDE, Macworld Norge, Multimediaworld, PC World Ekspress, PC World Nettverk, PC World Norge, PC World's Produktguide, Windows World Spesial; Pakistan: Computerworld Pakistan, PC World Pakistan; Panama: PC World Panama; P. R. of China: China Computer Users, China Computerworld, China Infoworld, China Telecom World Weekly, Computer & Communication, Electronic Design China, Electronics Today, Electronics Weekly, Game Camp, Game Soft, Network World China, PC World China, Popular Computer Weekly, Software Weekly, Software World, Telecom World; Peru: Computerworld Peru, PC World Profesional Peru, PC World Peru; Poland: Computerworld Poland, Computerworld Special Report, Macworld, Networld, PC World Komputer; Philippines: Computerworld Philippines, PC World Philippines, Publish in Asia; Portugal: Cerebro/PC World, Computerworld/Correio Informático, Dealer World Portugal, Mac*In/PC*In, Multimedia World Portugal; Puerto Rico: PC World Puerto Rico; Romania: Computerworld Romania, PC World Romania, Telecom Romania; Russia: Computerworld Russia, Mir PK, Sety; Singapore: Computerworld Singapore, PC World Singapore, Publish in Asia; Slovenia: MONITOR; South Africa: Computing S.A., InfoWorld S.A., Network World S.A., Software World; Spain: Computerworld Espa-a, COMUNICACIONES WORLD, Dealer World, Macworld Espa-a, PC World Espa-a; Sweden: CAP&Design, Computer Sweden, Corporate Computing, MacWorld, Maxi Data, MikroDatorn, Nätverk & Kommunikation, PC/Aktiv, PC World, Windows World; Switzerland: Computerworld Schweiz, Macworld Schweiz, PCtip; Taiwan: Computerworld Taiwan, Macworld Taiwan, PC World Taiwan, Publish Taiwan, Windows World; Thailand: Thai Computerworld, Publish in Asia; Turkey: Computerworld Turkiye, MACWORLD Turkiye, PC WORLD Turkiye; Ukraine: Computerworld Kiev, Computers & Software, Multimedia World Ukraine, PC World Ukraine; United Kingdom: Acorn User, Amiga Action, Amiga Computing, Appletalk, Computing, GamePro, Macworld, Network News, Parents and Computers, PC Advisor, PC Home, PSX Pro UK, The WEB; United States: Cable in the Classroom, CD Review, CIO Magazine, Computerworld, Computerworld Client/Server Journal, Digital Video Magazine, DOS World, Federal Computer Week, GamePro, InfoWorld, I-Way, JavaWorld, Macworld, Multimedia World, Netscape World Online, Network World, PC Entertainment, PC World, Publish, SunWorld Online, SWATPro Magazine, Video Event, WebMaster; Uruguay: PC World Uruguay; Venezuela: Computerworld Venezuela, PC World Venezuela; and Vietnam: PC World Vietnam.

Every maranGraphics book represents the extraordinary vision and commitment of a unique family: the Maran family of Toronto, Canada.

Back Row (from left to right): *Sherry Maran, Rob Maran, Richard Maran, Maxine Maran, Jill Maran.*
Front Row (from left to right): *Judy Maran, Ruth Maran.*

Richard Maran is the company founder and its inspirational leader. He developed maranGraphics' proprietary communication technology called "visual grammar." This book is built on that technology—empowering readers with the easiest and quickest way to learn about computers.

Ruth Maran is the Author and Architect—a role Richard established that now bears Ruth's distinctive touch. She creates the words and visual structure that are the basis for the books.

Judy Maran is Senior Editor. She works with Ruth, Richard and the highly talented maranGraphics illustrators, designers and editors to transform Ruth's material into its final form.

Rob Maran is the Technical and Production Specialist. He makes sure the state-of-the-art technology used to create these books always performs as it should.

Sherry Maran manages the Reception, Order Desk and any number of areas that require immediate attention and a helping hand.

Jill Maran is a jack-of-all-trades and dynamo who fills in anywhere she's needed anytime she's back from university.

Maxine Maran is the Business Manager and family sage. She maintains order in the business and family—and keeps everything running smoothly.

Oh, and three other family members are seated on the sofa. These graphic disk characters help make it fun and easy to learn about computers. They're part of the extended maranGraphics family.

Credits

Author & Architect:
Ruth Maran

Technical Consultant:
Wendi Blouin Ewbank

Project Manager:
Judy Maran

Editors:
Brad Hilderley
Alison MacAlpine
Paul Lofthouse

Proofreader:
Lorena Zupancic

Layout & Cover Design:
Christie Van Duin

Illustrator & Layout Reviser:
Tamara Poliquin

Illustrators:
Chris K.C. Leung
Russell Marini
Andrew Trowbridge

Screen Artist:
Greg Midensky

Indexer:
Kelleigh Wing

Post Production:
Robert Maran

Acknowledgments

Thanks to Dave Carter of Microsoft Canada for ensuring the technical accuracy of this book.

Thanks to the dedicated staff of maranGraphics, including Francisco Ferreira, Brad Hilderley, Chris K.C. Leung, Paul Lofthouse, Alison MacAlpine, Jill Maran, Judy Maran, Maxine Maran, Robert Maran, Sherry Maran, Russ Marini, Greg Midensky, Tamara Poliquin, Andrew Trowbridge, Christie Van Duin and Kelleigh Wing.

Finally, to Richard Maran who originated the easy-to-use graphic format of this guide. Thank you for your inspiration and guidance.

TABLE OF CONTENTS

— CHAPTER 1 —

REVIEW OF WINDOWS BASICS

— CHAPTER 2 —

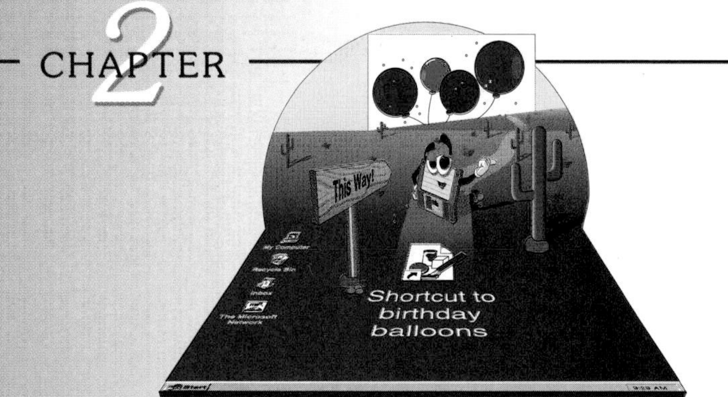

TIME-SAVING FEATURES

— CHAPTER 3 —

PERSONALIZE WINDOWS

— CHAPTER 4

ENTERTAINING FEATURES

— CHAPTER 5

OBJECT LINKING AND EMBEDDING

— CHAPTER 6

ADD HARDWARE AND SOFTWARE

TABLE OF CONTENTS

— CHAPTER 7 —

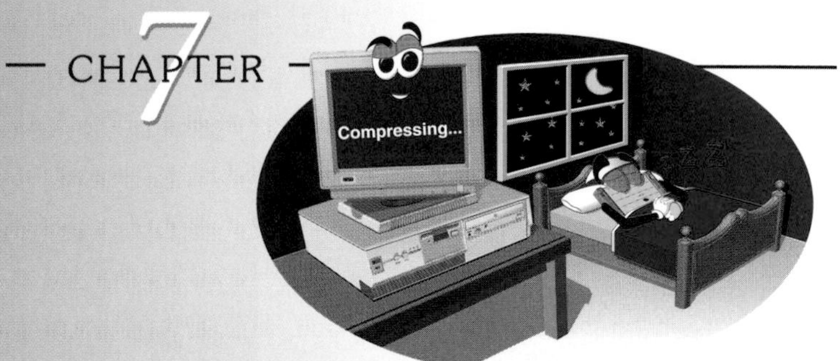

MAINTAIN YOUR COMPUTER

— CHAPTER 8 —

THE MICROSOFT NETWORK

— CHAPTER 9 —

BRIEFCASE

CHAPTER 10

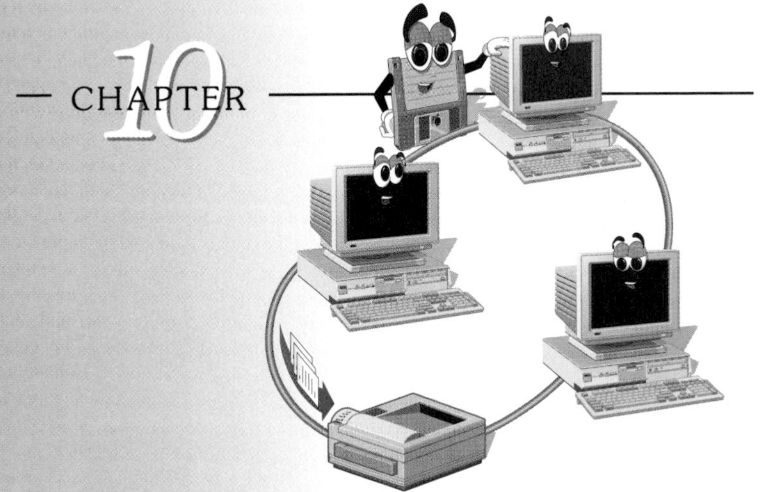

NETWORKS

CHAPTER 11

DIAL-UP NETWORKING

CHAPTER 12

DIRECT CABLE CONNECTION

In this chapter you will review the basic skills you need to work in Windows 95.
My Computer
Recycle Bin
Inbox
The Microsoft Network
Welcome
Welcome to Windows95
Did you know...
You can use Paint in the Accessories folder to draw pictures and to view bitmap files.
Windows Tour
What's New
Online Registration
Product Catalog
Next Tip
Show this Welcome Screen next time you start Windows
Start
Welcome

CHAPTER 1

REVIEW OF WINDOWS BASICS

Windows Overview

Start a Program

Switch Between Windows

Close a Window

Minimize or Maximize a Window

Move or Size a Window

Close a Misbehaving Program

Shut Down Windows

Using the MS-DOS Prompt

Using Calculator

View Contents of Computer

Change Browsing Options

WINDOWS OVERVIEW

Microsoft® Windows® 95 is a program that controls the overall activity of your computer.

Like an orchestra conductor, Windows ensures that all parts of your computer work together smoothly and efficiently.

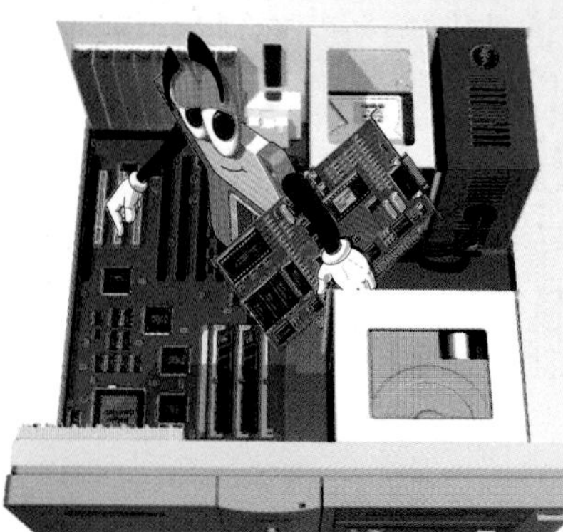

CONTROLS YOUR HARDWARE

Windows controls the different parts of your computer system, such as the printer and monitor, and enables them to work together.

RUNS YOUR PROGRAMS

Windows starts and operates programs, such as Microsoft Word and Lotus 1-2-3. Programs let you write letters, analyze numbers, manage finances, draw pictures and even play games.

ORGANIZES YOUR INFORMATION

Windows provides ways to organize and manage files stored on your computer. You can use Windows to sort, copy, move, delete and view your files.

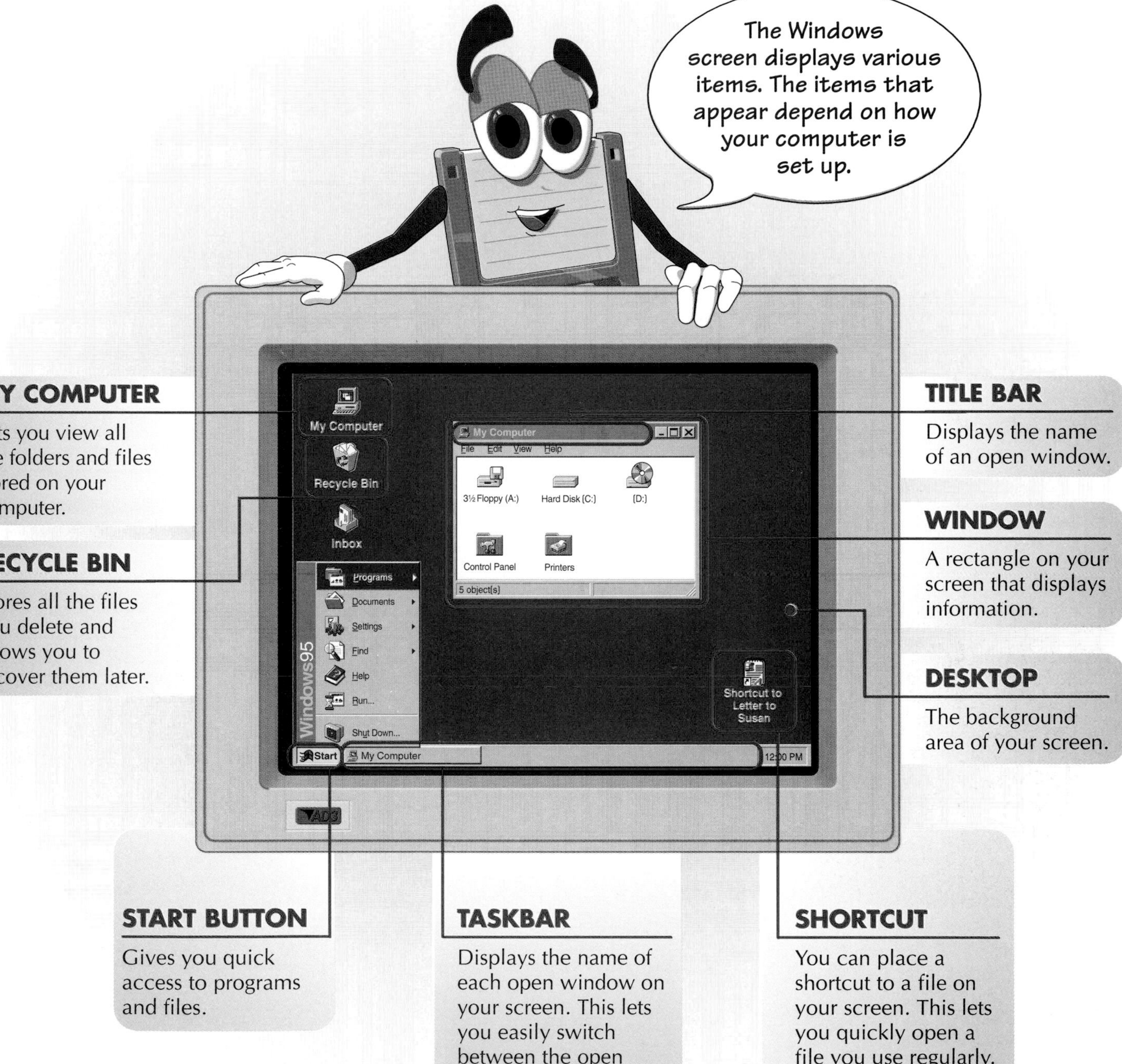
The Windows screen displays various items. The items that appear depend on how your computer is set up.
MY COMPUTER
Lets you view all the folders and files stored on your computer.
RECYCLE BIN
Stores all the files you delete and allows you to recover them later.
TITLE BAR
Displays the name of an open window.
WINDOW
A rectangle on your screen that displays information.
DESKTOP
The background area of your screen.
START BUTTON
Gives you quick access to programs and files.
TASKBAR
Displays the name of each open window on your screen. This lets you easily switch between the open windows.
SHORTCUT
You can place a shortcut to a file on your screen. This lets you quickly open a file you use regularly.
My Computer
Recycle Bin
Inbox
Programs
Documents
Settings
Find
Help
Run...
Shut Down...
Windows95
Start
12:00 PM
File Edit View Help
3½ Floppy (A:)
Hard Disk (C:)
(D:)
Control Panel
Printers
5 object(s)
Shortcut to Letter to Susan

START A PROGRAM

START A PROGRAM

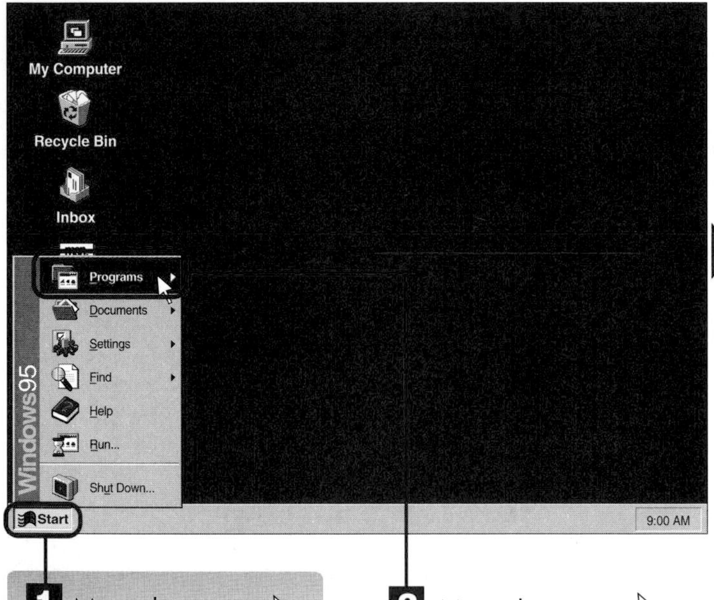

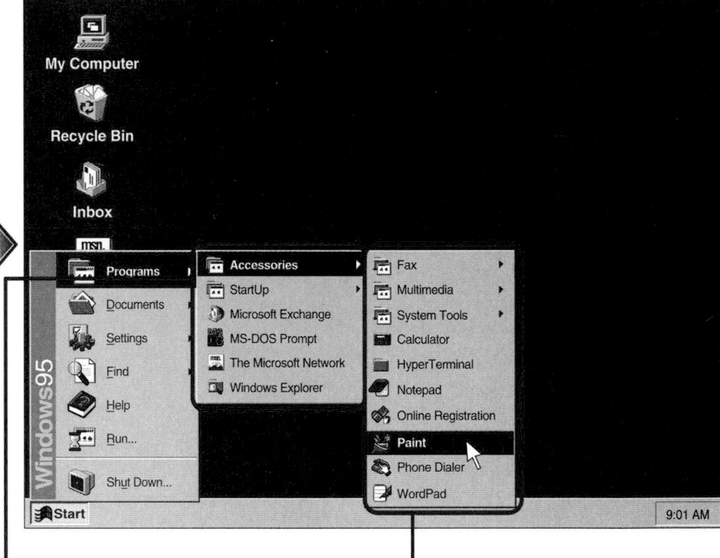

1 Move the mouse over **Start** and then press the left button. A menu appears.

Note: To display the ***Start*** *menu using the keyboard, press and hold down* **Ctrl** *and then press* **Esc**.

2 Move the mouse over **Programs**.

Note: To select a menu item using the keyboard, press the underlined letter (example: ***P*** *for* ***Programs****).*

■ A list of items appears.

3 To view the programs for an item displaying an arrow (▸), move the mouse over the item.

4 To start a program, move the mouse over the program and then press the left button.

Windows comes with many useful programs. Here are some examples.

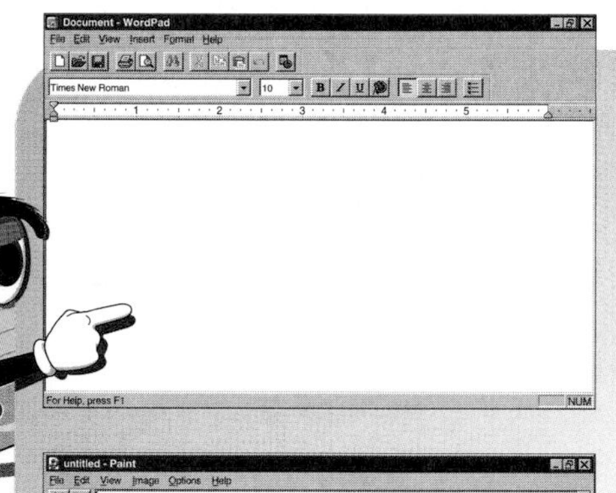

WordPad is a word processing program that lets you create letters, reports and memos.

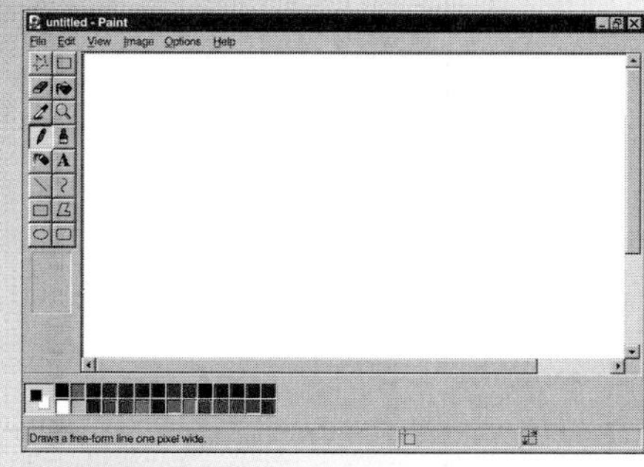

Paint is a drawing program that lets you draw pictures and maps.

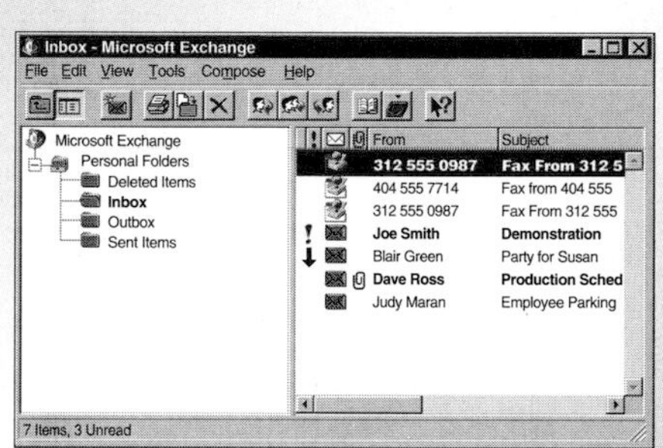

Microsoft Exchange is a program that lets you exchange electronic mail and faxes.

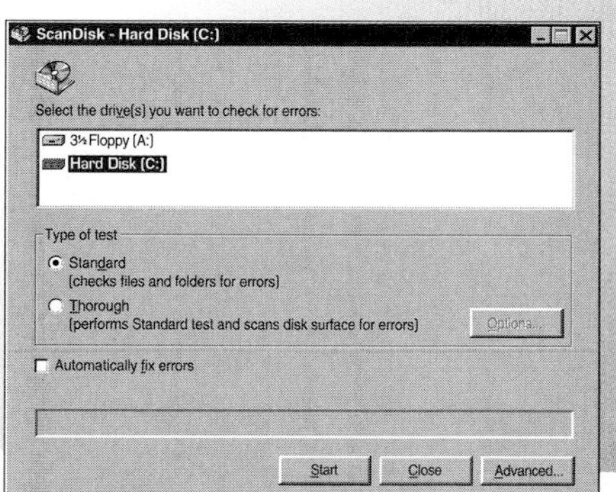

ScanDisk is a program that searches for and repairs disk errors.

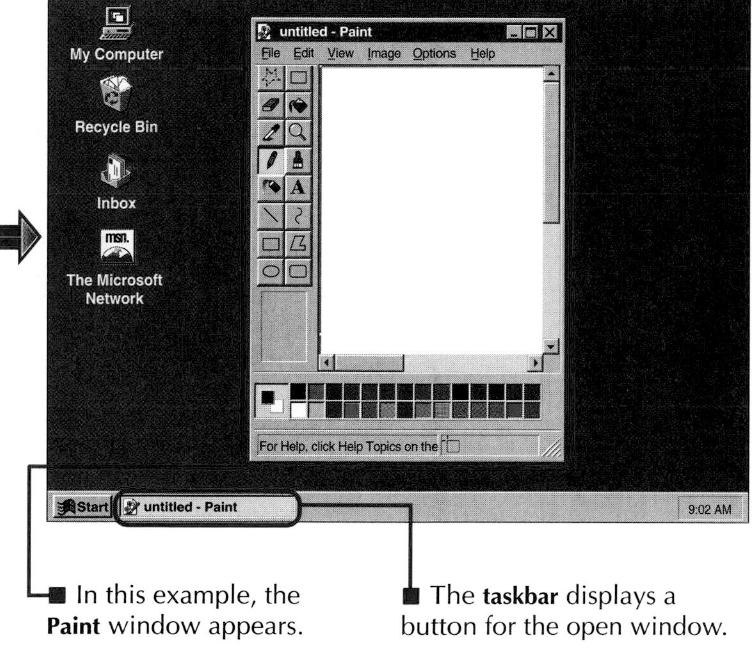

■ In this example, the **Paint** window appears.

■ The **taskbar** displays a button for the open window.

SWITCH BETWEEN WINDOWS

You can have more than one window open at a time. Windows lets you easily switch between the windows.

SWITCH BETWEEN WINDOWS

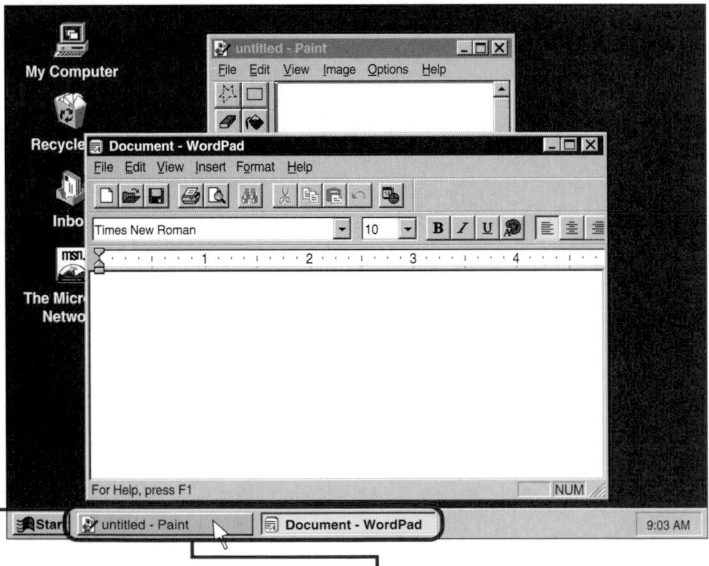

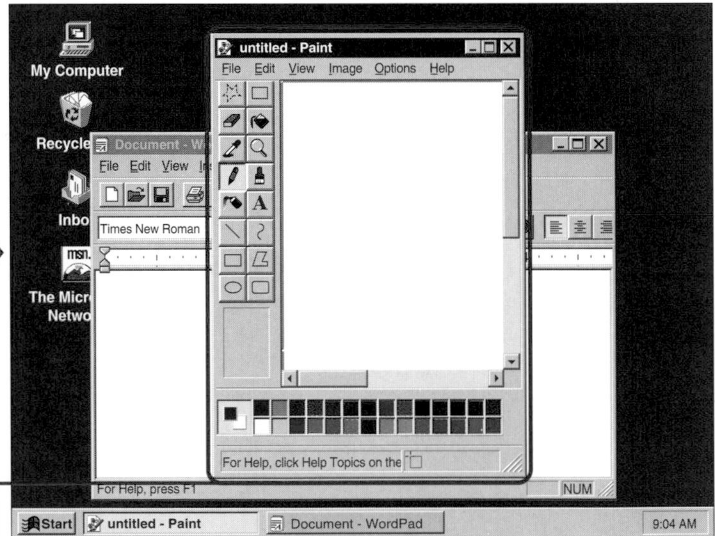

■ The taskbar displays a button for each open window on your screen.

Note: The WordPad and Paint programs come with Windows. To start these programs, refer to page 6.

1 To move the window you want to work with to the front, move the mouse over its button on the taskbar and then press the left button.

■ The window appears in front of all other windows. This lets you clearly view its contents.

CLOSE A WINDOW

When you finish working with a window, you can close the window to remove it from your screen.

CLOSE A WINDOW

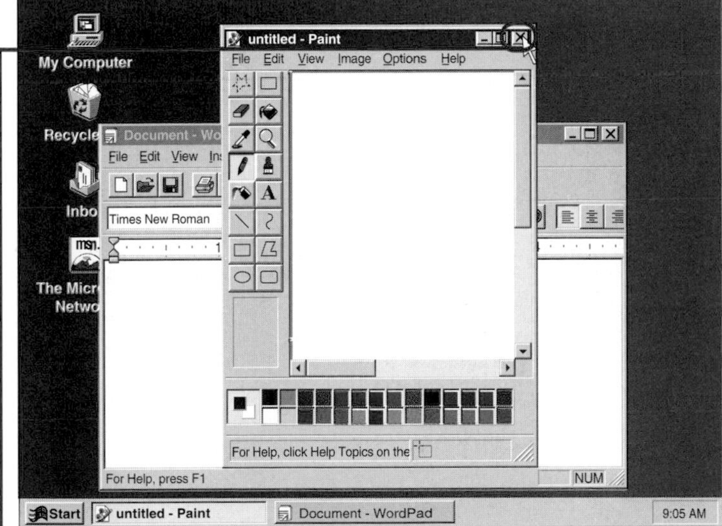

1 Move the mouse over ☒ in the window you want to close and then press the left button.

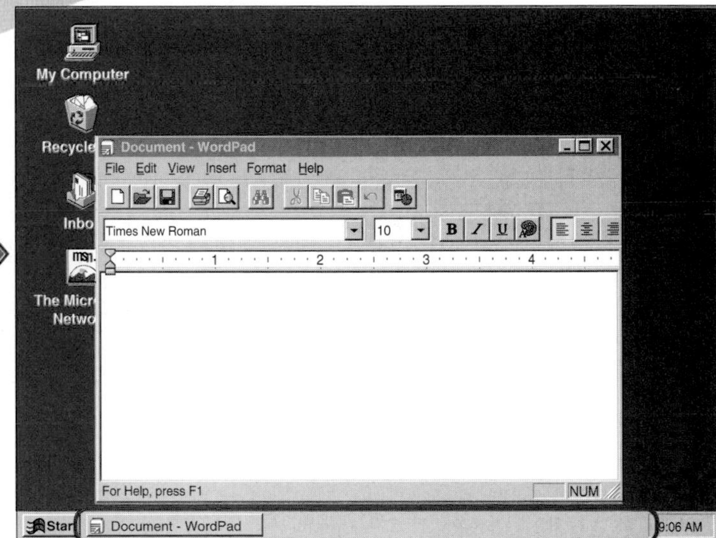

■ The window disappears from your screen.

■ The button for the window disappears from the taskbar.

MINIMIZE A WINDOW

If you are not using a window, you can minimize the window to remove it from your screen. You can redisplay the window at any time.
My Computer
Recycle Bin
Inbox
Start
Document - WordPad
9:16 AM

MINIMIZE A WINDOW

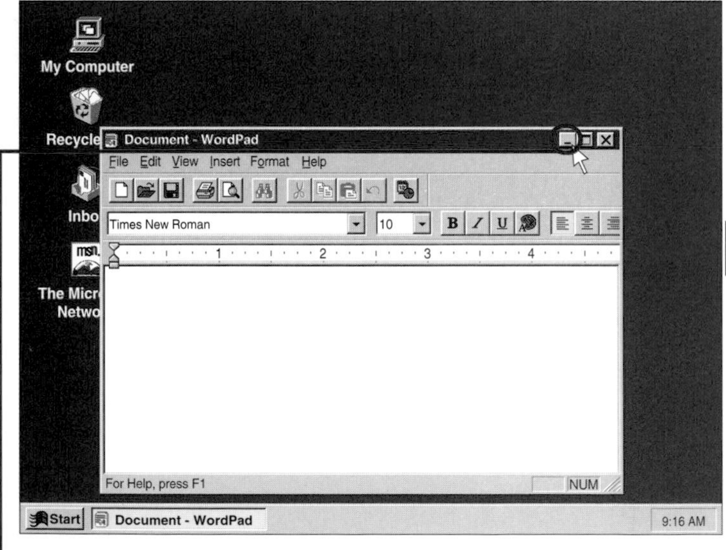

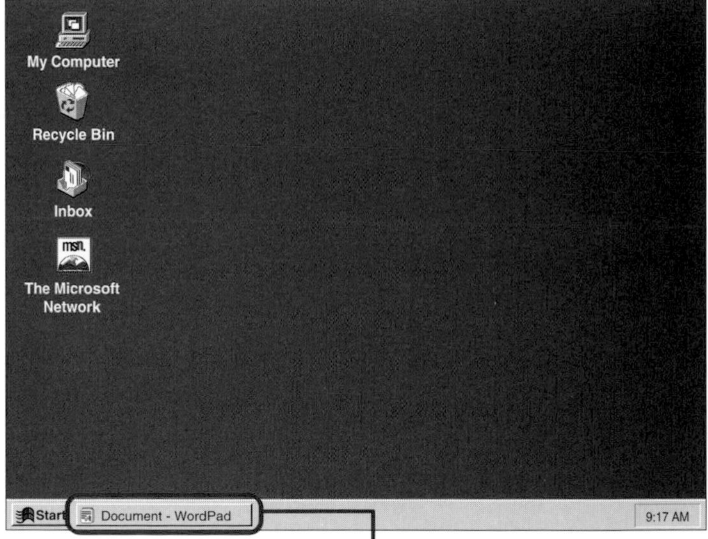

1 Move the mouse over ▁ in the window you want to minimize and then press the left button.

■ The window disappears.

■ To redisplay the window, move the mouse over its button on the taskbar and then press the left button.

MAXIMIZE A WINDOW

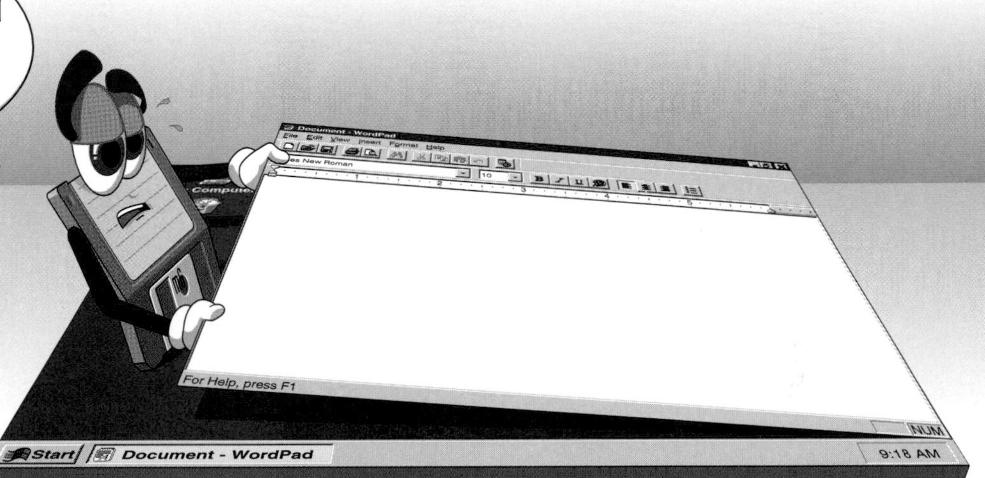

MAXIMIZE A WINDOW

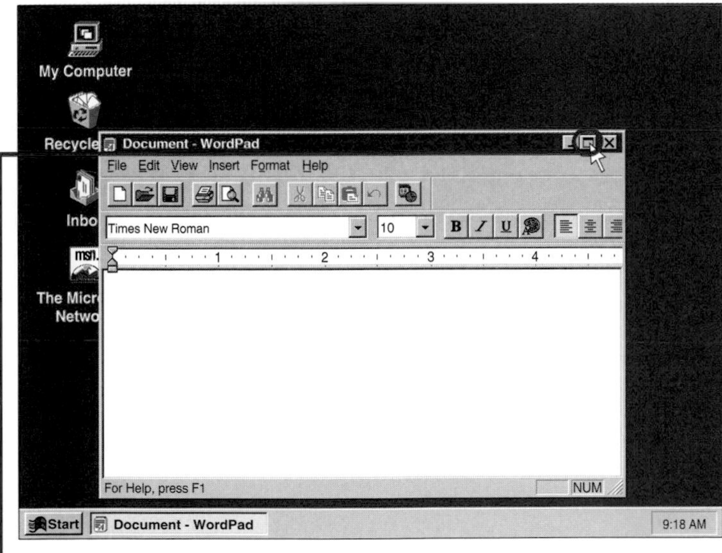

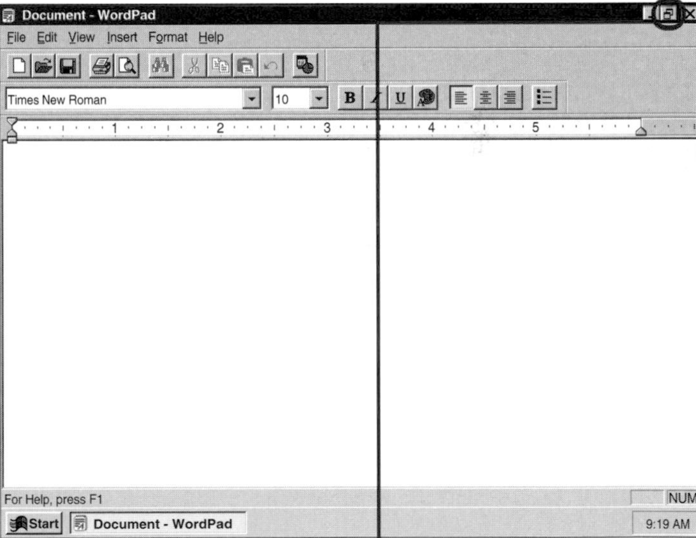

1 Move the mouse over in the window you want to enlarge and then press the left button.

■ The window fills your screen.

■ To return the window to its previous size, move the mouse over and then press the left button.

MOVE A WINDOW

If a window covers items on your screen, you can move the window to a different location.

MOVE A WINDOW

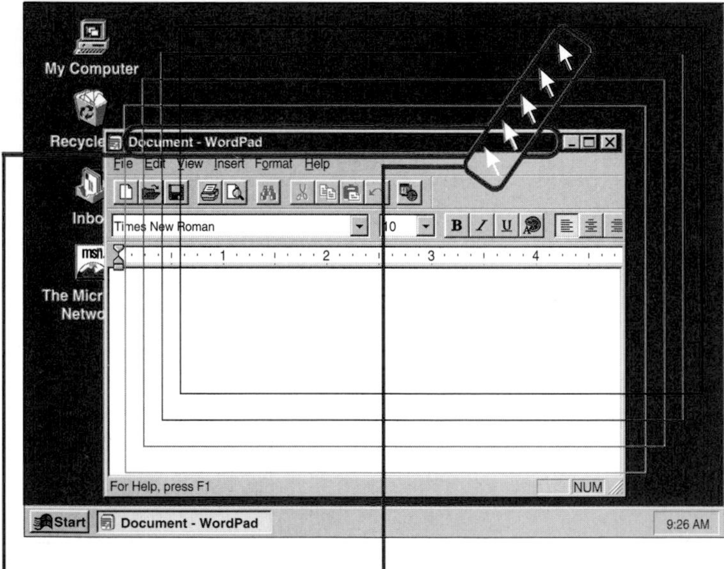

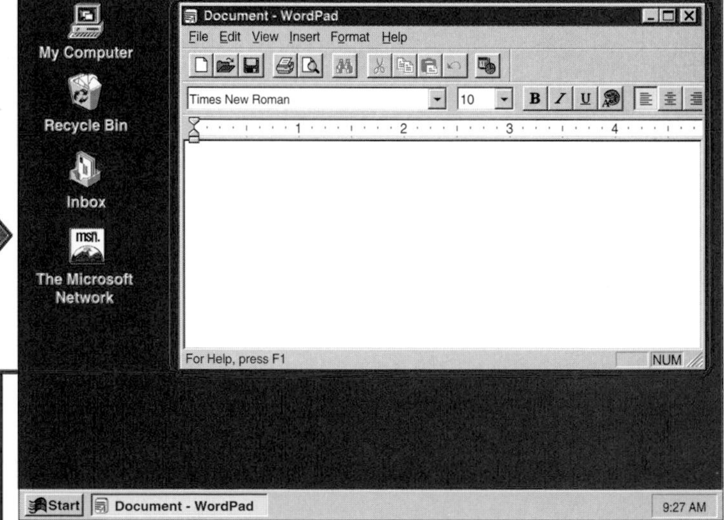

1 Move the mouse over the title bar of the window you want to move.

2 Press and hold down the left button as you drag the mouse to where you want to place the window.

■ An outline of the window indicates the new location.

3 Release the button and the window moves to the new location.

SIZE A WINDOW

- Enlarging a window lets you view more of its contents.
- Reducing a window lets you view items covered by the window.

SIZE A WINDOW

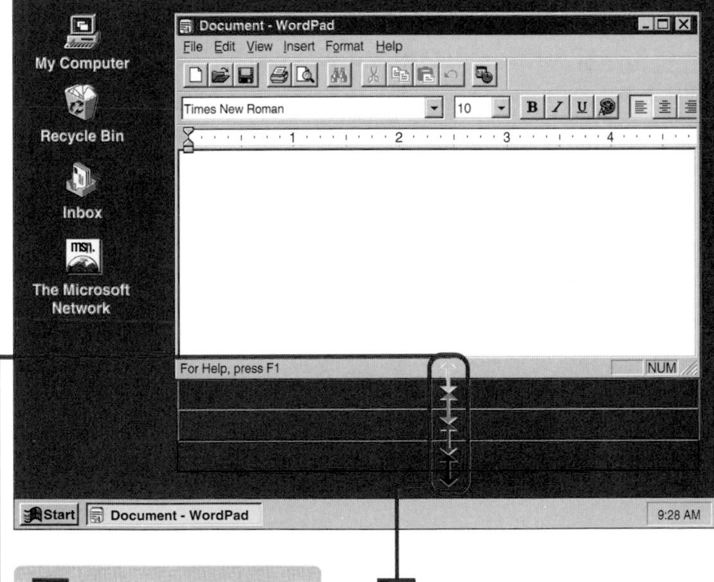

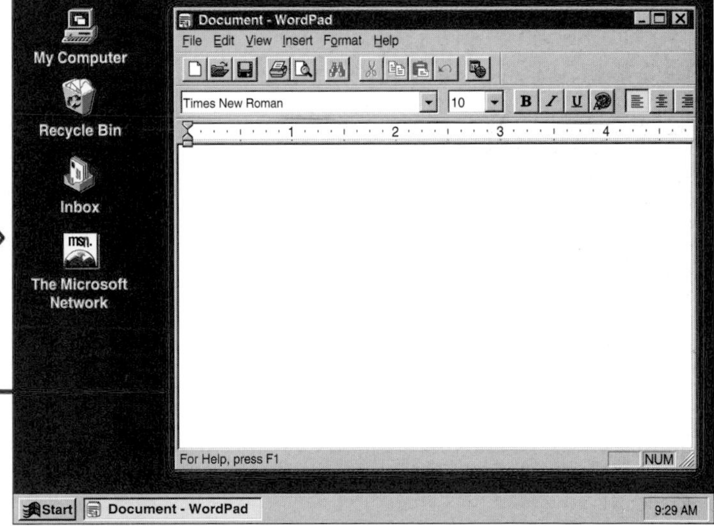

1 Move the mouse ↖ over an edge of the window you want to size and ↖ changes to ↕ or ↔.

2 Press and hold down the left button as you drag the mouse ↕ until the outline of the window displays the size you want. Then release the button.

- The window changes to the new size.

CLOSE A MISBEHAVING PROGRAM

If a program suddenly stops working, you can close the program.

CLOSE A MISBEHAVING PROGRAM

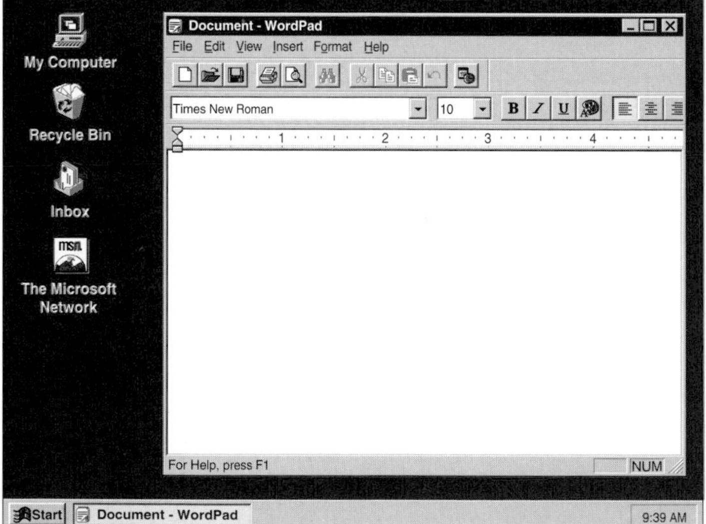

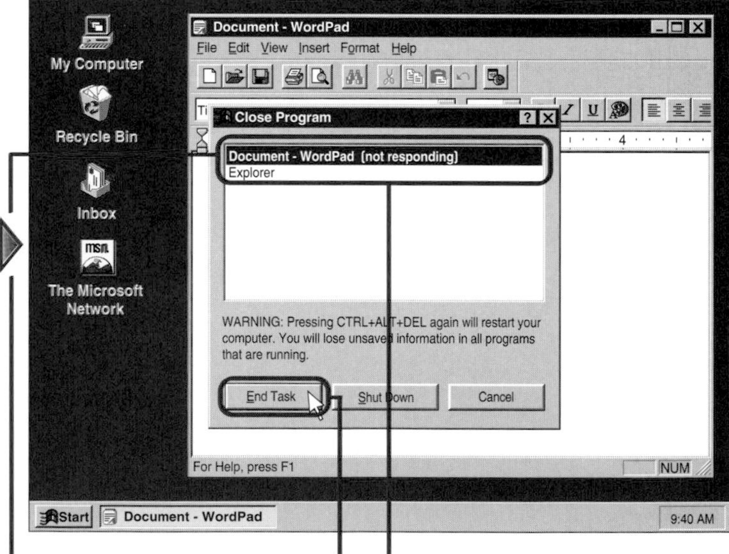

1 Press and hold down **Ctrl** and **Alt** on your keyboard and then press **Delete**.

■ The **Close Program** dialog box appears.

■ This area displays the programs that are currently running.

Note: Misbehaving programs display the words ***not responding****.*

2 Move the mouse over the program you want to close and then press the left button.

3 Move the mouse over **End Task** and then press the left button.

SHUT DOWN WINDOWS

When you finish using your computer, you should shut down Windows before turning the computer off.

■ Do not turn off your computer until this message appears on your screen.

SHUT DOWN WINDOWS

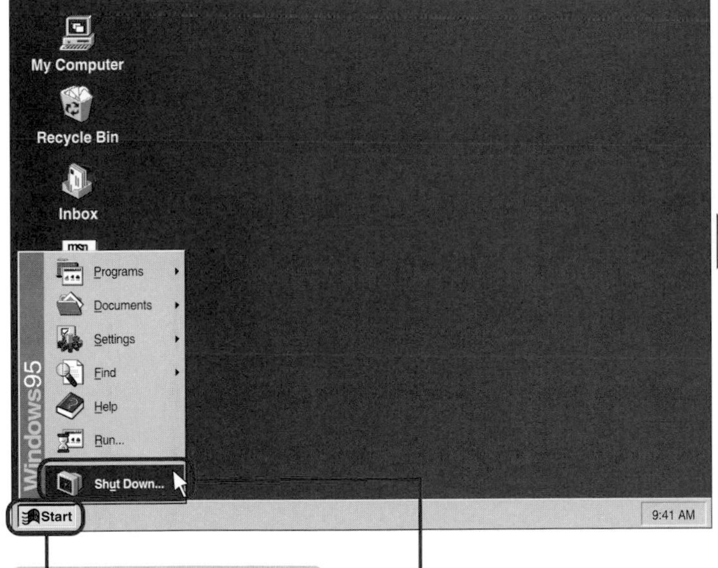

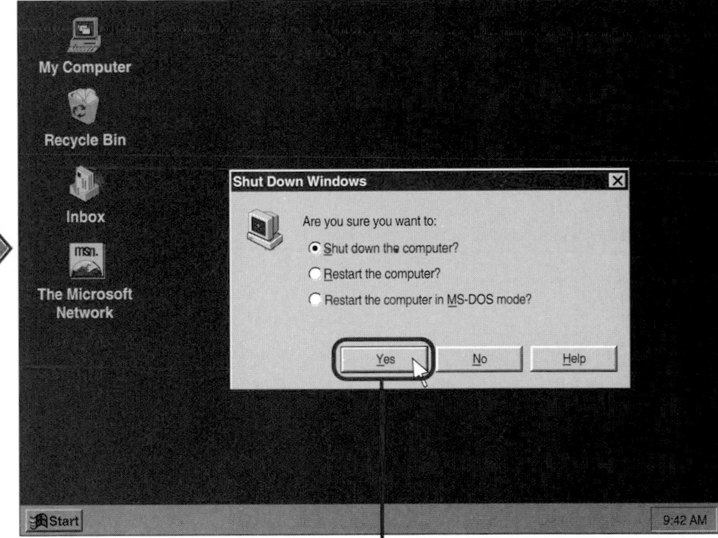

1 Move the mouse over **Start** and then press the left button.

2 Move the mouse over **Shut Down** and then press the left button.

■ The **Shut Down Windows** dialog box appears.

3 To shut down your computer, move the mouse over **Yes** and then press the left button.

USING THE MS-DOS PROMPT

USING THE MS-DOS PROMPT

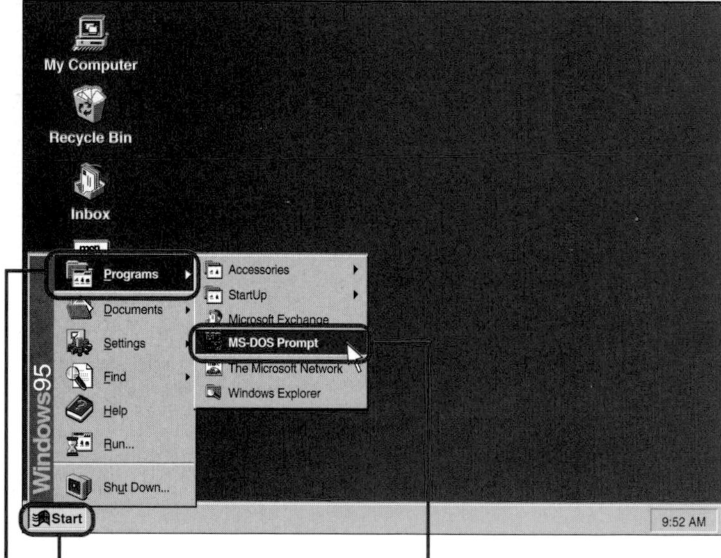

1 Move the mouse over **Start** and then press the left button.

2 Move the mouse over **Programs**.

3 Move the mouse over **MS-DOS Prompt** and then press the left button.

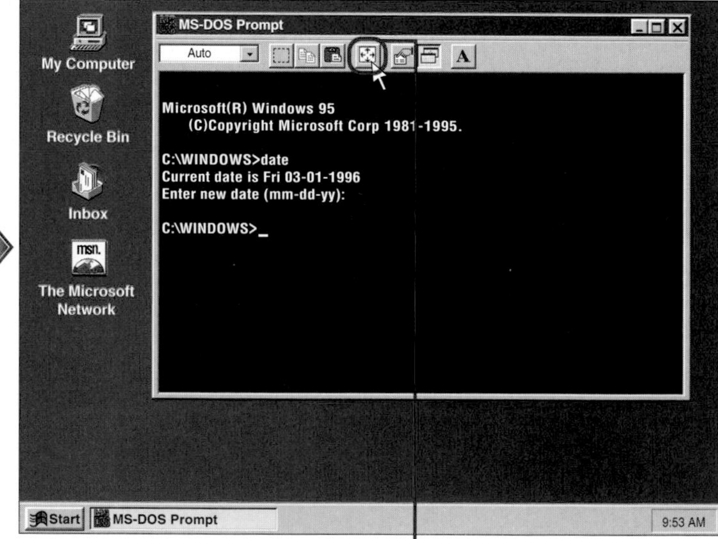

■ The **MS-DOS Prompt** window appears. You can enter DOS commands and start DOS programs in the window.

Note: In this example, we use the ***date*** *command to display the date set in the computer.*

4 To fill your screen with the MS-DOS prompt, move the mouse over [full screen button] and then press the left button.

Tip ***If a DOS program will not run in a window, try restarting the program in MS-DOS mode.***

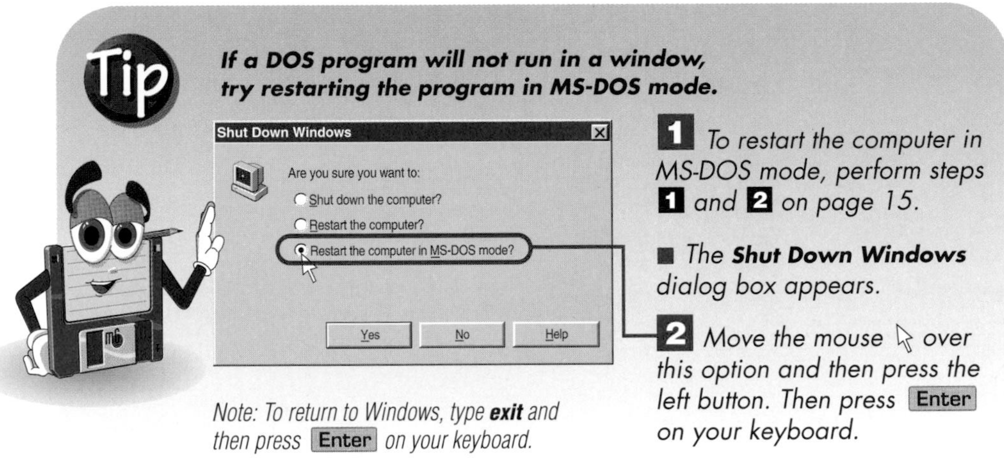

*Note: To return to Windows, type **exit** and then press Enter on your keyboard.*

1 To restart the computer in MS-DOS mode, perform steps 1 and 2 on page 15.

*■ The **Shut Down Windows** dialog box appears.*

2 Move the mouse over this option and then press the left button. Then press Enter on your keyboard.

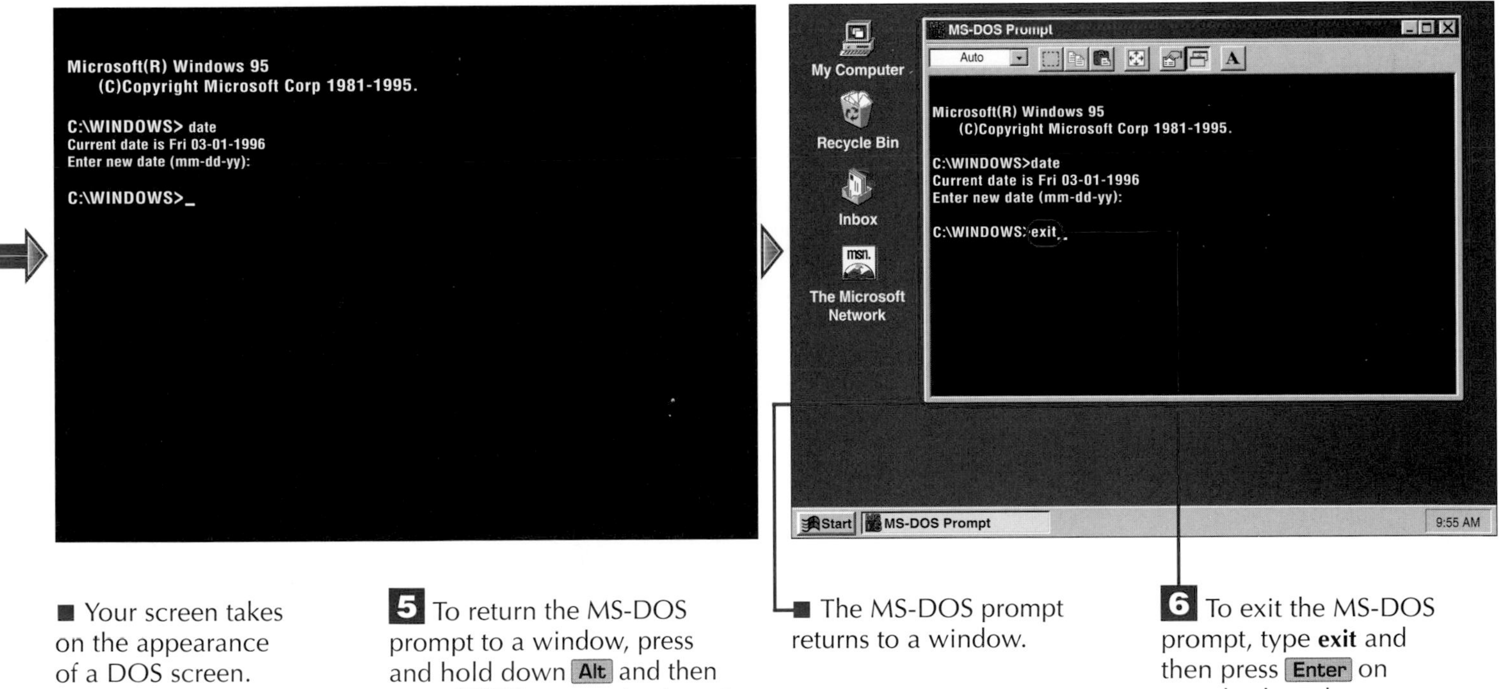

■ Your screen takes on the appearance of a DOS screen.

5 To return the MS-DOS prompt to a window, press and hold down Alt and then press Enter on your keyboard.

■ The MS-DOS prompt returns to a window.

6 To exit the MS-DOS prompt, type **exit** and then press Enter on your keyboard.

USING CALCULATOR

Windows provides a calculator you can use to perform calculations.

USING CALCULATOR

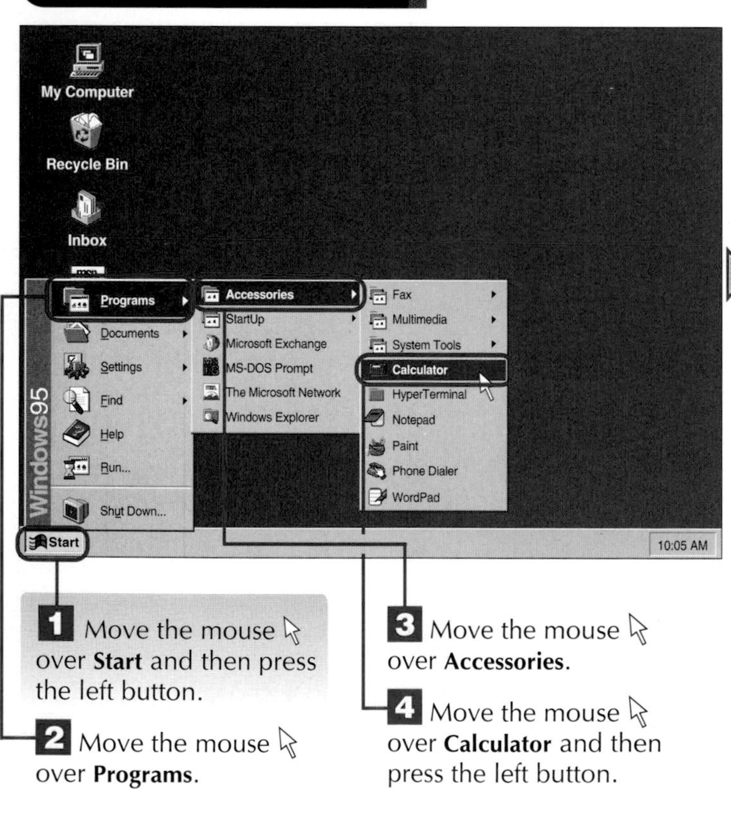

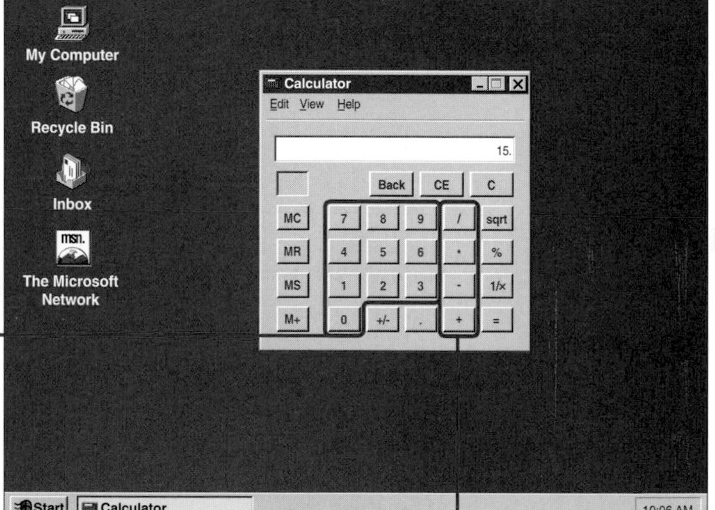

1 Move the mouse over **Start** and then press the left button.

2 Move the mouse over **Programs**.

3 Move the mouse over **Accessories**.

4 Move the mouse over **Calculator** and then press the left button.

■ The **Calculator** window appears.

5 To enter a number, move the mouse over the first digit and then press the left button. Repeat this step until you finish entering the number (example: **12**).

6 Move the mouse over the operator you want to use (example: *) and then press the left button.

7 Repeat steps **5** and **6** until you finish entering the numbers and operators in the calculation (example: **12*15**).

Tip ***You can also use your keyboard to enter numbers and operators into Calculator.***

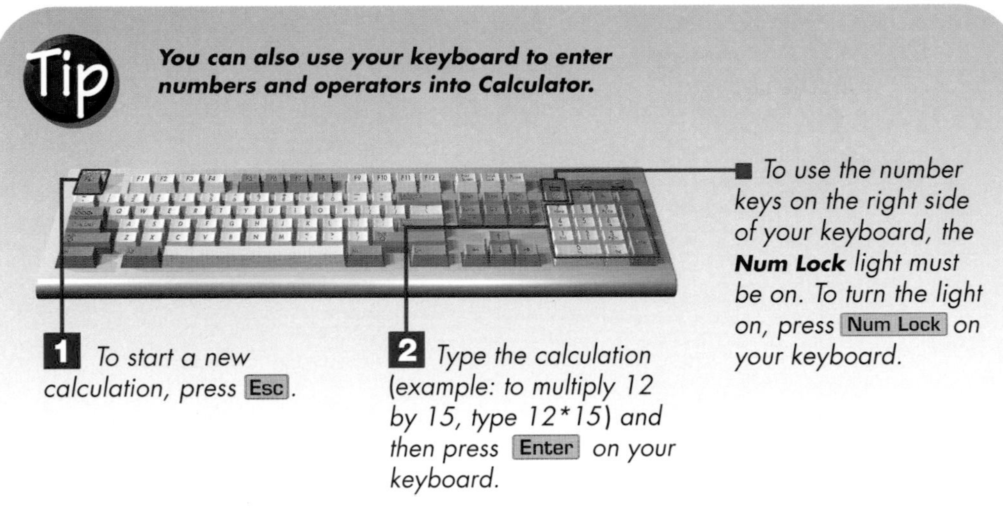

■ *To use the number keys on the right side of your keyboard, the* ***Num Lock*** *light must be on. To turn the light on, press* Num Lock *on your keyboard.*

1 *To start a new calculation, press* Esc.

2 *Type the calculation (example: to multiply 12 by 15, type 12*15) and then press* Enter *on your keyboard.*

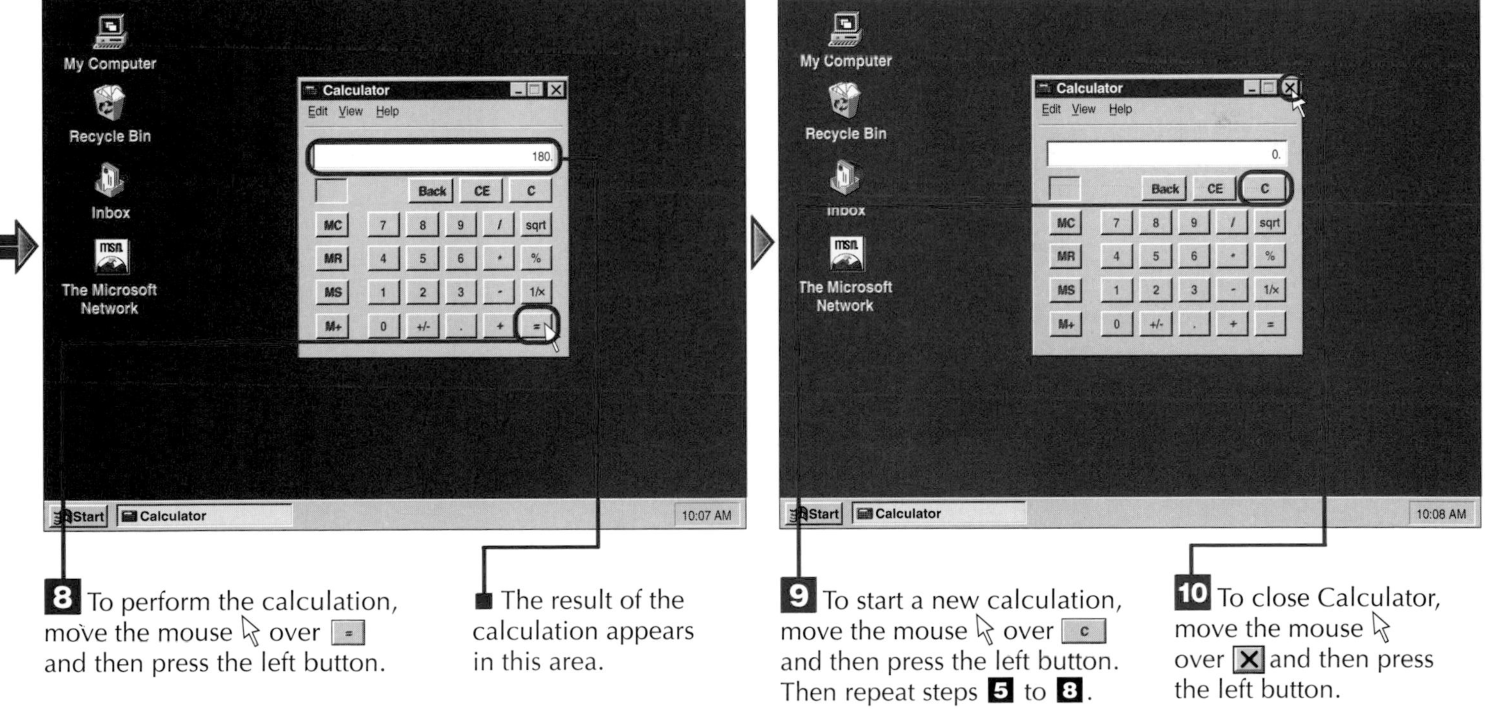

8 To perform the calculation, move the mouse over = and then press the left button.

■ The result of the calculation appears in this area.

9 To start a new calculation, move the mouse over C and then press the left button. Then repeat steps **5** to **8**.

10 To close Calculator, move the mouse over ☒ and then press the left button.

VIEW CONTENTS OF COMPUTER

Like a filing cabinet, your computer uses folders to organize information.

VIEW CONTENTS OF COMPUTER

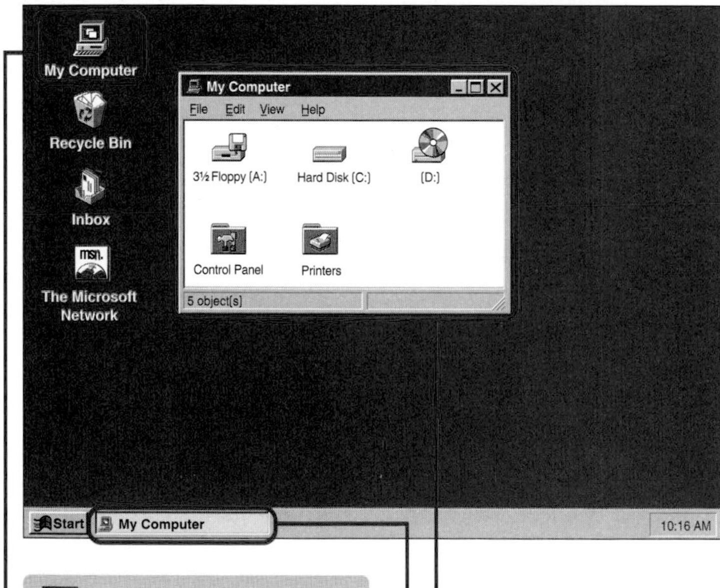

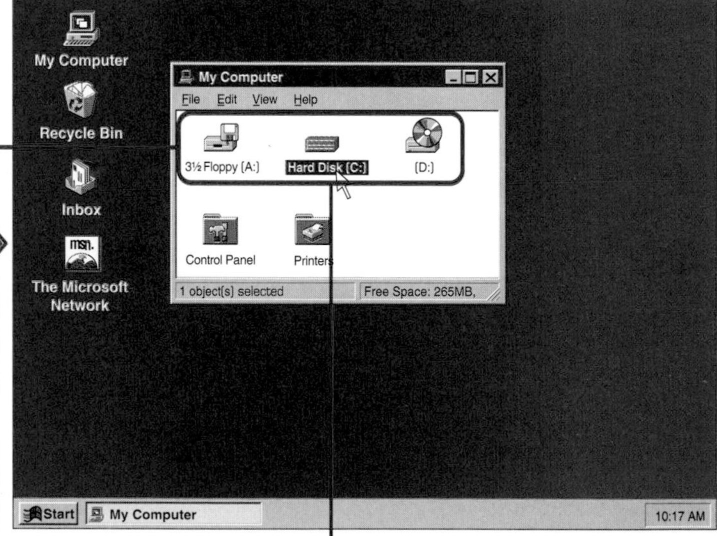

1 To view the contents of your computer, move the mouse over **My Computer** and then quickly press the left button twice.

■ The **My Computer** window appears.

■ The taskbar displays the name of the open window.

■ These objects represent the drives on your computer.

2 To display the contents of a drive, move the mouse over the drive (example: **C:**) and then quickly press the left button twice.

Note: If you want to view the contents of a floppy or CD-ROM drive, make sure you insert a floppy disk or CD-ROM disc before performing step **2**.

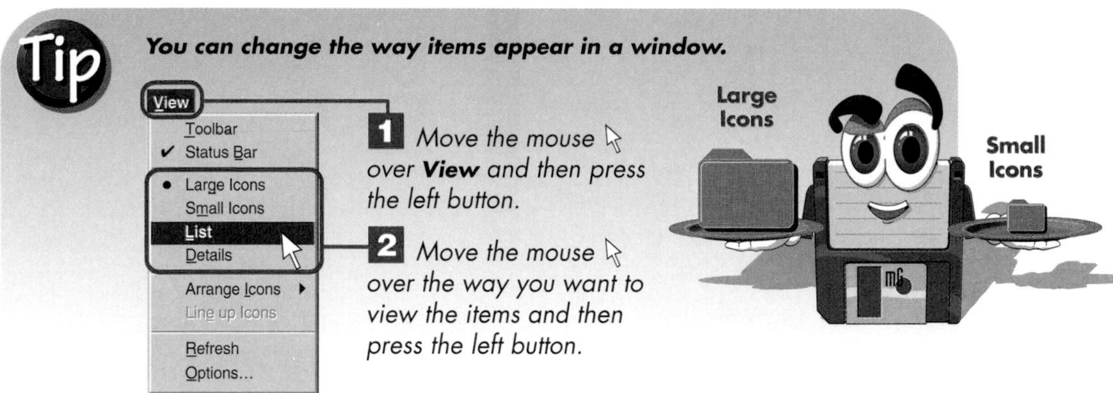

Tip
You can change the way items appear in a window.
View
Toolbar
Status Bar
Large Icons
Small Icons
List
Details
Arrange Icons
Line up Icons
Refresh
Options...
1 Move the mouse over **View** and then press the left button.
2 Move the mouse over the way you want to view the items and then press the left button.
Large Icons
Small Icons

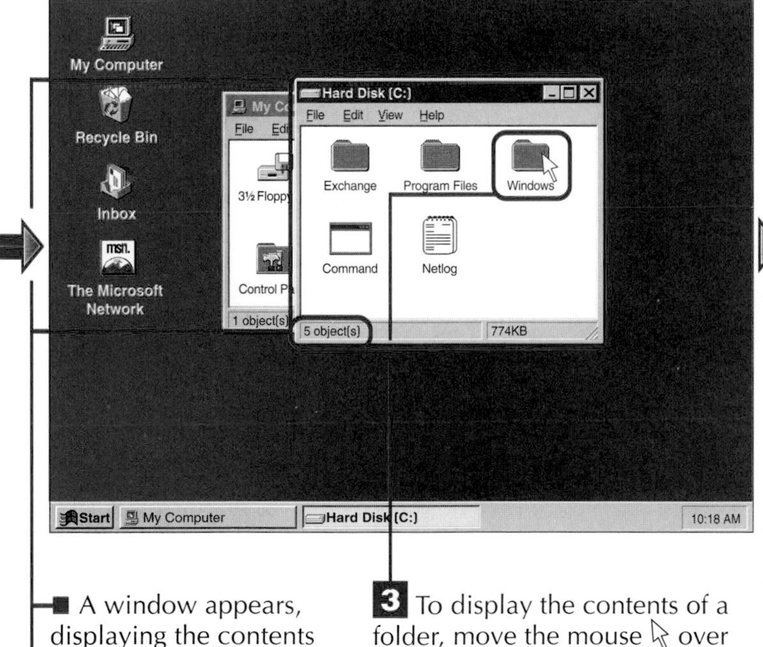

■ A window appears, displaying the contents of the drive.

■ This area tells you how many objects are in the window.

3 To display the contents of a folder, move the mouse over the folder (example: **Windows**) and then quickly press the left button twice.

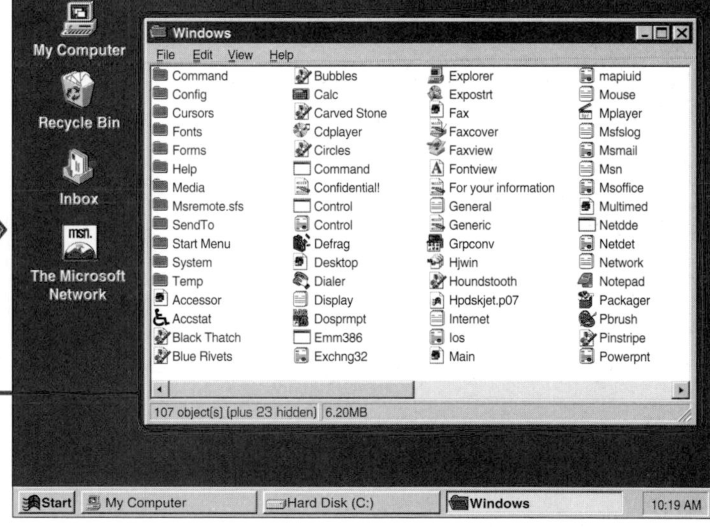

■ A new window appears, displaying the contents of the folder.

Note: To return to the previous window, press **←Backspace** *on your keyboard.*

CHANGE BROWSING OPTIONS

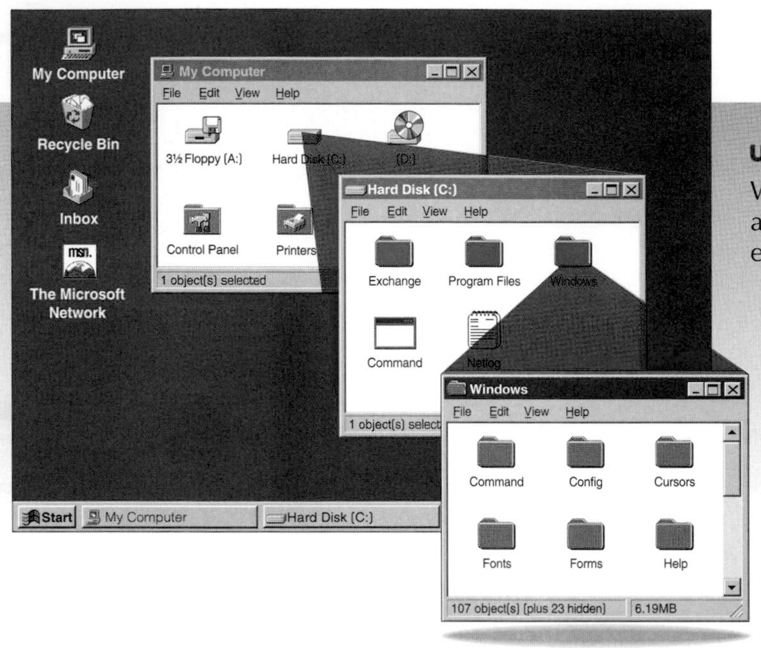

Use Separate Windows

Windows displays a separate window for each folder you open.

CHANGE BROWSING OPTIONS

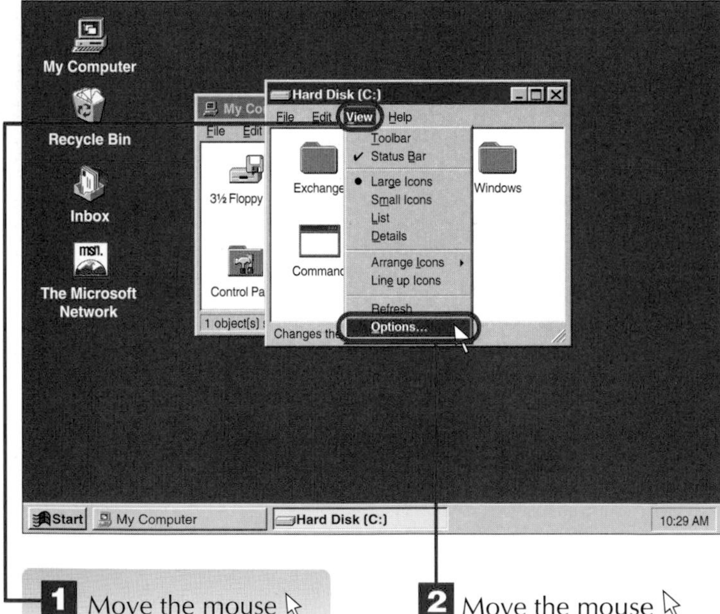

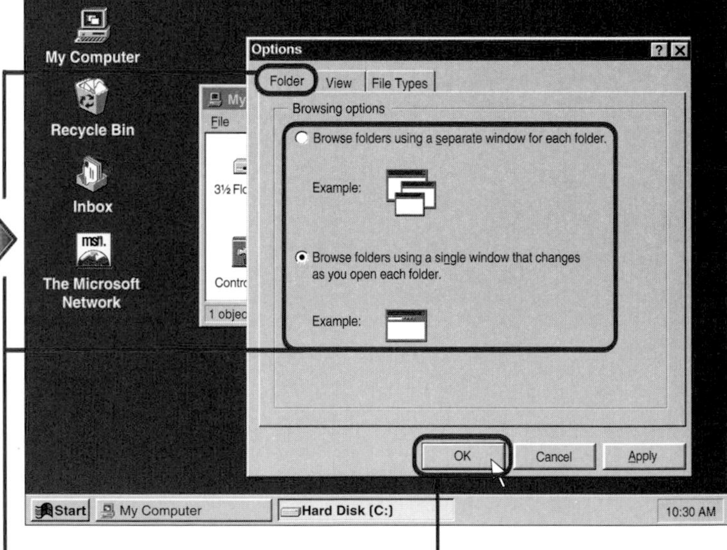

1 Move the mouse over **View** and then press the left button.

2 Move the mouse over **Options** and then press the left button.

■ The **Options** dialog box appears.

3 Move the mouse over the **Folder** tab and then press the left button.

4 Move the mouse over the browsing option you want to use and then press the left button (○ changes to ◉).

5 Move the mouse over **OK** and then press the left button.

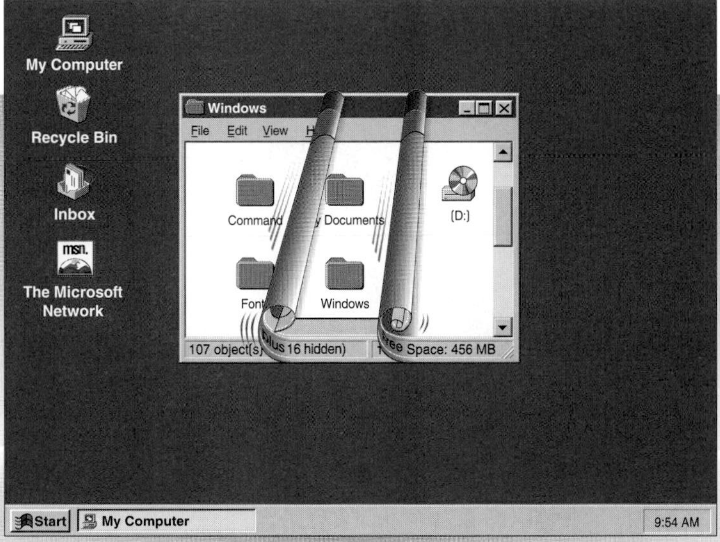

Use a Single Window

Windows displays a single window that changes as you open each folder. This option prevents your screen from becoming cluttered with windows. The option also prevents your taskbar from becoming cluttered with the name of each window you open.

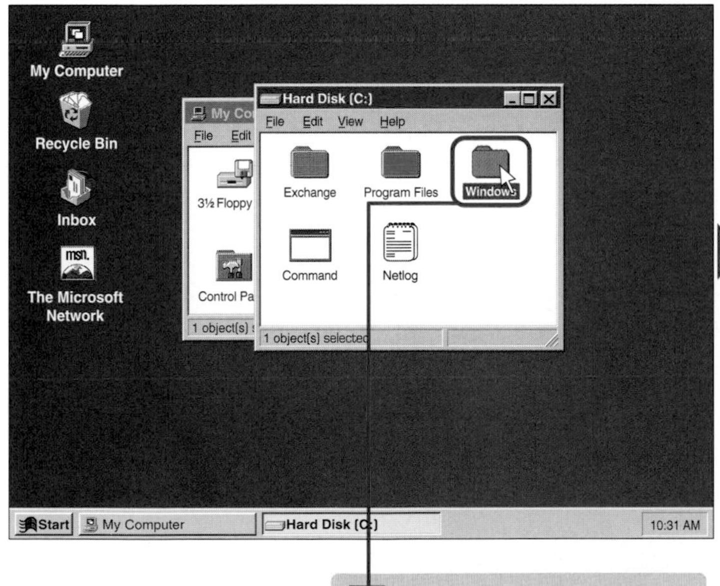

You can easily test the browsing option you selected.

1 To display the contents of a folder, move the mouse over the folder and then quickly press the left button twice.

■ In this example, the contents of the folder appear in the same window. A new window does not appear.

■ To return to the previous window, press **Backspace** on your keyboard.

In this chapter you will learn how to use several Windows features that will save you time.
This Way!
My Computer
Recycle Bin
Inbox
The Microsoft Network
Shortcut to birthday balloons
Start

TIME-SAVING FEATURES

Open a Recently Used File

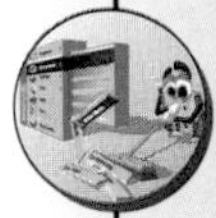

Clear List of Recently Used Files

Find a File

Add a Shortcut to the Desktop

Put Part of a Document on the Desktop

Add a Program to the Start Menu

Have a Program Start Automatically

OPEN A RECENTLY USED FILE

OPEN A RECENTLY USED FILE

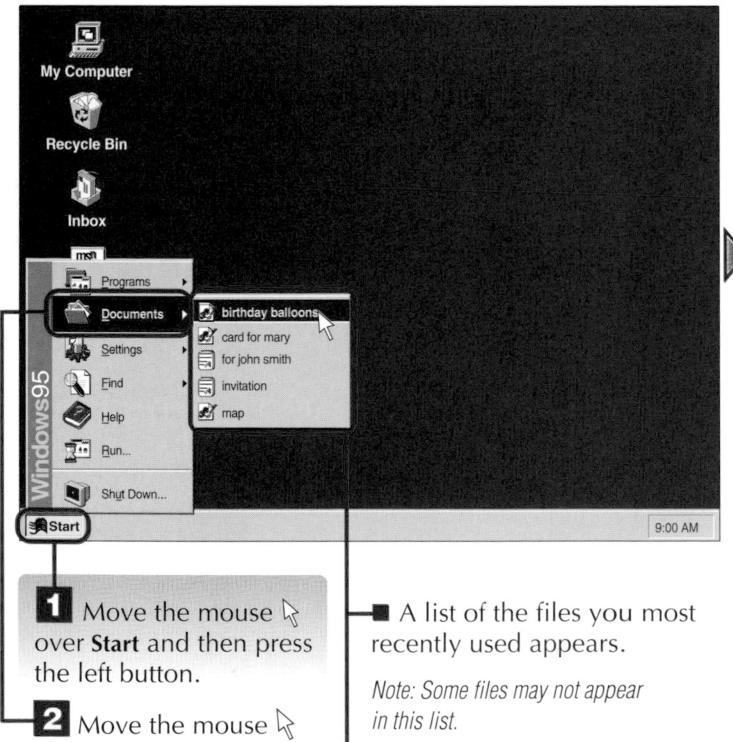

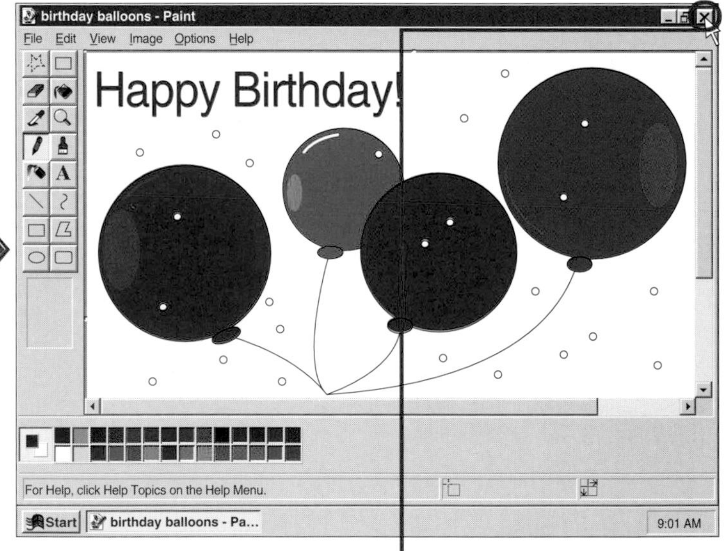

1 Move the mouse over **Start** and then press the left button.

2 Move the mouse over **Documents**.

■ A list of the files you most recently used appears.

Note: Some files may not appear in this list.

3 Move the mouse over the file you want to open and then press the left button.

■ The file opens. You can review and make changes to the file.

4 To close the file, move the mouse over ☒ and then press the left button.

CLEAR LIST OF RECENTLY USED FILES

You can clear the list of your recently used files. This is useful if the list gets cluttered with files you no longer use.

CLEAR LIST OF RECENTLY USED FILES

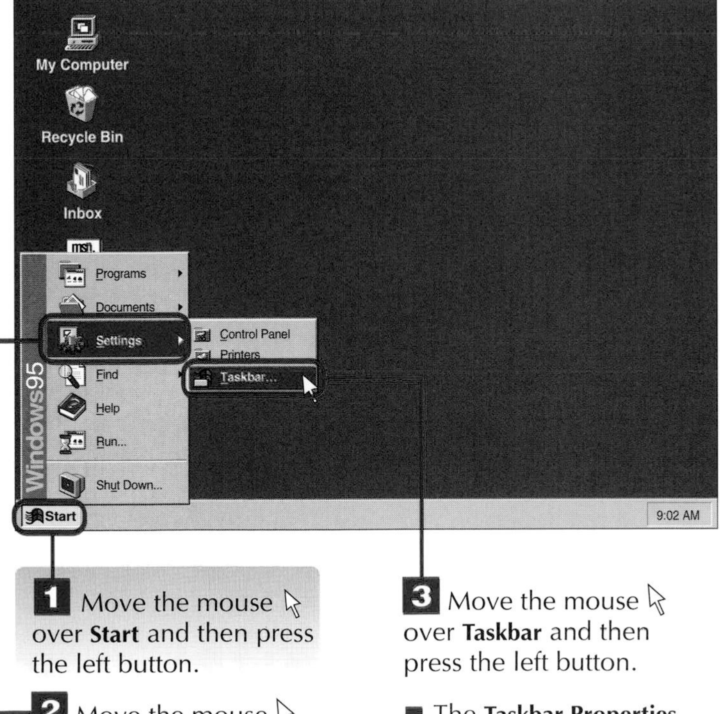

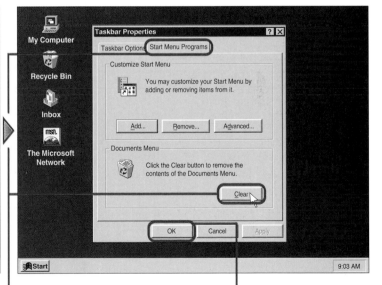

1 Move the mouse over **Start** and then press the left button.

2 Move the mouse over **Settings**.

3 Move the mouse over **Taskbar** and then press the left button.

■ The **Taskbar Properties** dialog box appears.

4 Move the mouse over the **Start Menu Programs** tab and then press the left button.

5 Move the mouse over **Clear** and then press the left button.

6 Move the mouse over **OK** and then press the left button.

FIND A FILE

If you cannot remember the name or location of a file you want to work with, you can have Windows search for the file.

FIND A FILE

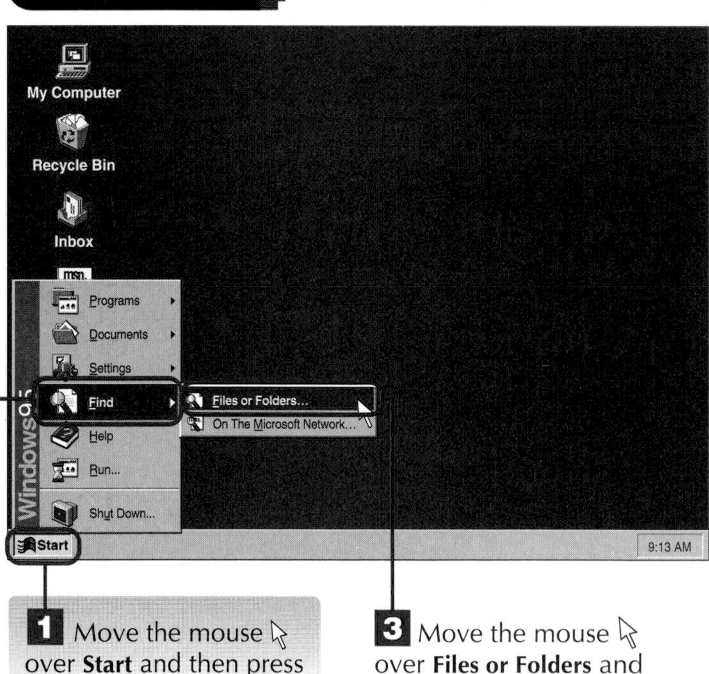

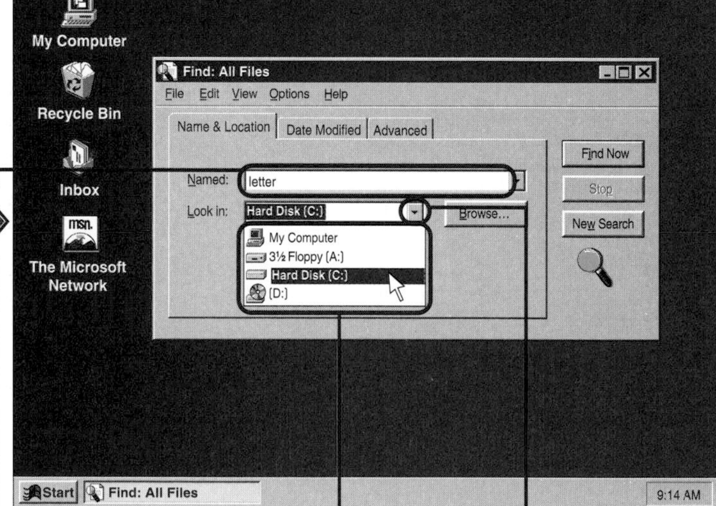

1 Move the mouse over **Start** and then press the left button.

2 Move the mouse over **Find**.

3 Move the mouse over **Files or Folders** and then press the left button.

■ The **Find: All Files** dialog box appears.

4 If you know all or part of the name of the file you want to find, type the name (example: **letter**).

5 To specify where you want Windows to search for the file, move the mouse over ▼ in this area and then press the left button.

6 Move the mouse over the location you want to search and then press the left button.

You can search for a specific type of file, such as an application.

*Note: An application is a program that lets you perform tasks (example: **WordPad**).*

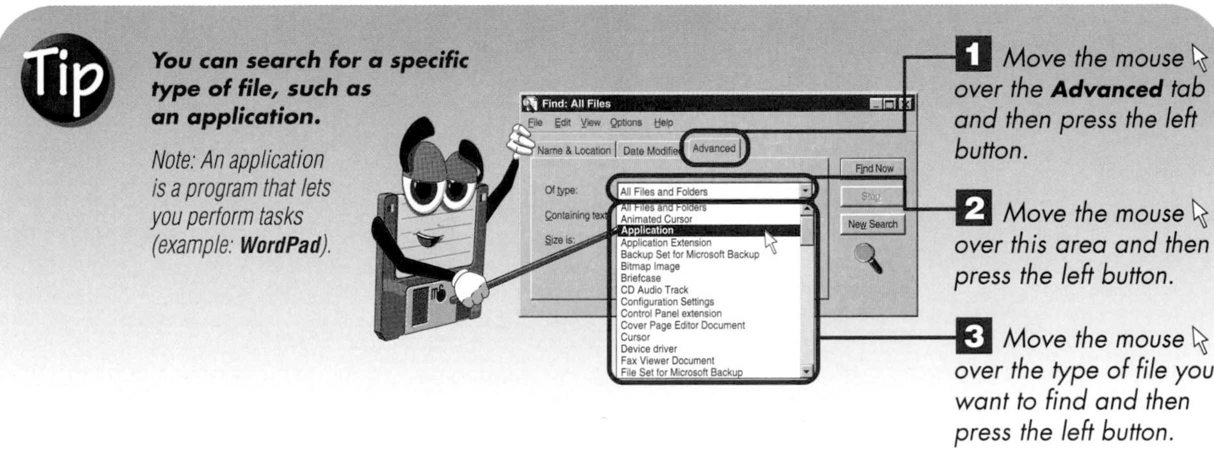

1 Move the mouse over the **Advanced** tab and then press the left button.

2 Move the mouse over this area and then press the left button.

3 Move the mouse over the type of file you want to find and then press the left button.

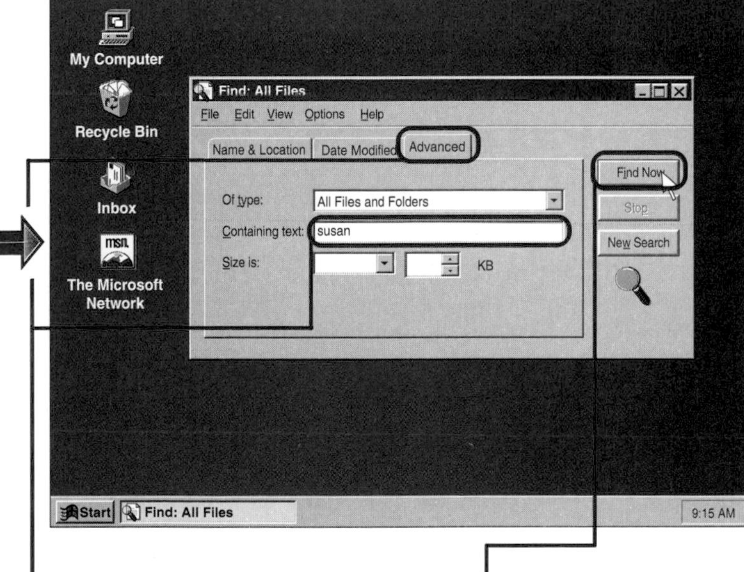

7 If you know a word or phrase in the file you want to find, move the mouse over the **Advanced** tab and then press the left button.

8 Move the mouse over the box beside **Containing text:** and then press the left button. Type the word or phrase (example: **susan**).

9 To start the search, move the mouse over **Find Now** and then press the left button.

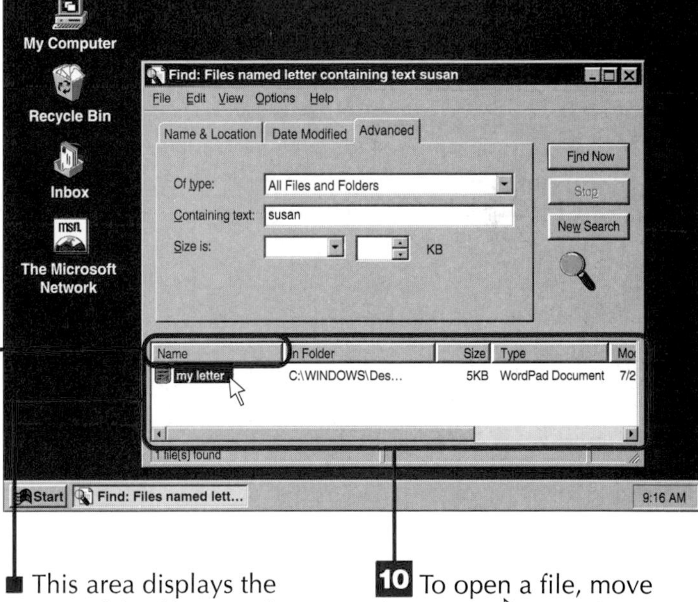

■ This area displays the names of the files Windows found and information about each file.

■ If Windows found several files, you can sort the files alphabetically. To do so, move the mouse over **Name** and then press the left button.

10 To open a file, move the mouse over the name of the file and then quickly press the left button twice.

ADD A SHORTCUT TO THE DESKTOP

You can add a shortcut to the desktop to provide a quick way of opening a file you use regularly.

ADD A SHORTCUT TO THE DESKTOP

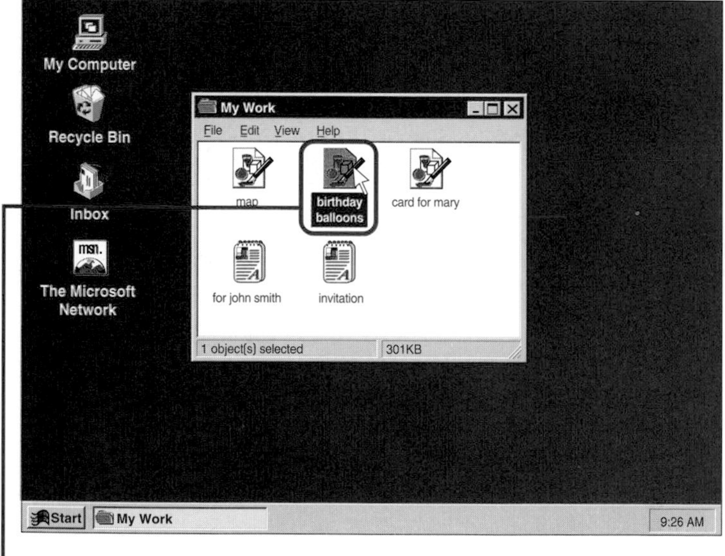

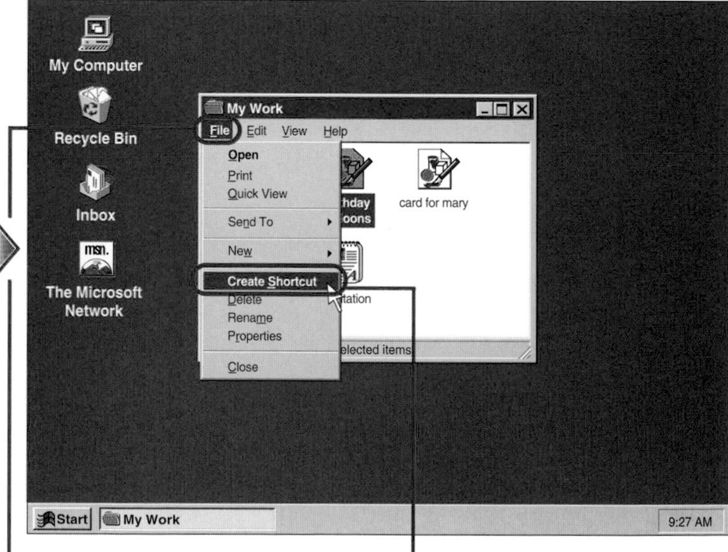

1 Move the mouse over the file you want to create a shortcut to and then press the left button.

2 Move the mouse over **File** and then press the left button.

3 Move the mouse over **Create Shortcut** and then press the left button.

Tip
You can easily tell the difference between the original file and the shortcut.
Original File
birthday balloons
Shortcut to birthday balloons
Shortcut
A shortcut looks like the original file, but displays an arrow (↗).

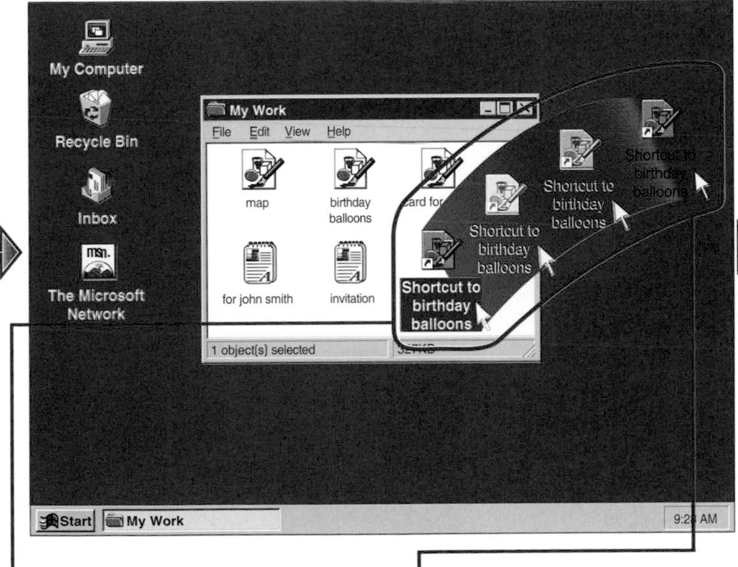

■ Windows creates a shortcut to the file.

4 To add the shortcut to the desktop, move the mouse ↖ over the shortcut.

5 Press and hold down the left button as you move the shortcut to an empty area on your desktop. Then release the button.

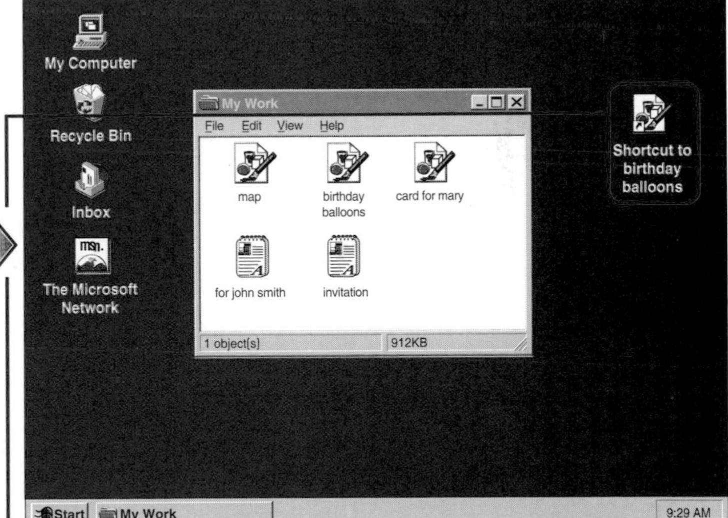

■ The shortcut appears on the desktop.

■ To open the file and display its contents on your screen, move the mouse ↖ over the shortcut and then quickly press the left button twice.

Note: When you add a shortcut to the desktop, the original file does not move. The original file remains in the same place on your hard disk.

PUT PART OF A DOCUMENT ON THE DESKTOP

■ Information you place on the desktop is called a **scrap**.

PUT PART OF A DOCUMENT ON THE DESKTOP

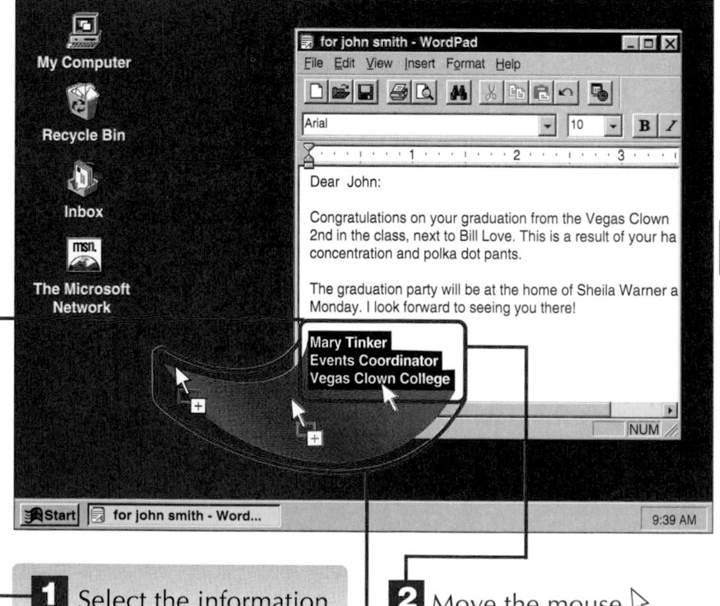

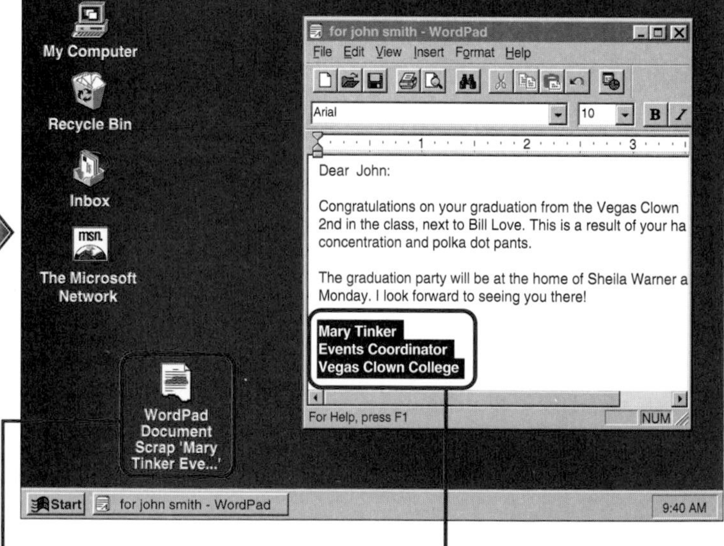

1 Select the information you want to place on the desktop.

Note: To start the WordPad program, refer to page 6.

2 Move the mouse over the information.

3 Press and hold down the left button as you move the mouse to a blank area on your desktop. Then release the button.

■ Windows creates an icon, called a **scrap**, to represent the information from the document.

Note: Some programs cannot create scraps.

■ The information does not move from the document.

Tip You can create scraps for information you frequently use in documents, such as your name and address or company logo.

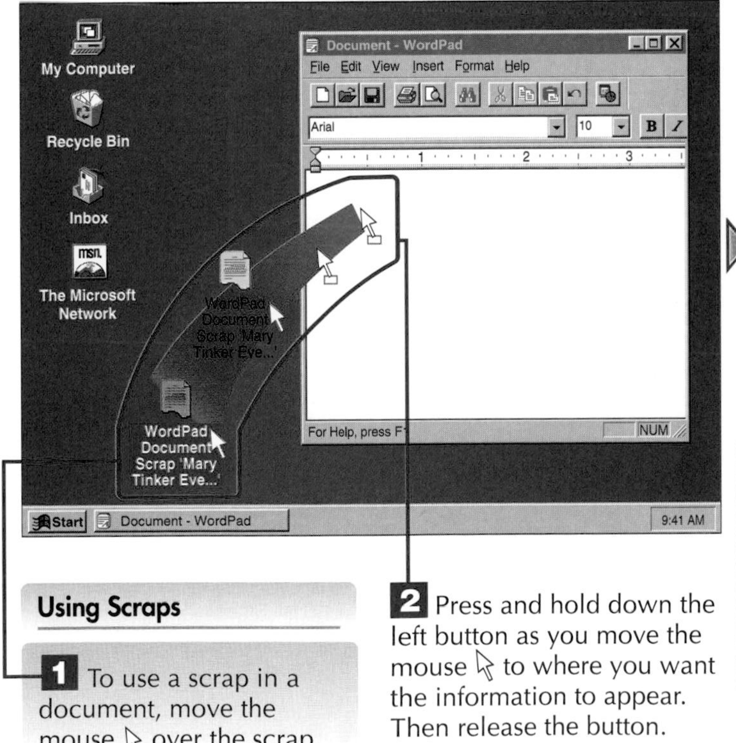

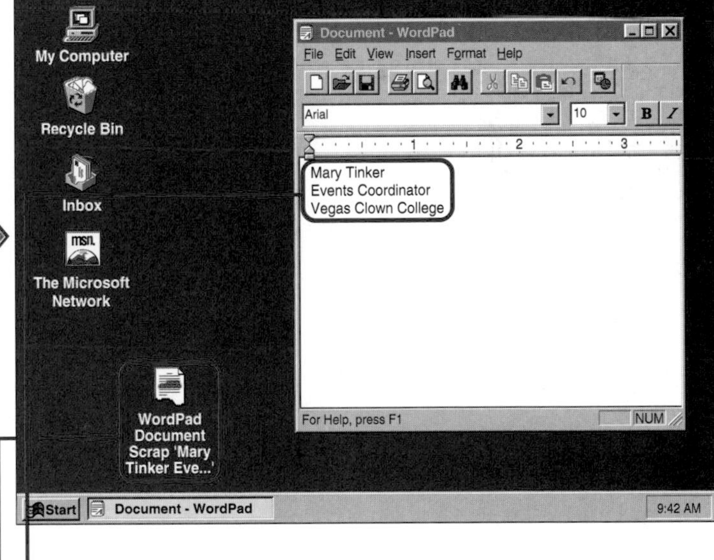

Using Scraps

1 To use a scrap in a document, move the mouse over the scrap.

2 Press and hold down the left button as you move the mouse to where you want the information to appear. Then release the button.

■ The information appears in the document.

■ The scrap remains on your desktop. This lets you place the information in as many documents as you wish.

Note: You can delete a scrap from your screen as you would delete any file.

ADD A PROGRAM TO THE START MENU

ADD A PROGRAM TO THE START MENU

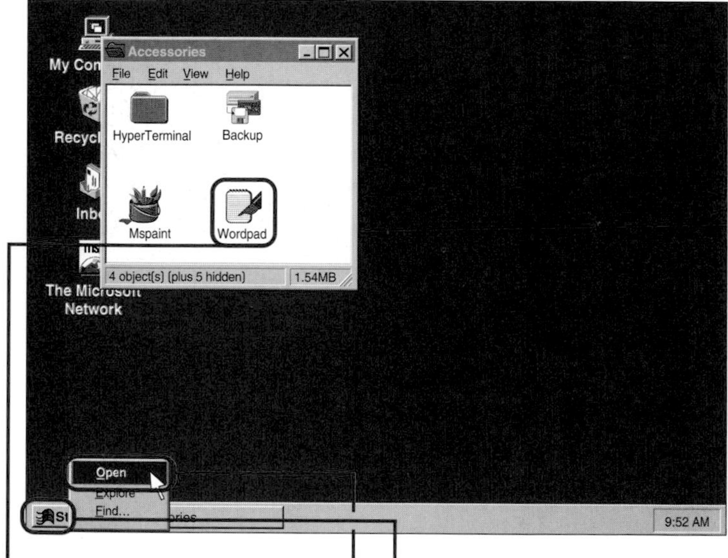

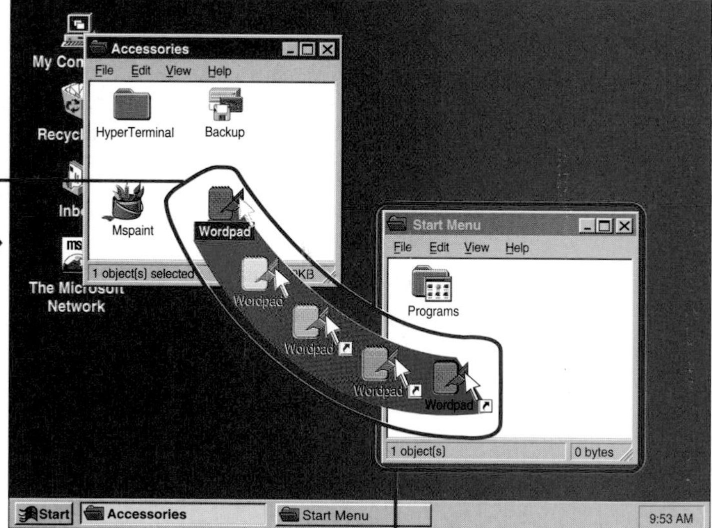

1 Locate a program you want to add to the Start menu.

*Note: To find a program, refer to the **Tip** on page 29.*

2 Move the mouse over **Start** and then press the **right** button. A menu appears.

3 Move the mouse over **Open** and then press the left button.

■ The **Start Menu** window appears.

4 To place a copy of the program in the **Start Menu** window, move the mouse over the program.

5 Press and hold down the left button as you move the program to a blank area in the **Start Menu** window. Then release the button.

If you no longer want a program to appear in the Start menu, delete the program from the Start Menu window as you would delete any file.

Removing a program from the Start Menu window does not delete the program from your hard disk.

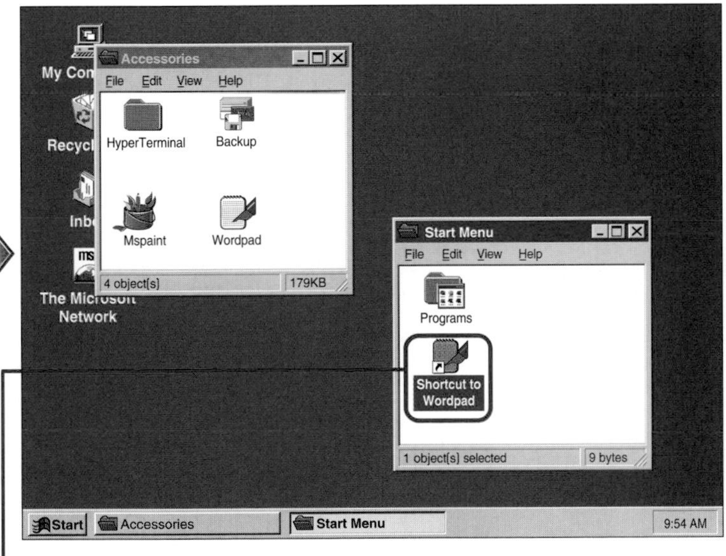

■ A copy of the program appears in the **Start Menu** window.

■ When you copy a program to the **Start Menu** window, you do not change the location of the program on your hard disk.

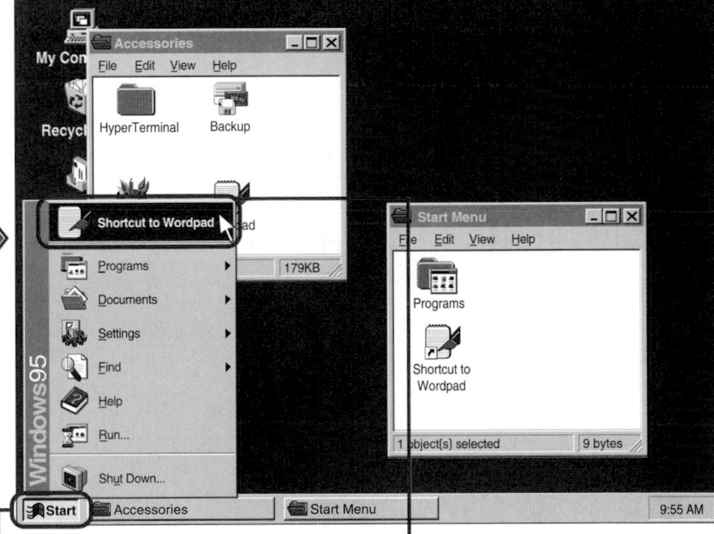

Start the Program

1 To start the program, move the mouse over **Start** and then press the left button.

■ The program you added to the Start menu appears at the top of the menu.

2 Move the mouse over the name of the program and then press the left button.

HAVE A PROGRAM START AUTOMATICALLY

If you use the same programs every day, you can have the programs start automatically every time you turn on your computer.

HAVE A PROGRAM START AUTOMATICALLY

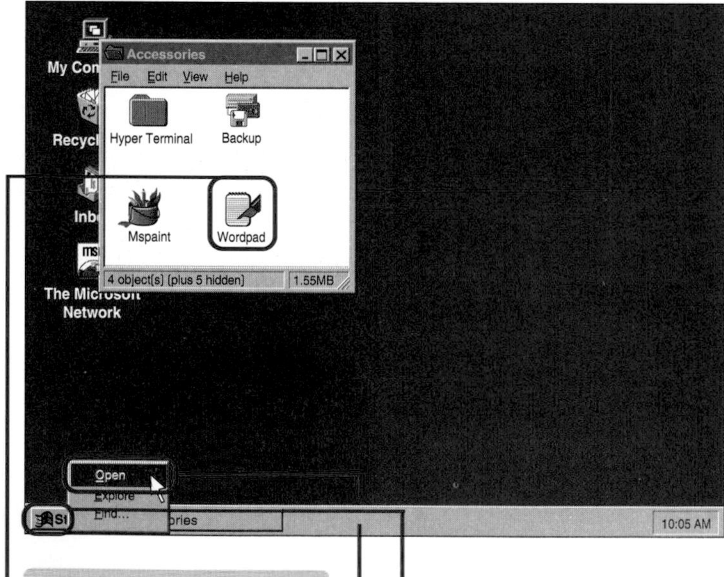

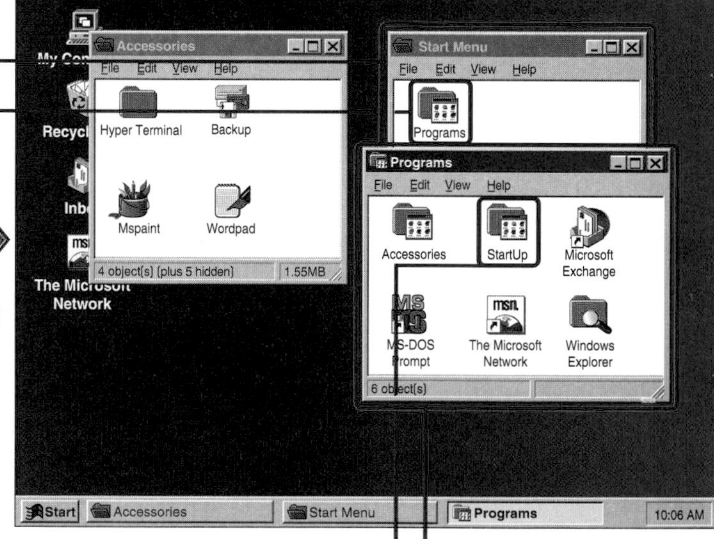

1 Locate the program you want to start automatically.

Note: To find a program, refer to the ***Tip*** *on page 29.*

2 Move the mouse over **Start** and then press the **right** button. A menu appears.

3 Move the mouse over **Open** and then press the left button.

■ The **Start Menu** window appears.

4 To display the contents of the **Programs** folder, move the mouse over the folder and then quickly press the left button twice.

■ The **Programs** window appears.

■ The **StartUp** folder contains all the programs that start automatically when you turn on your computer.

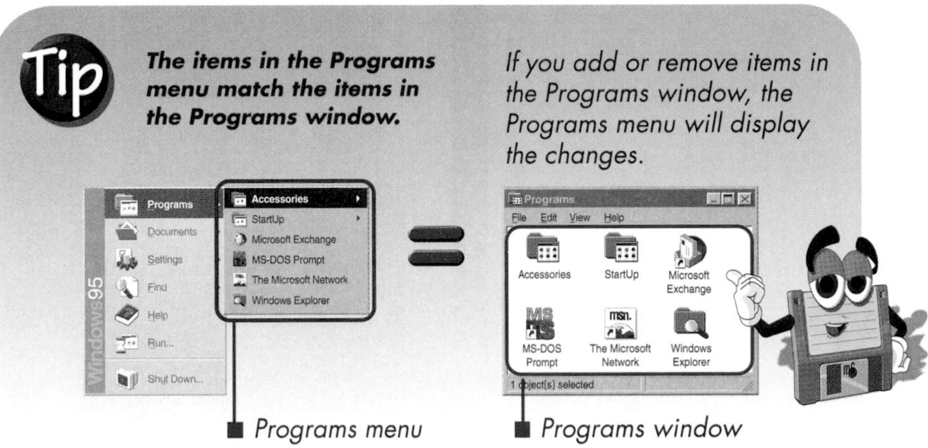

Tip
The items in the Programs menu match the items in the Programs window.
If you add or remove items in the Programs window, the Programs menu will display the changes.
Programs menu
Programs window

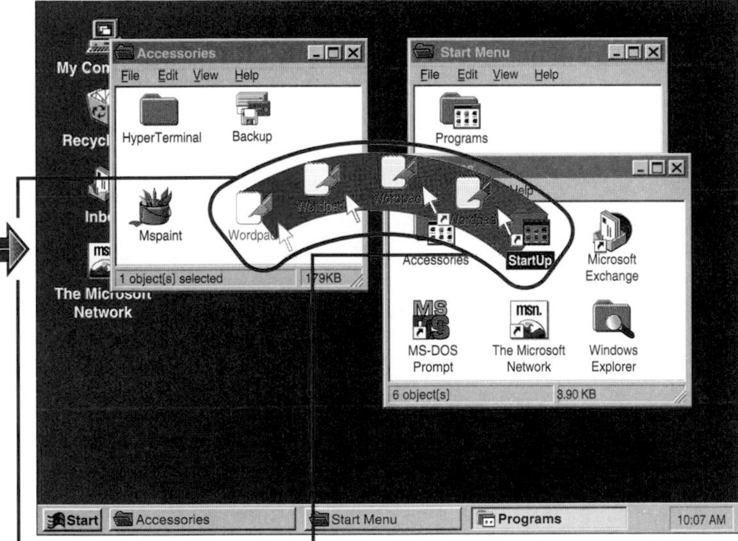

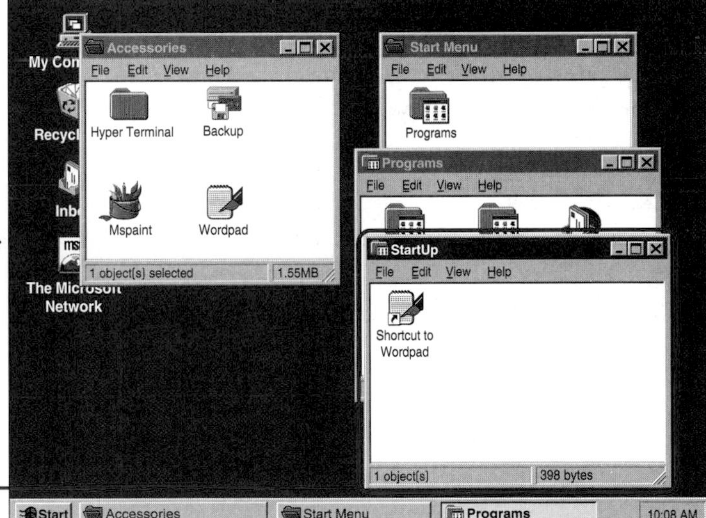

5 To add a copy of a program to the **StartUp** folder, move the mouse over the program.

6 Press and hold down the left button as you move the program over the **StartUp** folder. Then release the button.

7 To display the contents of the **StartUp** folder, move the mouse over the folder and then quickly press the left button twice.

■ The **StartUp** window appears. The programs in this window will start automatically every time you turn on your computer.

■ If you no longer want a program to start automatically, delete the program from the **StartUp** window as you would delete any file.

In this chapter you will learn how to change the appearance of your screen and the way your keyboard operates.

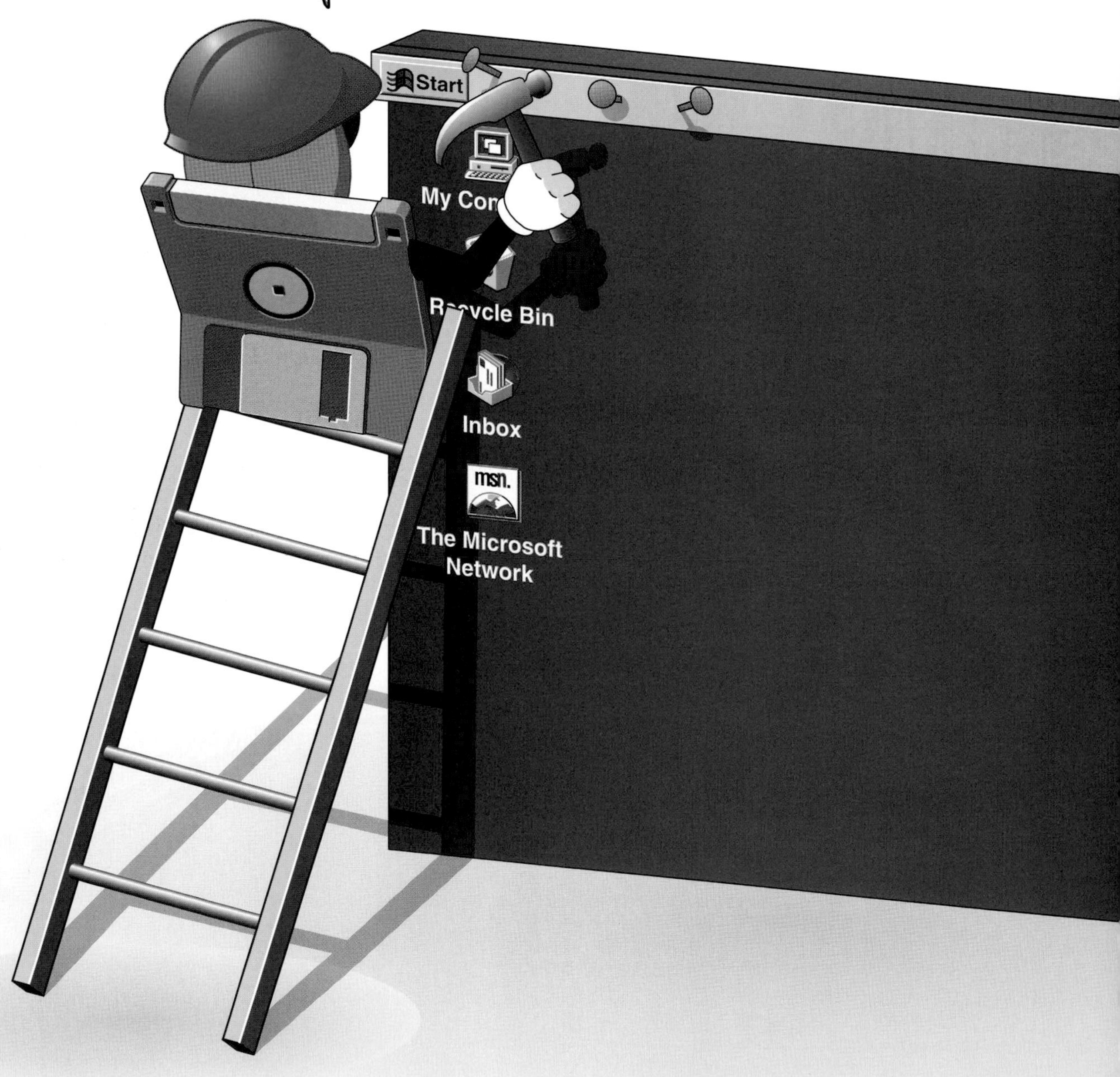

PERSONALIZE WINDOWS

MOVE THE TASKBAR

You can move the taskbar to a more convenient location on your screen.

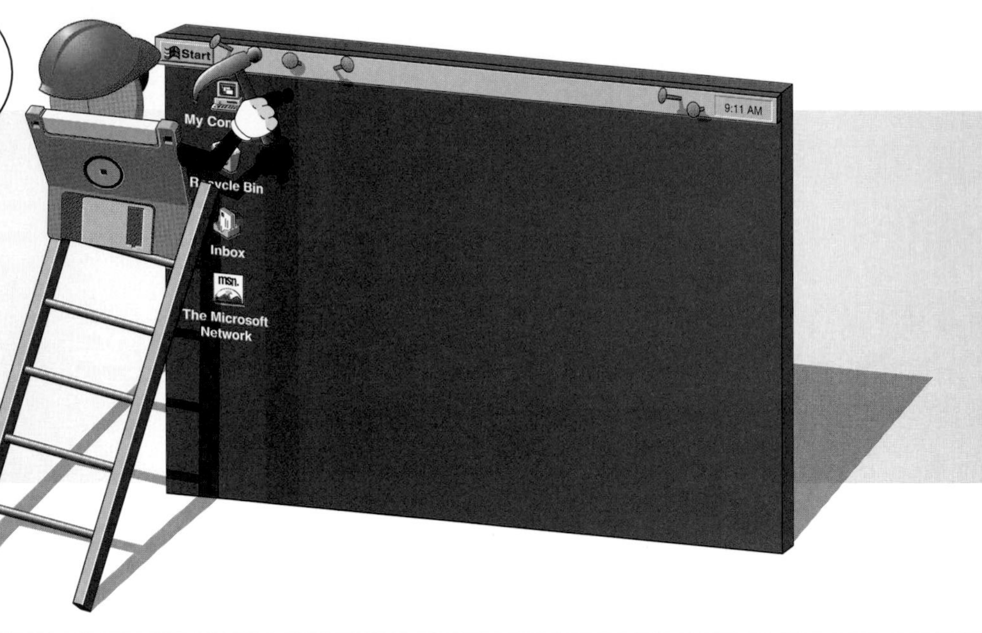

MOVE THE TASKBAR

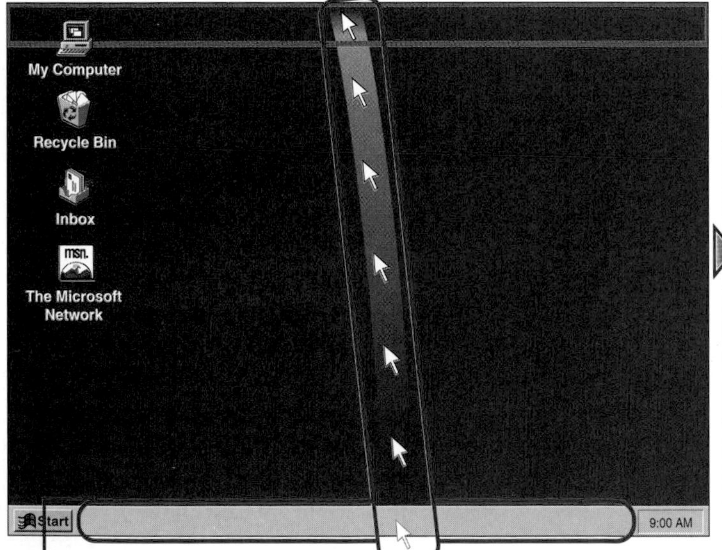

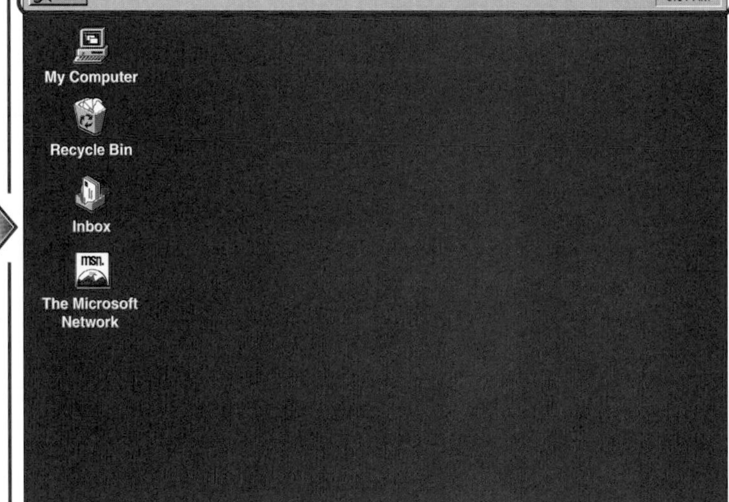

1 Move the mouse over a blank area on the taskbar.

2 Press and hold down the left button as you move the taskbar to a new location on your screen. Then release the button.

■ The taskbar moves to the new location.

Note: You can move the taskbar to the top, bottom, left or right side of your screen.

SIZE THE TASKBAR

You can change the size of the taskbar so it can display more information.
Start
Document - WordPad
Untitled - Paint
Calculator
9:26 AM

SIZE THE TASKBAR

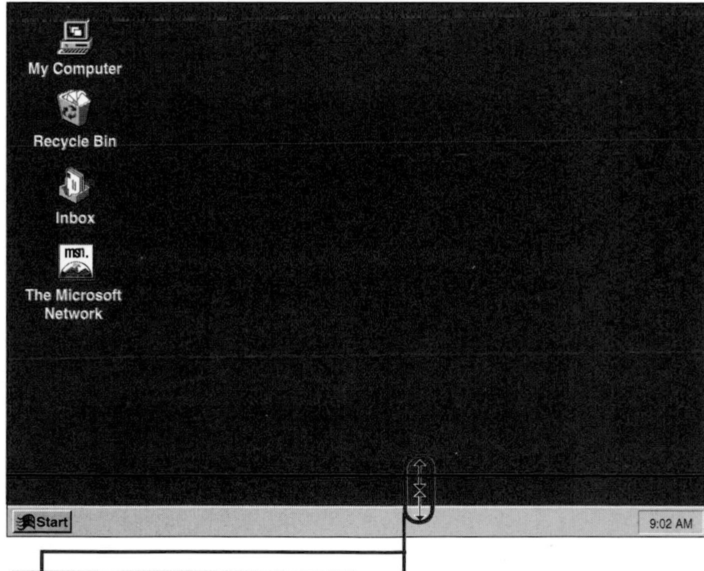

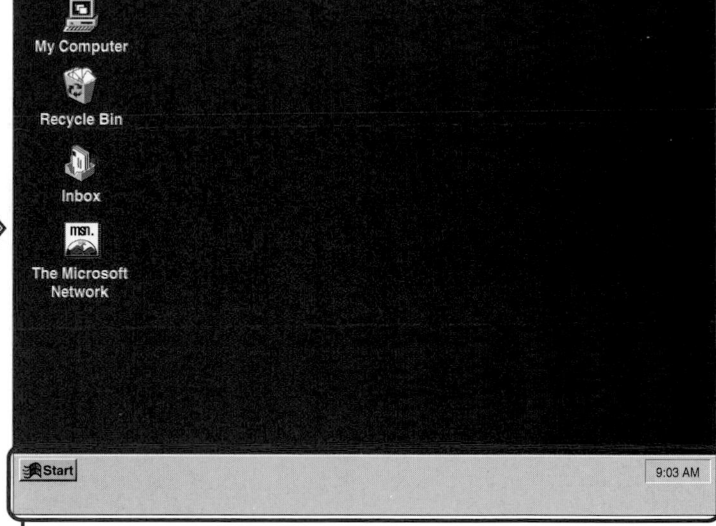

1 Move the mouse ↖ over the edge of the taskbar and ↖ changes to ↕.

2 Press and hold down the left button as you move the mouse ↕ until the outline of the taskbar displays the size you want. Then release the button.

■ The taskbar changes to the new size.

HIDE THE TASKBAR

HIDE THE TASKBAR

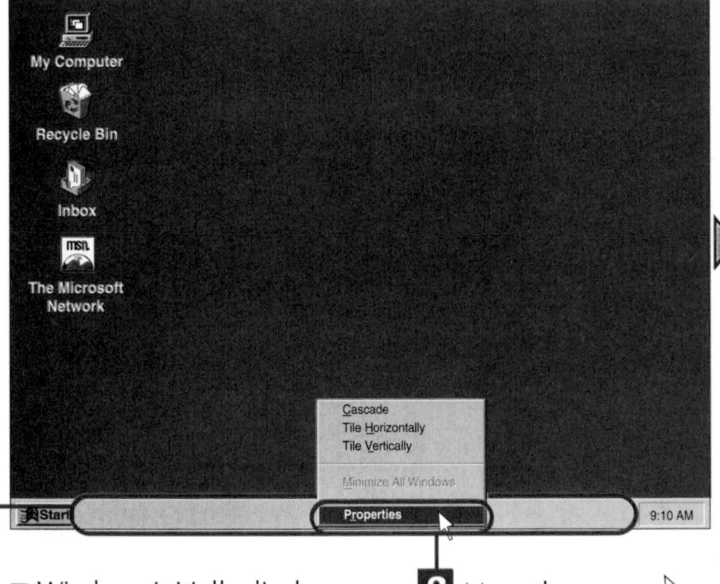

■ Windows initially displays the taskbar at all times.

1 To hide the taskbar, move the mouse over a blank area on the taskbar and then press the **right** button. A menu appears.

2 Move the mouse over **Properties** and then press the left button.

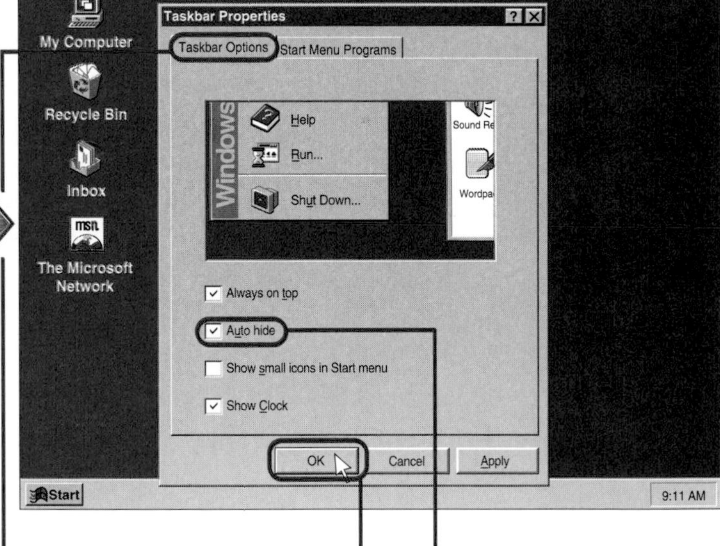

■ The **Taskbar Properties** dialog box appears.

3 Move the mouse over the **Taskbar Options** tab and then press the left button.

4 Move the mouse over **Auto hide** and then press the left button (☐ changes to ☑).

5 Move the mouse over **OK** and then press the left button.

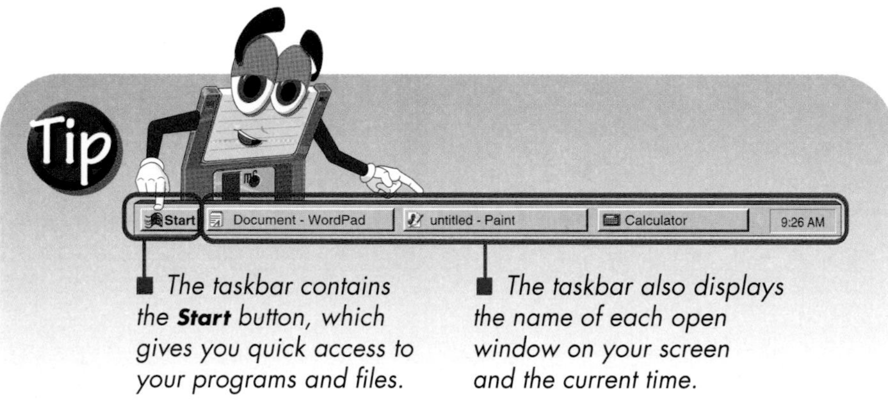

■ *The taskbar contains the* ***Start*** *button, which gives you quick access to your programs and files.*

■ *The taskbar also displays the name of each open window on your screen and the current time.*

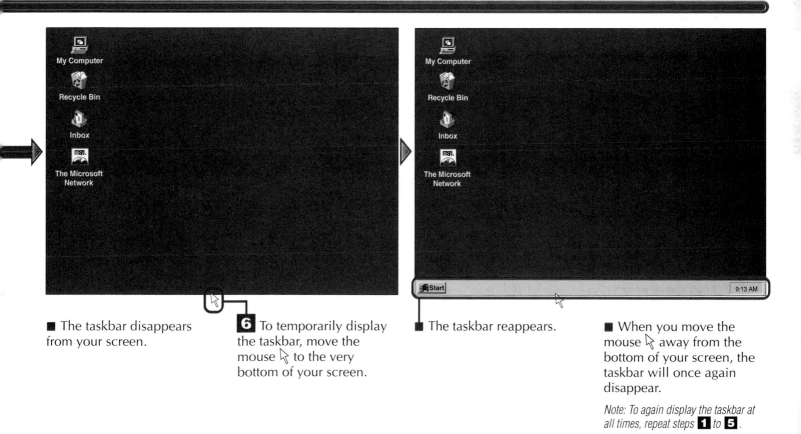

■ The taskbar disappears from your screen.

6 To temporarily display the taskbar, move the mouse ⇖ to the very bottom of your screen.

■ The taskbar reappears.

■ When you move the mouse ⇖ away from the bottom of your screen, the taskbar will once again disappear.

Note: To again display the taskbar at all times, repeat steps **1** *to* **5**.

CHANGE SCREEN RESOLUTION

You can change the amount of information that can fit on your screen.

You cannot change the screen resolution for some monitors.

CHANGE SCREEN RESOLUTION

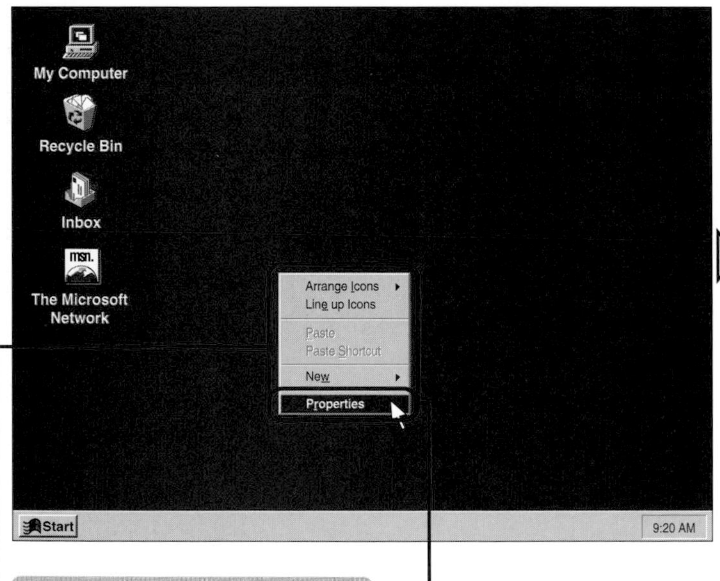

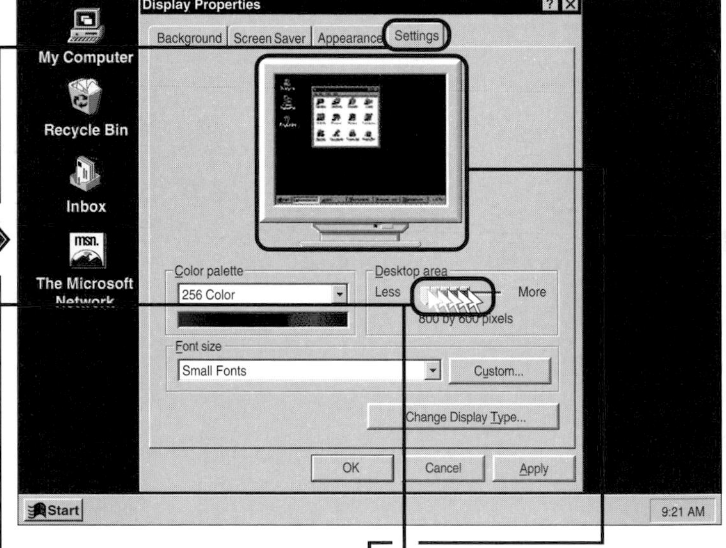

1 Move the mouse over a blank area on your desktop and then press the **right** button. A menu appears.

2 Move the mouse over **Properties** and then press the left button.

■ The **Display Properties** dialog box appears.

3 Move the mouse over the **Settings** tab and then press the left button.

4 To change the resolution, move the mouse over the slider.

5 Press and hold down the left button as you move the slider until you select the resolution you want to use. Then release the button.

■ This area displays how your screen will look at the new resolution.

640 x 480

Lower resolutions display larger images on the screen. This lets you see information more clearly.

800 x 600

1024 x 768

Higher resolutions display smaller images on the screen. This lets you display more information at once.

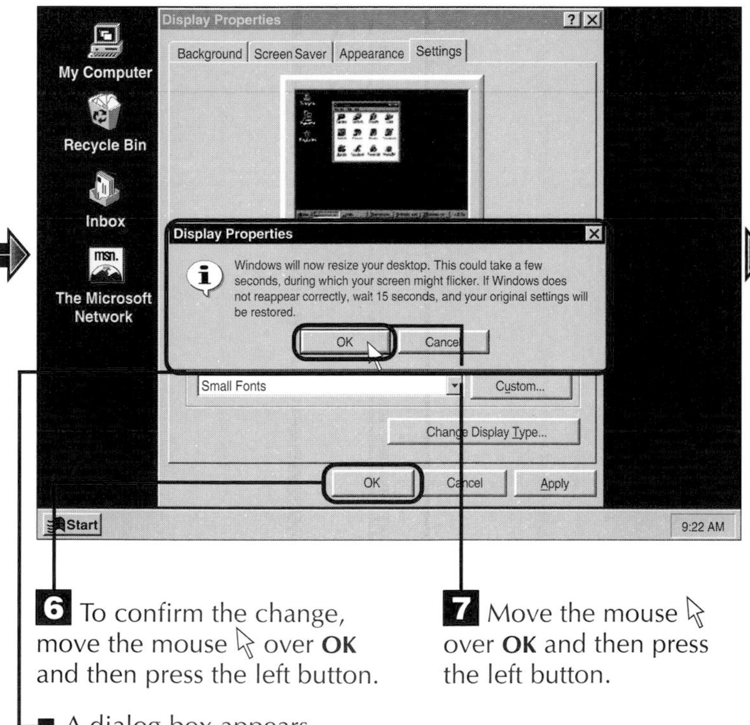

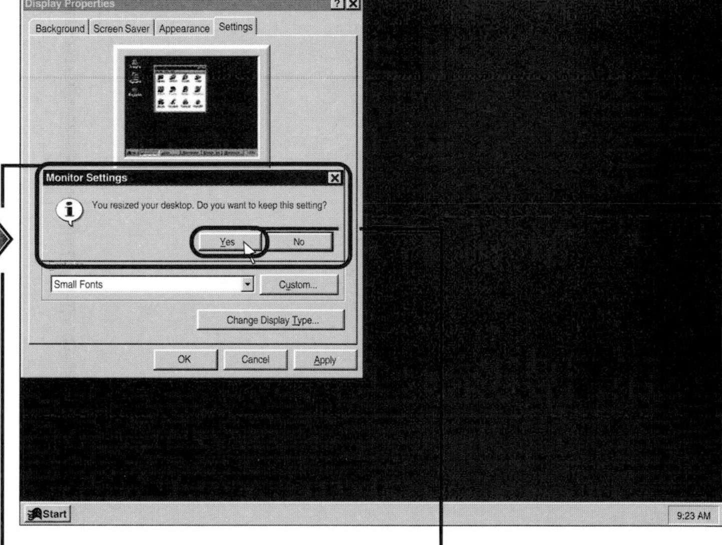

6 To confirm the change, move the mouse over **OK** and then press the left button.

■ A dialog box appears.

*Note: Some computers will ask you to restart your computer. To do so, move the mouse over **Yes** and then press the left button.*

7 Move the mouse over **OK** and then press the left button.

■ Windows resizes the information on your screen.

■ The **Monitor Settings** dialog box appears, asking if you want to keep the setting.

8 To keep the setting, move the mouse over **Yes** and then press the left button.

CHANGE COLOR DEPTH

You can change the number of colors displayed on your screen. More colors result in more realistic images.

CHANGE COLOR DEPTH

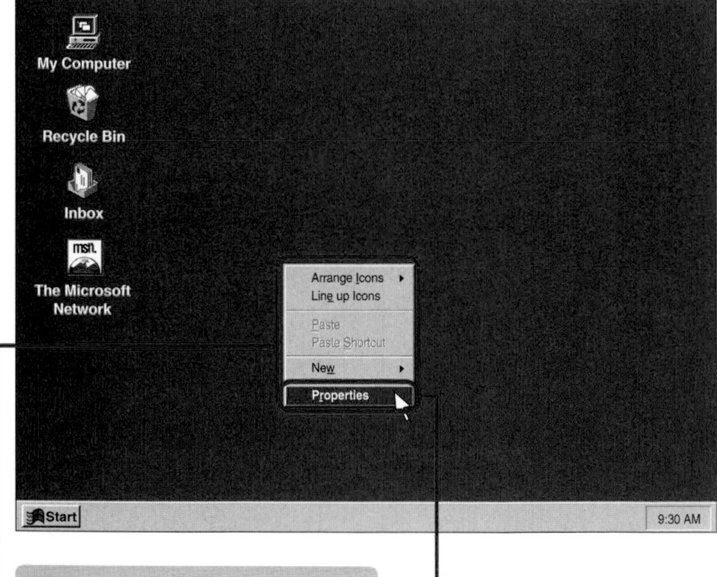

1 Move the mouse over a blank area on your desktop and then press the **right** button. A menu appears.

2 Move the mouse over **Properties** and then press the left button.

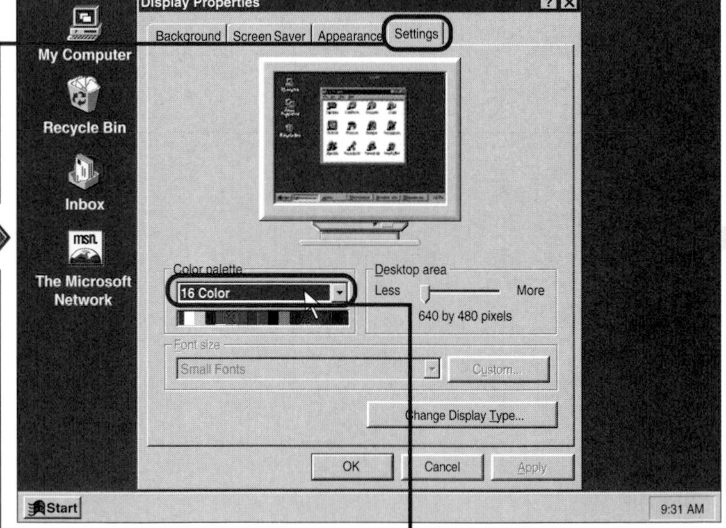

■ The **Display Properties** dialog box appears.

3 Move the mouse over the **Settings** tab and then press the left button.

4 To select a color depth, move the mouse over this area and then press the left button.

16 Color
Choppy-looking images.

256 Color
Ideal for most home and business applications.

High Color
Ideal for video and desktop publishing.

True Color
Ideal for high-end graphics programs and photo-retouching.

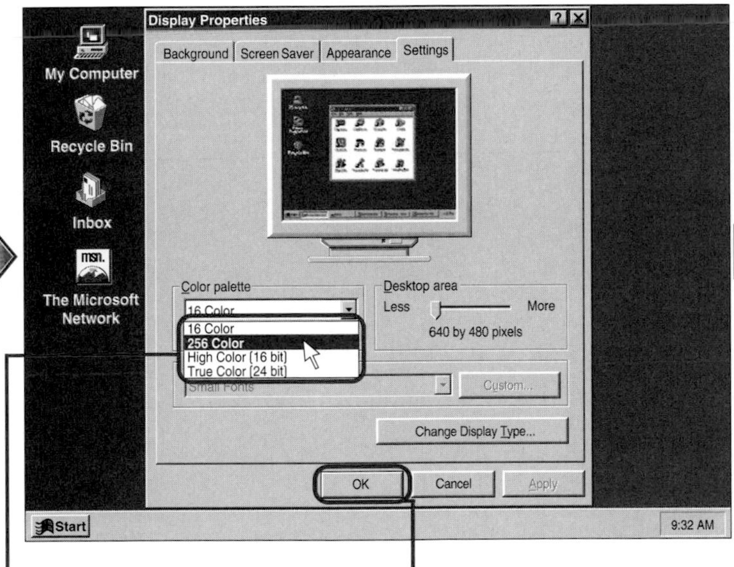

5 Move the mouse over the color depth you want to use and then press the left button.

Note: Make sure you select a color depth your computer system can handle.

6 To confirm the change, move the mouse over **OK** and then press the left button.

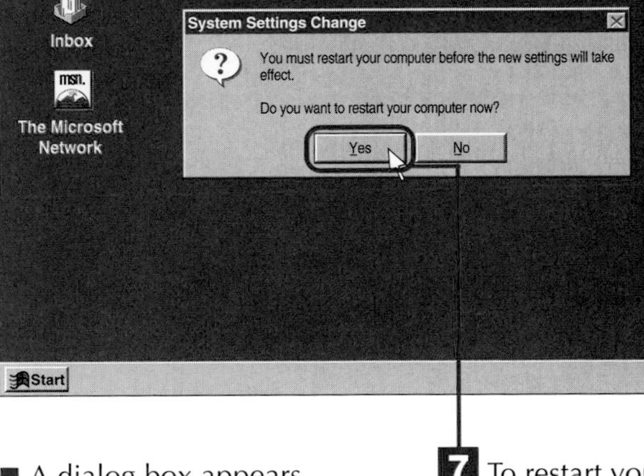

■ A dialog box appears, telling you that you must restart your computer before the color depth you selected will take effect.

7 To restart your computer, move the mouse over **Yes** and then press the left button.

CHANGE KEYBOARD SETTINGS

You can change the way your keyboard operates to suit your needs.

For more ways to customize your keyboard, refer to pages 54-57.

CHANGE KEYBOARD SETTINGS

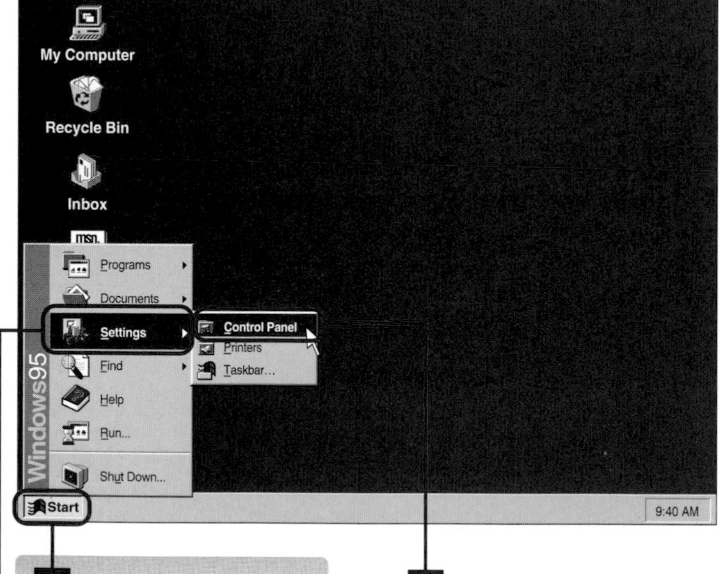

1 Move the mouse over **Start** and then press the left button.

2 Move the mouse over **Settings**.

3 Move the mouse over **Control Panel** and then press the left button.

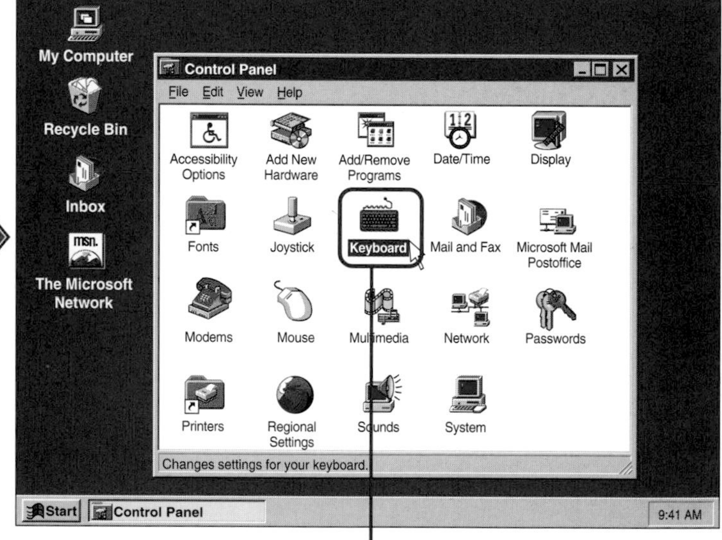

■ The **Control Panel** window appears.

4 Move the mouse over **Keyboard** and then quickly press the left button twice.

■ The **Keyboard Properties** dialog box appears.

To prevent injury, your elbows should be level with the keyboard when you are typing. Your wrists should be higher than your fingers and should remain straight at all times.

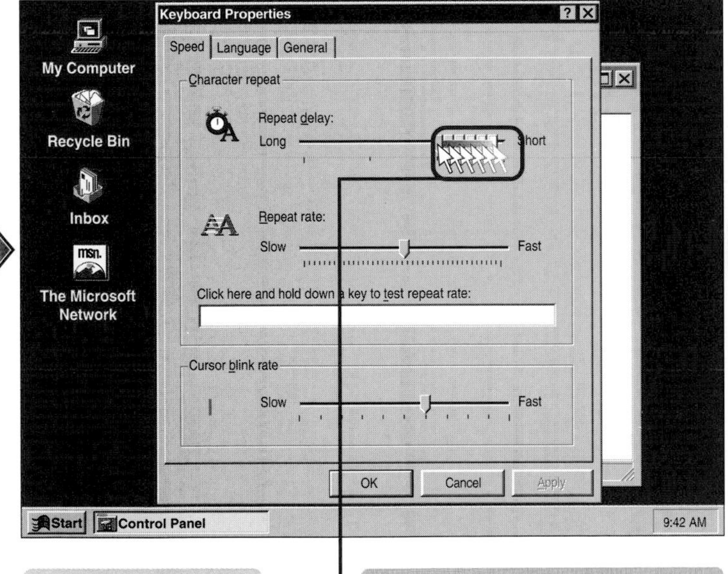

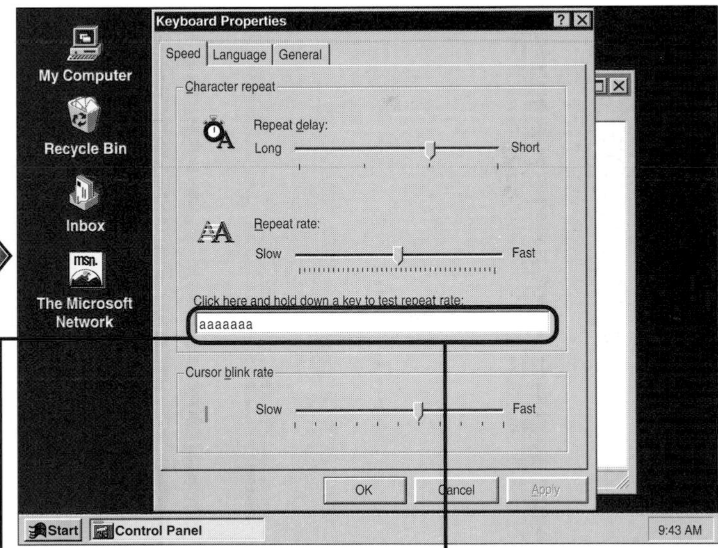

Repeat Delay

You can change how long you must hold down a key before a character starts repeating.

1 Move the mouse over this slider.

2 Press and hold down the left button as you move the slider to make the repeat delay longer or shorter. Then release the button.

3 To test the repeat delay, move the mouse over this area and then press the left button.

4 Press and hold down a key on your keyboard.

CHANGE KEYBOARD SETTINGS

You can further customize your keyboard by changing the repeat rate and cursor blink rate.

CHANGE KEYBOARD SETTINGS (CONTINUED)

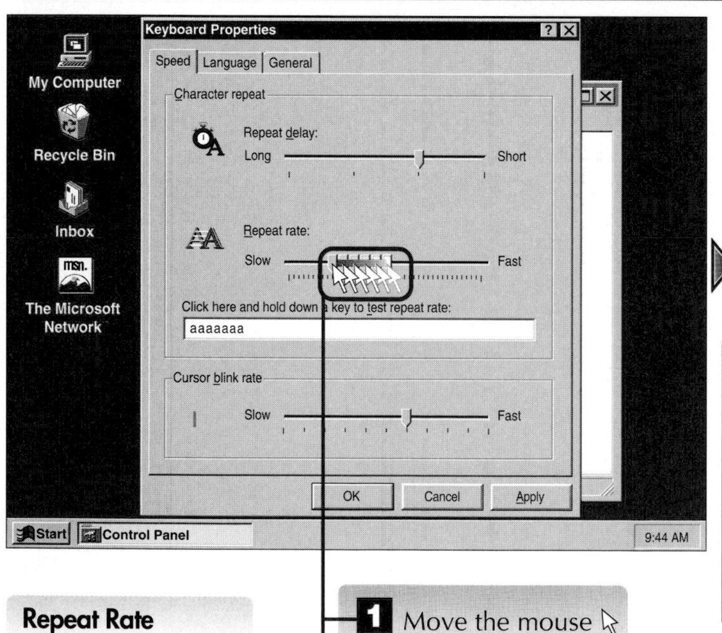

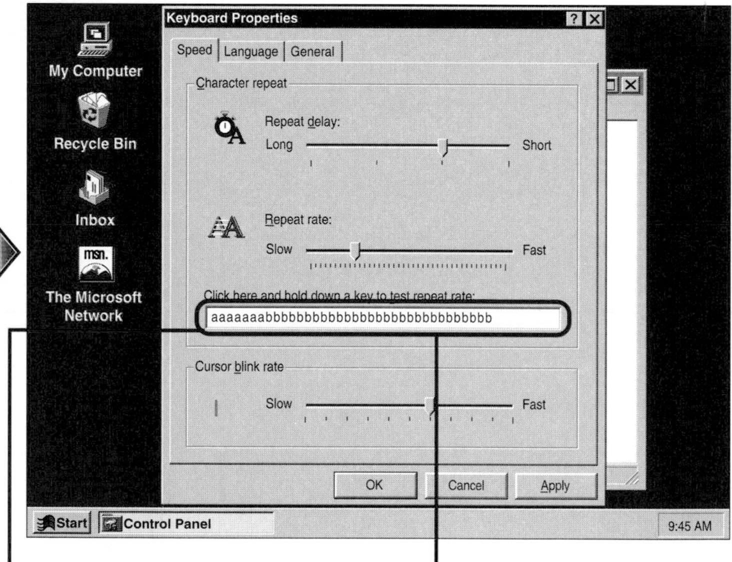

Repeat Rate

You can change how quickly characters repeat when you hold down a key.

1 Move the mouse over this slider.

2 Press and hold down the left button as you move the slider to make the repeat rate slower or faster. Then release the button.

3 To test the repeat rate, move the mouse over this area and then press the left button.

4 Press and hold down a key on your keyboard.

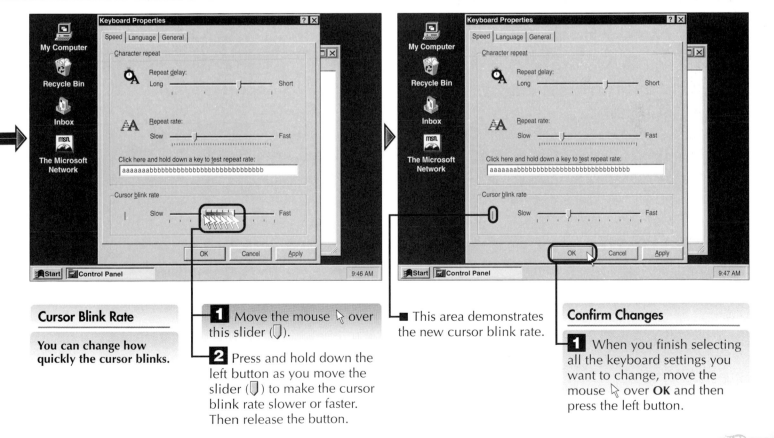

Tip
Most keyboards have small bumps on the D and K keys or on the F and J keys. These bumps help you position your fingers without looking at the keyboard.
D
K

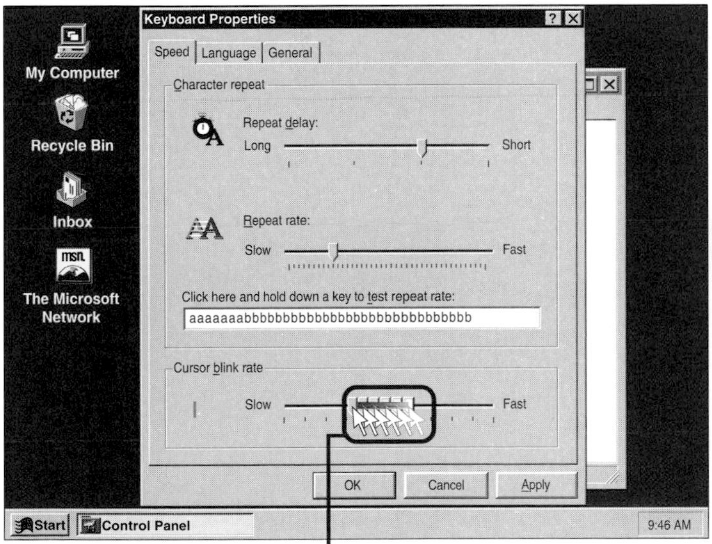

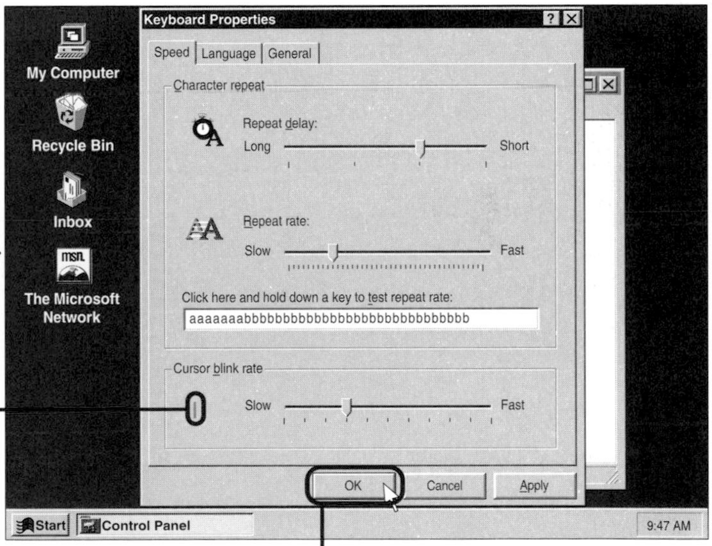

Cursor Blink Rate

You can change how quickly the cursor blinks.

1 Move the mouse over this slider.

2 Press and hold down the left button as you move the slider to make the cursor blink rate slower or faster. Then release the button.

■ This area demonstrates the new cursor blink rate.

Confirm Changes

1 When you finish selecting all the keyboard settings you want to change, move the mouse over **OK** and then press the left button.

ACCESSIBILITY OPTIONS

Windows offers many options for people with disabilities.

Even if you do not have a disability, you may find some of the accessibility options very useful.

DISPLAY ACCESSIBILITY OPTIONS

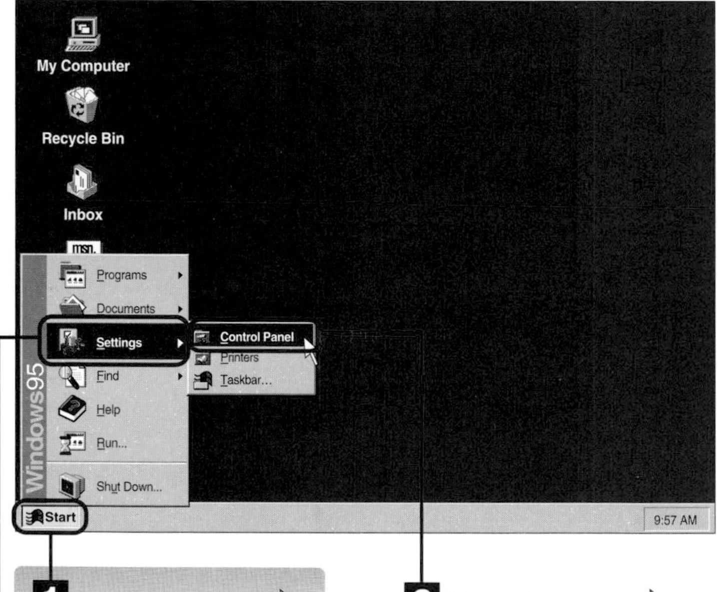

1 Move the mouse over **Start** and then press the left button.

2 Move the mouse over **Settings**.

3 Move the mouse over **Control Panel** and then press the left button.

■ The **Control Panel** window appears.

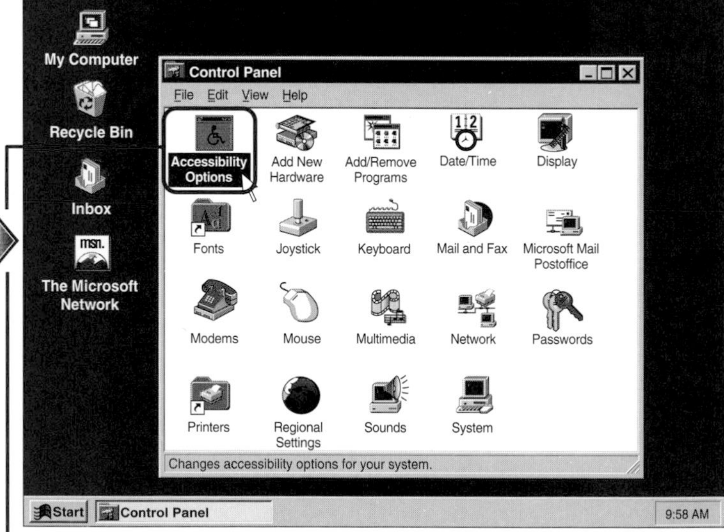

4 Move the mouse over **Accessibility Options** and then quickly press the left button twice.

*Note: If **Accessibility Options** is not available, you must add the Windows component, which is found in the Accessibility Options category. To do so, refer to page 96.*

■ The **Accessibility Properties** dialog box appears.

You can change the display to make your screen easier to read. This is ideal for people with vision problems.

CHANGE DISPLAY

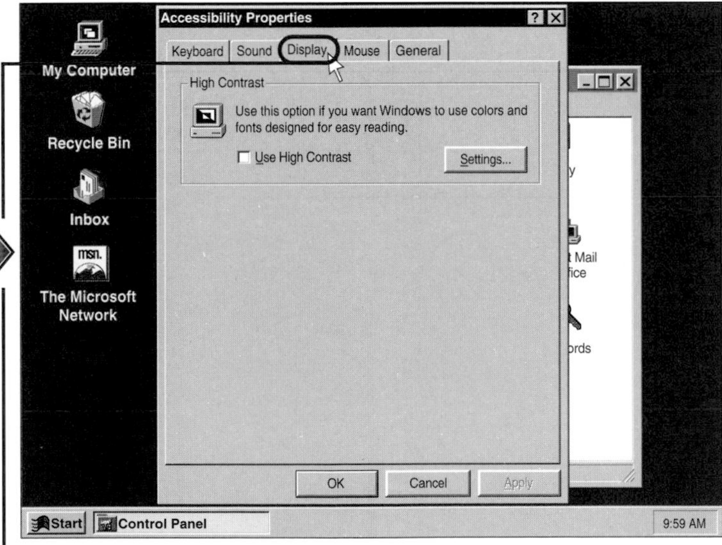

1 To make the screen easier to read, move the mouse ↖ over the **Display** tab and then press the left button.

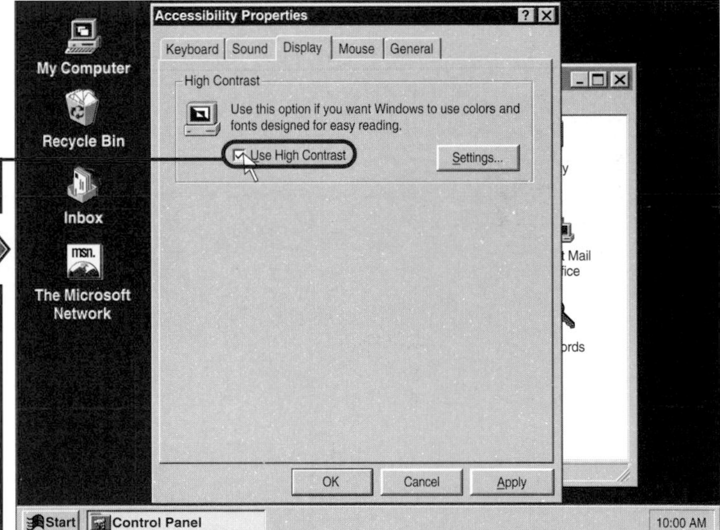

2 Move the mouse ↖ over this area and then press the left button (☐ changes to ☑).

Note: To confirm this change and skip all other accessibility options, refer to page 57.

ACCESSIBILITY OPTIONS

Windows offers several options to make your keyboard easier to use.

CUSTOMIZE YOUR KEYBOARD

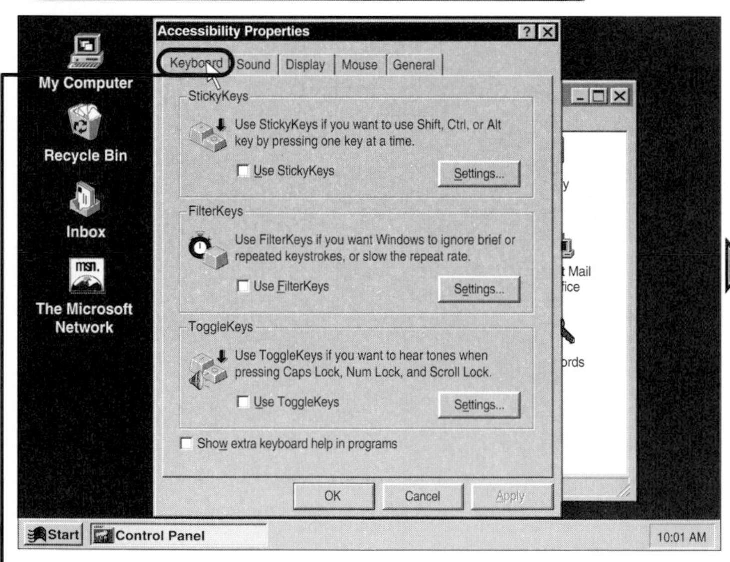

1 To change the keyboard settings, move the mouse over the **Keyboard** tab and then press the left button.

*Note: To display the **Accessibility Properties** dialog box, perform steps* **1** *to* **4** *on page 52.*

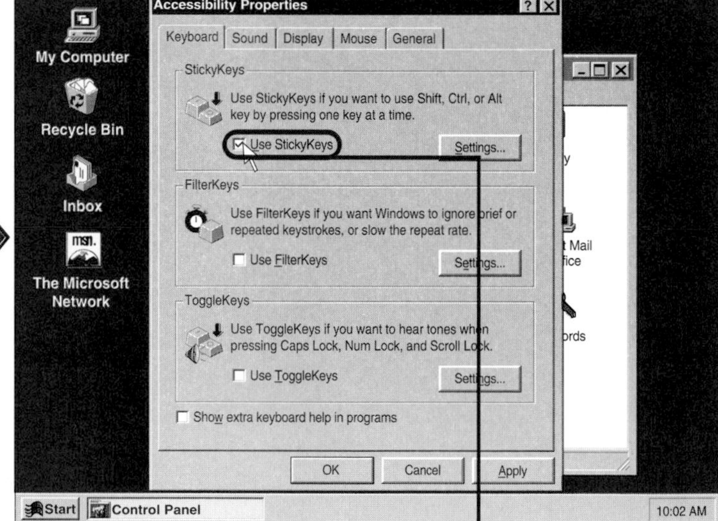

StickyKeys

■ **You can use this option if you have difficulty pressing two keys at the same time.**

■ When you press Shift, Ctrl or Alt on your keyboard, the key will remain active until you press the second key.

1 To turn on StickyKeys, move the mouse over this area and then press the left button (☐ changes to ☑).

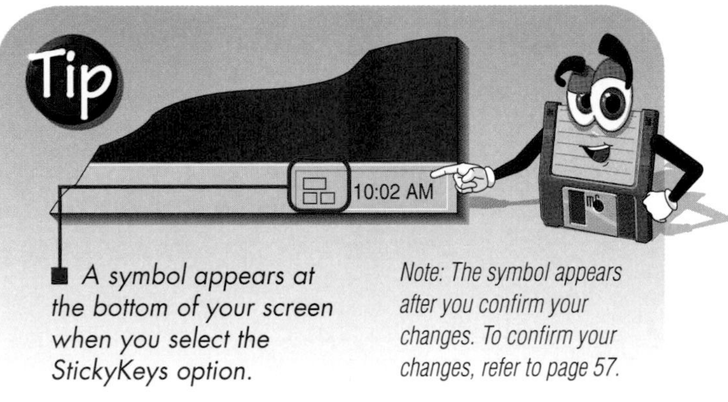

■ A symbol appears at the bottom of your screen when you select the StickyKeys option.

Note: The symbol appears after you confirm your changes. To confirm your changes, refer to page 57.

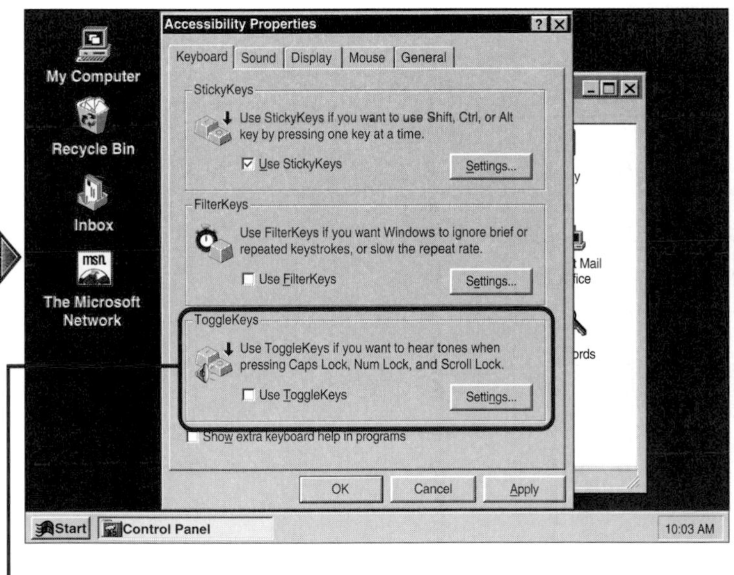

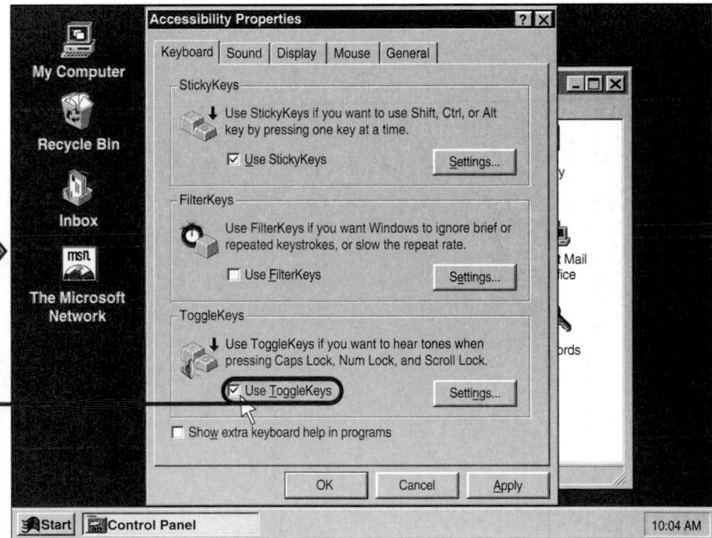

ToggleKeys

■ You can use this option if you want to hear a tone when you press Caps Lock, Num Lock or Scroll Lock on your keyboard.

■ Your computer will play a high sound when you turn a key on and a low sound when you turn a key off.

1 To turn on ToggleKeys, move the mouse over this area and then press the left button (☐ changes to ☑).

Note: To confirm the changes and skip all other accessibility options, refer to page 57.

ACCESSIBILITY OPTIONS

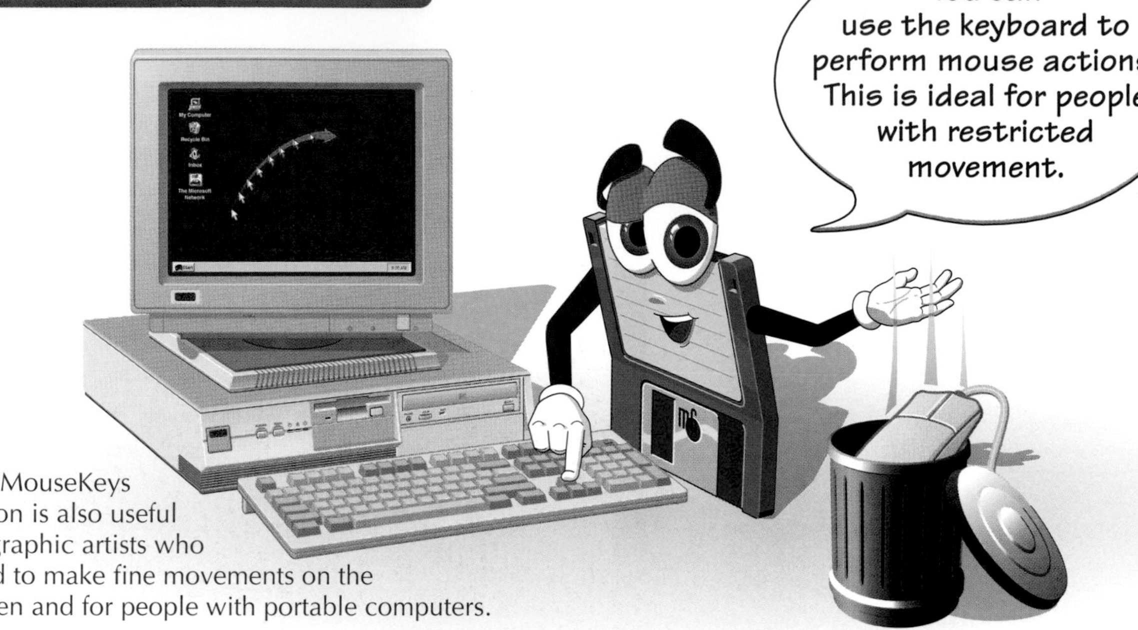

You can use the keyboard to perform mouse actions. This is ideal for people with restricted movement.

The MouseKeys option is also useful for graphic artists who need to make fine movements on the screen and for people with portable computers.

CHANGE MOUSE SETTINGS

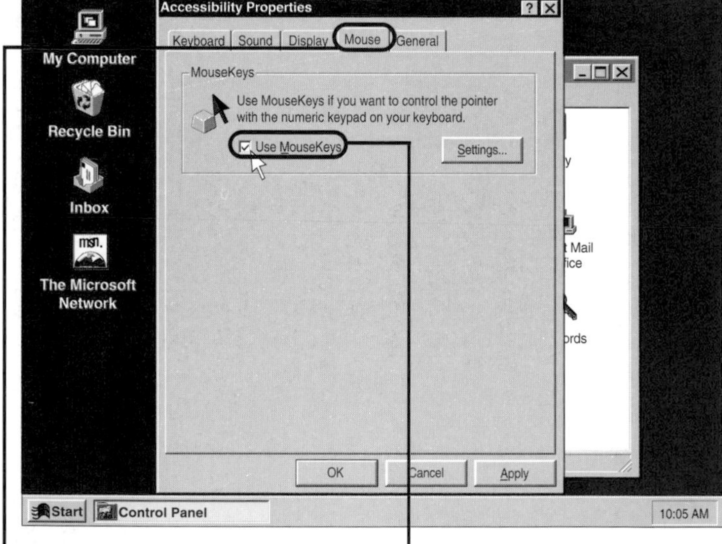

1 To use the keyboard to perform mouse actions, move the mouse ↖ over the **Mouse** tab and then press the left button.

Note: To display the ***Accessibility Properties*** *dialog box, perform steps* **1** *to* **4** *on page 52.*

2 To turn on MouseKeys, move the mouse ↖ over this area and then press the left button (☐ changes to ☑).

■ To confirm this change, refer to page 57.

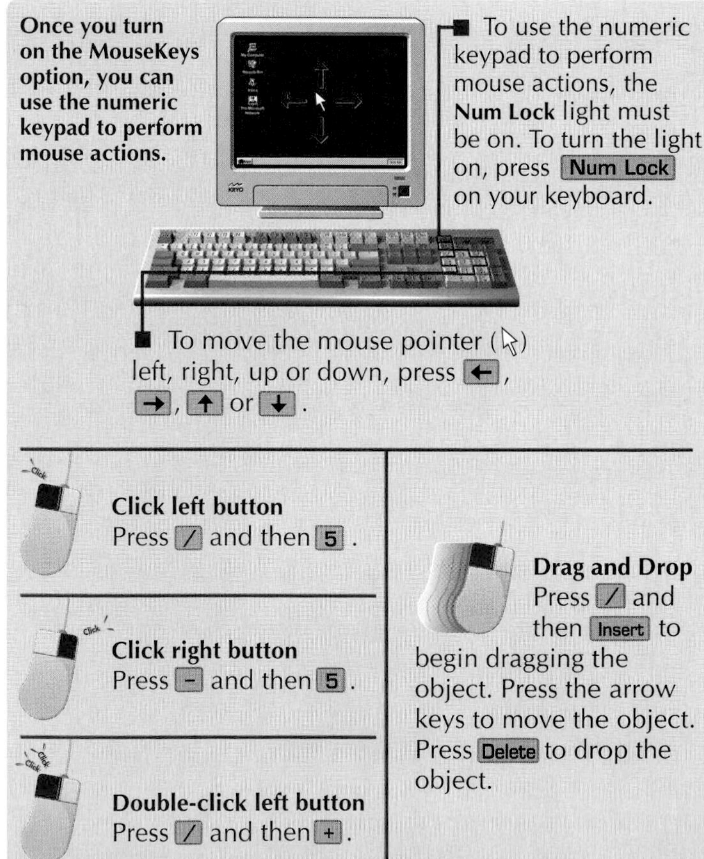

Once you turn on the MouseKeys option, you can use the numeric keypad to perform mouse actions.

■ To use the numeric keypad to perform mouse actions, the **Num Lock** light must be on. To turn the light on, press Num Lock on your keyboard.

■ To move the mouse pointer (↖) left, right, up or down, press ←, →, ↑ or ↓.

Click left button
Press / and then 5.

Click right button
Press - and then 5.

Double-click left button
Press / and then +.

Drag and Drop
Press / and then Insert to begin dragging the object. Press the arrow keys to move the object. Press Delete to drop the object.

CONFIRM CHANGES

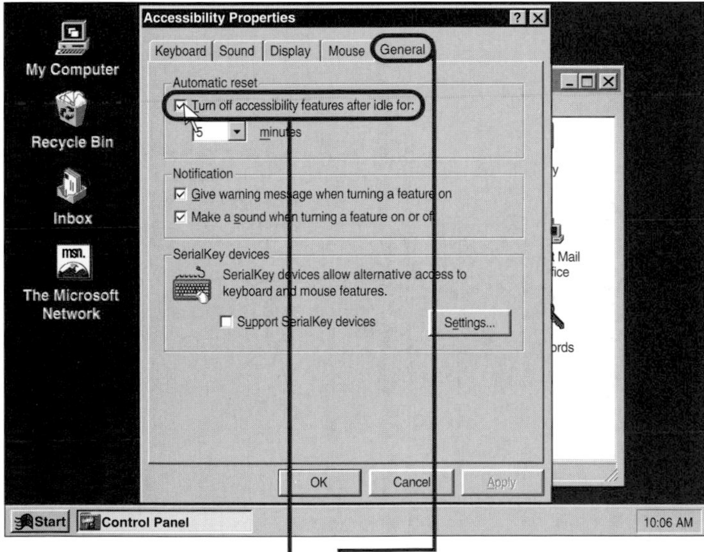

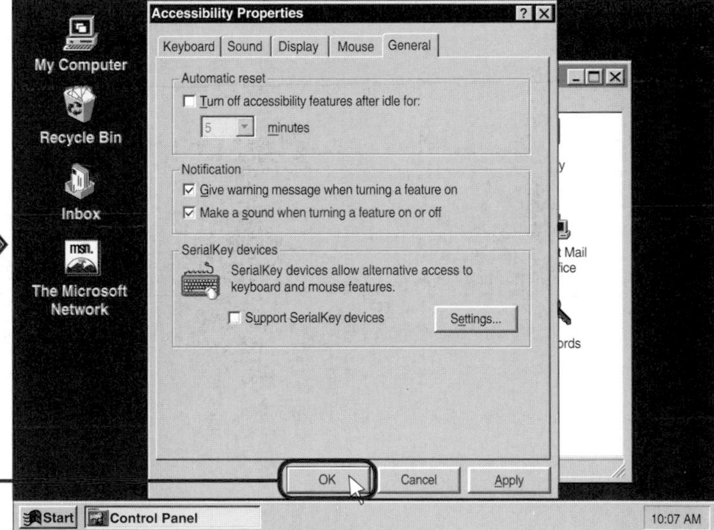

Windows automatically turns off the accessibility options when you do not use your computer for a certain period of time.

1 If you do not want your computer to turn off the accessibility options after a certain period of time, move the mouse over the **General** tab and then press the left button.

2 Move the mouse over this area and then press the left button (☑ changes to ☐).

3 When you finish selecting all the accessibility options you want to use, move the mouse over **OK** and then press the left button.

In this chapter you will learn how to view videos and hear and record sounds.
Document - WordPad
File Edit View Insert Format Help
Times New Roman
Dear Mr. President:
Inbox
Start
9:06 AM
NUM
Tap
Bass Treble
mG music
Jazz

CHAPTER 4

ENTERTAINING FEATURES

PLAY A GAME

Windows comes with several games to entertain you.

PLAY A GAME

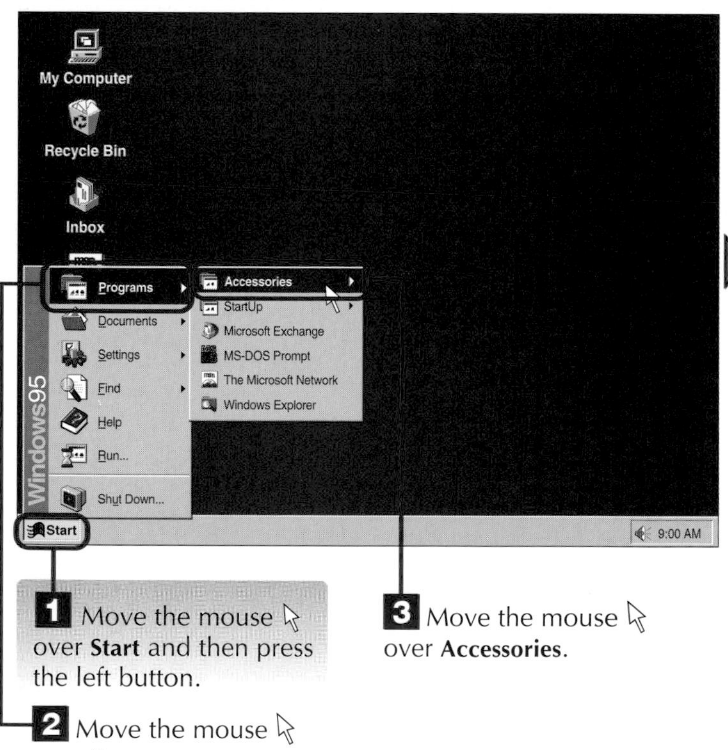

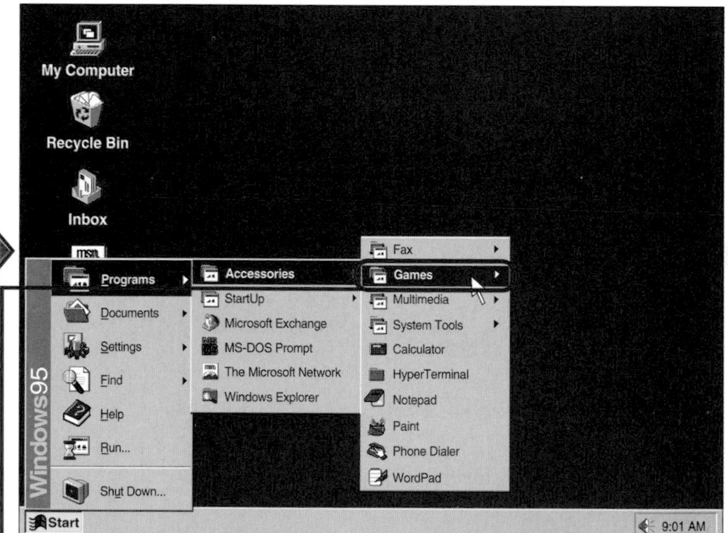

1 Move the mouse over **Start** and then press the left button.

2 Move the mouse over **Programs**.

3 Move the mouse over **Accessories**.

4 Move the mouse over **Games**.

*Note: If **Games** is not available, you must add the Windows component, which is found in the Accessories category. To do so, refer to page 96.*

Tip ***Windows offers these games.***

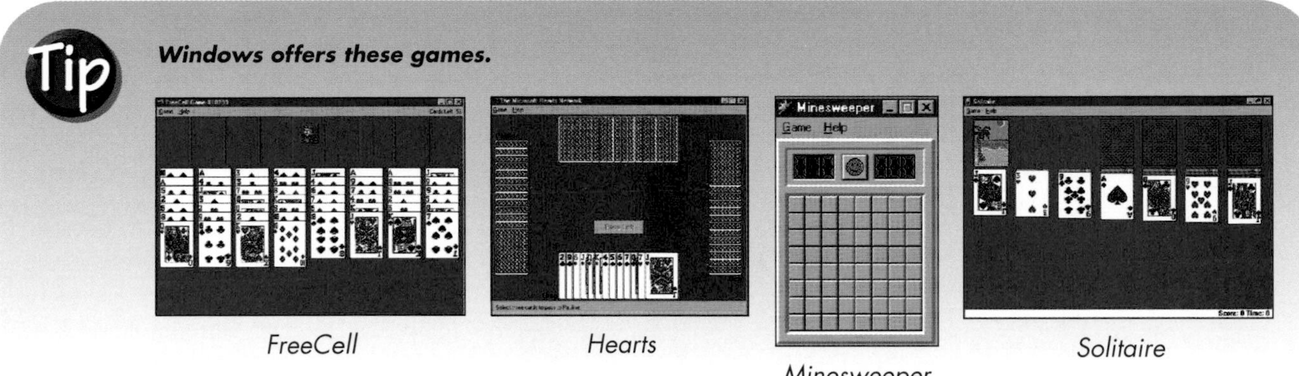

FreeCell *Hearts* *Minesweeper* *Solitaire*

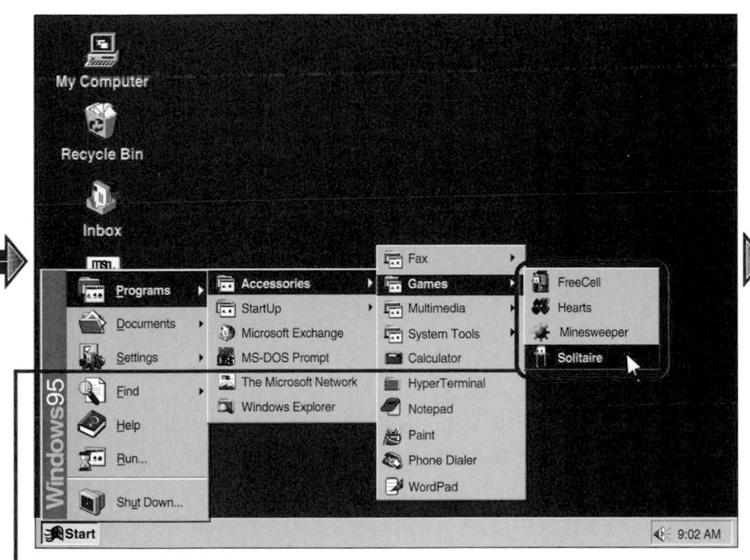

5 Move the mouse over the game you want to start and then press the left button.

■ The game appears (example: **Solitaire**).

Note: To enlarge a window to fill your screen, refer to page 11.

PLAY A MUSIC CD

You can use your computer to play music CDs while you work.

You need a CD-ROM drive, a sound card and speakers to play music CDs.

PLAY A MUSIC CD

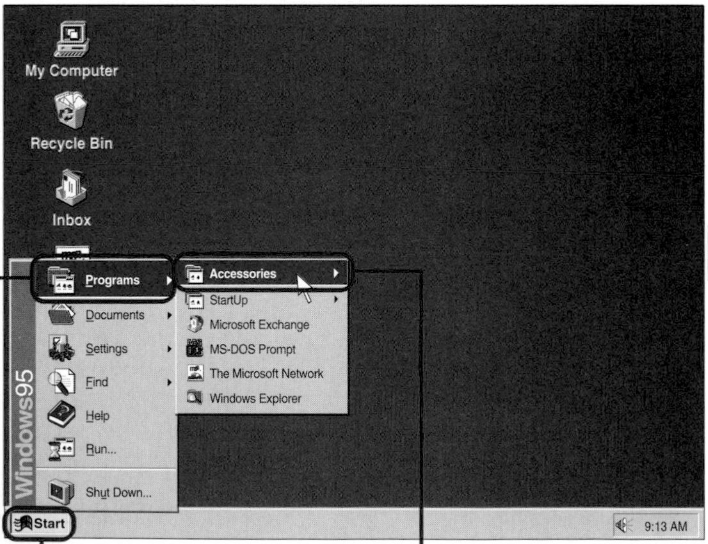

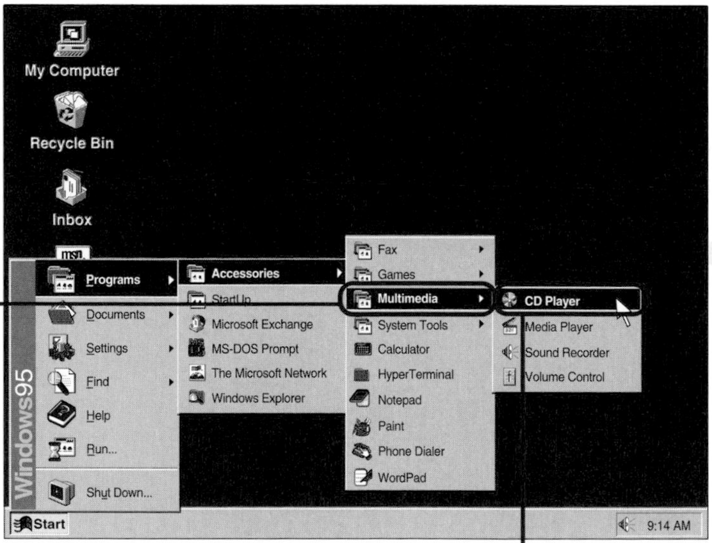

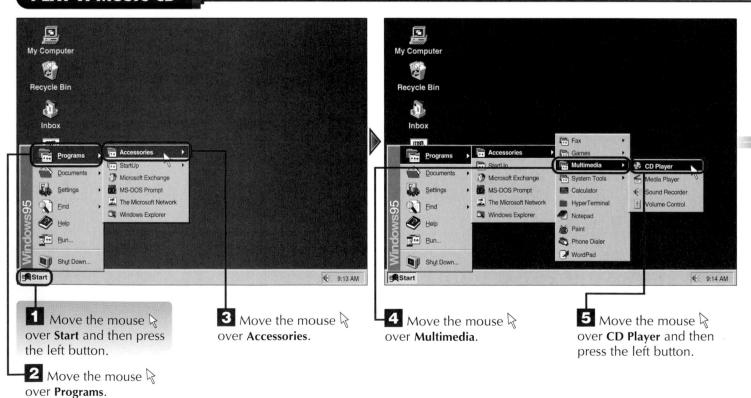

1 Move the mouse over **Start** and then press the left button.

2 Move the mouse over **Programs**.

3 Move the mouse over **Accessories**.

4 Move the mouse over **Multimedia**.

5 Move the mouse over **CD Player** and then press the left button.

Tip
You can also listen to music privately by plugging a headset into your CD-ROM drive.

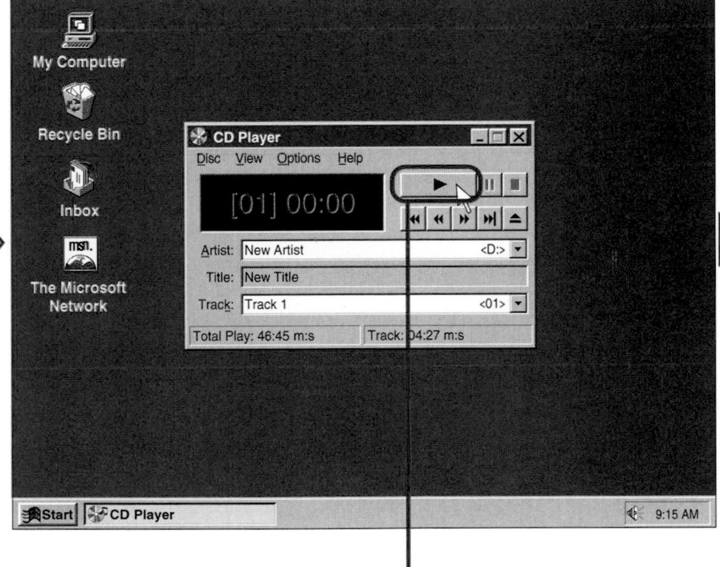

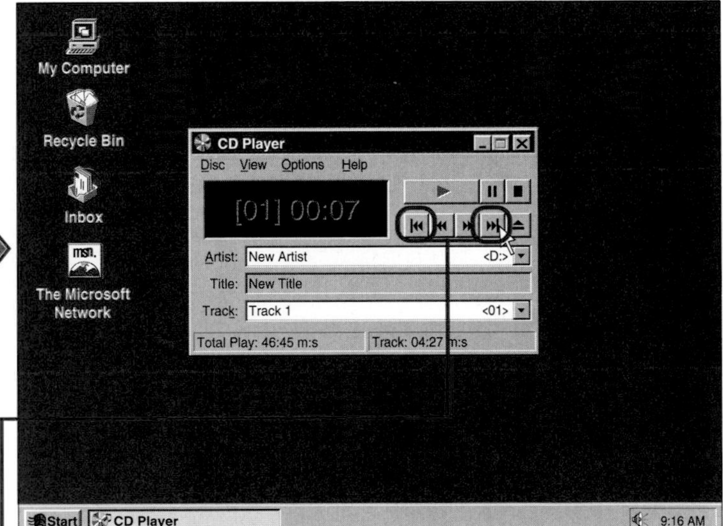

■ The **CD Player** window appears.

6 Insert a music CD into the CD-ROM drive.

7 To play the CD, move the mouse over ▶ and then press the left button.

Play Another Song

1 To play another song on the CD, move the mouse over one of these options and then press the left button.

⏮ Plays previous song.

⏭ Plays next song.

PLAY A MUSIC CD

You can have Windows pause or stop the music at any time and play songs in random order.

PLAY A MUSIC CD (CONTINUED)

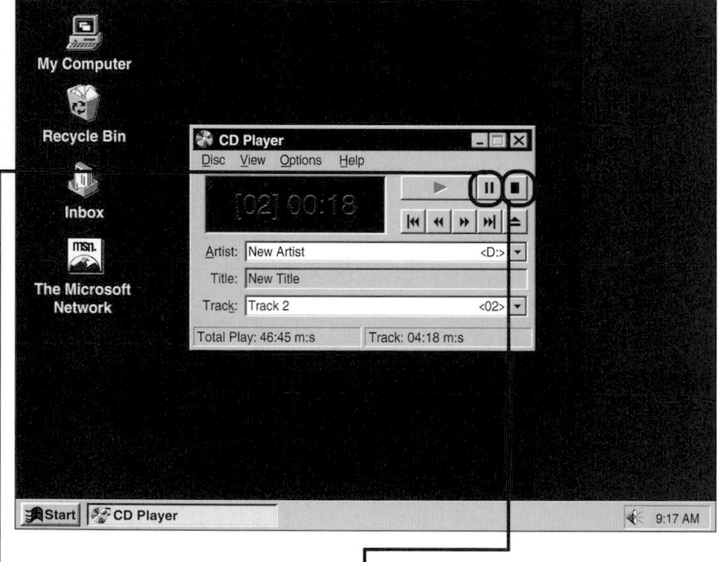

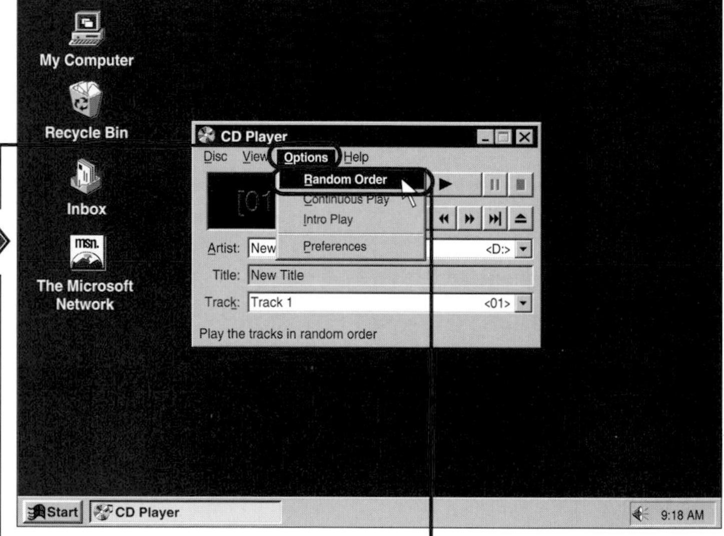

Pause Play

1 To temporarily stop playing the CD, move the mouse ↖ over ⏸ and then press the left button.

Note: To resume playing the CD, repeat the step above.

Stop Play

1 To stop playing the CD, move the mouse ↖ over ■ and then press the left button.

Play Songs in Random Order

1 To play the songs on a CD in random order, move the mouse ↖ over **Options** and then press the left button.

2 Move the mouse ↖ over **Random Order** and then press the left button.

*Note: To once again play the songs in order, repeat steps **1** and **2**.*

ADJUST THE VOLUME

You can easily adjust the volume of sound coming from your speakers.
Volume
Mute

ADJUST THE VOLUME

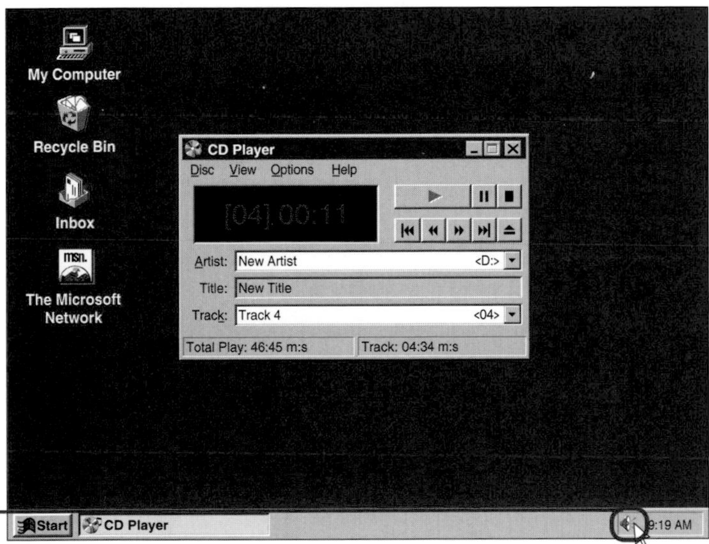

1 To display the **Volume** control box, move the mouse over and then press the left button.

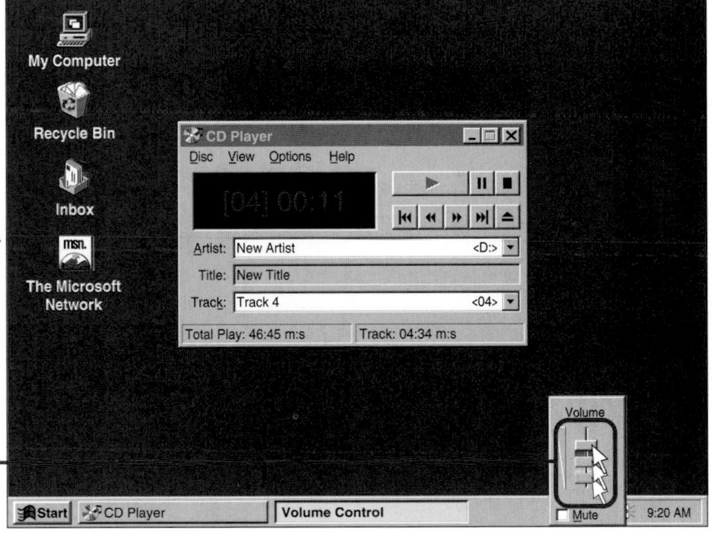

2 Move the mouse over the slider ( ).

3 Press and hold down the left button as you move the slider ( ) up or down to increase or decrease the volume. Then release the button.

4 To hide the **Volume** control box, move the mouse outside the box and then press the left button.

*Note: To close the **CD Player** window, move the mouse over ☒ and then press the left button.*

ASSIGN SOUNDS TO PROGRAM EVENTS

You can have Windows play sound effects when you perform certain tasks on your computer.

For example, you can hear a bird chirp when you close a program or a musical melody when you exit Windows.

ASSIGN SOUNDS TO PROGRAM EVENTS

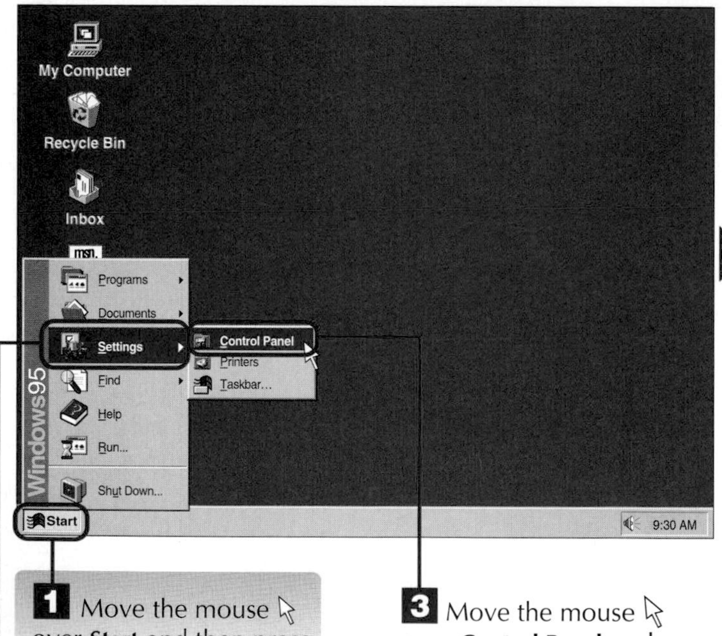

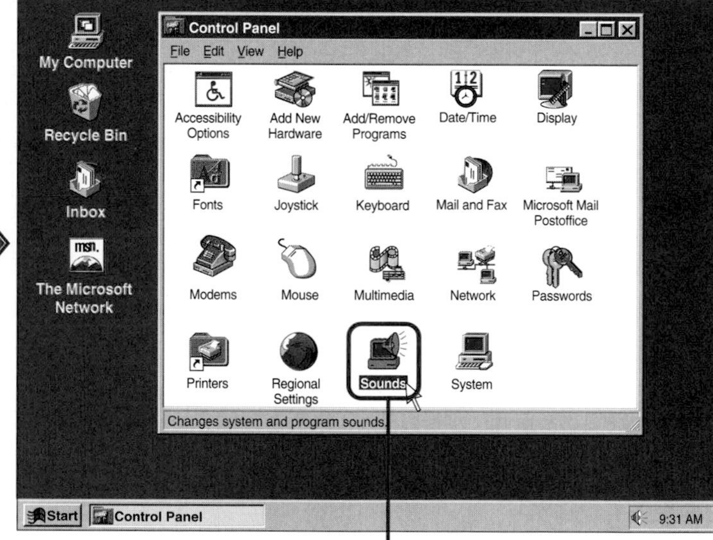

1 Move the mouse over **Start** and then press the left button.

2 Move the mouse over **Settings**.

3 Move the mouse over **Control Panel** and then press the left button.

■ The **Control Panel** window appears.

4 Move the mouse over **Sounds** and then quickly press the left button twice.

IMPORTANT

When you first set up Windows, not all the sound schemes that come with Windows are added to your computer. The schemes you can add later include:

Jungle

Musica

Robotz

Utopia

To add one or more sound schemes to your computer, refer to page 96. You can find these schemes in the Multimedia category.

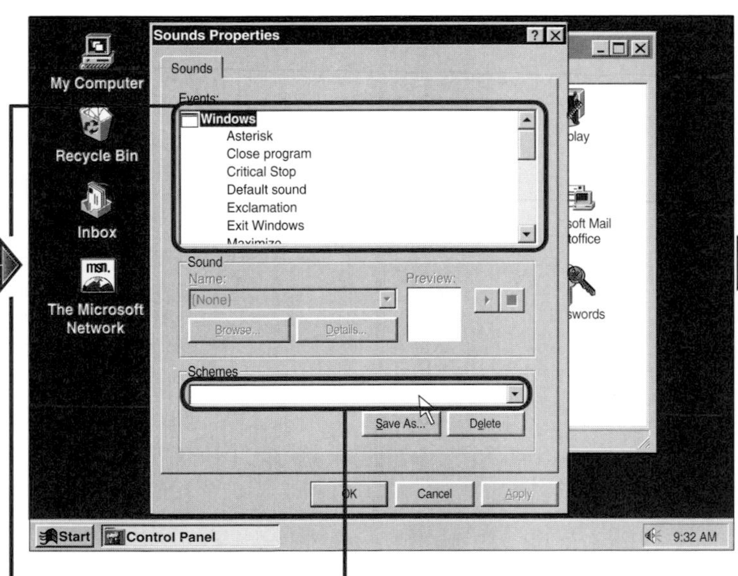

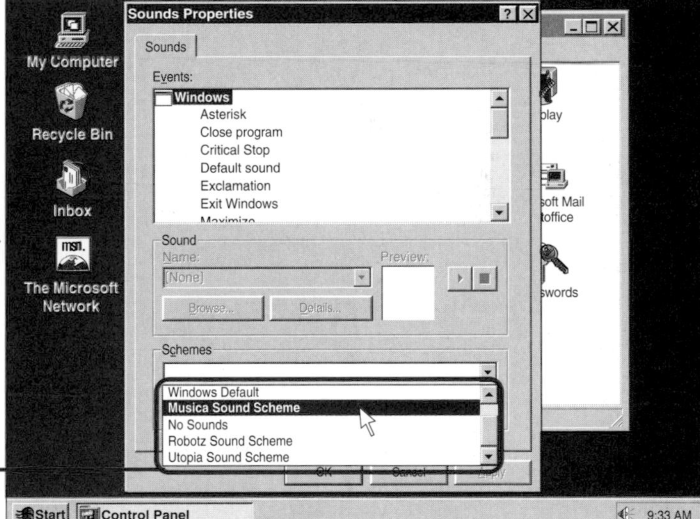

■ The **Sounds Properties** dialog box appears.

■ This area displays the events you can assign sounds to.

Assign Sounds to All Events

1 To have Windows assign sounds to all program events at once, move the mouse over this area and then press the left button.

Note: To assign a sound to only one event, refer to page 68.

2 Move the mouse over the sound scheme you want to use and then press the left button.

Note: The available sound schemes depend on the schemes you have installed on your computer. For more information, refer to the top of this page.

ASSIGN SOUNDS TO PROGRAM EVENTS

Assigning sounds to events can make Windows more fun and entertaining.
Empty Recycle Bin
Exit Windows
Menu popup

ASSIGN SOUNDS (CONTINUED)

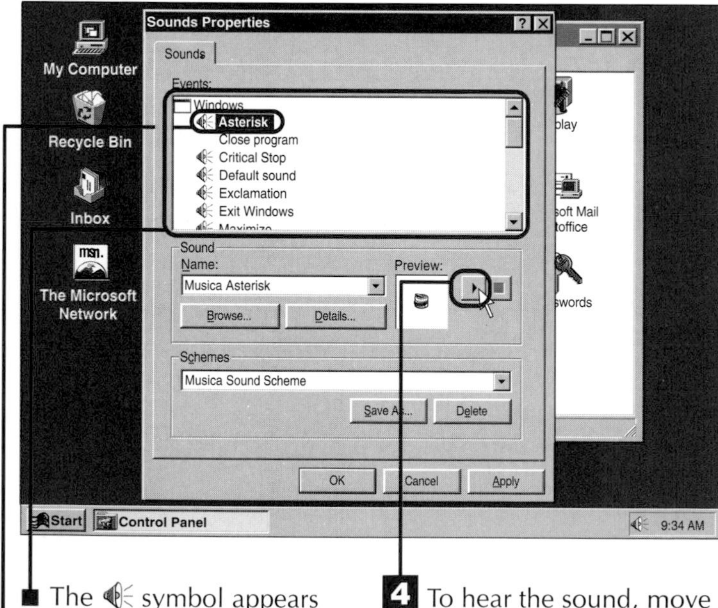

■ The 🔈 symbol appears beside each event that will now play a sound.

3 To hear the sound an event will play, move the mouse ↖ over the event and then press the left button.

4 To hear the sound, move the mouse ↖ over ▸ and then press the left button.

Note: To adjust the volume of sound coming from your speakers, refer to page 65.

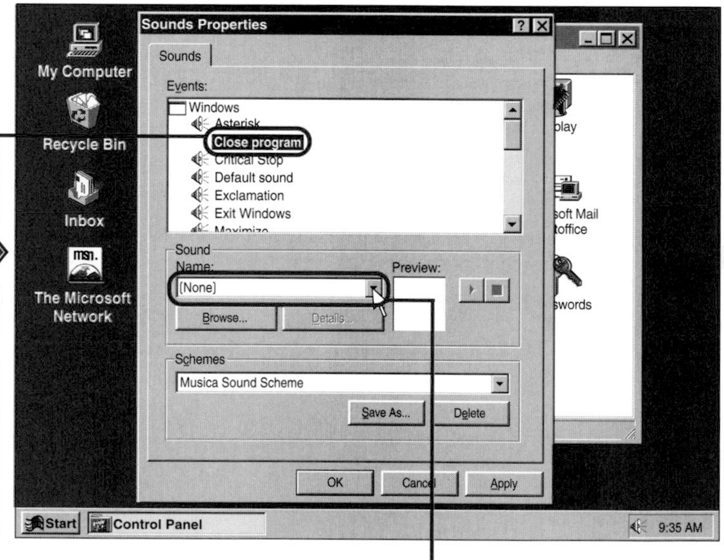

Assign a Sound to One Event

1 To assign a sound to one event, move the mouse ↖ over the event and then press the left button.

2 Move the mouse ↖ over ▾ in this area and then press the left button.

Tip
You need a sound card and speakers to hear sounds on your computer.

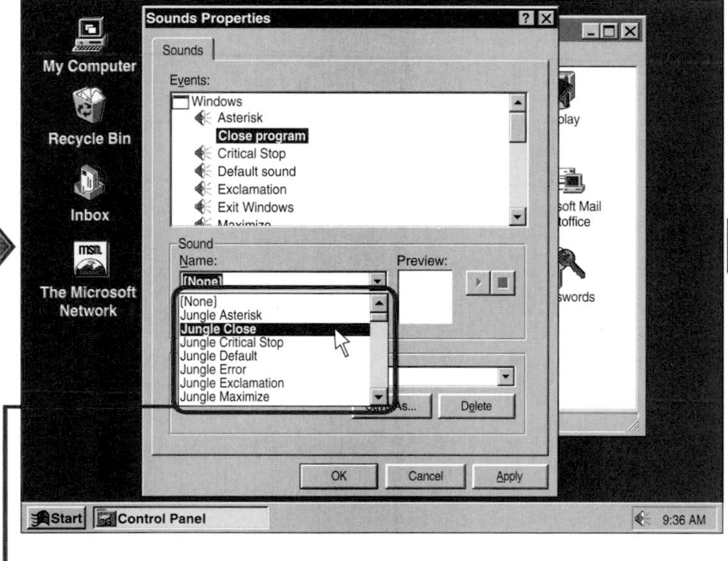

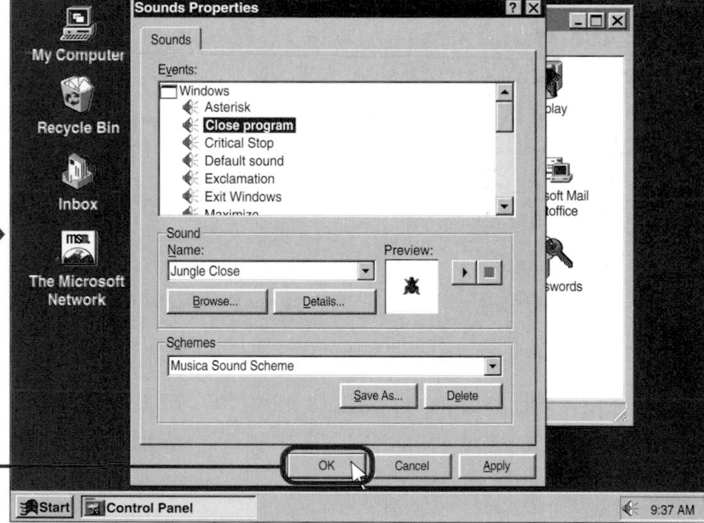

3 Move the mouse over the sound you want to hear every time the event occurs and then press the left button.

4 To assign sounds to other events, repeat steps **1** to **3** for each event.

5 To confirm the choices you have made, move the mouse over **OK** and then press the left button.

RECORD SOUNDS

You need a microphone to record live sounds.

You need a sound card and speakers to record and play sounds.

RECORD SOUNDS

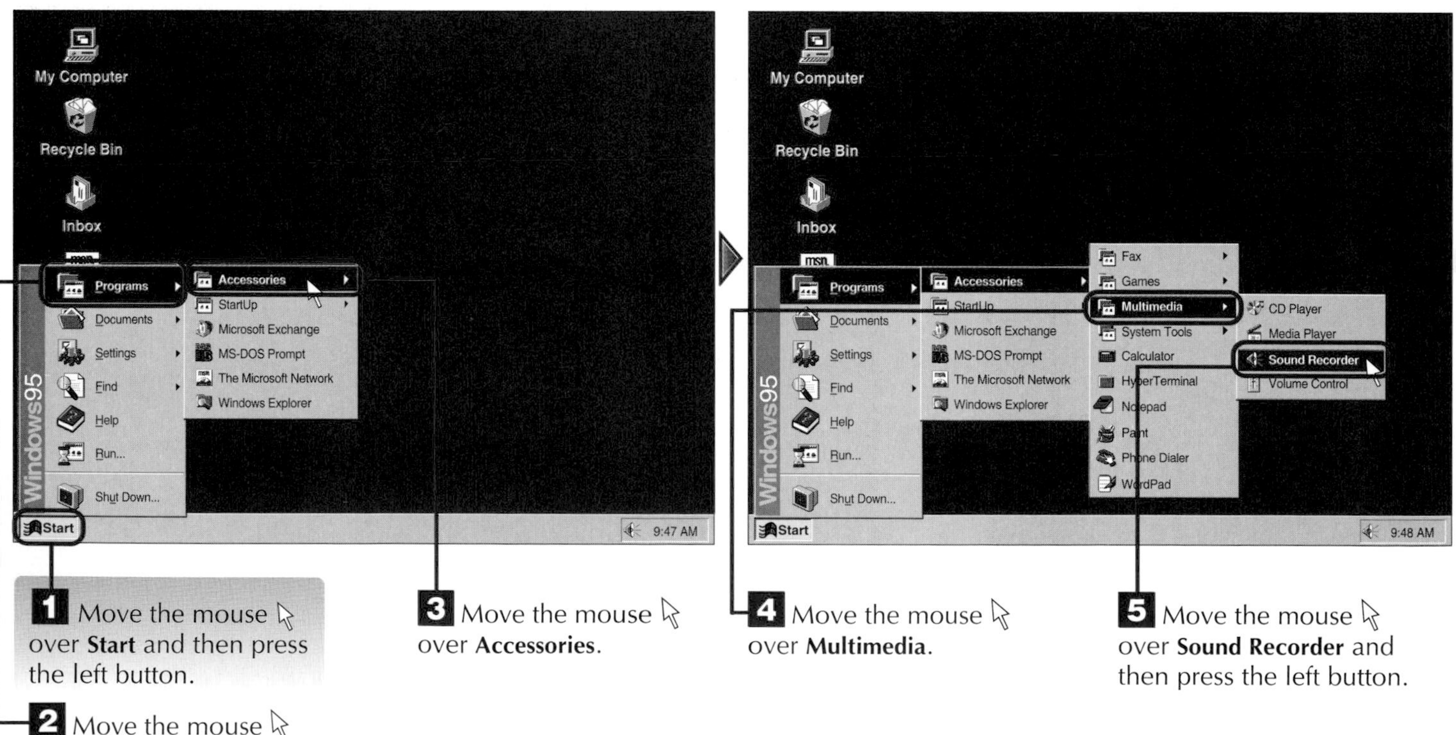

1 Move the mouse over **Start** and then press the left button.

2 Move the mouse over **Programs**.

3 Move the mouse over **Accessories**.

4 Move the mouse over **Multimedia**.

5 Move the mouse over **Sound Recorder** and then press the left button.

Tip
You can also record sounds from a stereo, VCR or tape recorder.
VCR

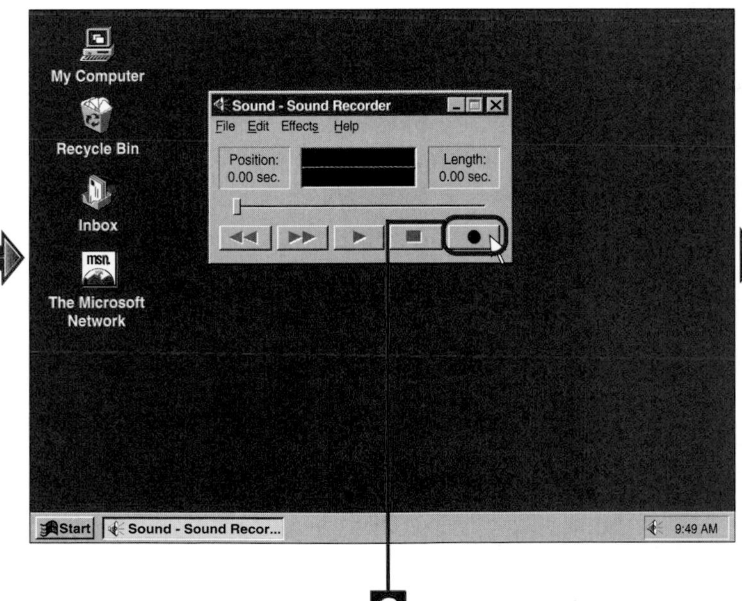

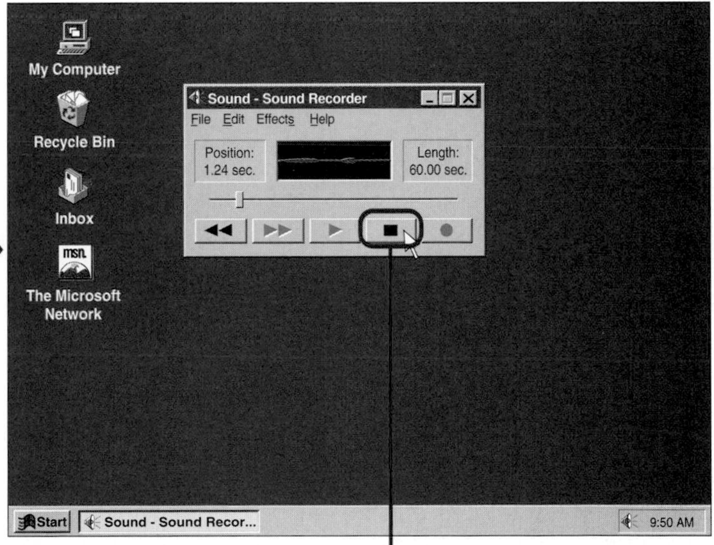

■ The **Sound Recorder** window appears.

6 To start recording, move the mouse over ● and then press the left button.

7 Use your microphone to record sounds.

8 To stop recording, move the mouse over ■ and then press the left button.

RECORD SOUNDS

You can store sounds you record and listen to them later.

RECORD SOUNDS (CONTINUED)

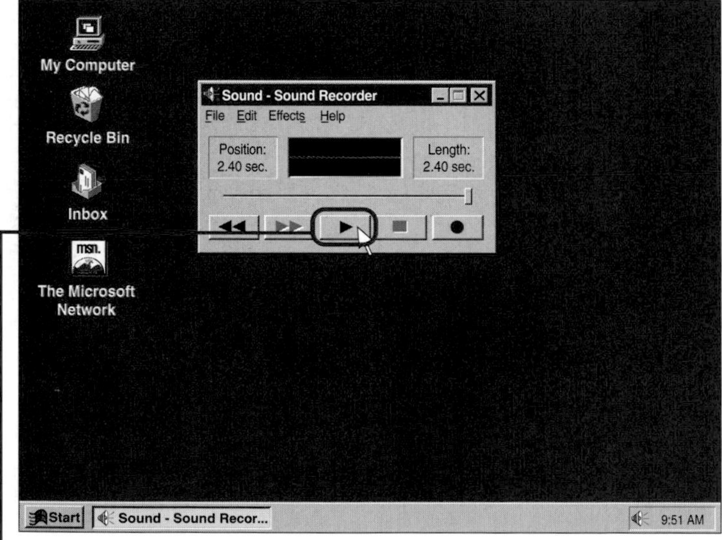

9 To play your recording, move the mouse over ▶ and then press the left button.

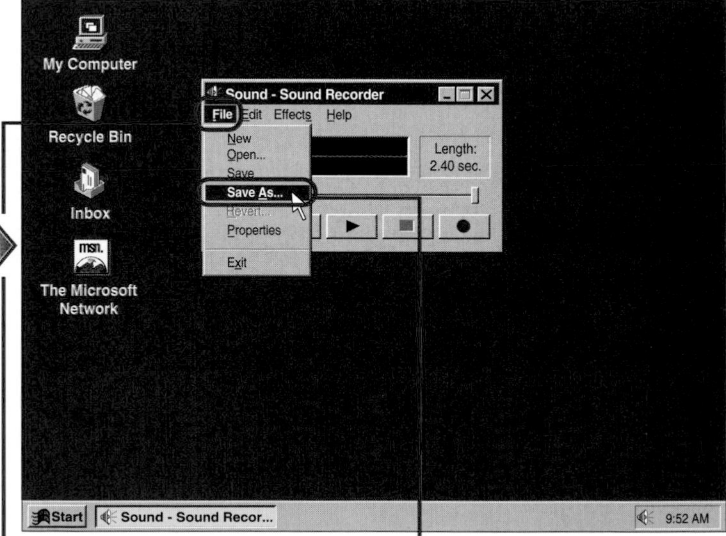

10 To save the recording, move the mouse over **File** and then press the left button.

11 Move the mouse over **Save As** and then press the left button.

■ The **Save As** dialog box appears.

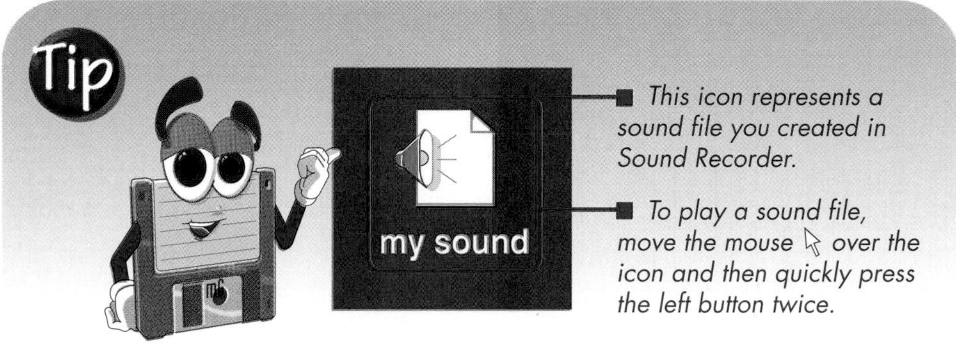

■ This icon represents a sound file you created in Sound Recorder.

■ To play a sound file, move the mouse ⇖ over the icon and then quickly press the left button twice.

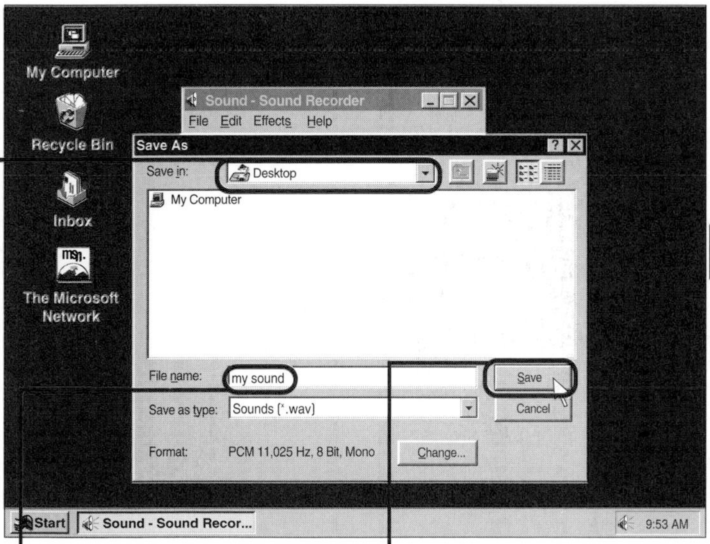

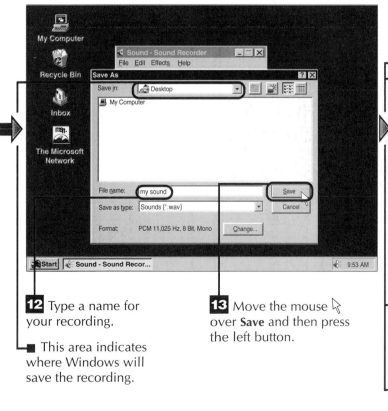

12 Type a name for your recording.

■ This area indicates where Windows will save the recording.

13 Move the mouse ⇖ over **Save** and then press the left button.

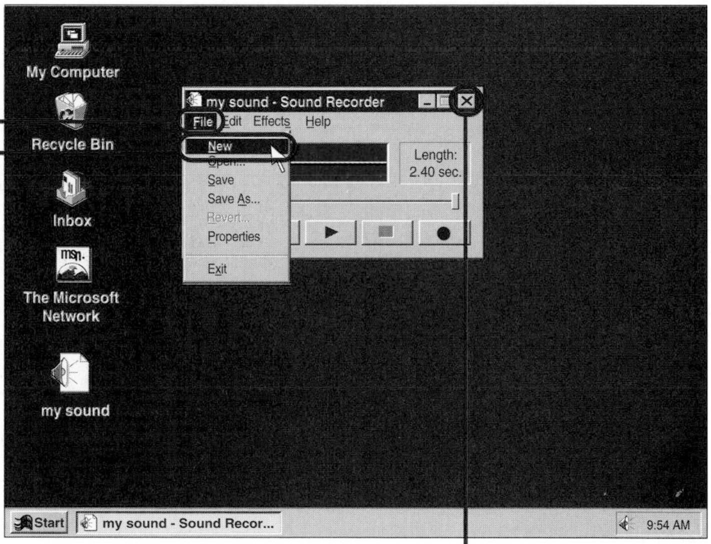

14 To make a new sound recording, move the mouse ⇖ over **File** and then press the left button.

15 Move the mouse ⇖ over **New** and then press the left button.

16 To record and save the new sound recording, repeat steps **6** to **13** starting on page 71.

17 To close the **Sound Recorder** window, move the mouse ⇖ over ☒ and then press the left button.

USING MEDIA PLAYER

Media Player lets you play sound, video and animation files.

USING MEDIA PLAYER

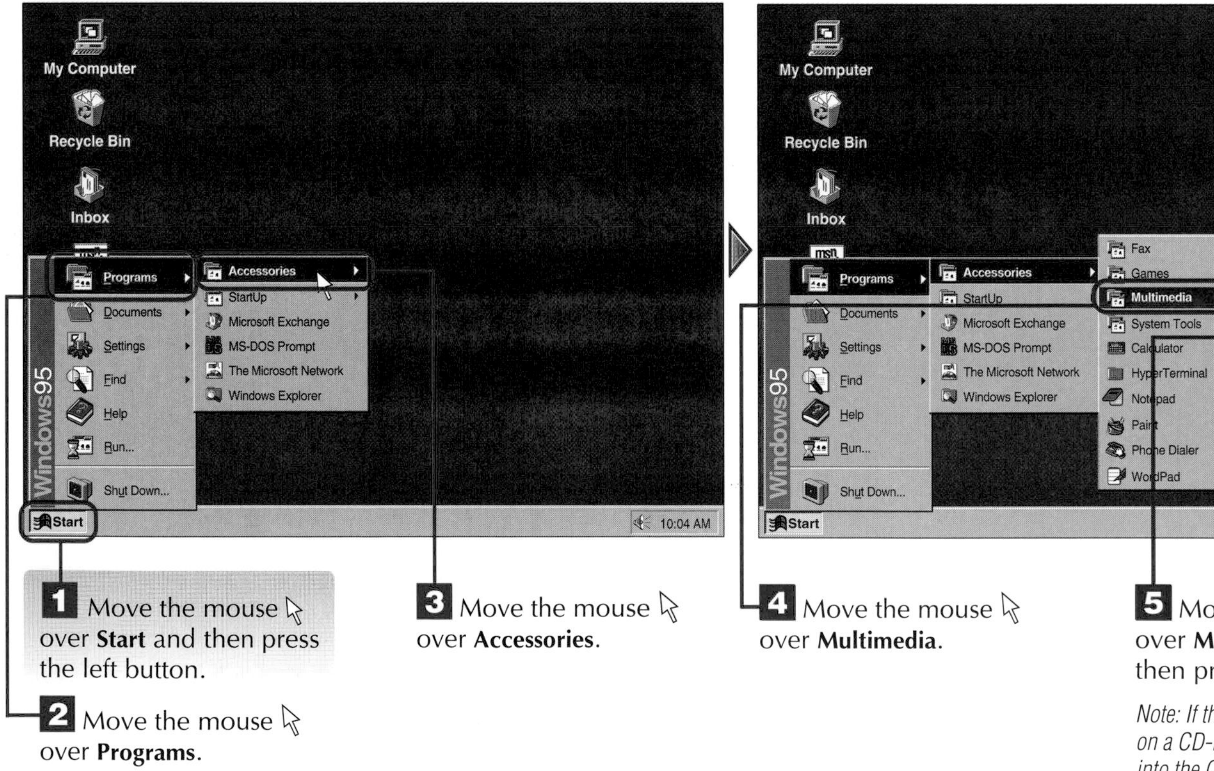

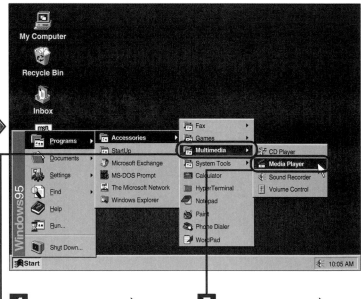

1 Move the mouse over **Start** and then press the left button.

2 Move the mouse over **Programs**.

3 Move the mouse over **Accessories**.

4 Move the mouse over **Multimedia**.

5 Move the mouse over **Media Player** and then press the left button.

Note: If the file you want to play is on a CD-ROM disc, insert the disc into the CD-ROM drive.

Tip
The Windows 95 CD-ROM disc includes several video files you can play.
WINDOWS 95 PROGRAM

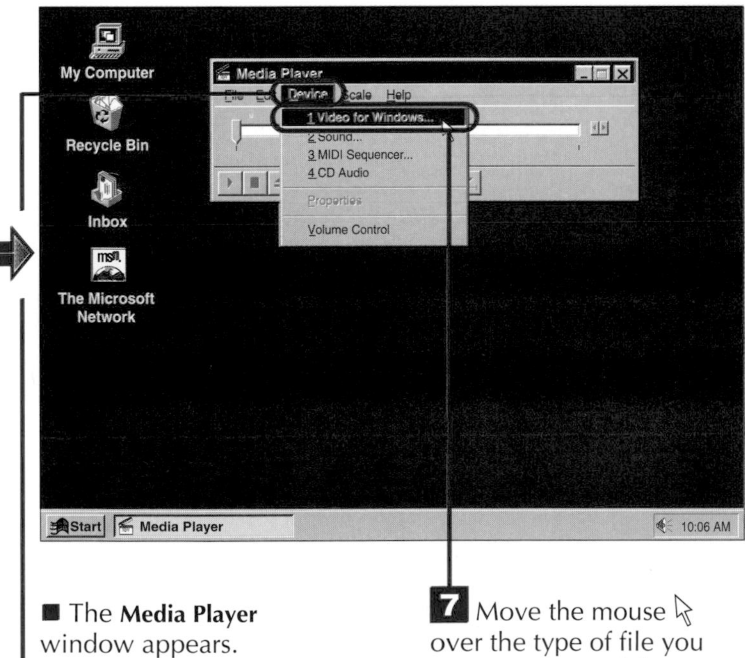

■ The **Media Player** window appears.

6 Move the mouse over **Device** and then press the left button.

7 Move the mouse over the type of file you want to play and then press the left button.

Note: In this example, we play a video from the Windows 95 CD-ROM disc.

■ The **Open** dialog box appears.

■ This area indicates where Windows will search for the file you want to play.

8 Move the mouse over the file you want to play and then press the left button.

9 Move the mouse over **Open** and then press the left button.

USING MEDIA PLAYER

You can use Media Player to play files you get from the Internet.

USING MEDIA PLAYER (CONTINUED)

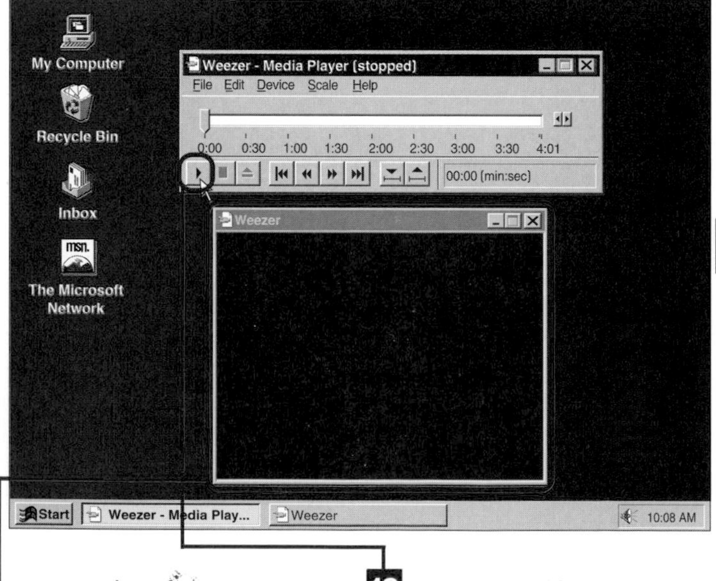

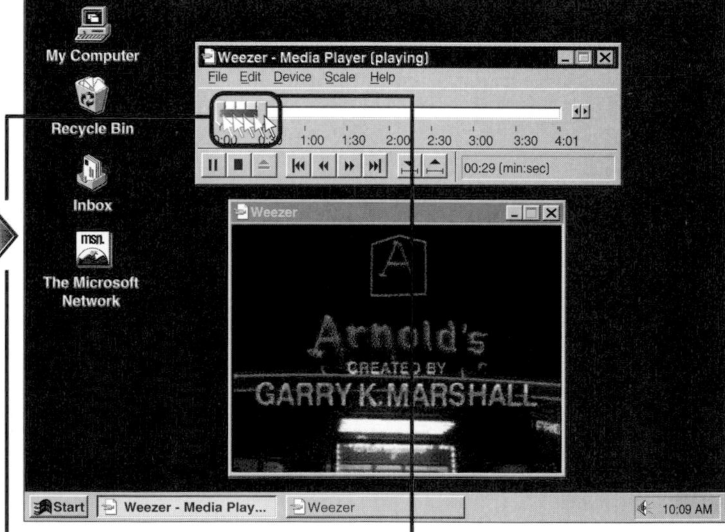

■ A window for viewing the file appears.

10 To play the file, move the mouse over ▶ and then press the left button.

11 To fast forward or rewind the playing of the file, move the mouse over the slider (▯).

12 Press and hold down the left button as you move the slider to a new location. Then release the button.

Tip

*Media Player can play animation, video, sound and MIDI files. You can tell the type of file by the three letters at the end of the file name. For example, **musical.wav** is a sound file.*

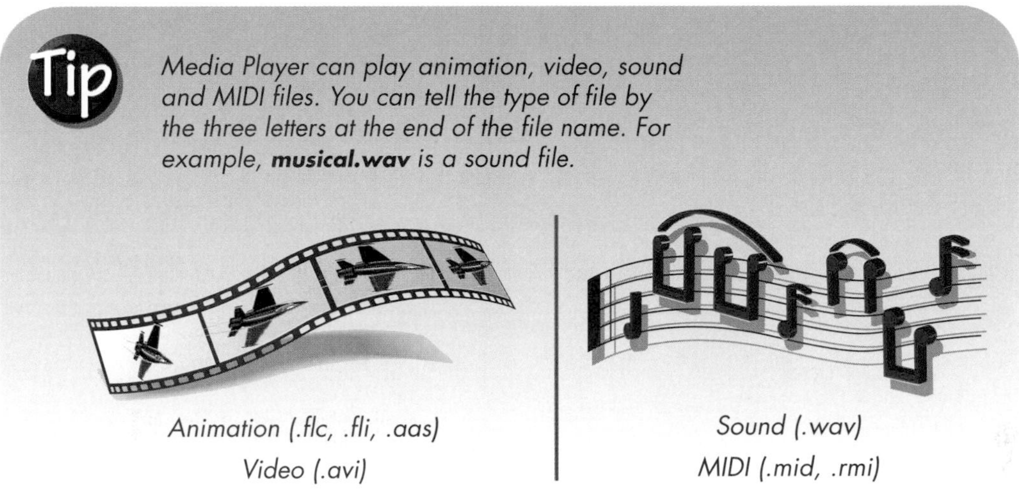

Animation (.flc, .fli, .aas)
Video (.avi)

Sound (.wav)
MIDI (.mid, .rmi)

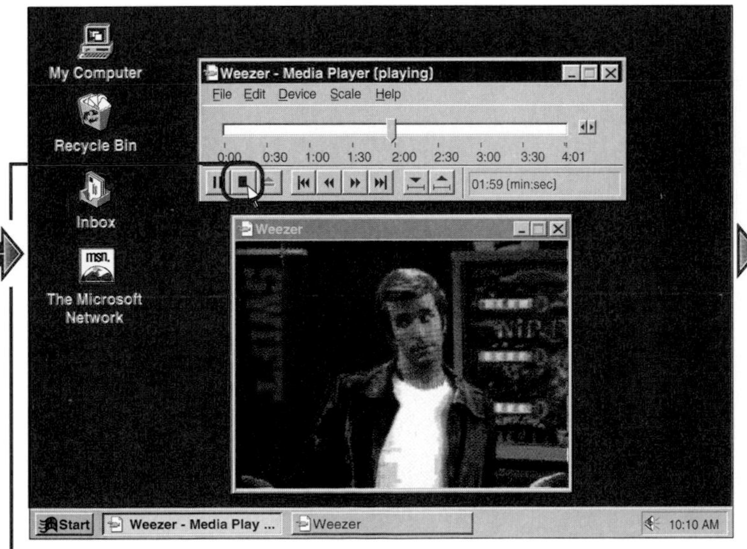

13 To stop playing the file, move the mouse over ■ and then press the left button.

14 To close the file, move the mouse over ☒ and then press the left button.

15 To close Media Player, move the mouse over ☒ and then press the left button.

In this chapter you will learn how to exchange information between programs.

CHAPTER 5

OBJECT LINKING AND EMBEDDING

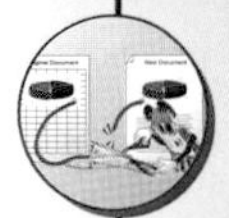

Embed or Link Information

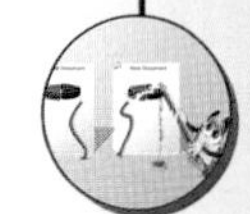

Edit Embedded Information

Edit Linked Information

EMBED OR LINK INFORMATION

When you embed information, the information becomes part of the new document.

EMBED INFORMATION
The original document is no longer needed, since the new document now contains the information.

EMBED OR LINK INFORMATION

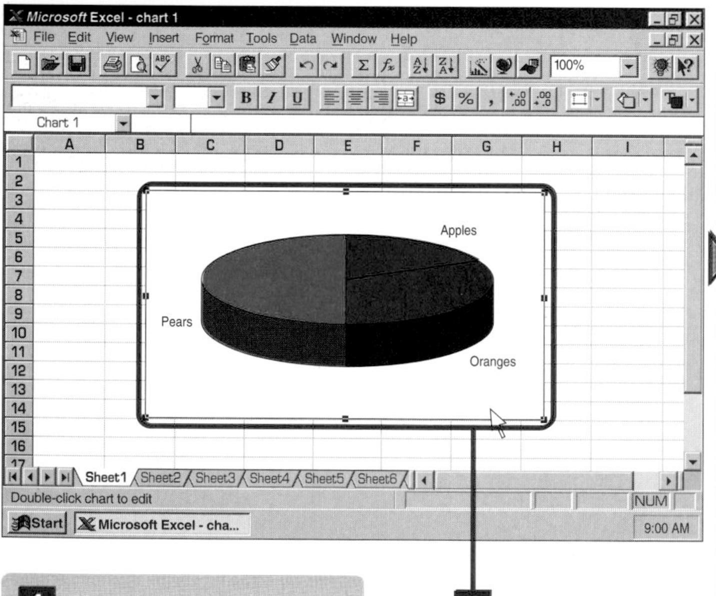

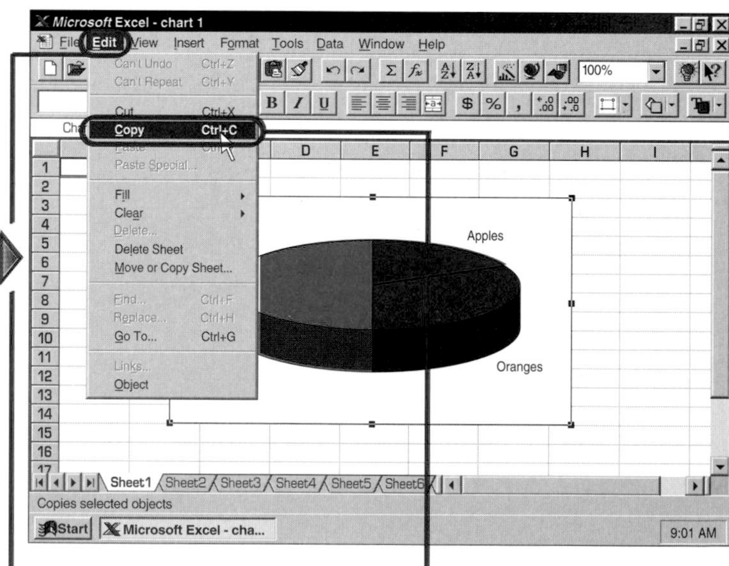

1 Open the document containing the information you want to place in another document.

2 Select the information.

3 Move the mouse over **Edit** and then press the left button.

4 Move the mouse over **Copy** and then press the left button.

LINK INFORMATION

Since the new document only contains a "screen image" of the information, a connection exists between the two documents.

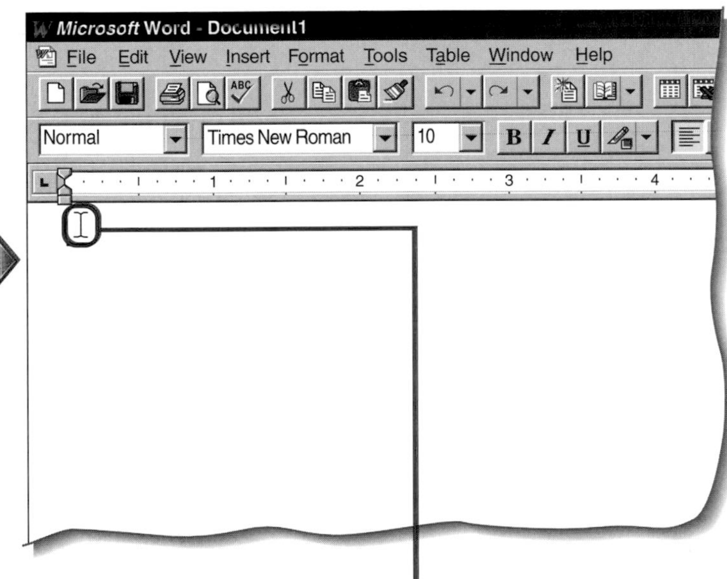

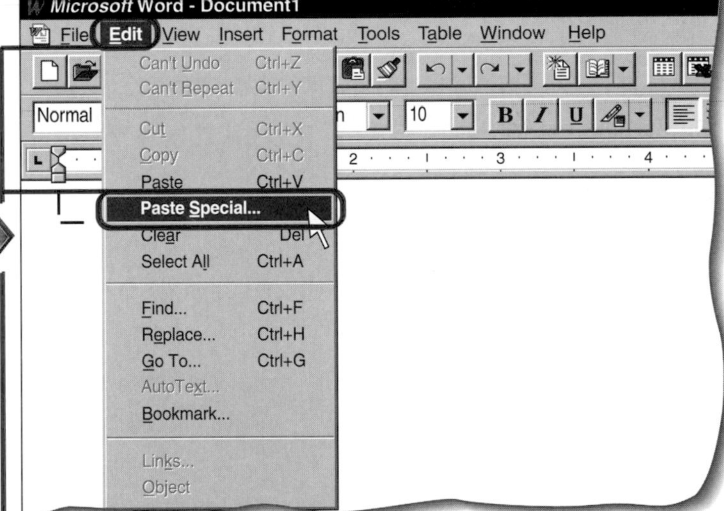

5 Open the document you want to receive the information.

6 Move the mouse I to where you want to place the information and then press the left button.

7 Move the mouse over **Edit** and then press the left button.

8 Move the mouse over **Paste Special** and then press the left button.

■ The **Paste Special** dialog box appears.

EMBED OR LINK INFORMATION

You can exchange pictures, charts, text, slides and spreadsheets between documents.
TEXT

EMBED OR LINK INFORMATION (CONTINUED)

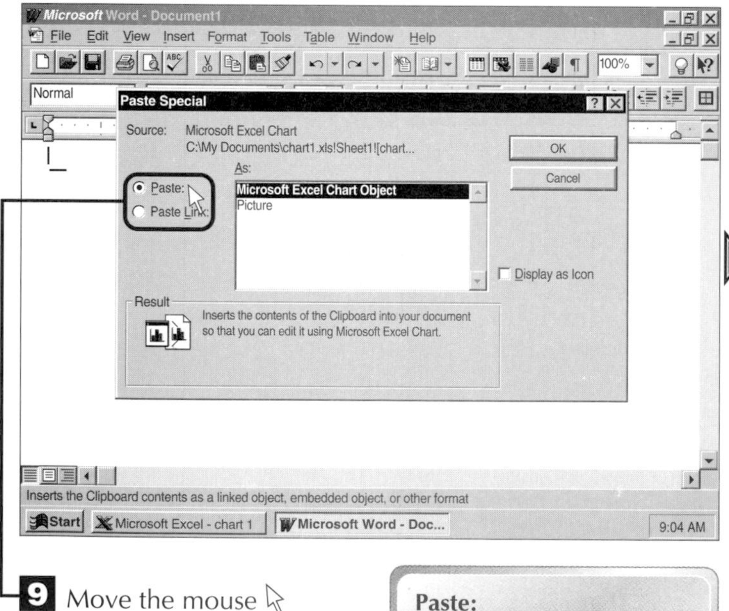

9 Move the mouse over one of these options and then press the left button (○ changes to ◉).

Paste:
Embeds the information.

Paste Link:
Links the information.

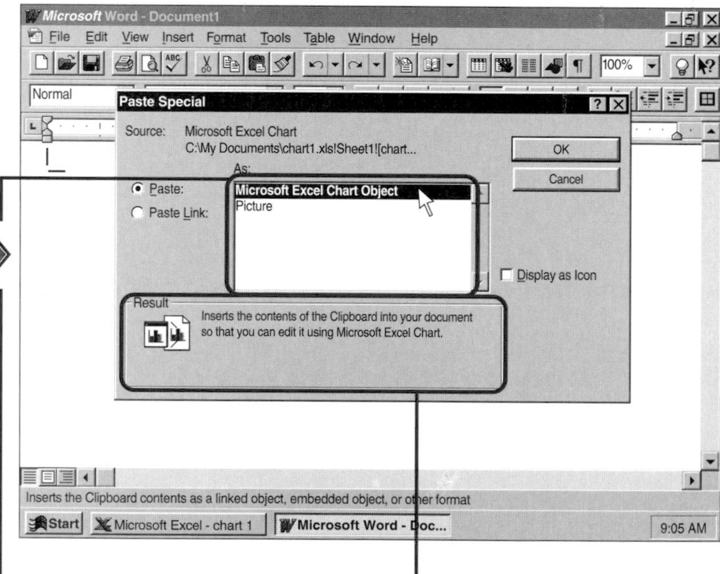

10 Move the mouse over the way you want to insert the information and then press the left button.

■ This area describes how the program will insert the information.

Tip

A document containing embedded information takes up more space on your computer than a document containing linked information.

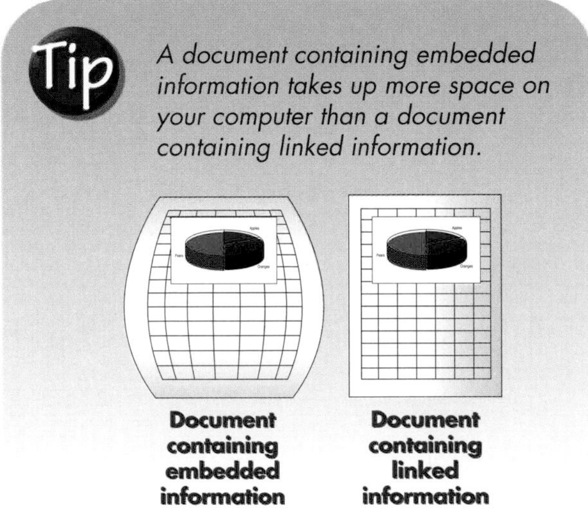

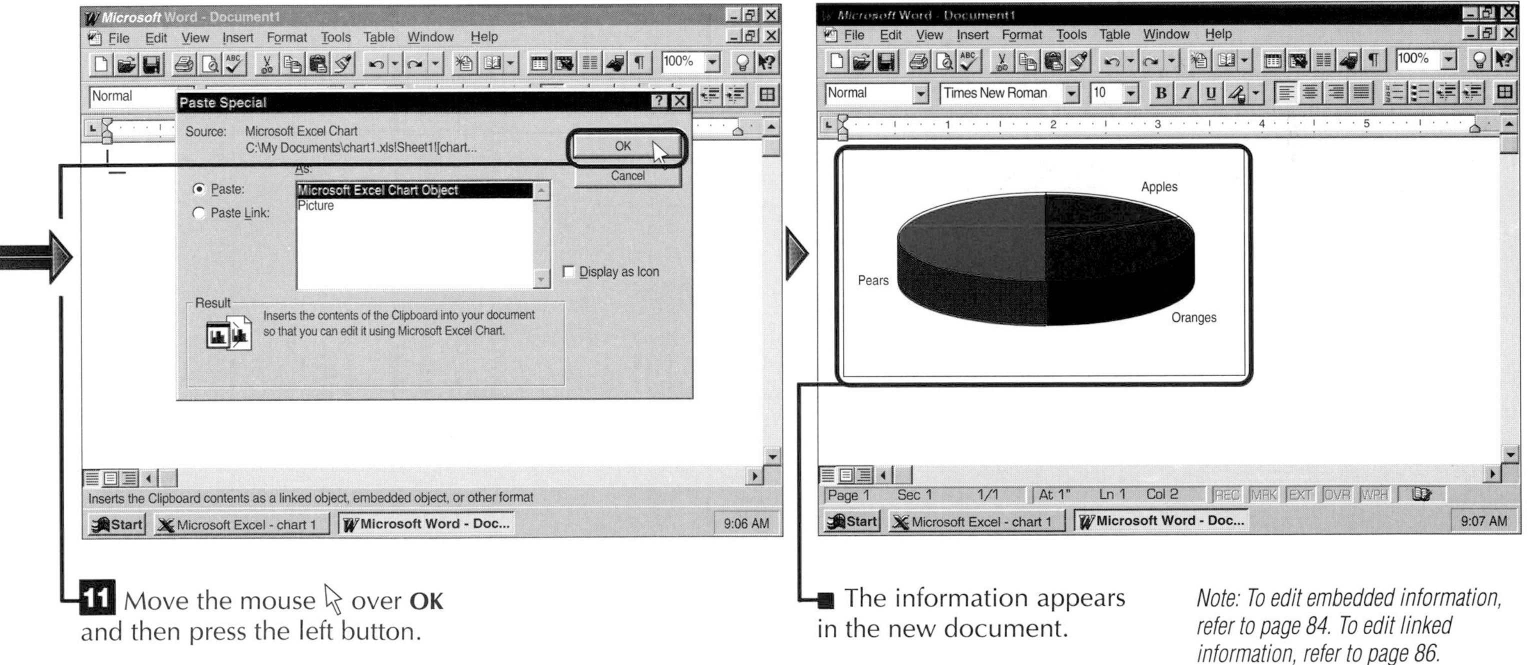

11 Move the mouse over **OK** and then press the left button.

■ The information appears in the new document.

Note: To edit embedded information, refer to page 84. To edit linked information, refer to page 86.

EDIT EMBEDDED INFORMATION

Original Document
Apples
Pears
Oranges
New Document
Pears
When you change embedded information, the original document does not change.

EDIT EMBEDDED INFORMATION

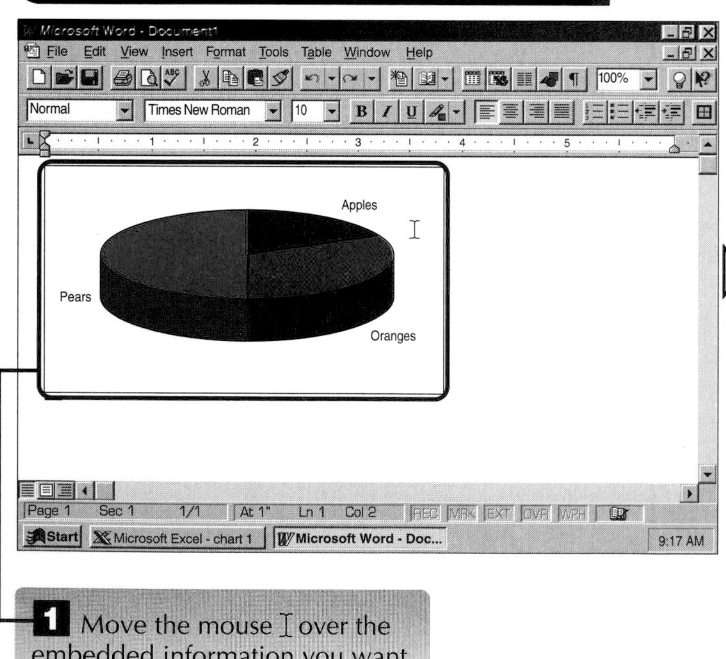

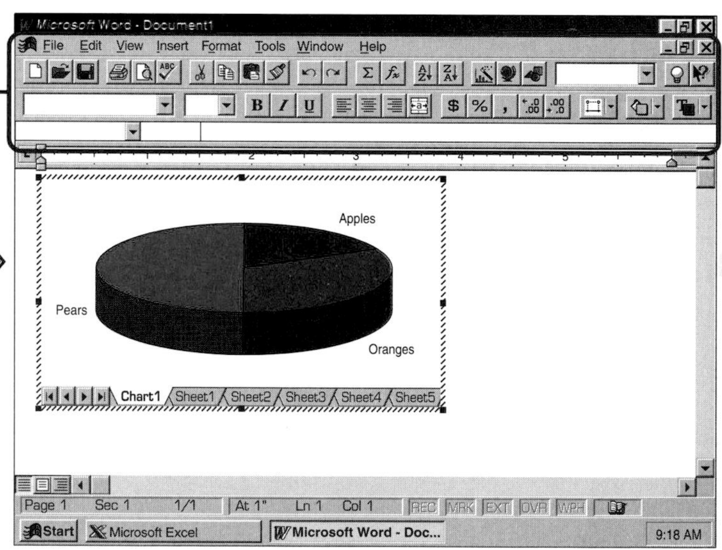

1 Move the mouse I over the embedded information you want to change and then quickly press the left button twice.

■ The toolbars and menus from the program you used to create the information appear. This lets you access all the commands you need to make the necessary changes.

Tip
A program that can link and embed information supports OLE—Object Linking and Embedding.
OLE

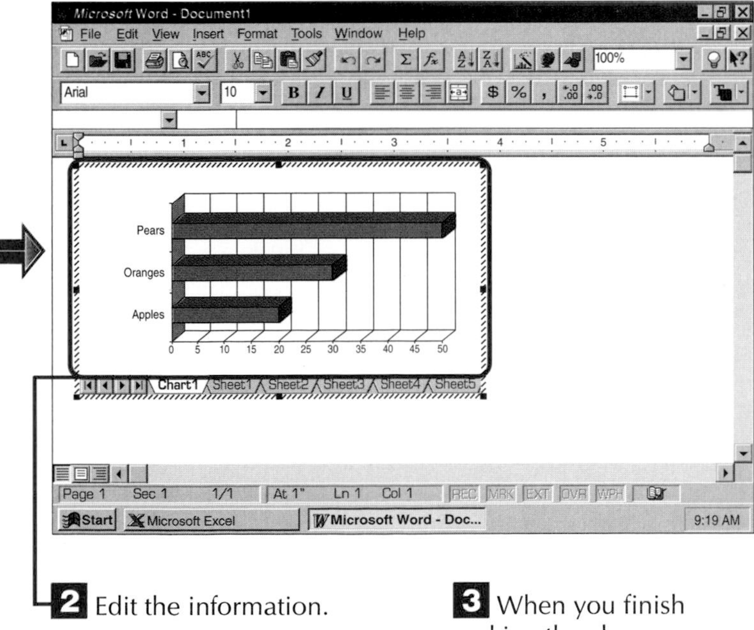

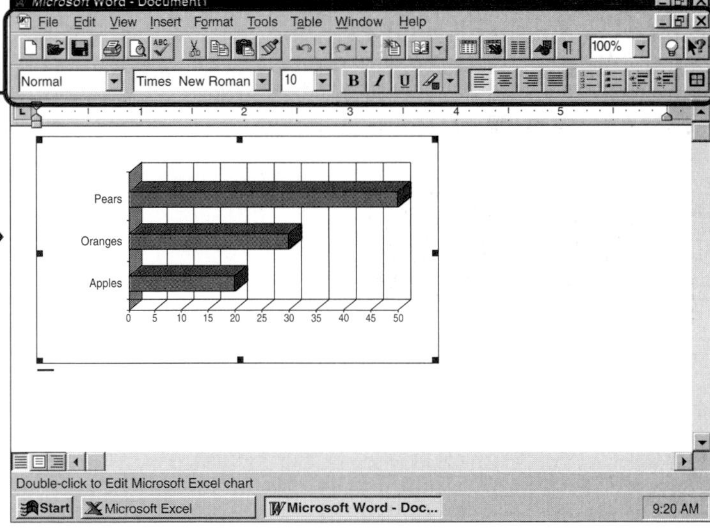

2 Edit the information.

Note: In this example, the pie chart is changed to a bar chart.

3 When you finish making the changes, move the mouse I anywhere outside the information and then press the left button.

■ The original toolbars and menus reappear.

EDIT LINKED INFORMATION

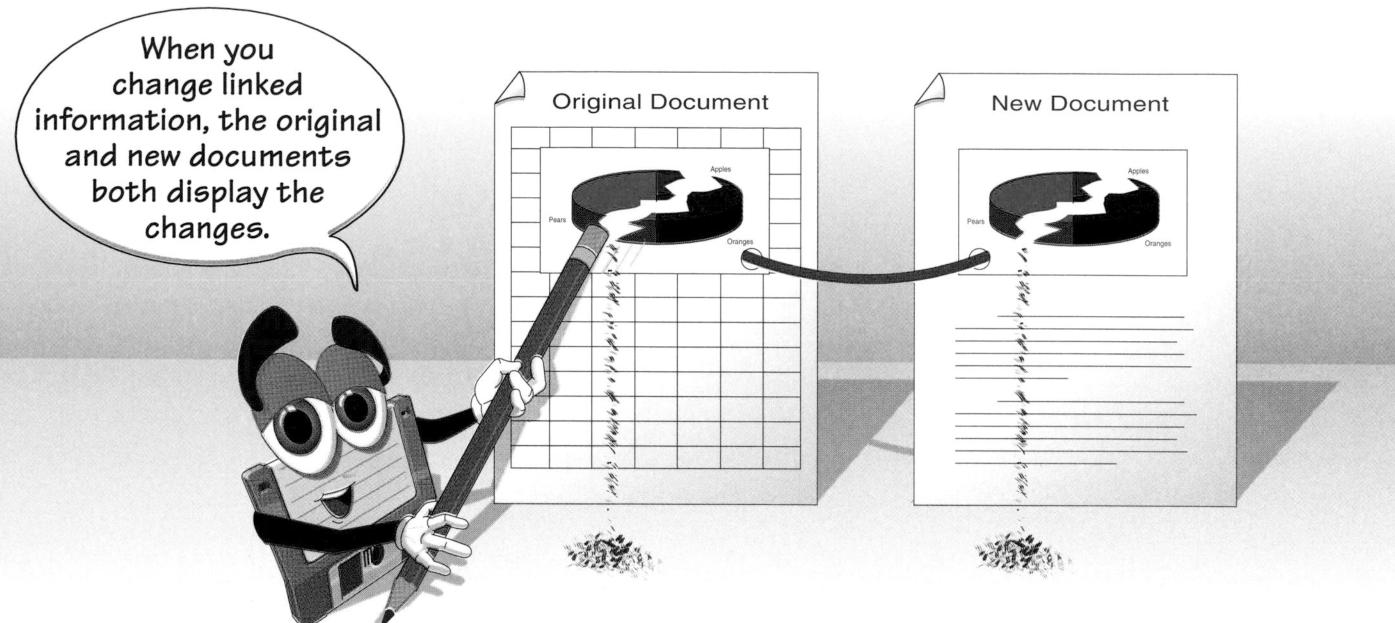

When you change linked information, the original and new documents both display the changes.
Original Document
New Document
Apples
Pears
Oranges

EDIT LINKED INFORMATION

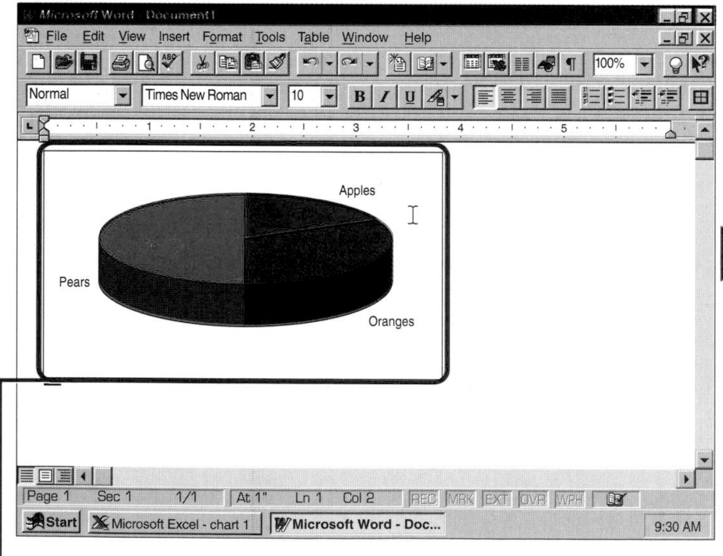

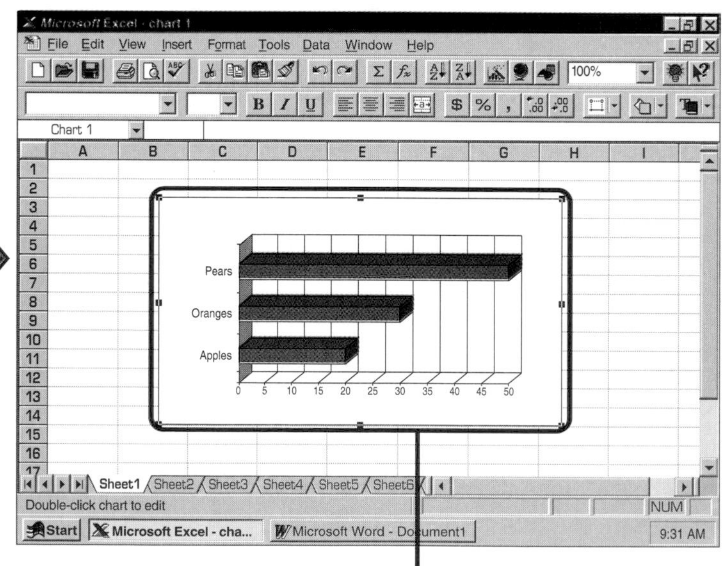

1 Move the mouse I over the linked information you want to change and then quickly press the left button twice.

■ The program you used to create the information opens. This lets you access all the commands you need to make the necessary changes.

2 Edit the information.

Note: In this example, the pie chart is changed to a bar chart.

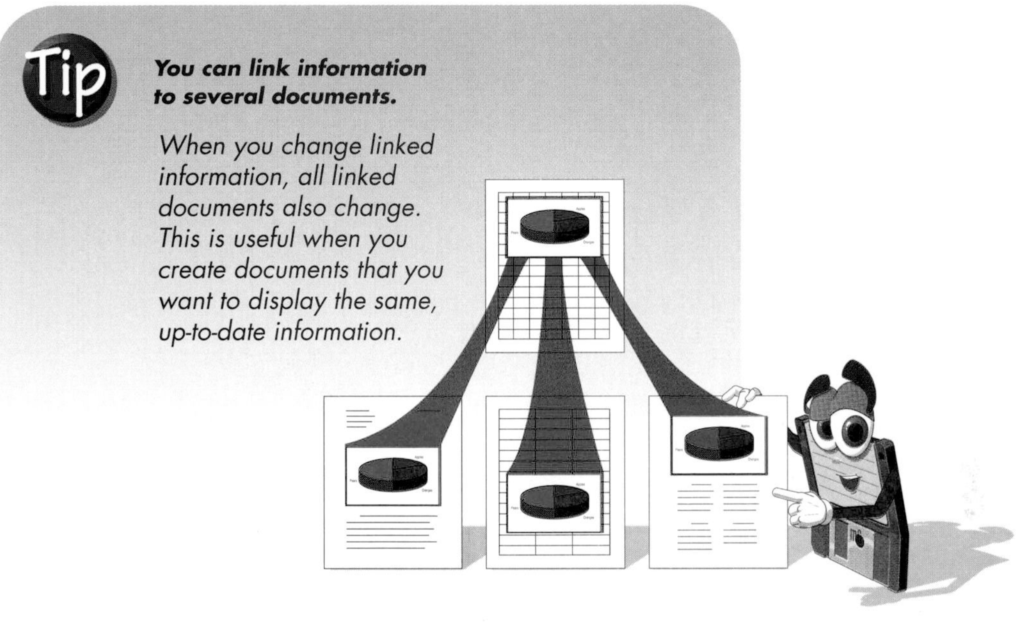

Tip

You can link information to several documents.

When you change linked information, all linked documents also change. This is useful when you create documents that you want to display the same, up-to-date information.

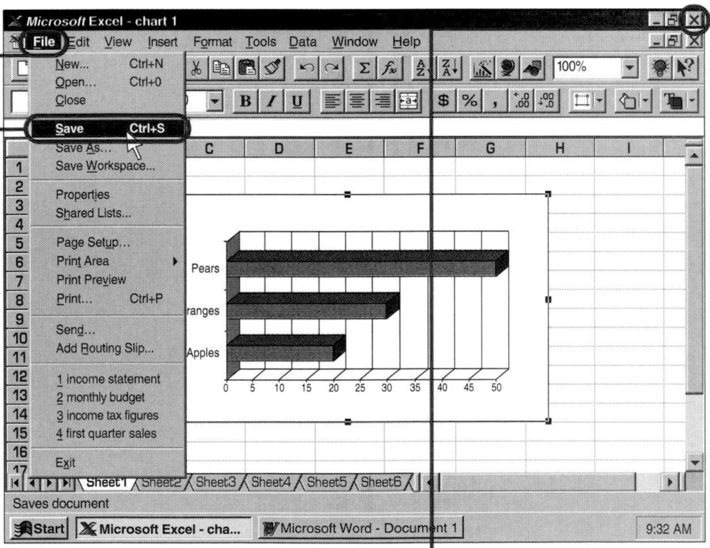

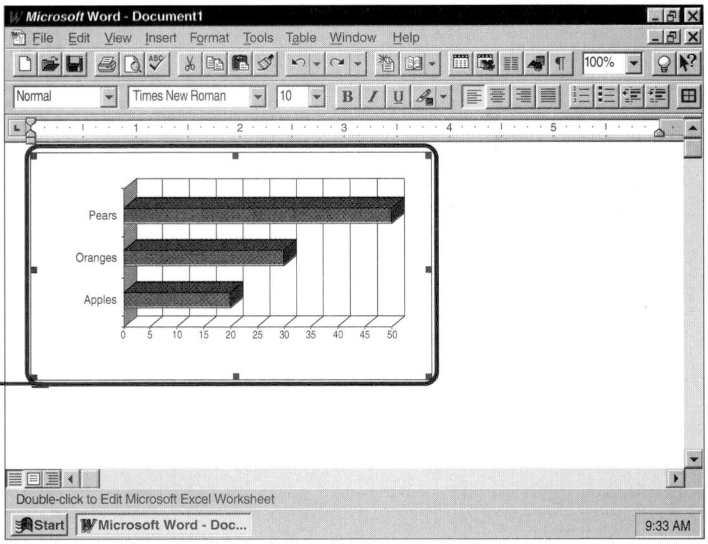

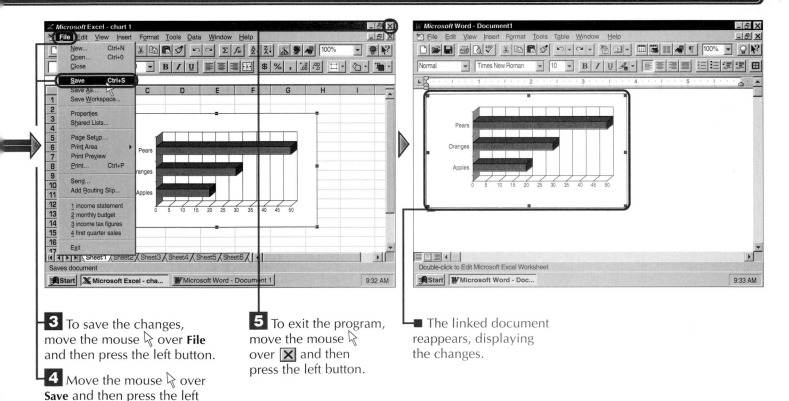

3 To save the changes, move the mouse over **File** and then press the left button.

4 Move the mouse over **Save** and then press the left button.

5 To exit the program, move the mouse over ☒ and then press the left button.

■ The linked document reappears, displaying the changes.

In this
chapter you will
learn how to add new fonts,
Windows components,
programs and hardware
to your computer.

ADD HARDWARE AND SOFTWARE

View Fonts

Add Fonts

Add Windows Components

Add a New Program

Set Up New Hardware Automatically

Set Up New Hardware Manually

VIEW FONTS

You can view a sample of every font available on your computer. This can help you decide which fonts to use in your documents.
Arial
Times New Roman
Courier

A font is a set of characters with a particular design.

VIEW FONTS

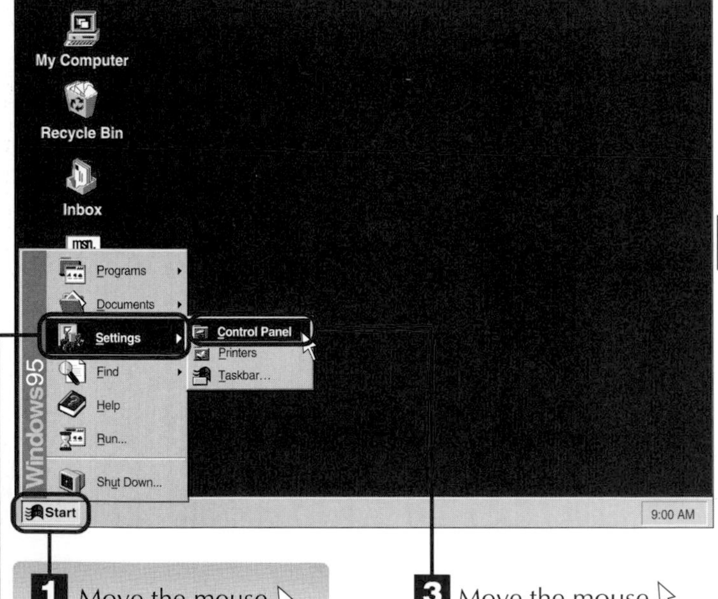

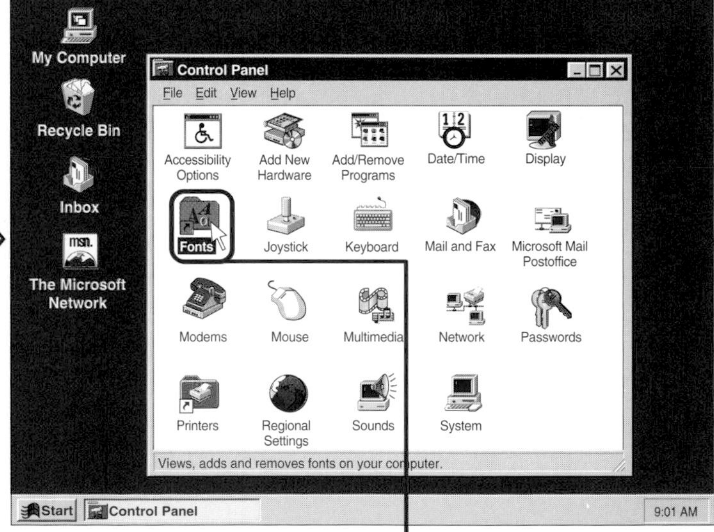

1 Move the mouse over **Start** and then press the left button.

2 Move the mouse over **Settings**.

3 Move the mouse over **Control Panel** and then press the left button.

■ The **Control Panel** window appears.

4 To view the fonts stored on your computer, move the mouse over **Fonts** and then quickly press the left button twice.

Tip
TrueType fonts look clear at any size. Try to use TrueType fonts whenever possible.
Screen fonts look clear at only a few sizes.

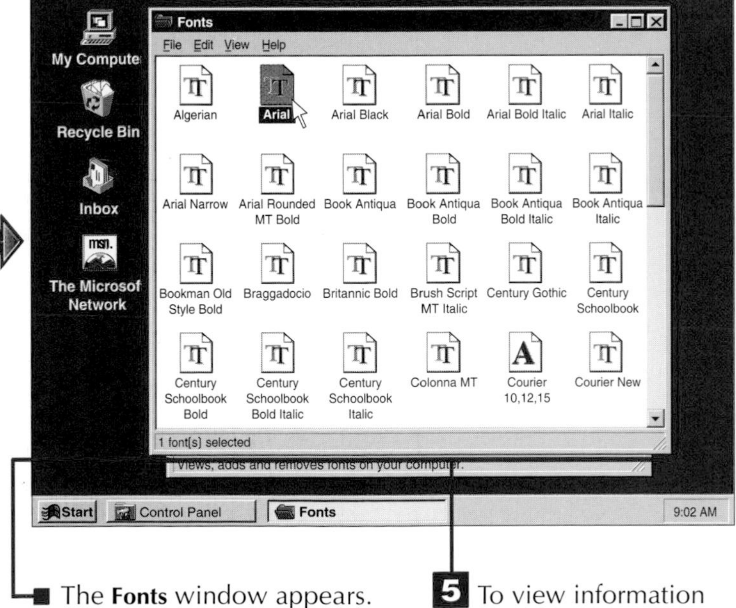

■ The **Fonts** window appears. Each icon represents a font stored on your computer.

5 To view information about a font, move the mouse ⇖ over the font and then quickly press the left button twice.

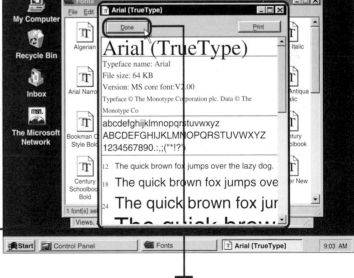

■ A window appears, displaying information about the font. You can see a sample of the font and all its available sizes.

6 When you finish viewing the information, move the mouse ⇖ over **Done** and then press the left button.

ADD FONTS

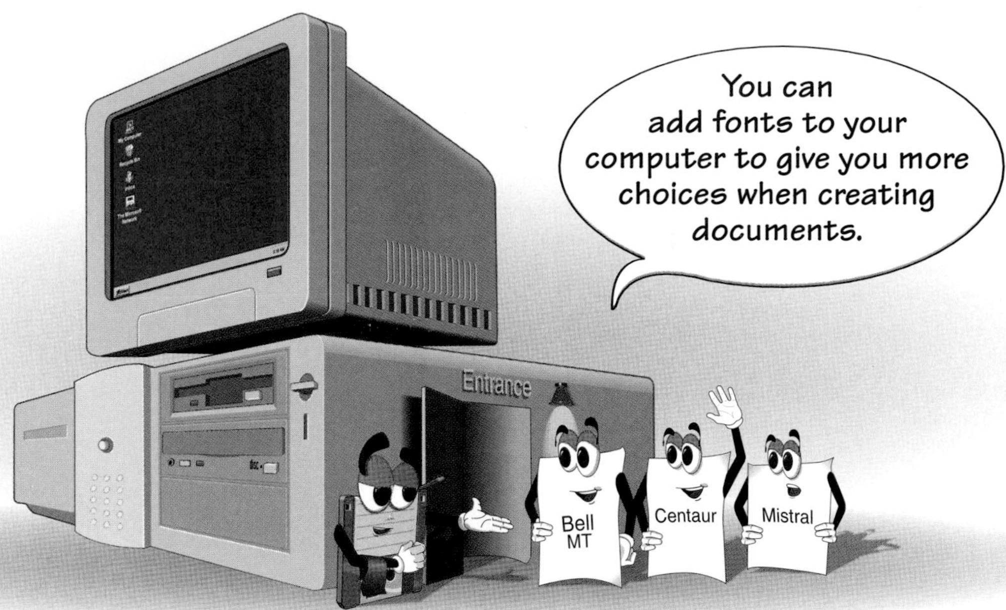

You can add fonts to your computer to give you more choices when creating documents.
Entrance
Bell MT
Centaur
Mistral

ADD FONTS

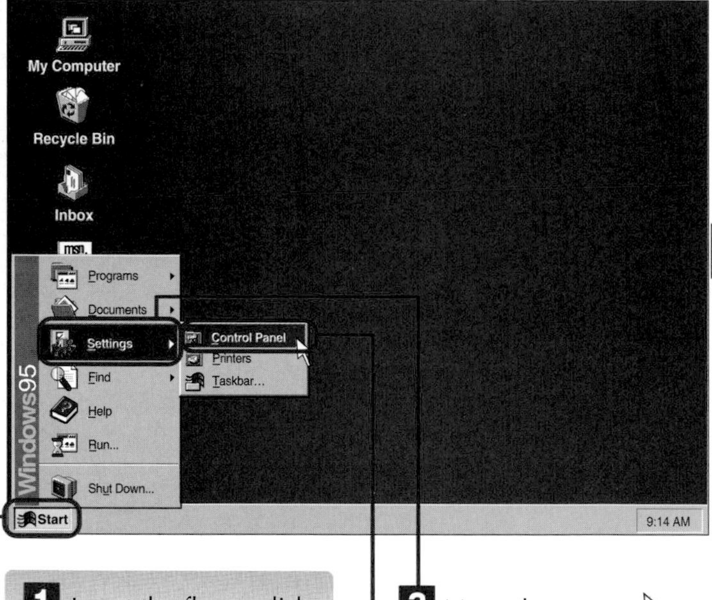

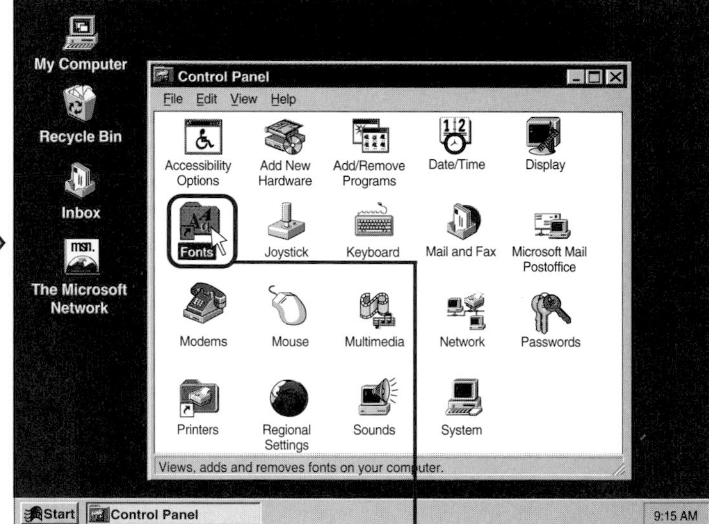

1 Insert the floppy disk containing the fonts into a drive.

2 Move the mouse over **Start** and then press the left button.

3 Move the mouse over **Settings**.

4 Move the mouse over **Control Panel** and then press the left button.

■ The **Control Panel** window appears.

5 To view the fonts stored on your computer, move the mouse over **Fonts** and then quickly press the left button twice.

Tip
You can buy fonts to add to your computer at most computer stores.
Computer Store
Midnight Madness
Fonts Fonts Fonts
We Sell Fonts

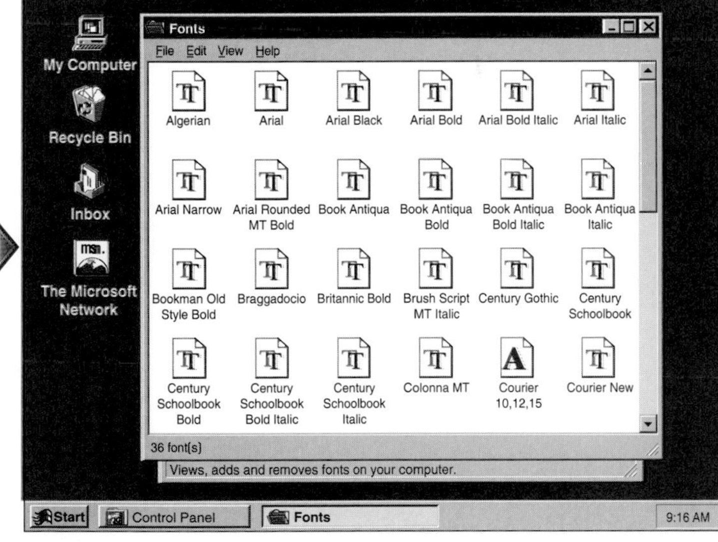

■ The **Fonts** window appears. Each icon represents a font stored on your computer.

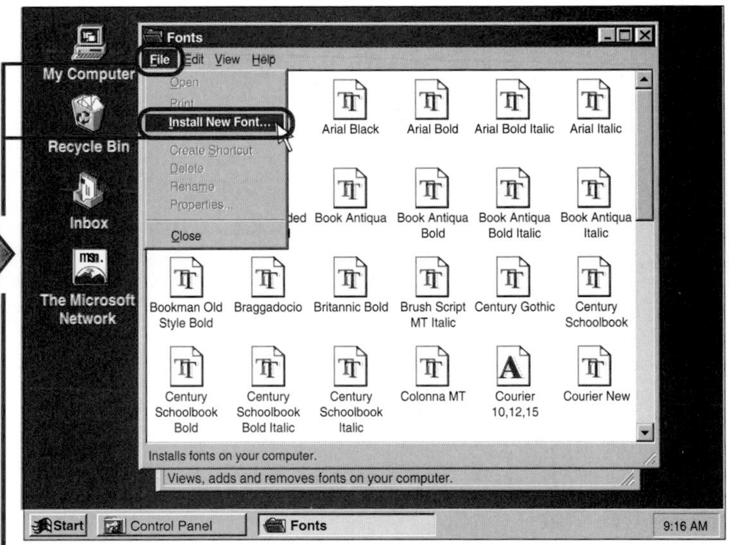

6 Move the mouse over **File** and then press the left button.

7 Move the mouse over **Install New Font** and then press the left button.

■ The **Add Fonts** dialog box appears.

ADD FONTS

When you add fonts to your computer, the fonts will be available for use in all your programs.

ADD FONTS (CONTINUED)

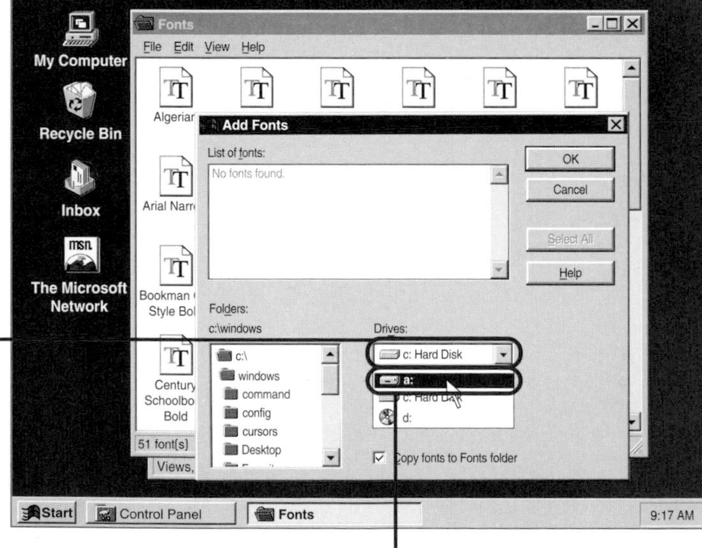

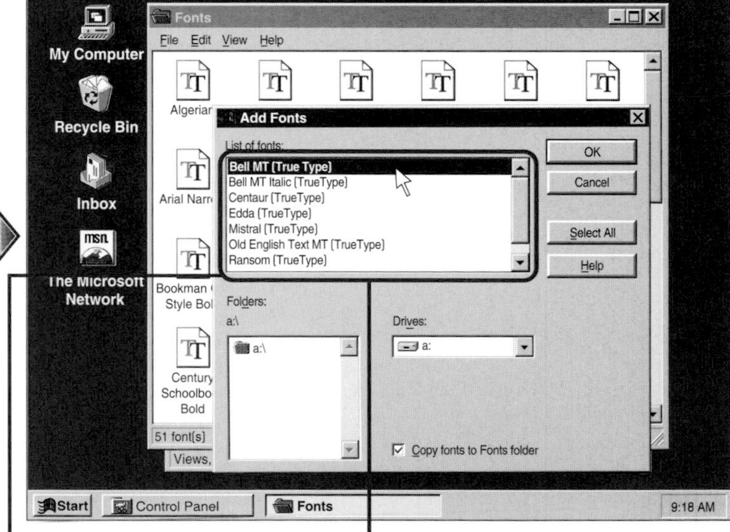

8 To view the fonts stored on the floppy disk, move the mouse over this area and then press the left button.

9 Move the mouse over the drive containing the floppy disk and then press the left button.

■ This area now displays the fonts stored on the floppy disk.

10 To select a font you want to add to your computer, move the mouse over the font and then press the left button.

Tip
Fonts take up space on your hard drive. If you do not use fonts you added to your computer, delete them as you would delete any file. Do not delete fonts that come with Windows.
Bell MT

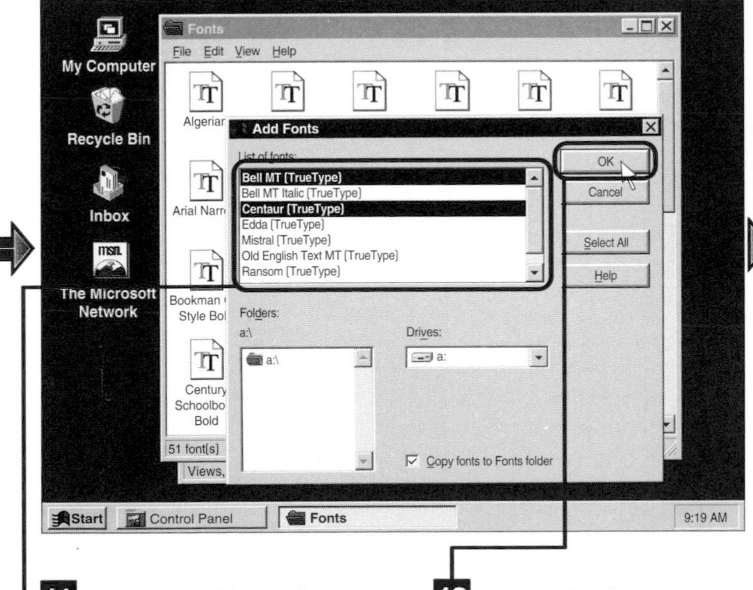

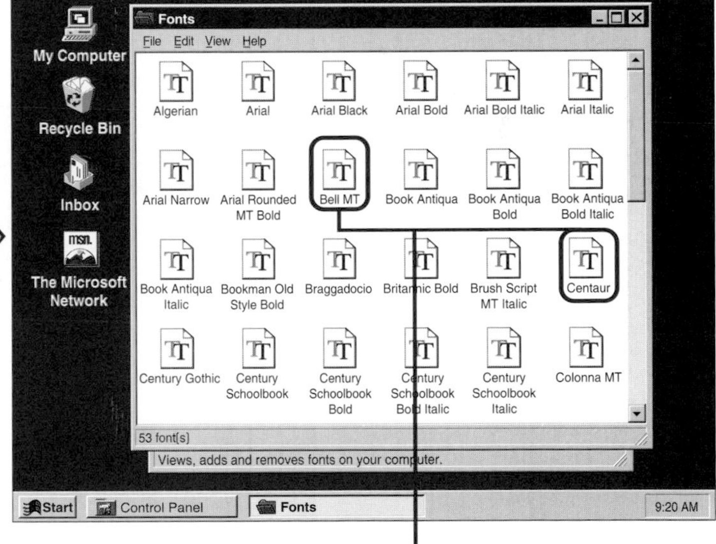

11 To select additional fonts, press and hold down **Ctrl** on your keyboard as you repeat step **10** for each font.

Note: To select all the fonts stored on the floppy disk, move the mouse over Select All and then press the left button.

12 To add the fonts to your computer, move the mouse over **OK** and then press the left button.

■ Windows copies the fonts to your computer.

■ The fonts now appear in the **Fonts** window.

ADD WINDOWS COMPONENTS

You can add components to your computer you did not add when you first set up Windows.

When setting up Windows, most people do not install all the components that come with the program. This avoids taking up storage space with components they do not plan to use.

ADD WINDOWS COMPONENTS

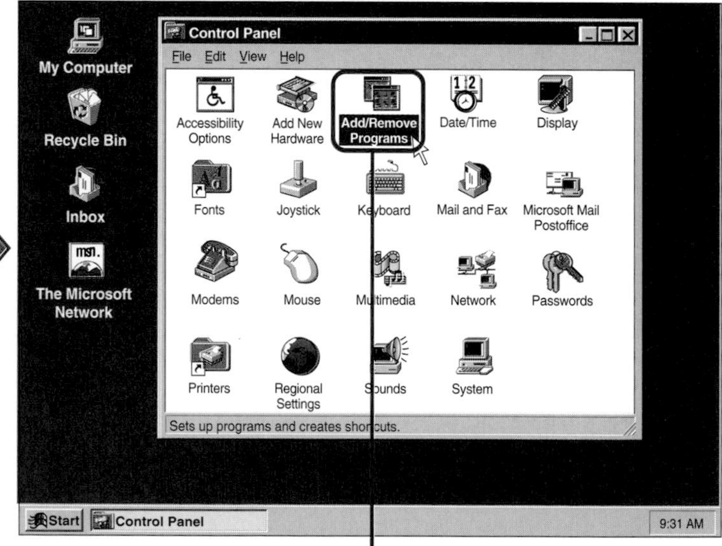

1 Move the mouse over **Start** and then press the left button.

2 Move the mouse over **Settings**.

3 Move the mouse over **Control Panel** and then press the left button.

■ The **Control Panel** window appears.

4 Move the mouse over **Add/Remove Programs** and then quickly press the left button twice.

■ The **Add/Remove Programs Properties** dialog box appears.

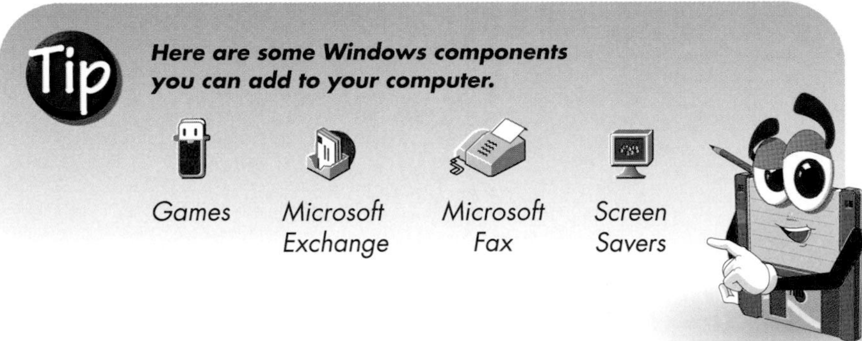

Tip
Here are some Windows components you can add to your computer.
Games
Microsoft Exchange
Microsoft Fax
Screen Savers

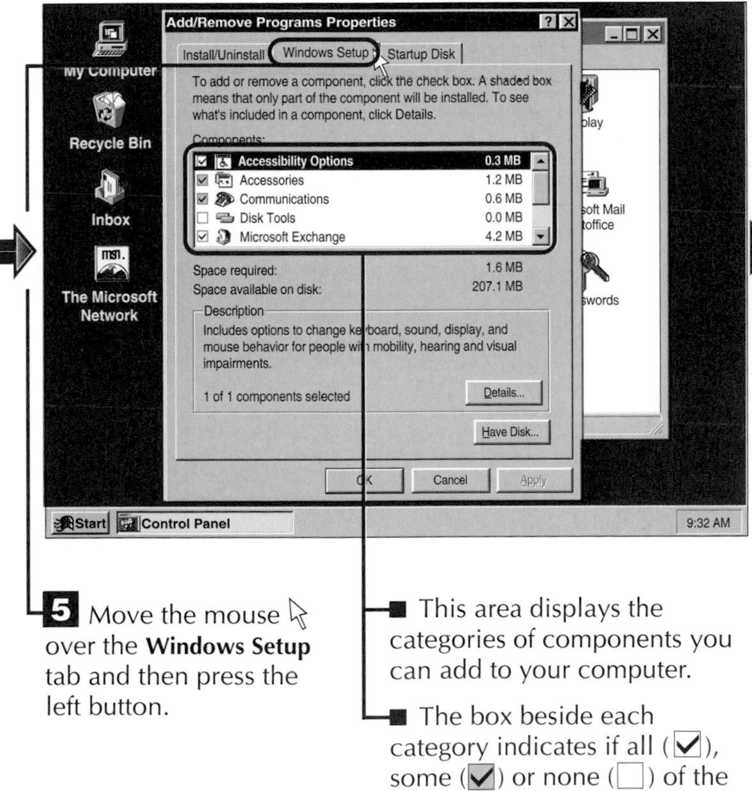

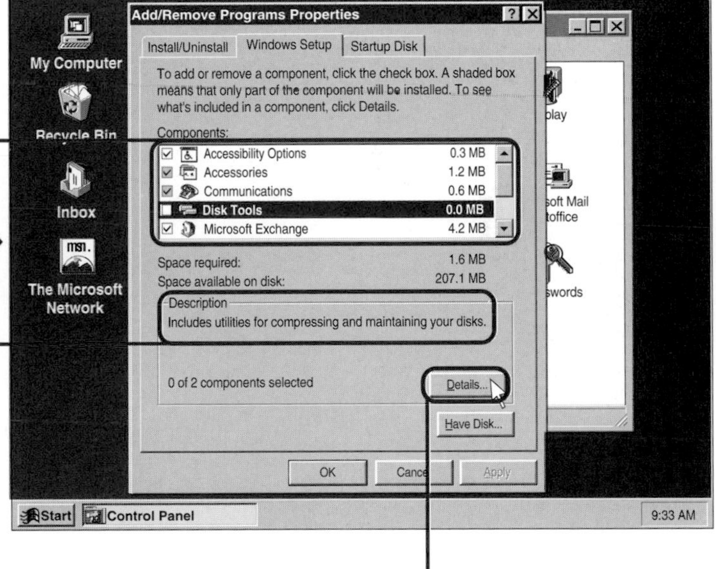

5 Move the mouse over the **Windows Setup** tab and then press the left button.

■ This area displays the categories of components you can add to your computer.

■ The box beside each category indicates if all (☑), some (☑) or none (☐) of the components in the category exist on your computer.

6 To display a description of the components in a category, move the mouse over the category and then press the left button.

■ This area displays a description of the components in the category.

7 To display the components in the category, move the mouse over **Details** and then press the left button.

ADD WINDOWS COMPONENTS

When adding Windows components, you must insert the installation CD-ROM disc or floppy disks that come with Windows.

Some components, such as CD Player and Quick View, are available on the Windows CD-ROM disc but not on the Windows floppy disks.

ADD WINDOWS COMPONENTS (CONTINUED)

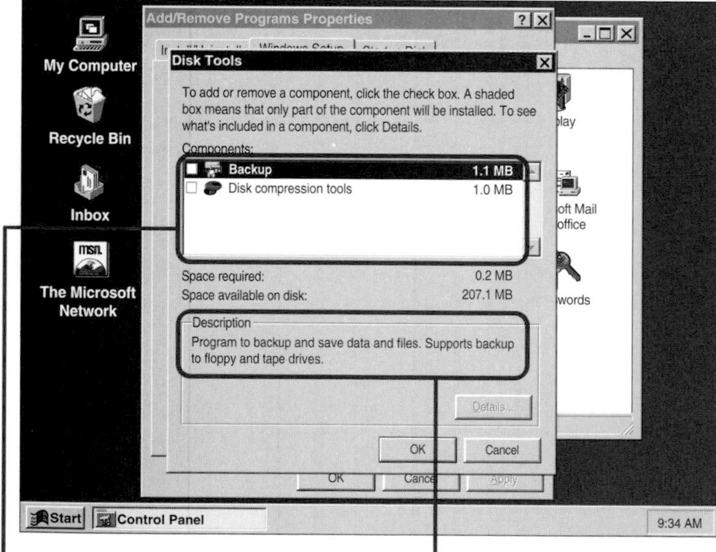

■ The components in the category appear. The box beside each component indicates if the component exists (☑) or does not exist (☐) on your computer.

■ This area displays a description of the highlighted component.

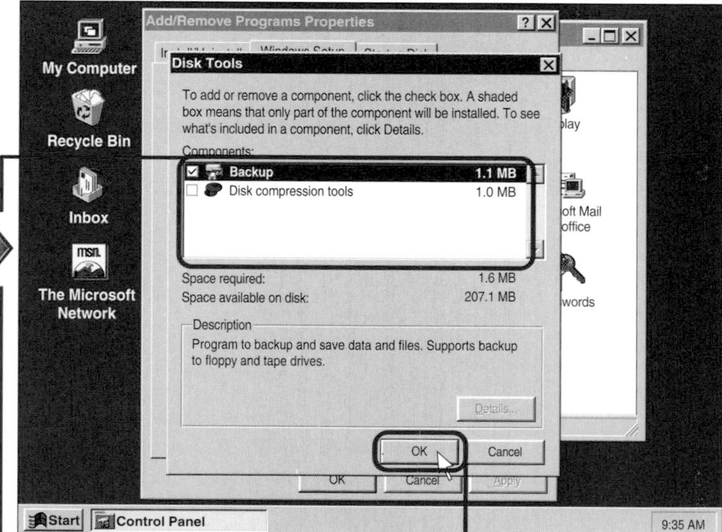

8 To select a component, move the mouse over the box (☐) beside the component and then press the left button (☐ changes to ☑).

9 Repeat step **8** for each component in the category you want to add to your computer.

10 Move the mouse over **OK** and then press the left button.

Tip *You can delete a component you do not use by performing steps* **1** *to* **12** *starting on page 96. When you select a component you want to remove,* ☑ *changes to* ☐ *in step* **8**.

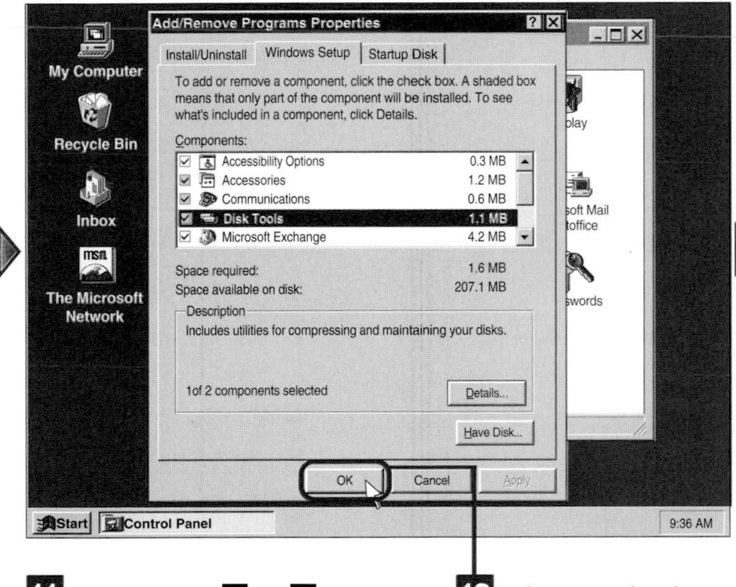

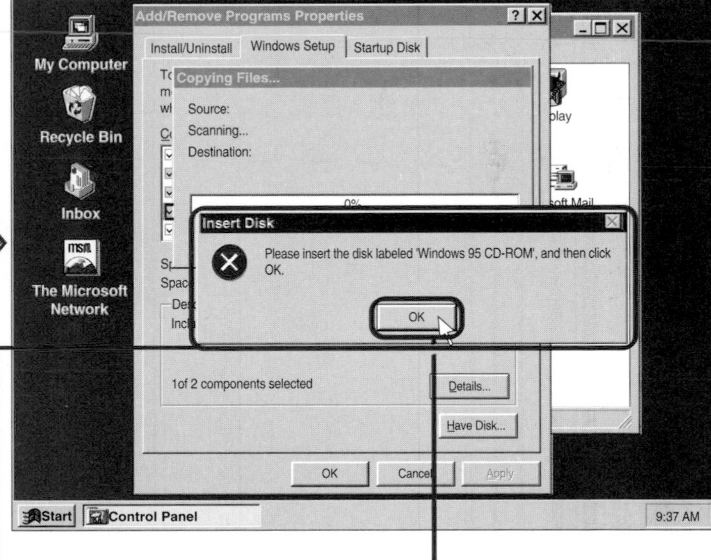

11 Repeat steps **6** to **10** starting on page 97 for any other component you want to add.

12 When you finish selecting all the components, move the mouse ↖ over **OK** and then press the left button.

■ A dialog box appears, asking you to insert the Windows CD-ROM disc or floppy disk.

13 Move the mouse ↖ over **OK** and then press the left button.

ADD A NEW PROGRAM

MAIN TYPES OF PROGRAMS

WORD PROCESSORS

A word processor helps you create documents quickly and efficiently. Popular word processors include Word and WordPerfect.

SPREADSHEETS

A spreadsheet program helps you manage, analyze and present financial information. Popular spreadsheet programs include Excel and Lotus 1-2-3.

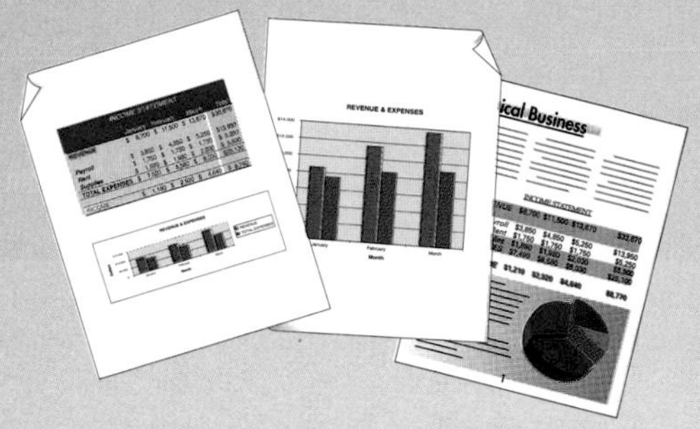

DATABASES

A database helps you manage large collections of information. Popular databases include Access and dBASE.

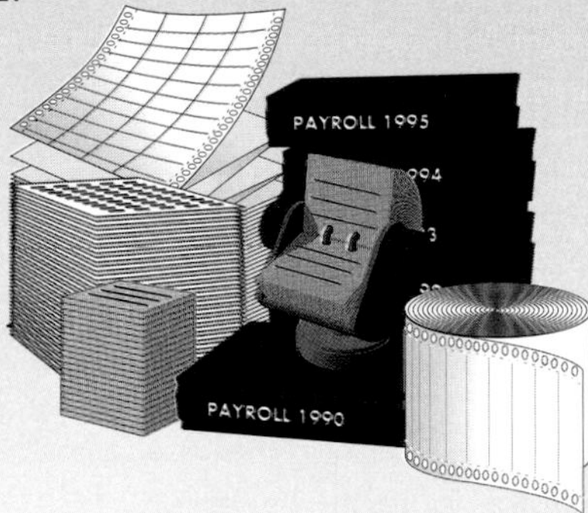

DESKTOP PUBLISHING

A desktop publishing program helps you create sophisticated documents by combining text and graphics on a page. Popular desktop publishing programs include PageMaker and QuarkXPress.

GAMES

There are thousands of games to entertain you. Popular games include Doom and Golf.

GRAPHICS

A graphics program helps you create and manipulate illustrations. Popular graphics programs include CorelDRAW! and Adobe Illustrator.

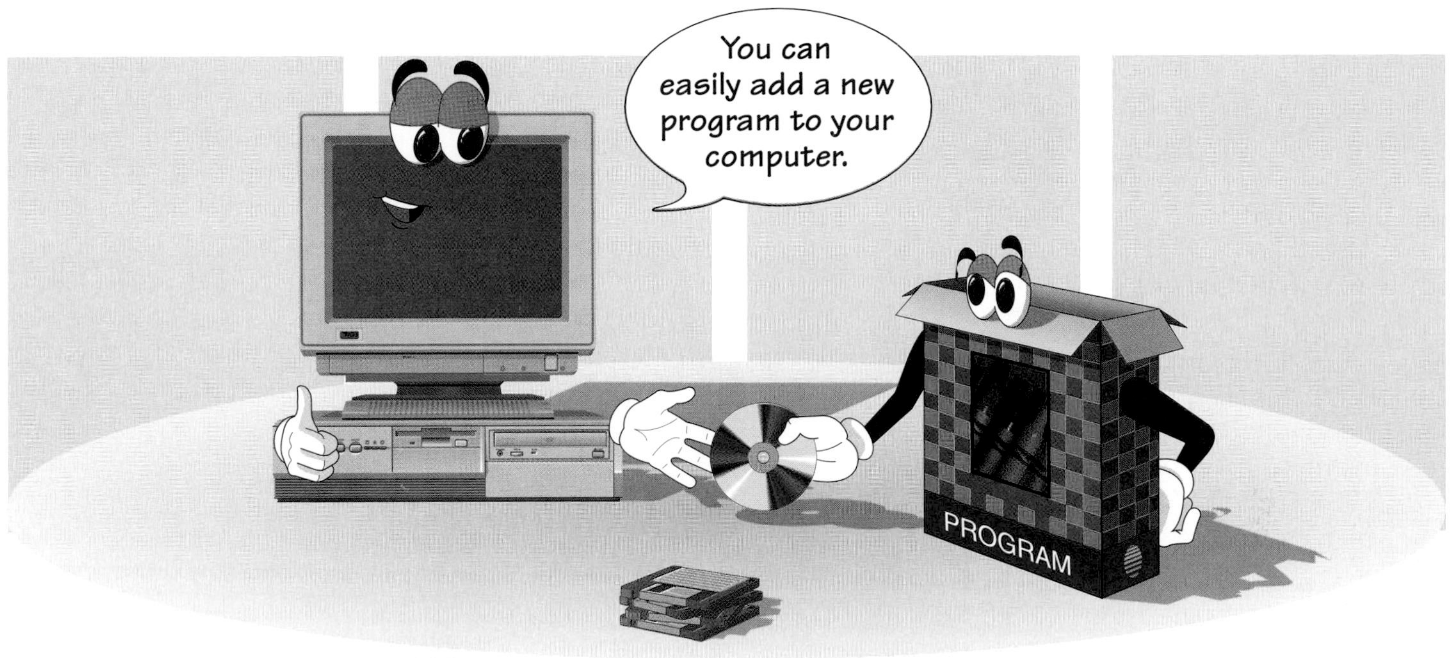

You can easily add a new program to your computer.
PROGRAM

ADD A NEW PROGRAM

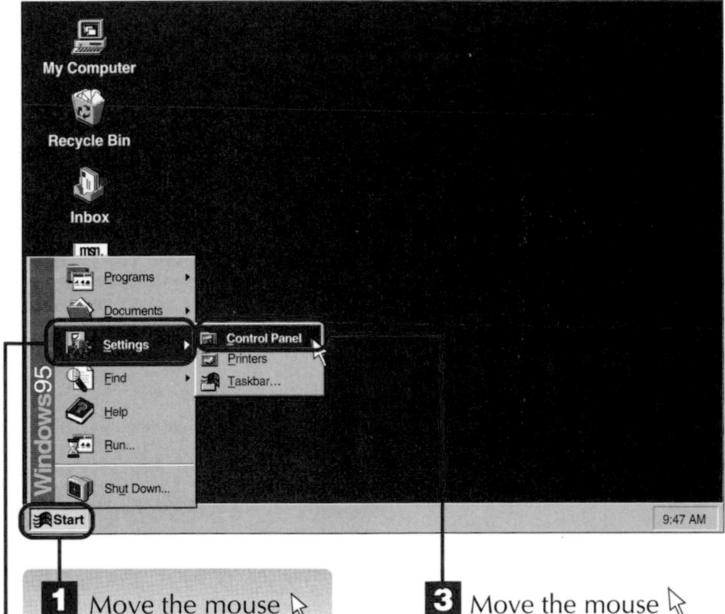

1 Move the mouse over **Start** and then press the left button.

2 Move the mouse over **Settings**.

3 Move the mouse over **Control Panel** and then press the left button.

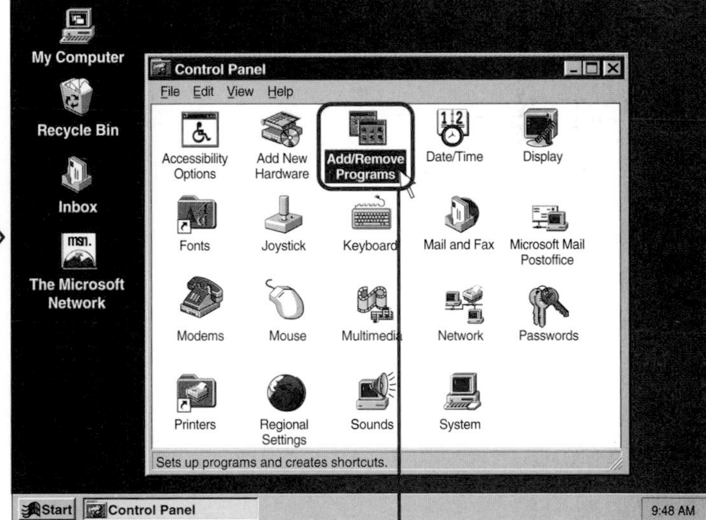

■ The **Control Panel** window appears.

4 Move the mouse over **Add/Remove Programs** and then quickly press the left button twice.

ADD A NEW PROGRAM

Programs come on either a CD-ROM disc or floppy disks.

When you finish installing a program, make sure you keep the CD-ROM disc or floppy disks in a safe place. If your computer fails or if you accidentally erase the program files, you may need to install the program again.

ADD A NEW PROGRAM (CONTINUED)

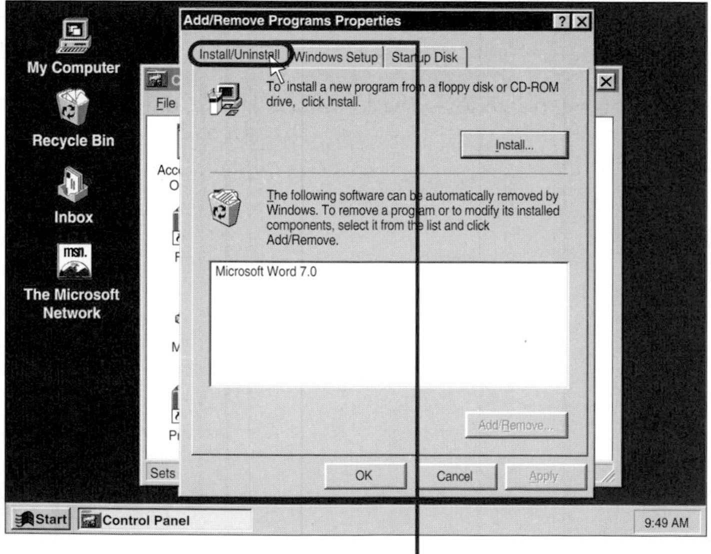

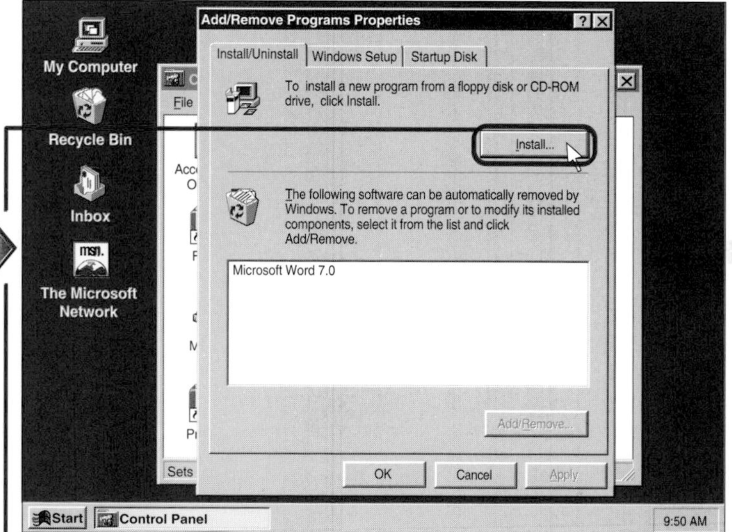

■ The **Add/Remove Programs Properties** dialog box appears.

5 Move the mouse over the **Install/Uninstall** tab and then press the left button.

6 Move the mouse over **Install** and then press the left button.

■ A dialog box appears.

You can often select the way you want to install a program. Common options include:

***Typical**—Installs the program as recommended for most people.*

***Custom**—Lets you customize the program to suit your specific needs.*

***Minimum**—Installs the minimum amount of the program needed. This is ideal for portable computers or computers with limited disk space.*

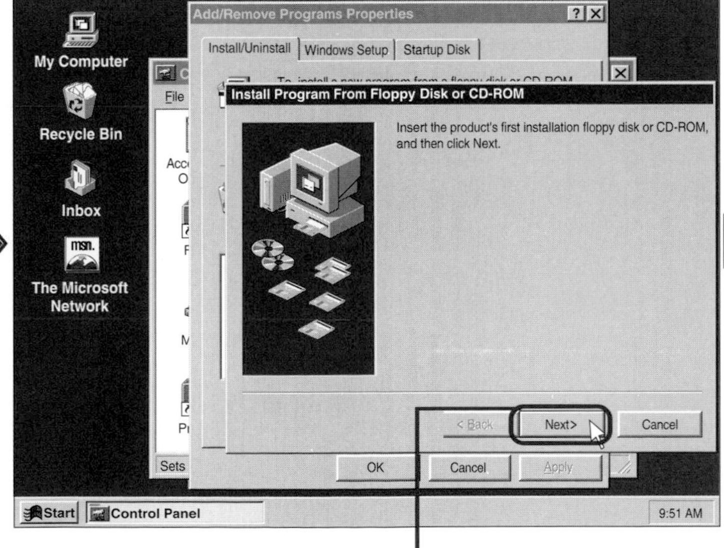

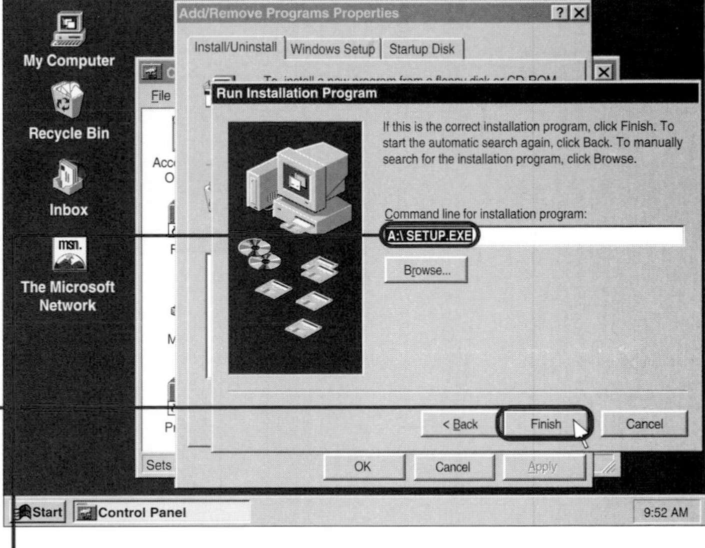

7 Insert the CD-ROM disc or the floppy disk labeled **Disk 1** into your computer.

8 To continue, move the mouse over **Next** and then press the left button.

■ Windows locates the file needed to install the program.

9 To install the program, move the mouse over **Finish** and then press the left button.

10 Follow the instructions on your screen. Every program sets itself up differently.

SET UP NEW HARDWARE AUTOMATICALLY

You can have Windows detect and install new hardware for you. This is extremely helpful if you do not know the details about the new hardware.
Sound Card

If you know the details about the new hardware, you can save time by telling Windows exactly what you added. For more information, refer to page 108.

SET UP NEW HARDWARE AUTOMATICALLY

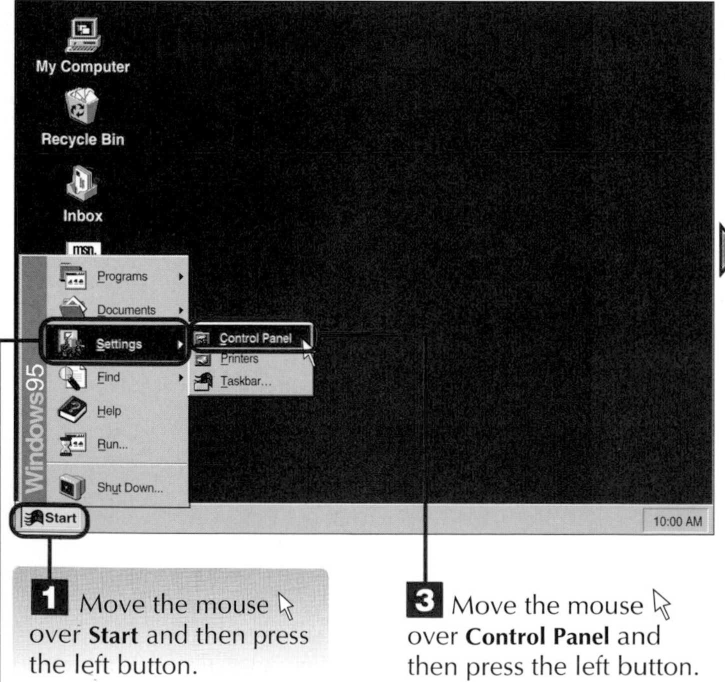

1 Move the mouse over **Start** and then press the left button.

2 Move the mouse over **Settings**.

3 Move the mouse over **Control Panel** and then press the left button.

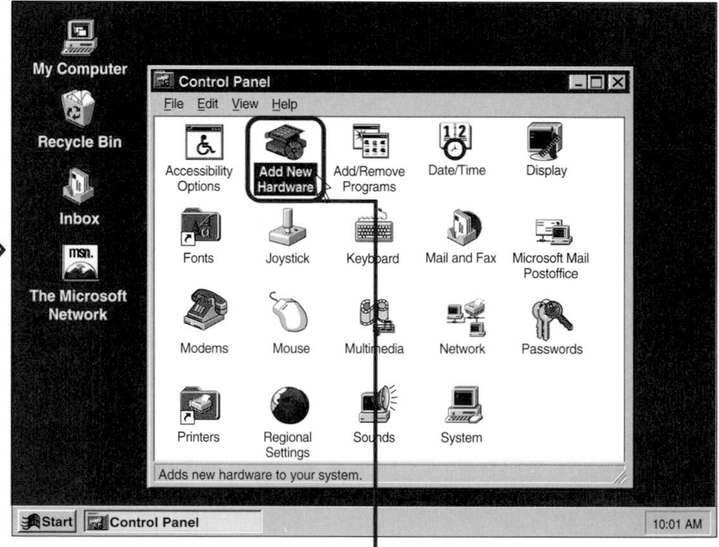

■ The **Control Panel** window appears.

4 Move the mouse over **Add New Hardware** and then quickly press the left button twice.

Tip
You can add a new CD-ROM drive, keyboard, modem, mouse, printer and much more to your computer.

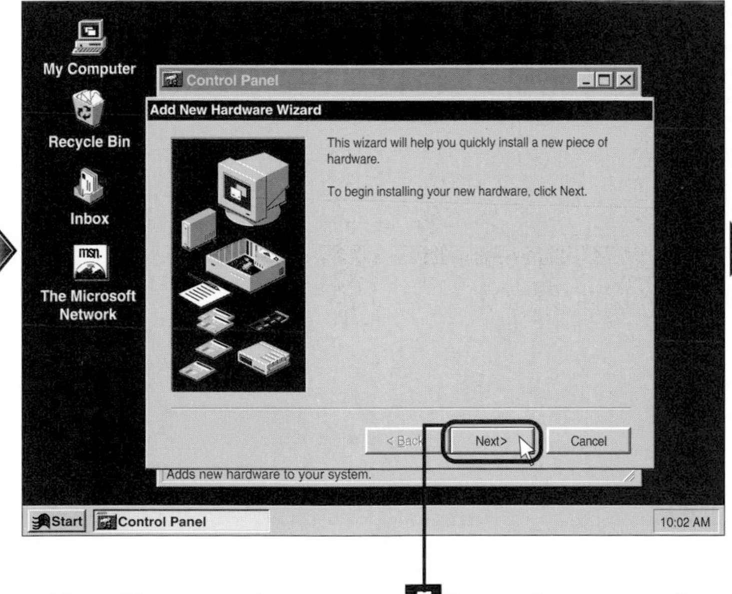

■ The **Add New Hardware Wizard** dialog box appears.

5 To continue, move the mouse over **Next** and then press the left button.

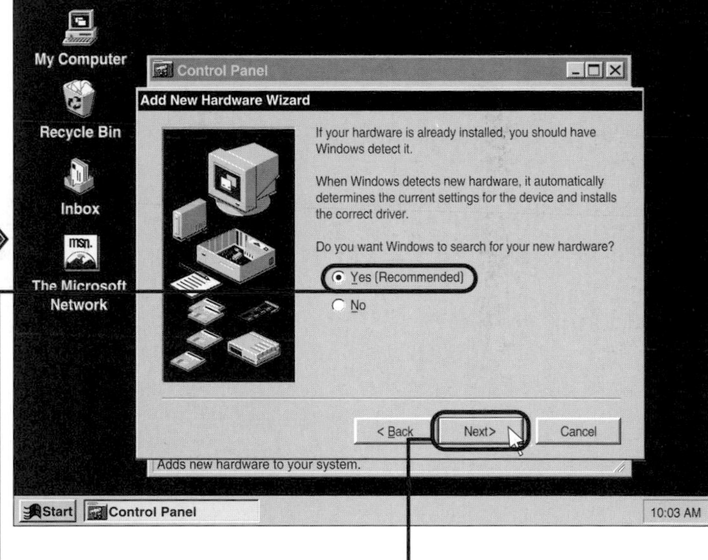

6 To have Windows search for the new hardware, move the mouse over **Yes** and then press the left button.

7 To continue, move the mouse over **Next** and then press the left button.

SET UP NEW HARDWARE AUTOMATICALLY

SET UP NEW HARDWARE AUTOMATICALLY (CONTINUED)

8 To start the search for the new hardware, move the mouse over **Next** and then press the left button.

■ This area displays the progress of the search.

■ If the progress indicator stops for a long time, you will need to restart your computer. Turn your computer off, wait a minute and then turn your computer on again. Try installing the hardware using the method described on page 108.

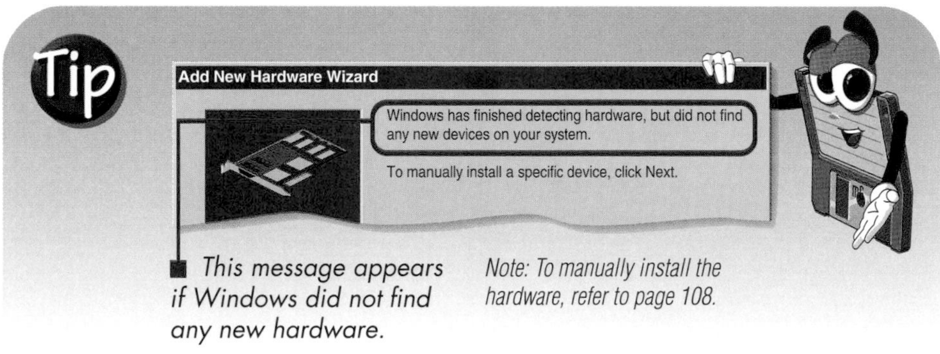

■ *This message appears if Windows did not find any new hardware.*

Note: To manually install the hardware, refer to page 108.

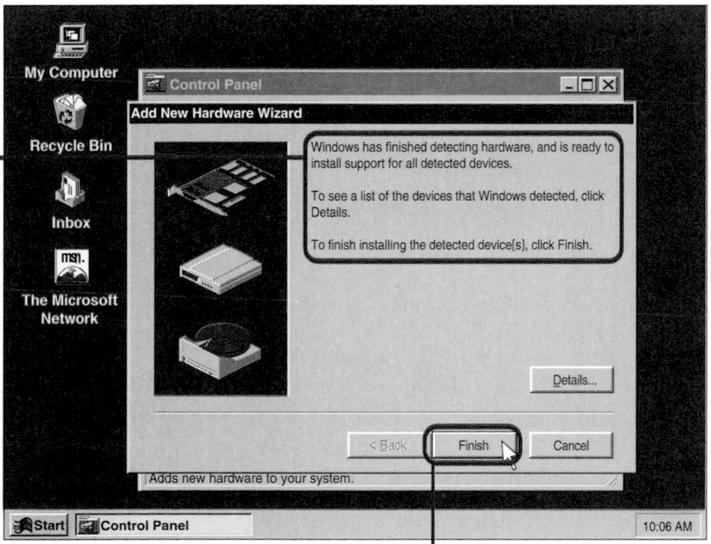

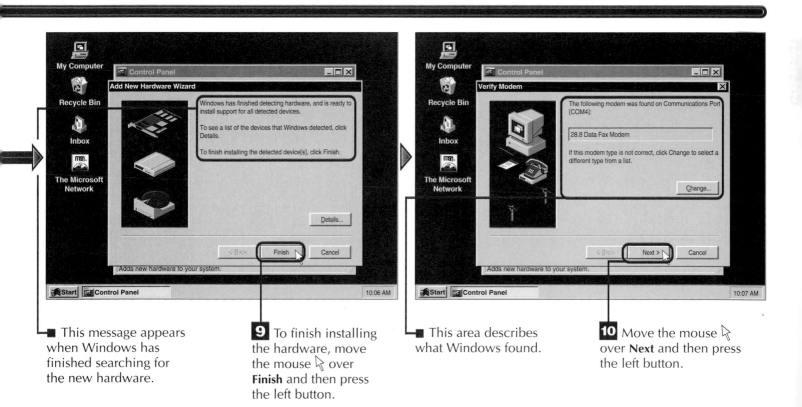

■ This message appears when Windows has finished searching for the new hardware.

9 To finish installing the hardware, move the mouse ⇖ over **Finish** and then press the left button.

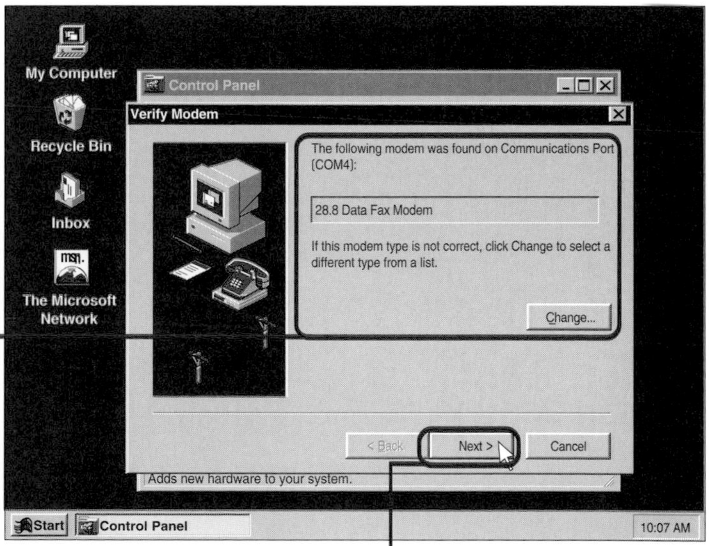

■ This area describes what Windows found.

10 Move the mouse ⇖ over **Next** and then press the left button.

SET UP NEW HARDWARE MANUALLY

If you do not know the details about the new hardware, you can have Windows detect and install the hardware for you. For more information, refer to page 104.

SET UP NEW HARDWARE MANUALLY

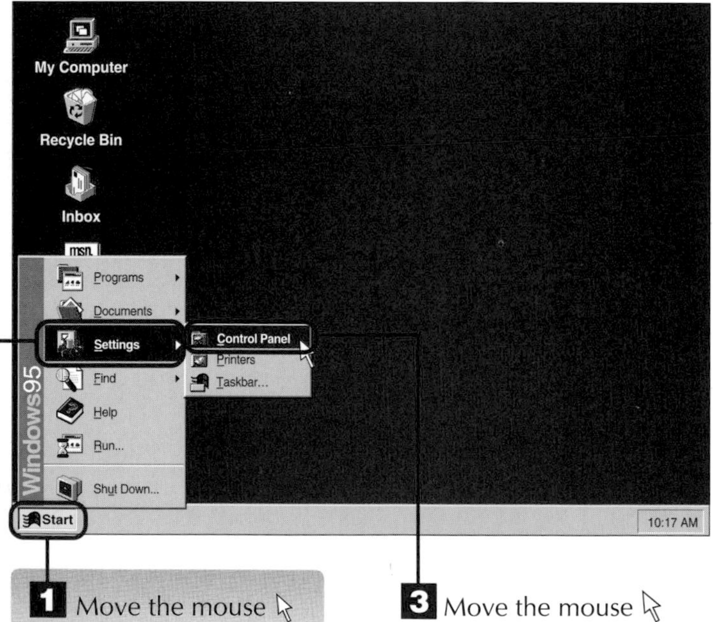

1 Move the mouse over **Start** and then press the left button.

2 Move the mouse over **Settings**.

3 Move the mouse over **Control Panel** and then press the left button.

■ The **Control Panel** window appears.

4 Move the mouse over **Add New Hardware** and then quickly press the left button twice.

Tip
For your computer to use new hardware, you have to install special software, called a **driver**. A driver is a program that helps the computer communicate with the hardware. Windows provides the most popular drivers and helps you install them.

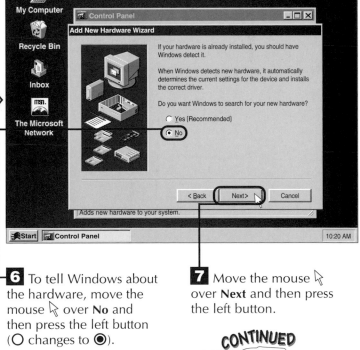

■ The **Add New Hardware Wizard** dialog box appears.

5 To continue, move the mouse over **Next** and then press the left button.

6 To tell Windows about the hardware, move the mouse over **No** and then press the left button (○ changes to ◉).

7 Move the mouse over **Next** and then press the left button.

CONTINUED

SET UP NEW HARDWARE MANUALLY

When adding new hardware, you must specify the manufacturer and model of the hardware.

SET UP NEW HARDWARE MANUALLY (CONTINUED)

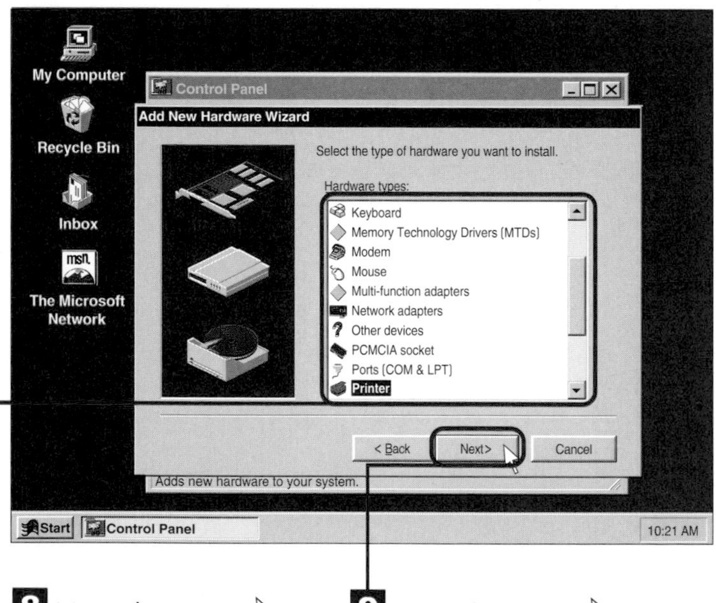

8 Move the mouse over the type of hardware you want to install and then press the left button.

9 Move the mouse over **Next** and then press the left button.

■ The remaining steps depend on the type of hardware you selected in step 8. In this example, we install a new printer.

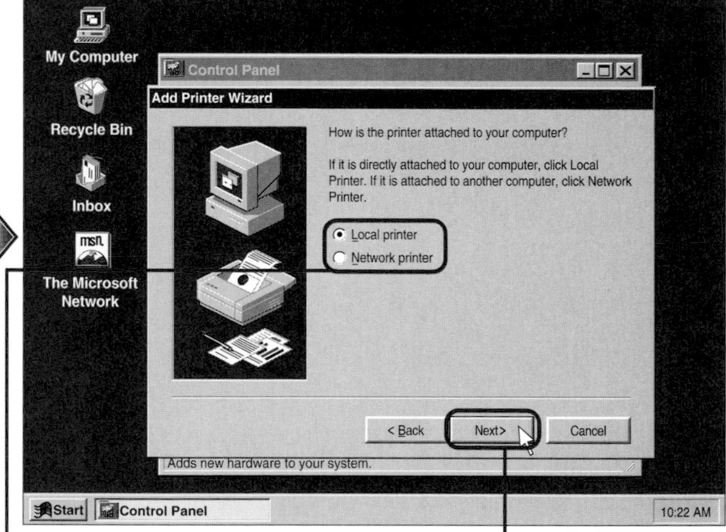

10 You may be asked to tell Windows how the printer connects to your computer. To do so, move the mouse over one of the following options and then press the left button (○ changes to ◉).

Local printer - Printer connected directly to your computer.

Network printer - Printer connected to another computer.

11 To continue, move the mouse over **Next** and then press the left button.

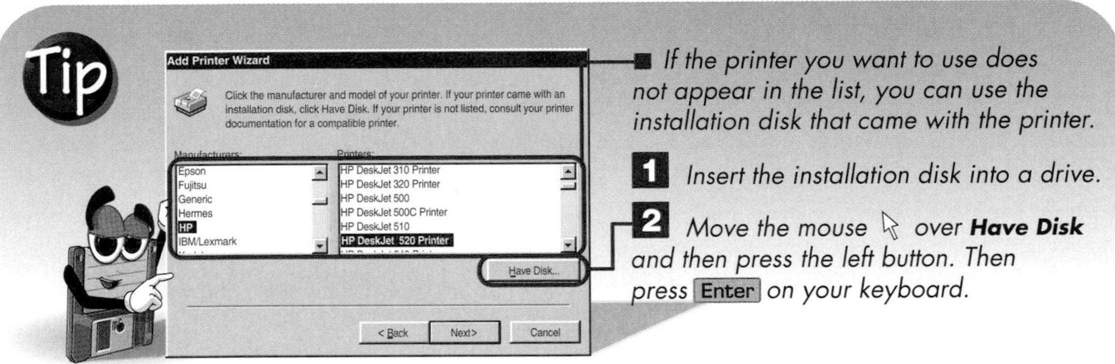

If the printer you want to use does not appear in the list, you can use the installation disk that came with the printer.

1 *Insert the installation disk into a drive.*

2 *Move the mouse over* ***Have Disk*** *and then press the left button. Then press* Enter *on your keyboard.*

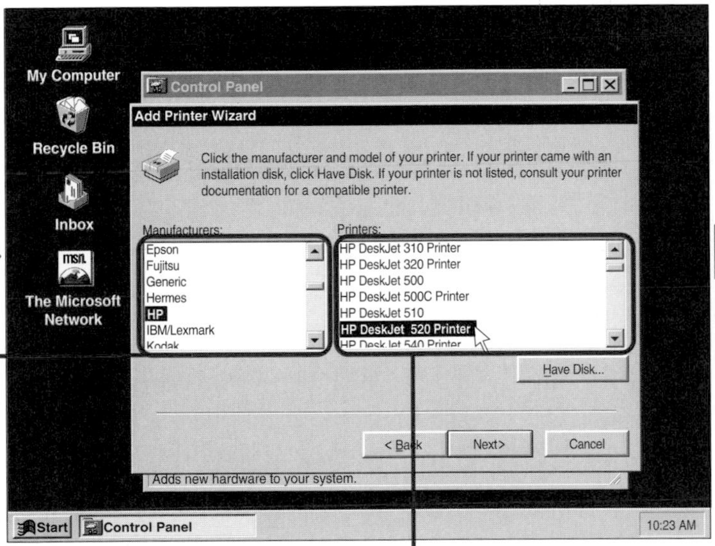

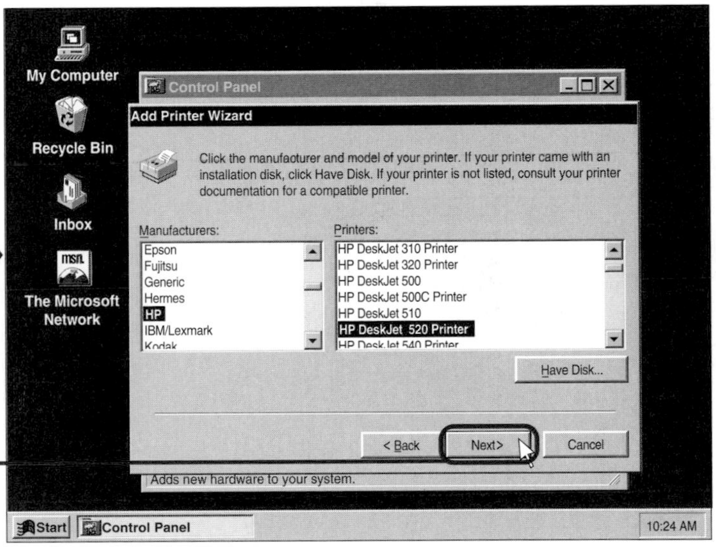

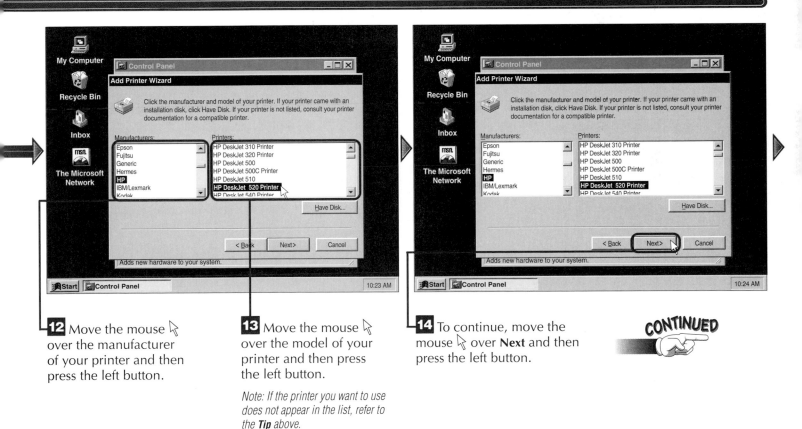

12 Move the mouse over the manufacturer of your printer and then press the left button.

13 Move the mouse over the model of your printer and then press the left button.

Note: If the printer you want to use does not appear in the list, refer to the ***Tip*** *above.*

14 To continue, move the mouse over **Next** and then press the left button.

CONTINUED

SET UP NEW HARDWARE MANUALLY

Windows asks you questions about the new hardware. This helps Windows set up the hardware to suit your specific needs.

SET UP NEW HARDWARE MANUALLY (CONTINUED)

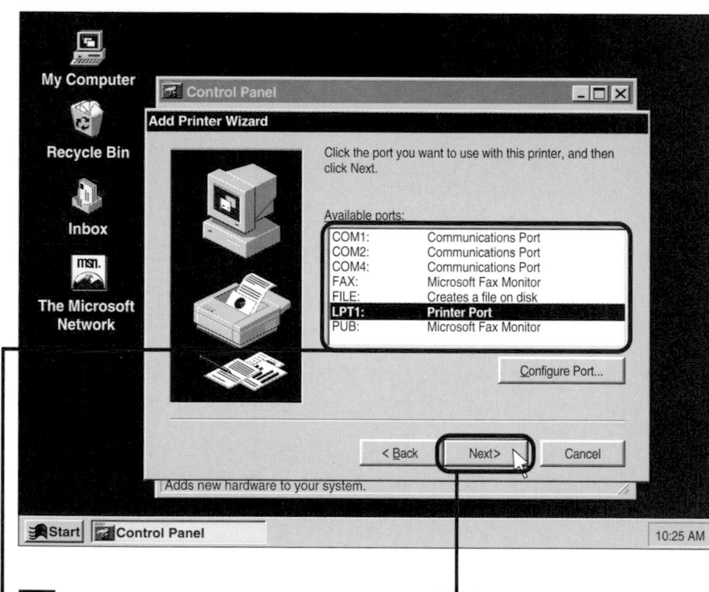

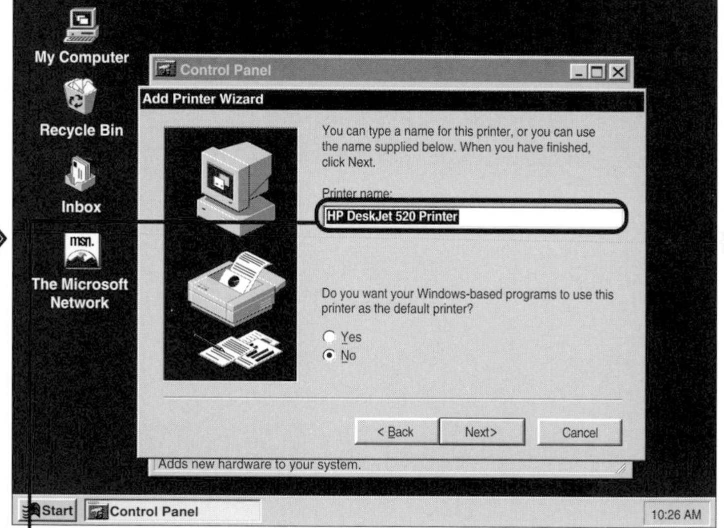

15 Move the mouse over the port you want to use with the printer and then press the left button.

Note: A port is a socket at the back of a computer where you plug in a device. LPT1 is the most commonly used port for printers.

16 To continue, move the mouse over **Next** and then press the left button.

17 Type a name for the printer.

Note: To use the name supplied by Windows, do not type a name.

*Windows 95 supports **Plug and Play**. Before Plug and Play, adding new features to a computer was difficult and frustrating. Plug and Play lets you quickly and easily add new features to a computer.*

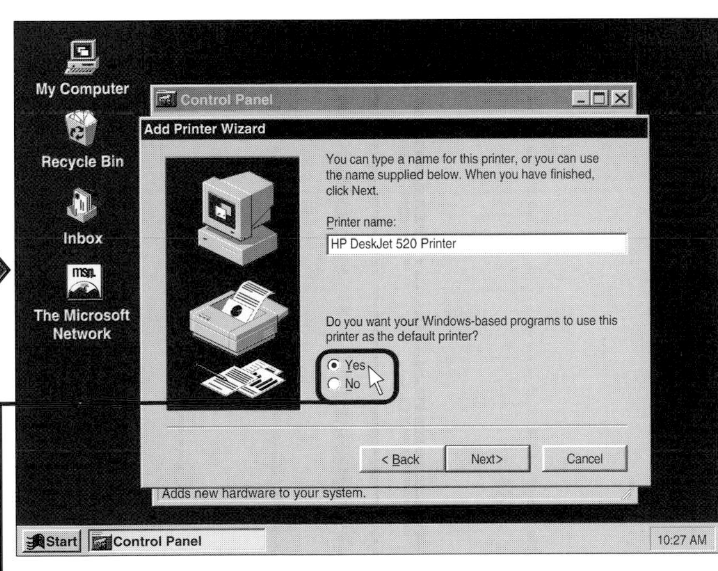

18 To specify if you want to use the printer as the default printer, move the mouse over one of these options and then press the left button (○ changes to ◉).

Yes - Documents will always print to this printer.

No - Documents will print to this printer only when you select the printer.

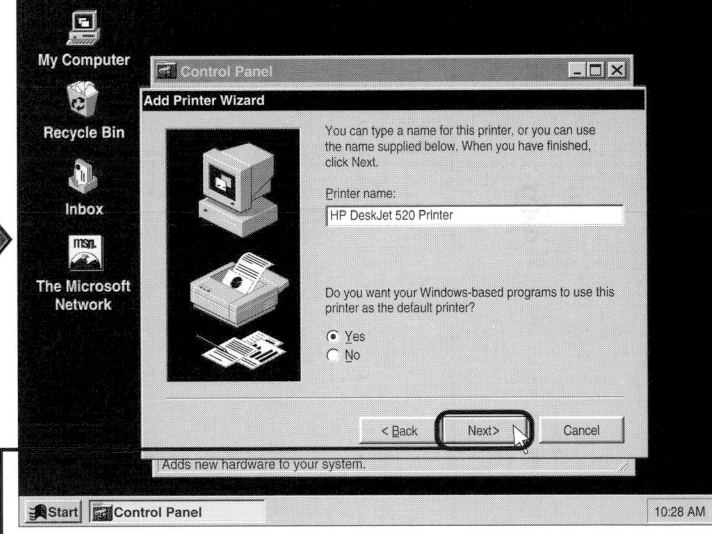

19 To continue, move the mouse over **Next** and then press the left button.

SET UP NEW HARDWARE MANUALLY

SET UP NEW HARDWARE MANUALLY (CONTINUED)

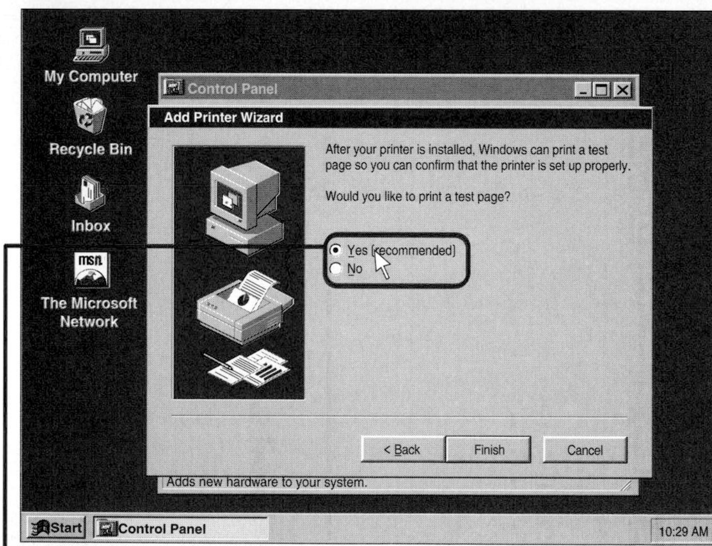

20 To specify if you want to print a test page, move the mouse over an option and then press the left button. A test page will confirm your printer is set up properly.

Yes - Print a test page.

No - Do not print a test page.

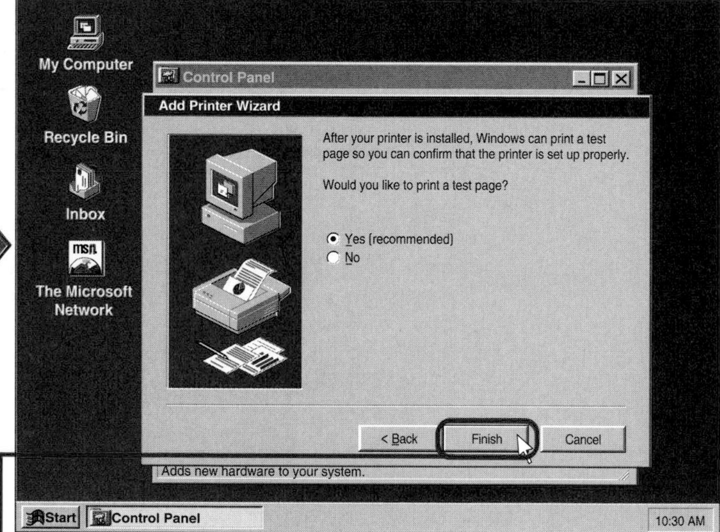

21 To complete the installation, move the mouse over **Finish** and then press the left button.

When you finish adding the new hardware, you can immediately start using the hardware.

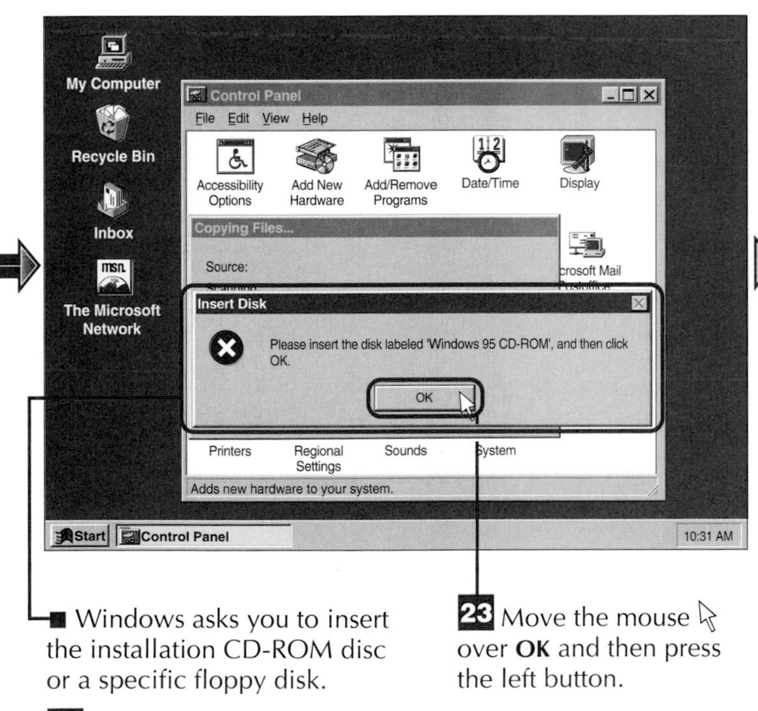

■ Windows asks you to insert the installation CD-ROM disc or a specific floppy disk.

22 Insert the CD-ROM disc or floppy disk into a drive.

23 Move the mouse over **OK** and then press the left button.

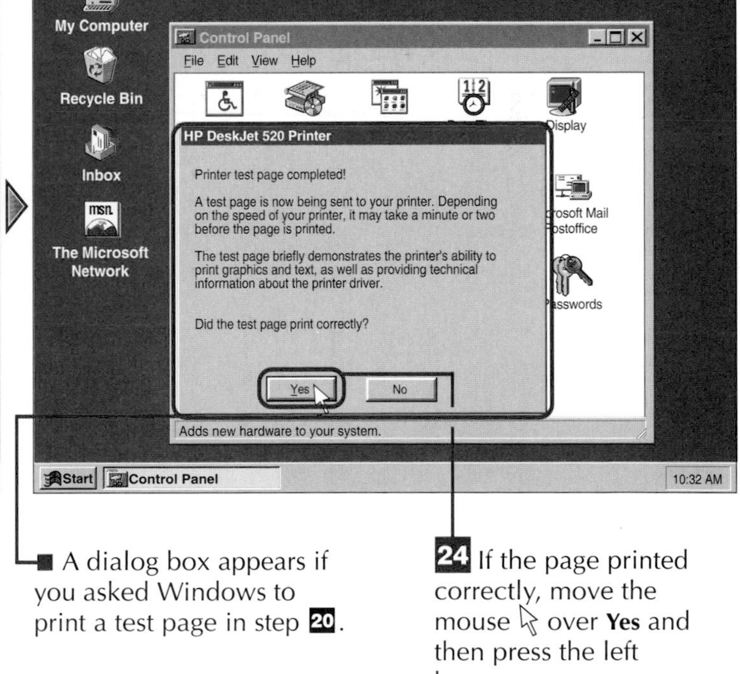

■ A dialog box appears if you asked Windows to print a test page in step **20**.

24 If the page printed correctly, move the mouse over **Yes** and then press the left button.

In this chapter you will learn how to copy a floppy disk and solve hardware and software problems. You will also learn how to view and create more free space on your hard disk.
Original
MicroFLOPPY
Double Sided
1.44 MB
Copy
MicroFLOPPY
Double Sided
1.44 MB

CHAPTER 7

MAINTAIN YOUR COMPUTER

COPY A FLOPPY DISK

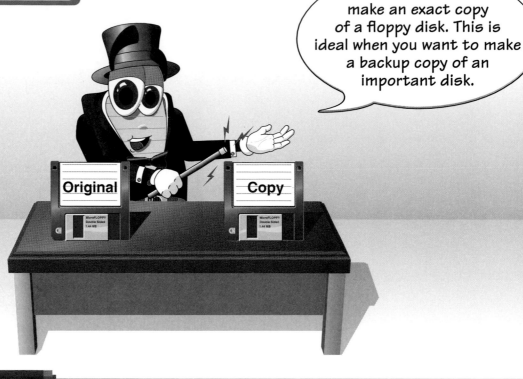

You can make an exact copy of a floppy disk. This is ideal when you want to make a backup copy of an important disk.

COPY A FLOPPY DISK

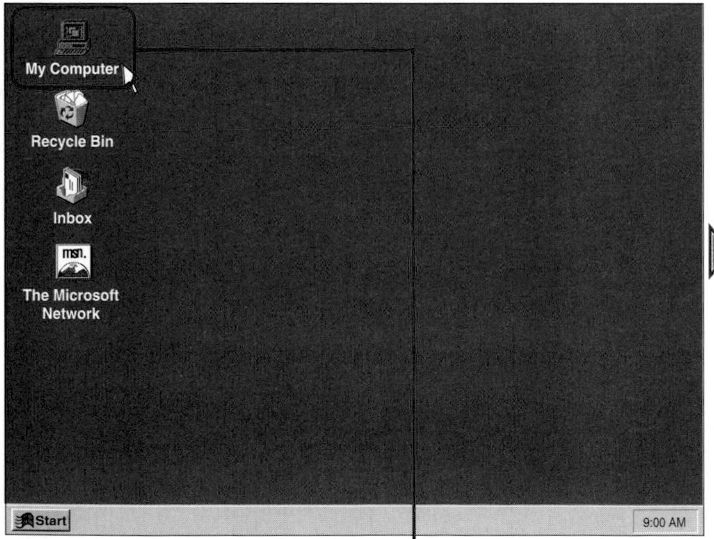

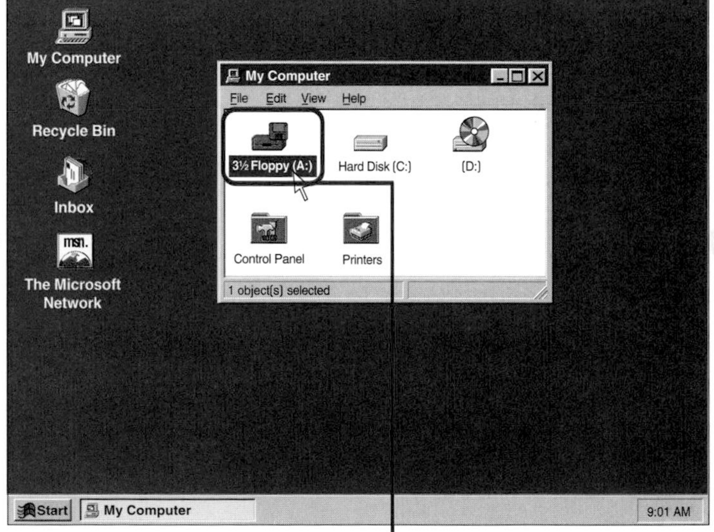

1 Insert the floppy disk you want to copy into a drive.

2 Move the mouse over **My Computer** and then quickly press the left button twice.

■ The **My Computer** window appears.

3 Move the mouse over the drive containing the floppy disk you want to copy and then press the left button.

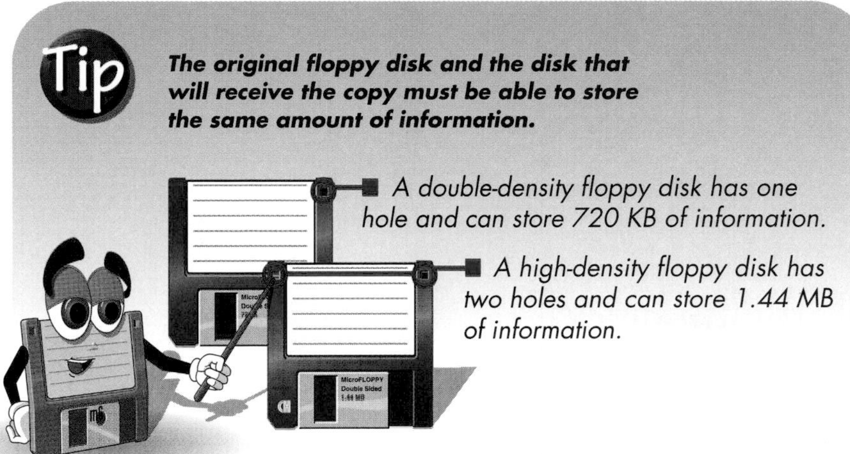

Tip
The original floppy disk and the disk that will receive the copy must be able to store the same amount of information.
■ A double-density floppy disk has one hole and can store 720 KB of information.
■ A high-density floppy disk has two holes and can store 1.44 MB of information.
MicroFLOPPY
Double Sided
1.44 MB

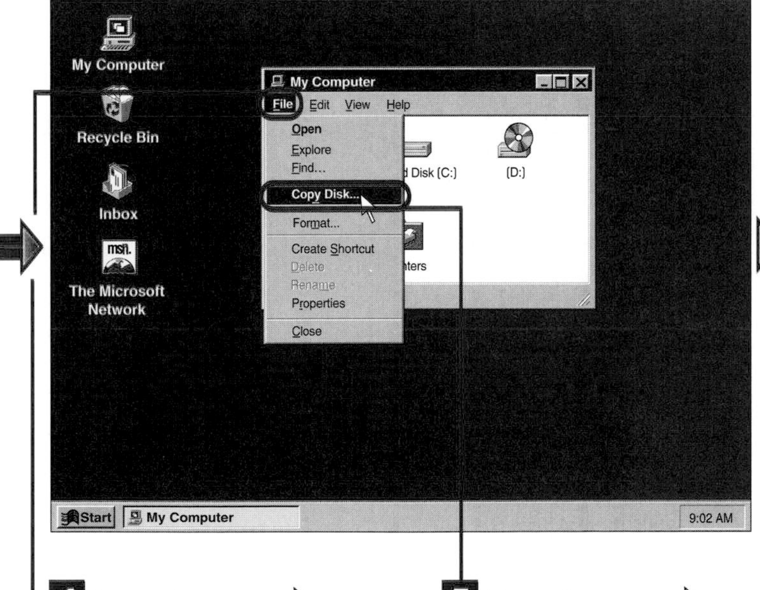

4 Move the mouse over **File** and then press the left button.

5 Move the mouse over **Copy Disk** and then press the left button.

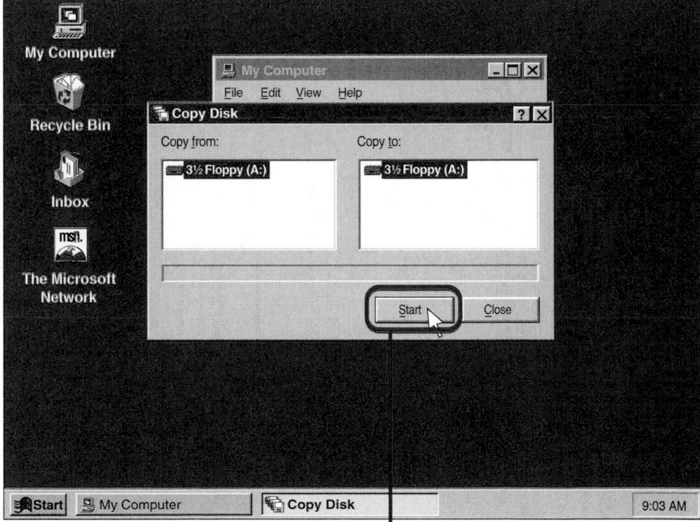

■ The **Copy Disk** dialog box appears.

6 To start the copy, move the mouse over **Start** and then press the left button.

COPY A FLOPPY DISK

Make sure the floppy disk receiving the copy does not contain information you want to keep. Copying will remove all the old information from the disk.

COPY A FLOPPY DISK (CONTINUED)

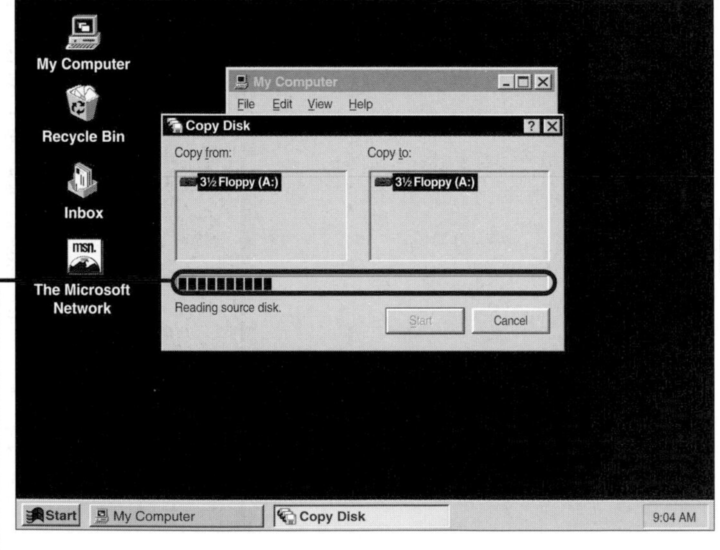

■ This area shows the progress of the copy.

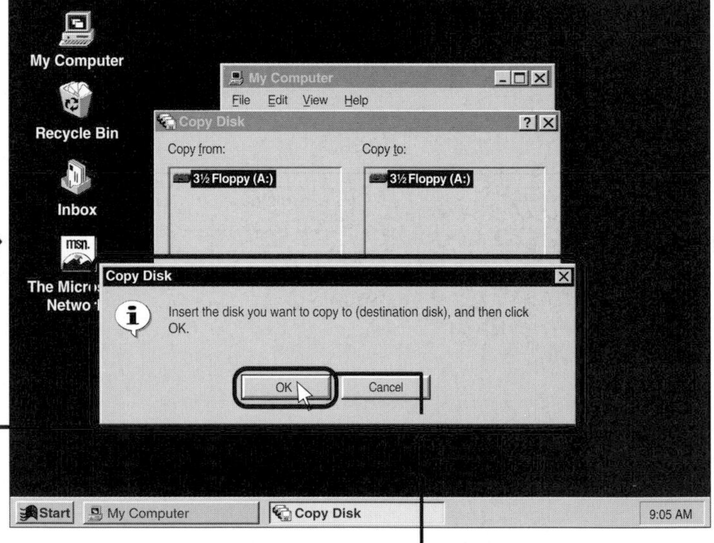

■ This dialog box appears, telling you to insert the floppy disk you want to receive the copy.

7 Remove the floppy disk currently in the drive and then insert the disk you want to receive the copy.

8 To continue, move the mouse over **OK** and then press the left button.

Tip
Keep floppy disks away from magnets, which can damage the information stored on the disks. Also be careful not to spill liquids such as coffee or soda on the disks.
Happy Birthday!

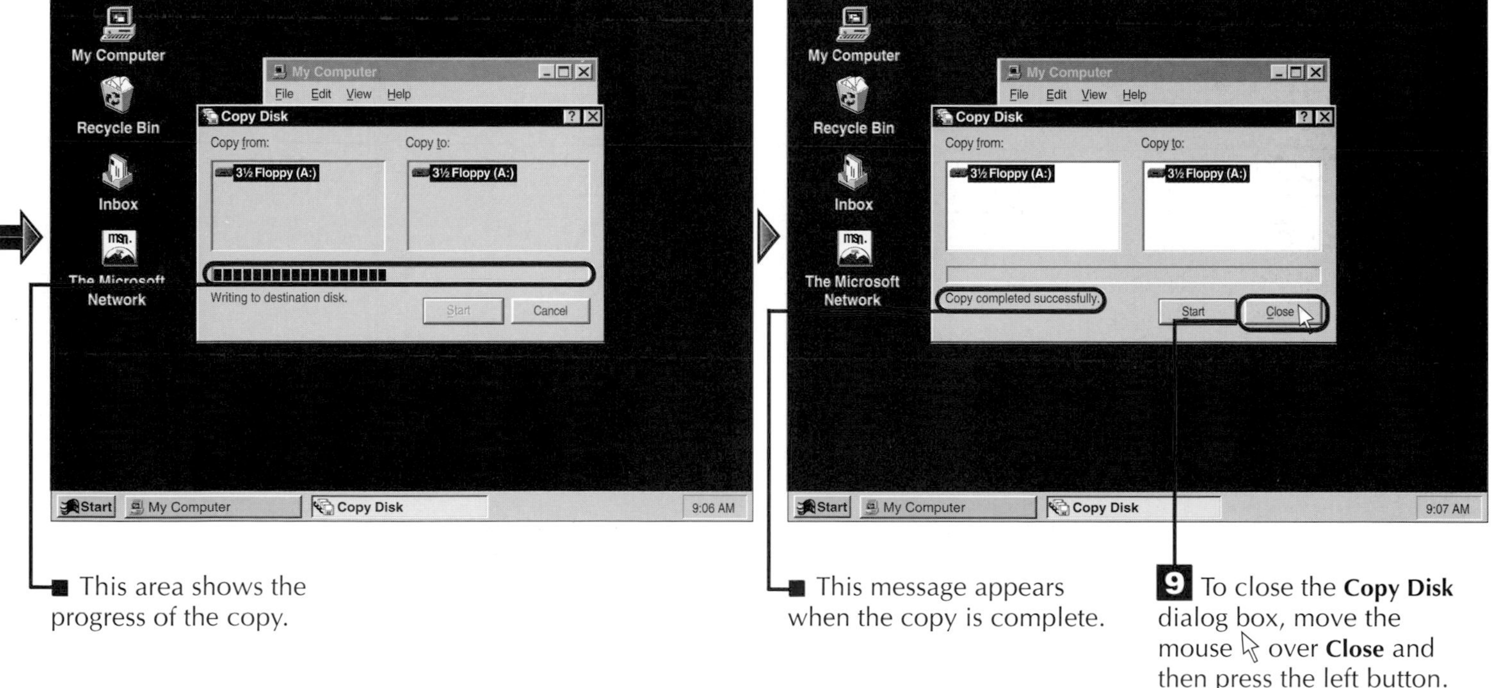

■ This area shows the progress of the copy.

■ This message appears when the copy is complete.

9 To close the **Copy Disk** dialog box, move the mouse ↖ over **Close** and then press the left button.

TROUBLESHOOTING

If hardware or software does not work as expected, Windows can help you solve the problem.

Windows asks you questions that will eventually lead to a solution.

TROUBLESHOOTING

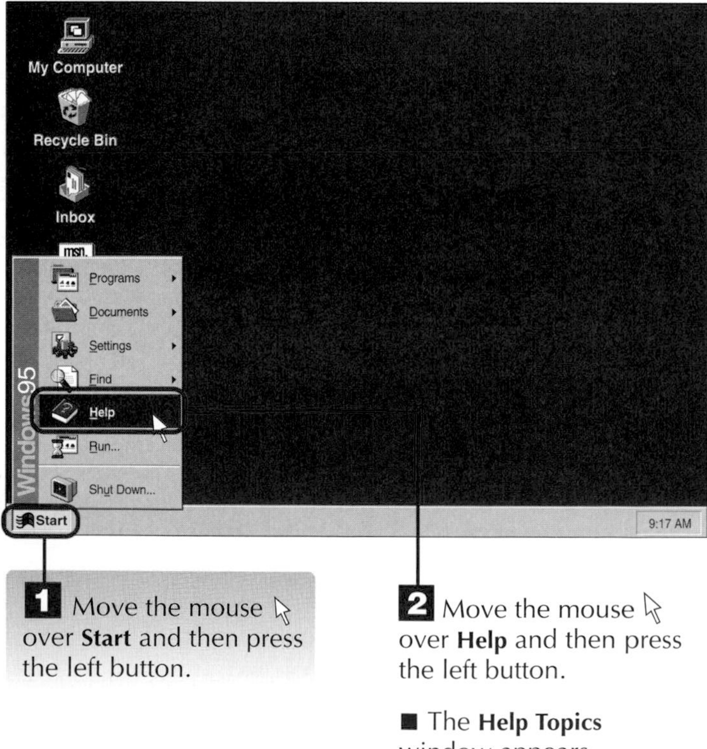

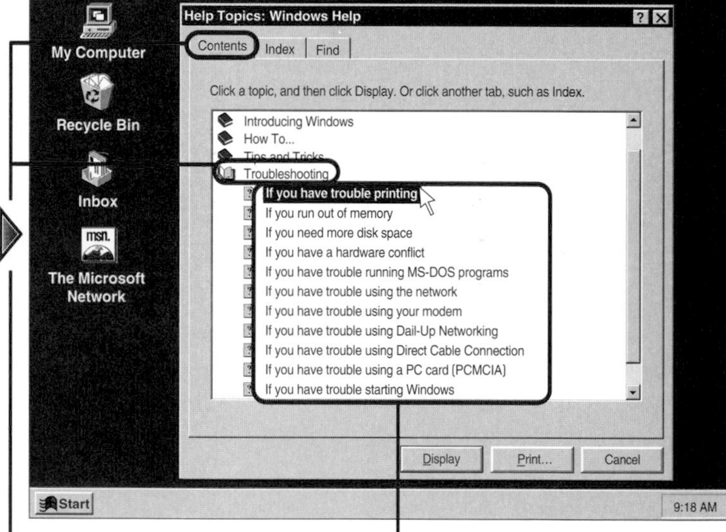

1 Move the mouse over **Start** and then press the left button.

2 Move the mouse over **Help** and then press the left button.

■ The **Help Topics** window appears.

3 Move the mouse over the **Contents** tab and then press the left button.

4 Move the mouse over **Troubleshooting** and then quickly press the left button twice.

■ A list of common problems appears.

5 Move the mouse over the problem you want to receive help on and then quickly press the left button twice.

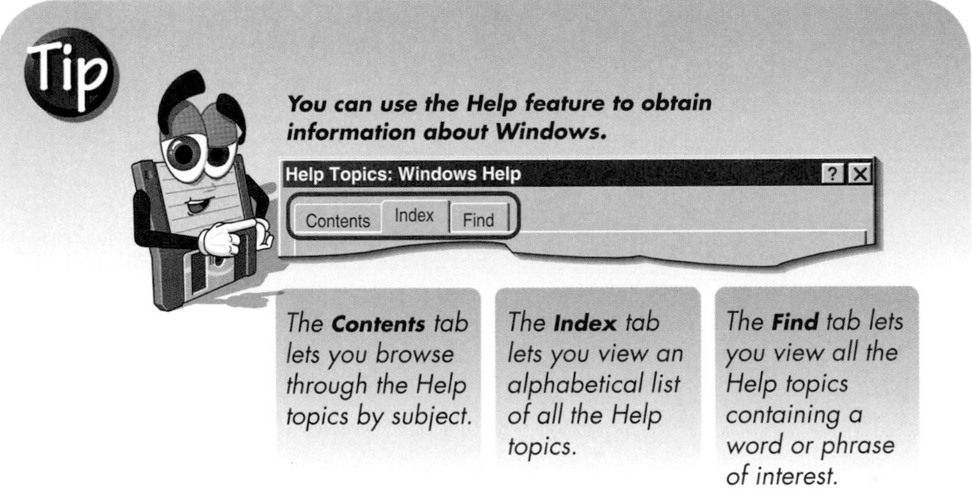

Tip
You can use the Help feature to obtain information about Windows.
Help Topics: Windows Help
Contents
Index
Find
The Contents tab lets you browse through the Help topics by subject.
The Index tab lets you view an alphabetical list of all the Help topics.
The Find tab lets you view all the Help topics containing a word or phrase of interest.

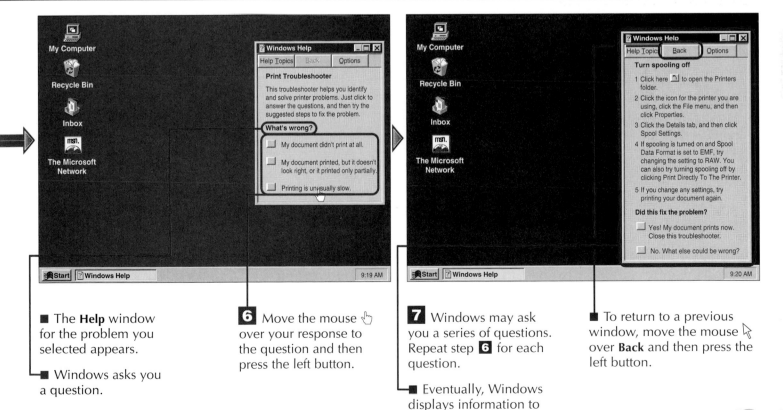

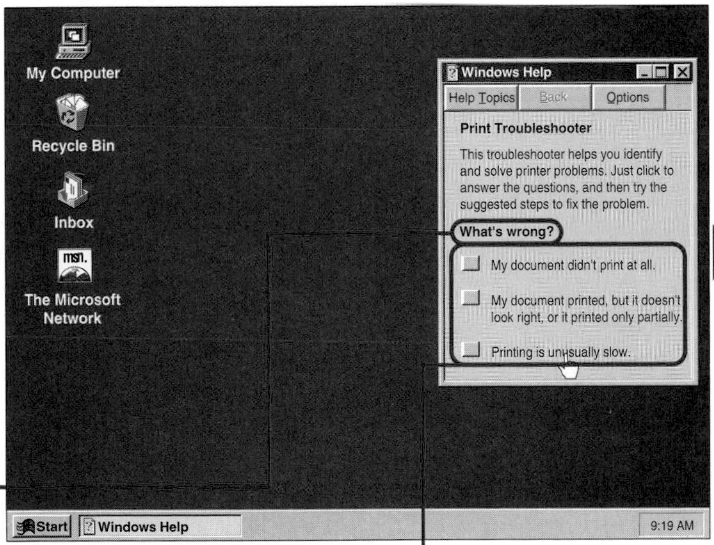

■ The **Help** window for the problem you selected appears.

■ Windows asks you a question.

6 Move the mouse over your response to the question and then press the left button.

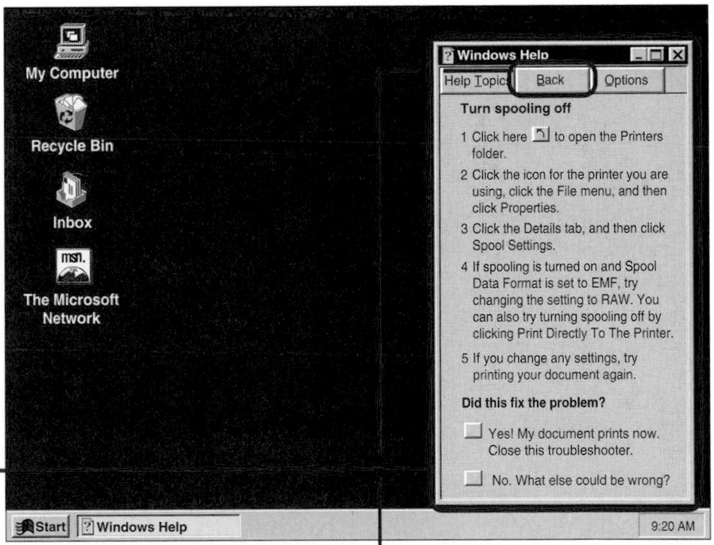

7 Windows may ask you a series of questions. Repeat step **6** for each question.

■ Eventually, Windows displays information to help you solve the problem.

■ To return to a previous window, move the mouse over **Back** and then press the left button.

VIEW AMOUNT OF DISK SPACE

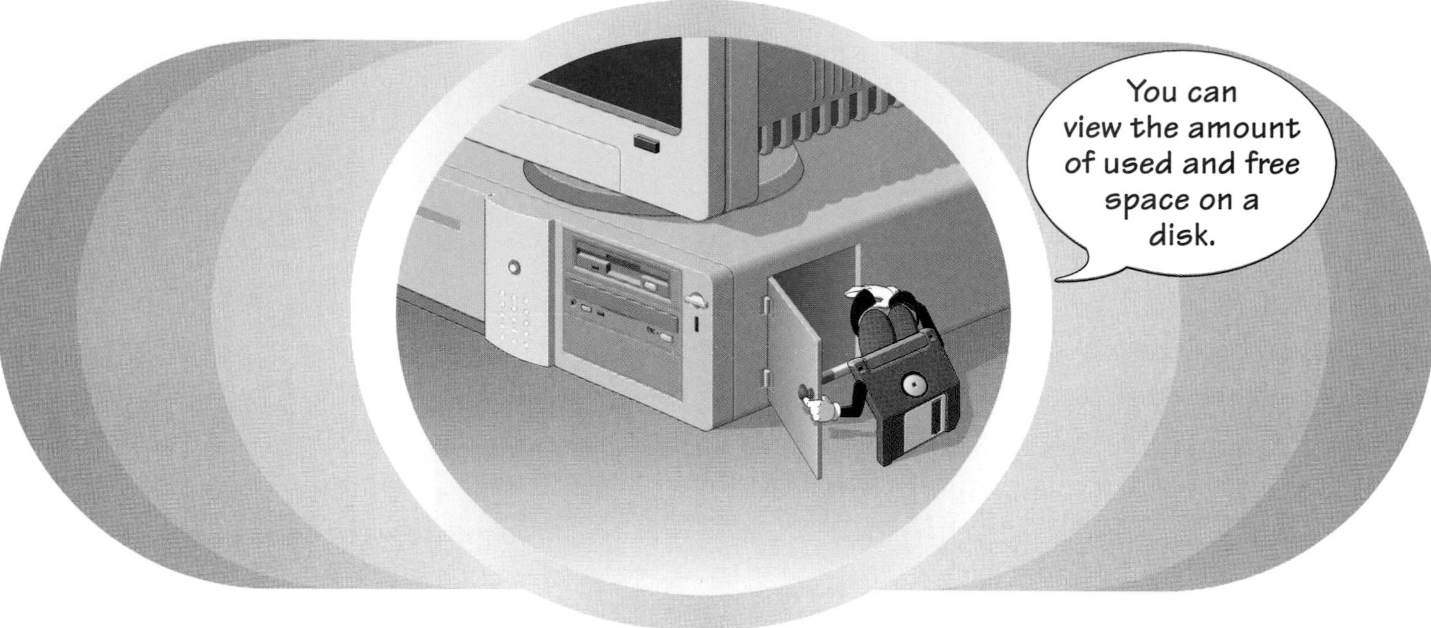

VIEW AMOUNT OF DISK SPACE

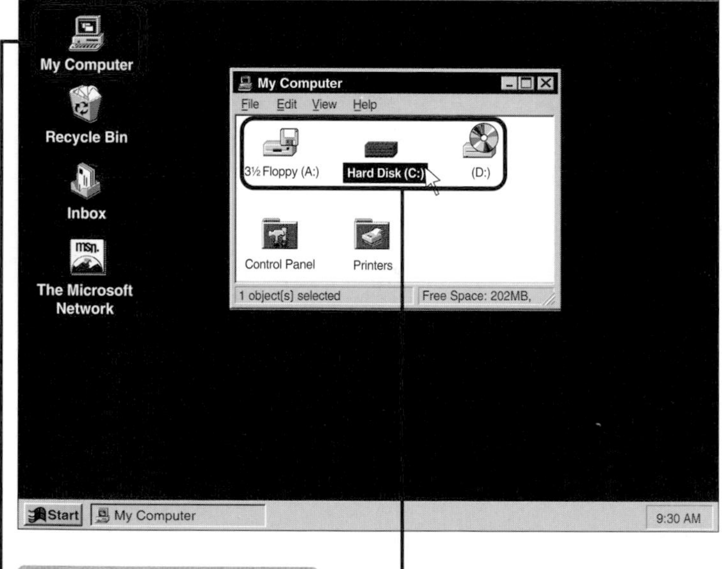

1 Move the mouse over **My Computer** and then quickly press the left button twice.

■ The **My Computer** window appears.

2 Move the mouse over the disk drive of interest and then press the left button.

Note: To view the disk space on a CD-ROM or floppy disk, insert the disk into the drive.

3 Move the mouse over **File** and then press the left button.

4 Move the mouse over **Properties** and then press the left button.

■ The **Properties** dialog box appears.

Tip **The amount of space on a disk is measured in bytes.**

Byte

One character.

Megabyte (MB)

Approximately one million characters, or one novel.

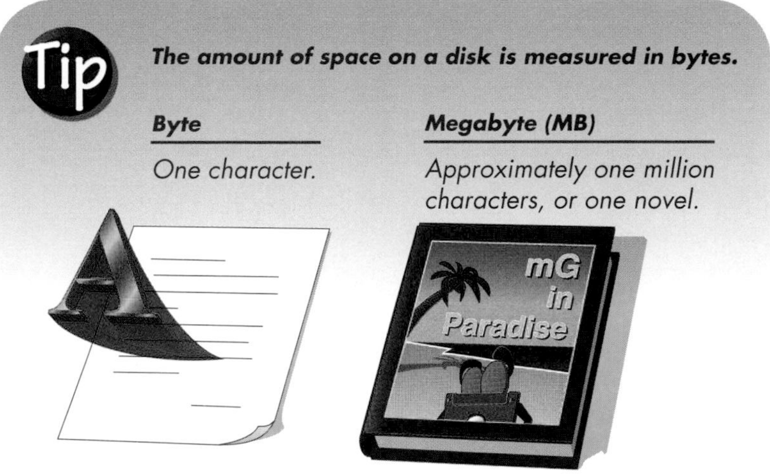

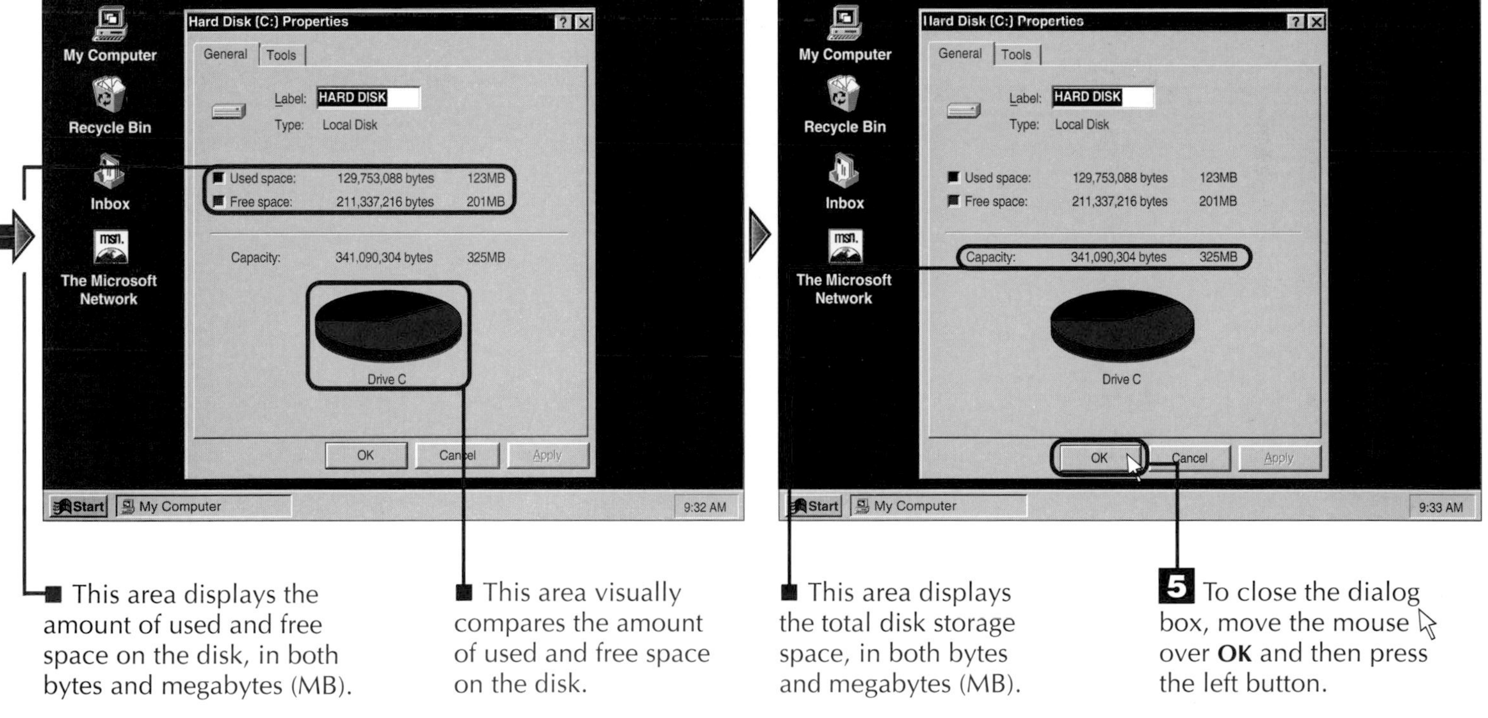

■ This area displays the amount of used and free space on the disk, in both bytes and megabytes (MB).

■ This area visually compares the amount of used and free space on the disk.

■ This area displays the total disk storage space, in both bytes and megabytes (MB).

5 To close the dialog box, move the mouse over **OK** and then press the left button.

COMPRESS A DISK

You can compress, or squeeze together, the information stored on your hard disk. This can double the amount of information the disk can store.

You can also compress floppy disks to store more information.

COMPRESS A DISK

Before compressing your hard disk, perform the following:

Exit all programs.

Back up the information on your hard disk.

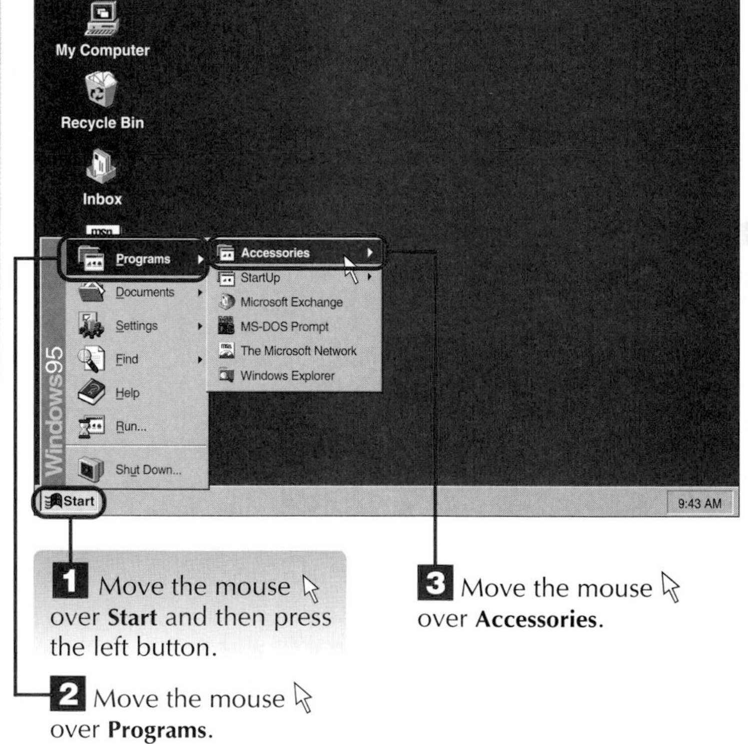

1 Move the mouse over **Start** and then press the left button.

2 Move the mouse over **Programs**.

3 Move the mouse over **Accessories**.

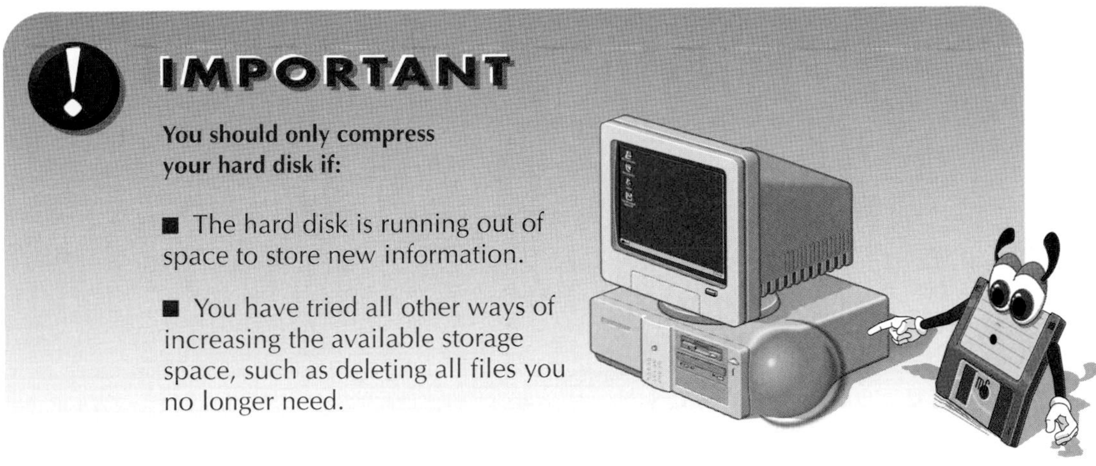

You should only compress your hard disk if:

- The hard disk is running out of space to store new information.
- You have tried all other ways of increasing the available storage space, such as deleting all files you no longer need.

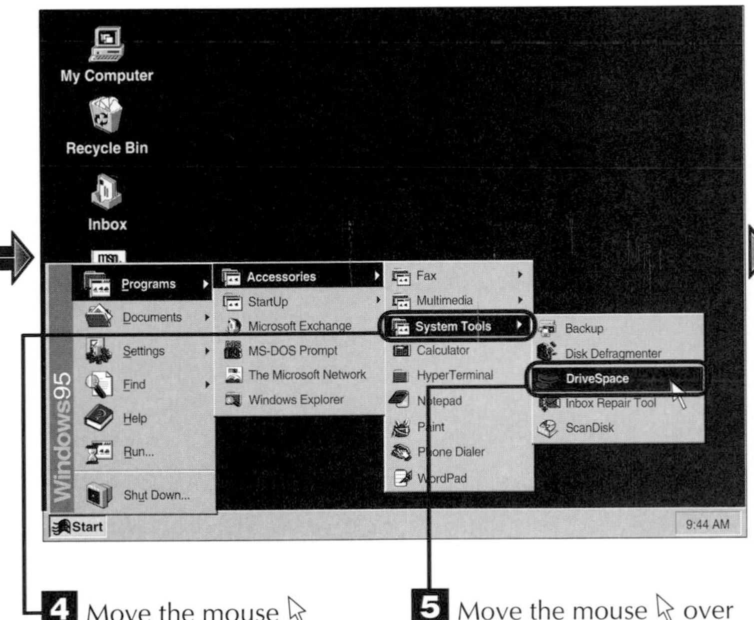

4 Move the mouse over **System Tools**.

5 Move the mouse over **DriveSpace** and then press the left button.

*Note: If **DriveSpace** is not available, you must add the Windows component called **Disk compression tools**. This component is found in the Disk Tools category. To add Windows components, refer to page 96.*

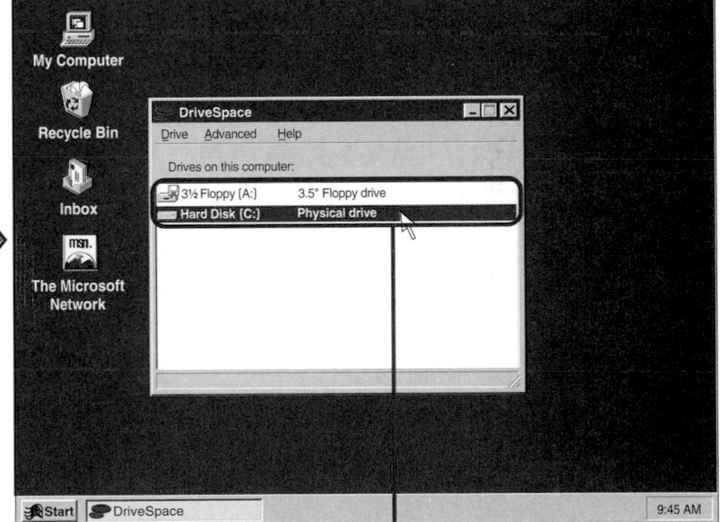

- The **DriveSpace** window appears.

6 To select the disk you want to compress, move the mouse over the disk and then press the left button.

COMPRESS A DISK

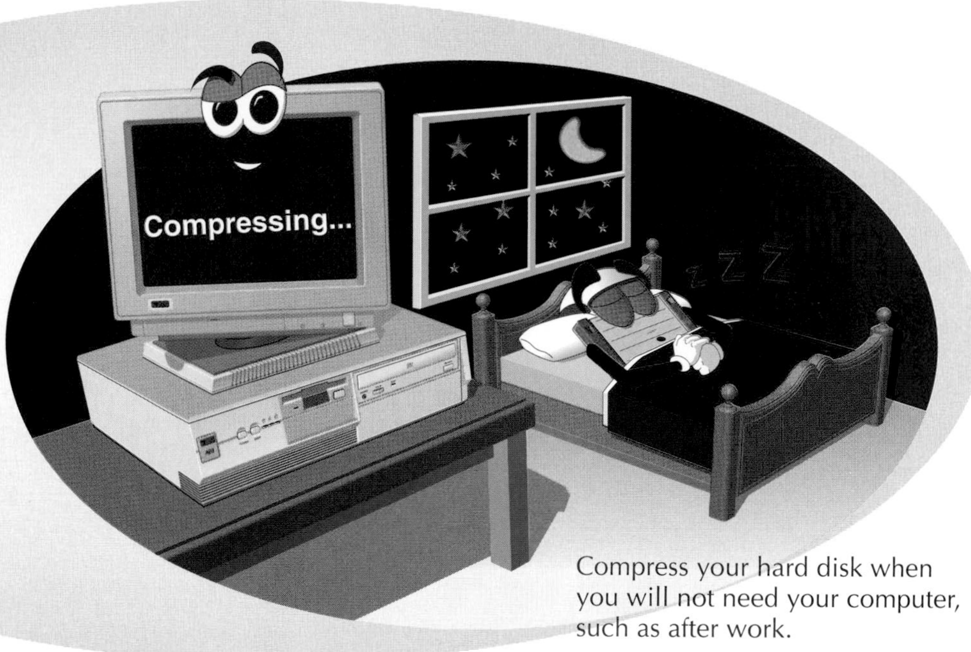

Compressing your hard disk can take several hours. During this time, you will not be able to use your computer.
Compressing...

Compress your hard disk when you will not need your computer, such as after work.

COMPRESS A DISK (CONTINUED)

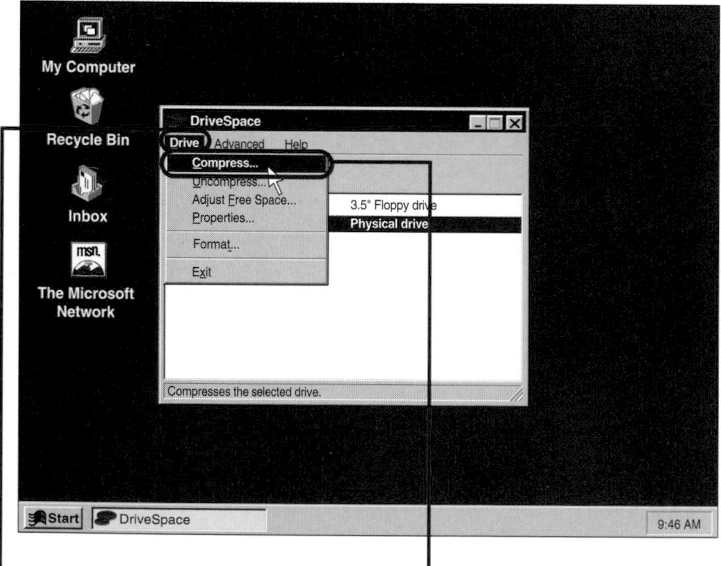

7 To compress the disk you selected, move the mouse over **Drive** and then press the left button.

8 Move the mouse over **Compress** and then press the left button.

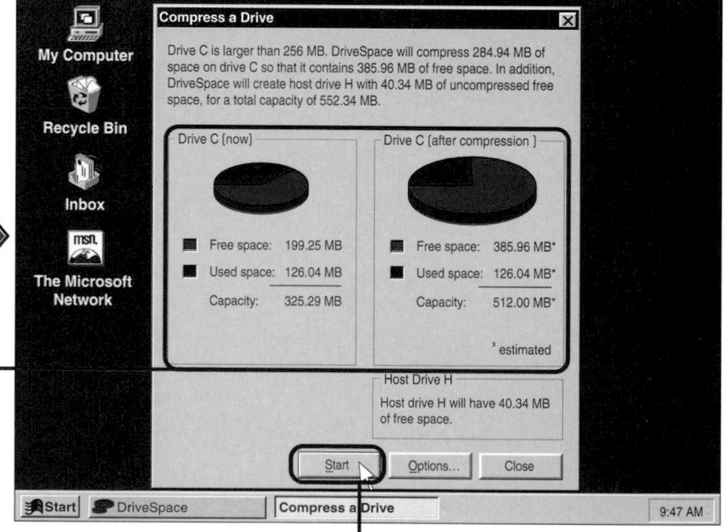

■ The **Compress a Drive** dialog box appears.

■ This area displays the amount of free and used space, before and after compression.

9 To continue, move the mouse over **Start** and then press the left button.

Tip
Before Windows compresses your disk, it uses ScanDisk to search for and repair any disk errors.

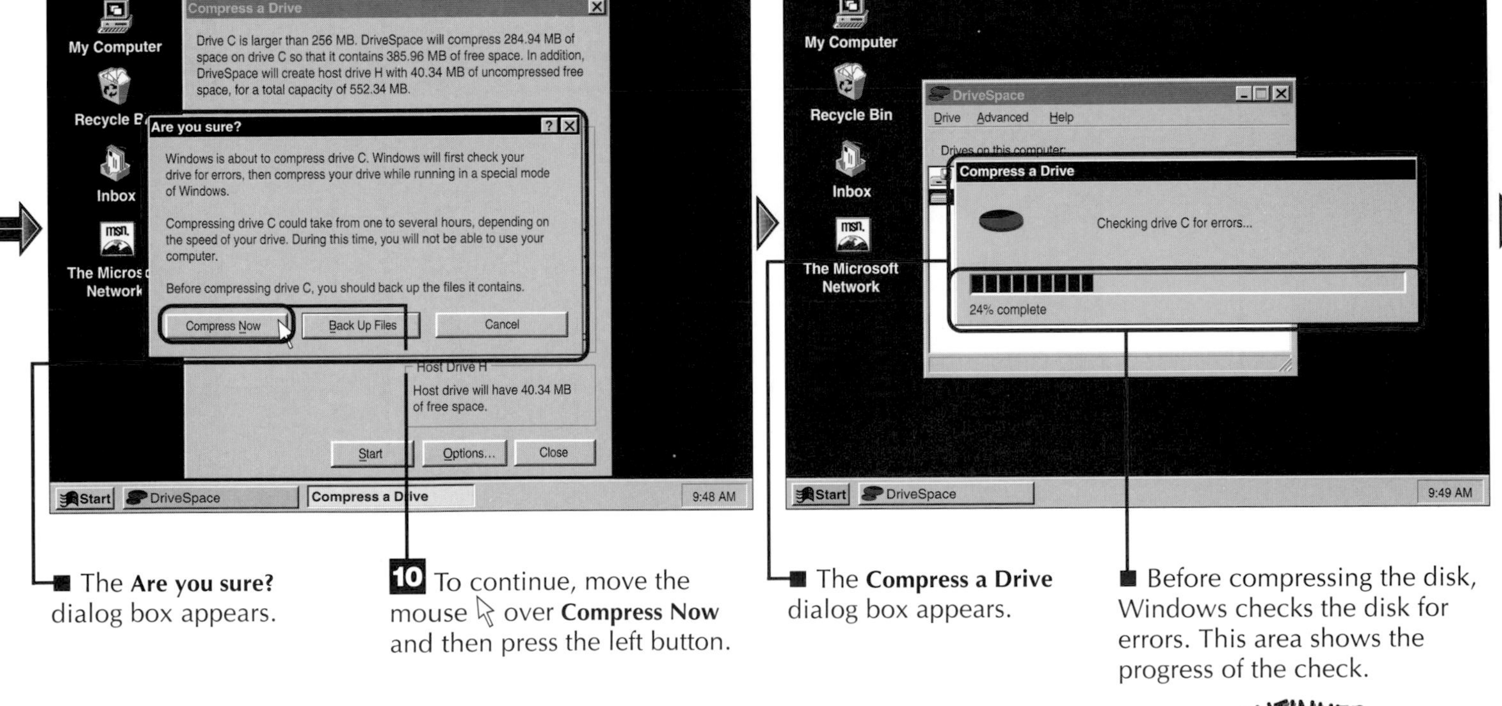

■ The **Are you sure?** dialog box appears.

10 To continue, move the mouse over **Compress Now** and then press the left button.

■ The **Compress a Drive** dialog box appears.

■ Before compressing the disk, Windows checks the disk for errors. This area shows the progress of the check.

CONTINUED

COMPRESS A DISK (CONTINUED)

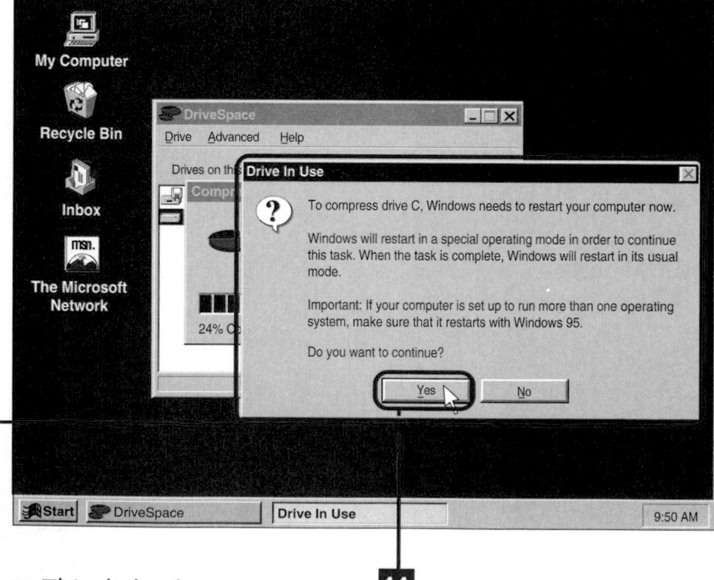

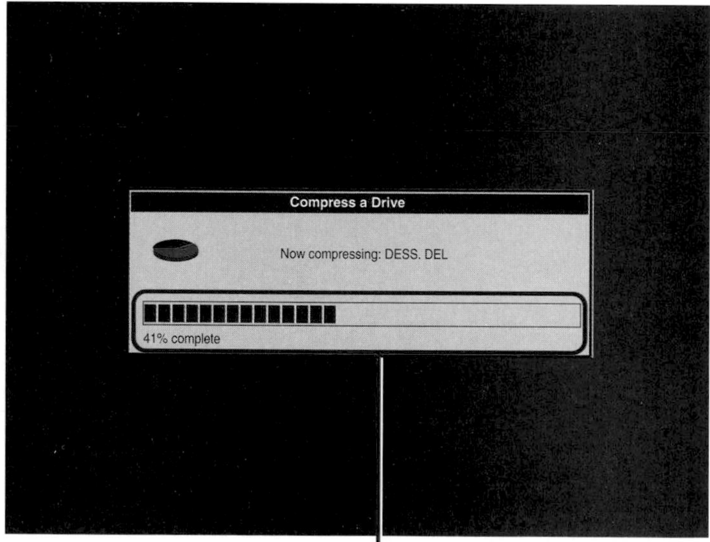

■ This dialog box appears if Windows needs to restart your computer before compressing the disk.

11 To continue, move the mouse over **Yes** and then press the left button.

■ Windows restarts your computer and then begins compressing your disk.

■ This area displays the progress of the compression.

Tip *After you compress your hard disk, the amount of free space added to your computer depends on the type of information stored on the disk.*

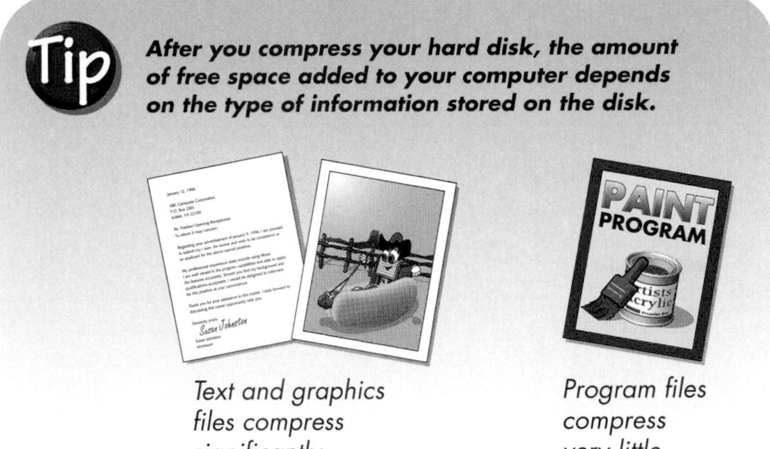

Text and graphics files compress significantly.

Program files compress very little.

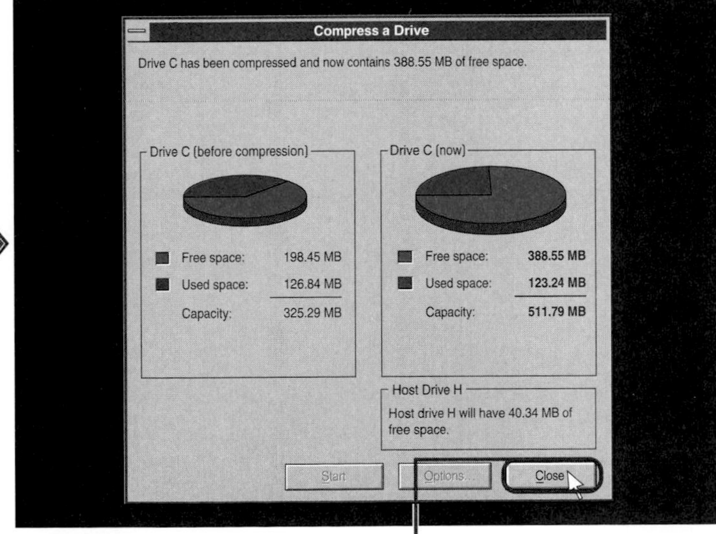

■ The **Compress a Drive** dialog box reappears when the compression is complete, displaying the results of the compression.

12 To close the dialog box, move the mouse over **Close** and then press the left button.

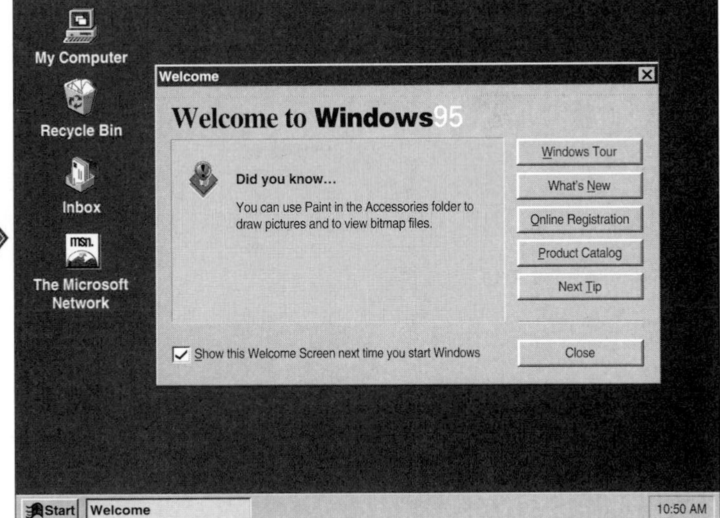

■ Windows restarts your computer.

■ You can now use your computer as usual.

In this chapter you will learn how to use The Microsoft Network to access information and communicate with people around the world.
mG

CHAPTER 8

THE MICROSOFT NETWORK

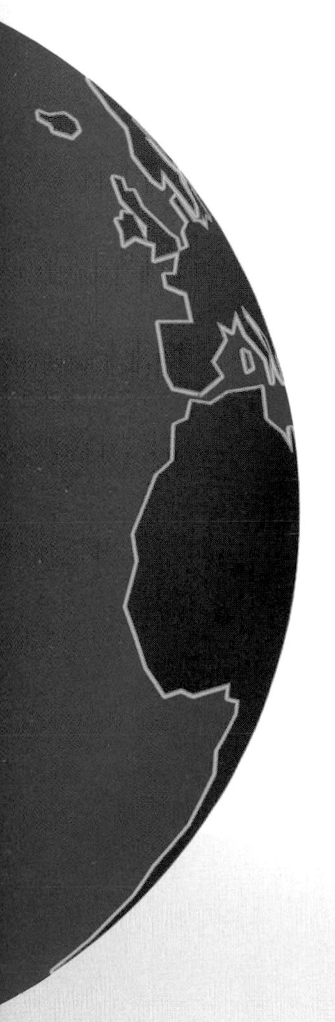

Introduction

Connect to The Microsoft Network

Browse Through Categories

Join a Chat Room

Display Bulletin Board Messages

Read Messages

Reply to a Message

Create a New Message

Add an Item to Favorite Places

Sign Out of the MSN

INTRODUCTION

The Microsoft Network (MSN) provides a vast amount of information and allows you to communicate with people around the world.

CHAT WITH OTHER MEMBERS

The Microsoft Network lets you have conversations with other members. You can observe ongoing conversations or make comments and ask questions that other members will see immediately.

EXCHANGE ELECTRONIC MAIL

You can exchange private messages with millions of people around the world. This includes MSN members, members of other online services and anyone using the Internet.

USE BULLETIN BOARDS

You can read and post (send) messages on public bulletin boards. A bulletin board is an area where you can communicate with other MSN members with similar interests. Bulletin board topics include sports, education, science, business, entertainment, hobbies and much more.

TRANSFER FILES

MSN provides useful files, such as documents, pictures and programs, that you can download (copy) to your computer.

Note: There may be a fee for copying some files.

USE THE INTERNET

You can exchange electronic messages with anyone connected to the Internet. You can also access thousands of newsgroups. Each newsgroup discusses a specific topic and allows people with common interests to communicate with each other. Windsurfing, politics, anthropology, religion, the environment, education and health are just a few of the newsgroup topics available.

Note: Newsgroups are similar to MSN bulletin boards, except they are available to everyone connected to the Internet.

CONNECT TO THE MICROSOFT NETWORK

msn
You must connect to The Microsoft Network to use the services it provides.

CONNECT TO THE MICROSOFT NETWORK

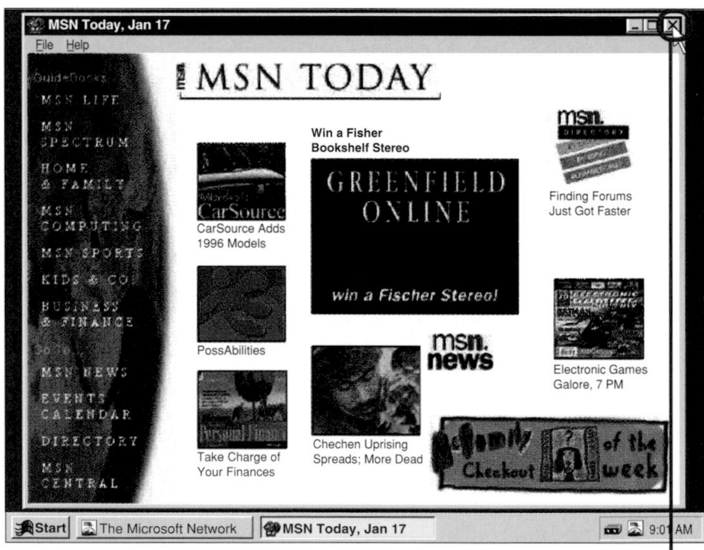

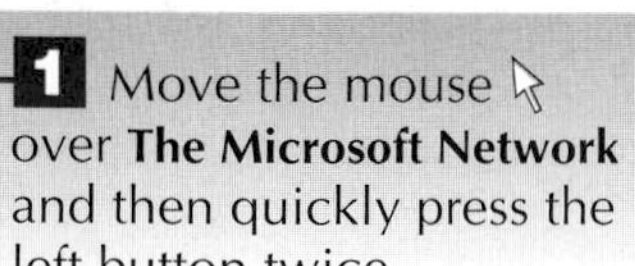

1 Move the mouse over **The Microsoft Network** and then quickly press the left button twice.

■ The **Sign In** dialog box appears.

2 To enter your password, move the mouse over this area and then press the left button.

3 Type your password and then press **Enter** on your keyboard.

Note: A symbol (x) appears for each character you type.

■ The **MSN Today** window appears.

4 To close the window, move the mouse over ☒ and then press the left button.

This dialog box appears if The Microsoft Network is not set up on your computer.

To set up The Microsoft Network, follow the instructions on your screen.

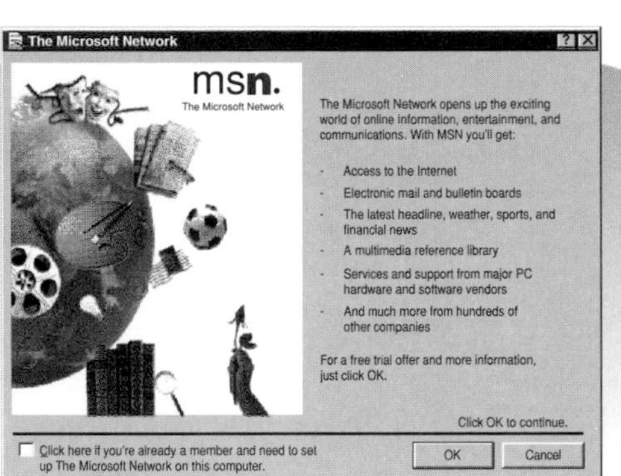

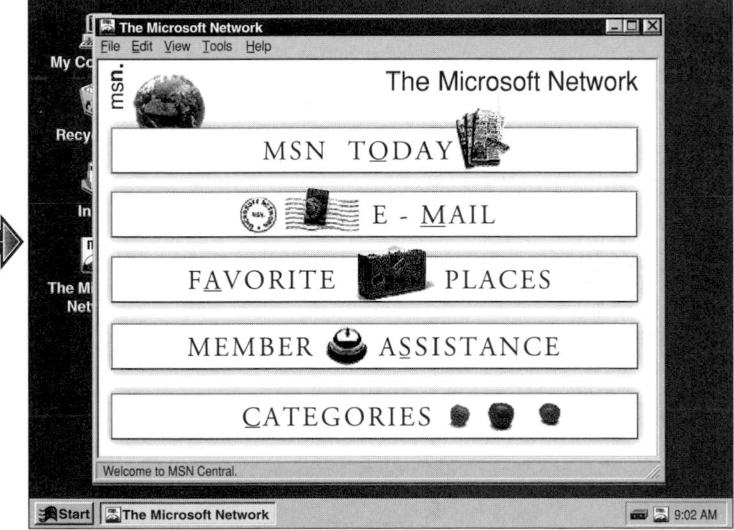

■ **The Microsoft Network** main window appears, displaying the five main areas available on the network.

There are five main areas on The Microsoft Network.

MSN TODAY	Provides new information about The Microsoft Network.
E-MAIL	Lets you send and receive electronic mail.
FAVORITE PLACES	Lets you quickly access the services on The Microsoft Network that you use most often.
MEMBER ASSISTANCE	Provides help to members of The Microsoft Network.
CATEGORIES	Lets you browse through the information on The Microsoft Network.

BROWSE THROUGH CATEGORIES

The Microsoft Network organizes information into categories. You can easily browse through the categories to find information of interest.

BROWSE THROUGH CATEGORIES

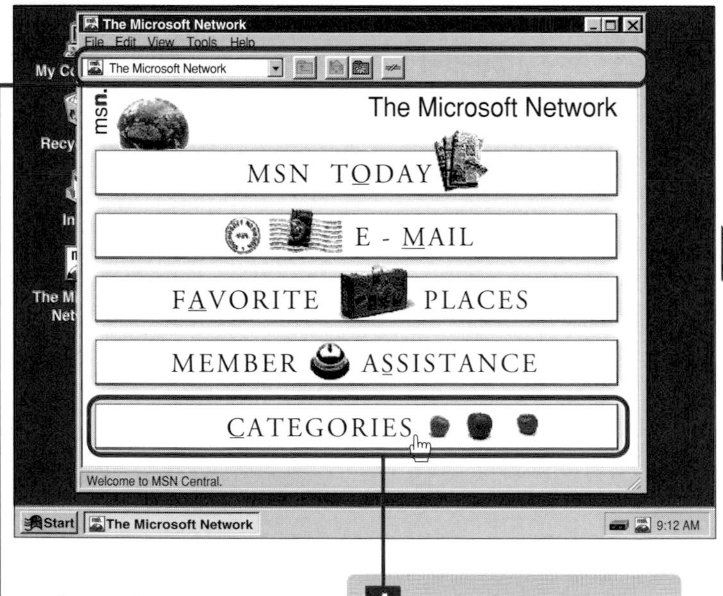

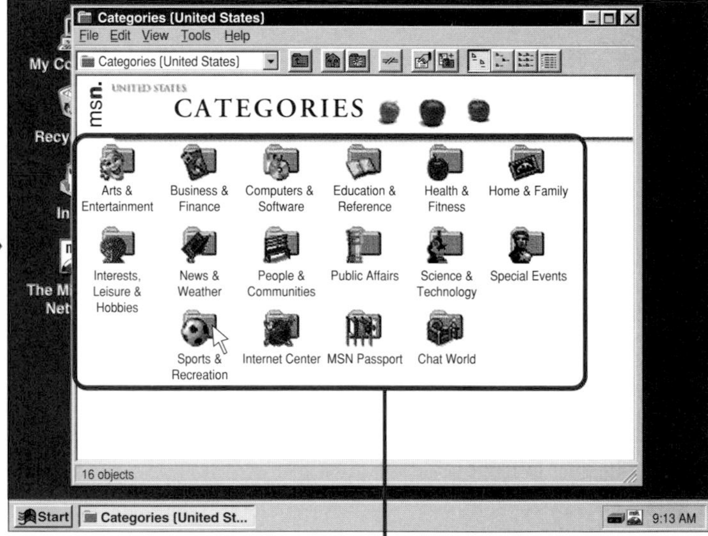

■ The toolbar displays buttons that let you quickly perform common tasks.

Note: To display the toolbar, refer to the ***Tip*** *on page 139.*

1 To display the main MSN categories, move the mouse over **Categories** and then press the left button.

■ The main MSN categories appear.

2 To select a category of interest, move the mouse over the category (example: **Sports & Recreation**) and then quickly press the left button twice.

Tip

You can easily display the toolbar on your screen. The toolbar lets you quickly perform common tasks.

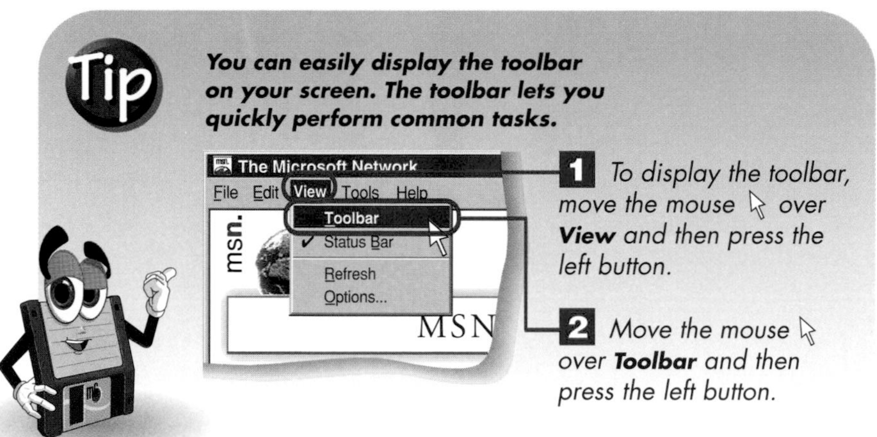

*1 To display the toolbar, move the mouse over **View** and then press the left button.*

*2 Move the mouse over **Toolbar** and then press the left button.*

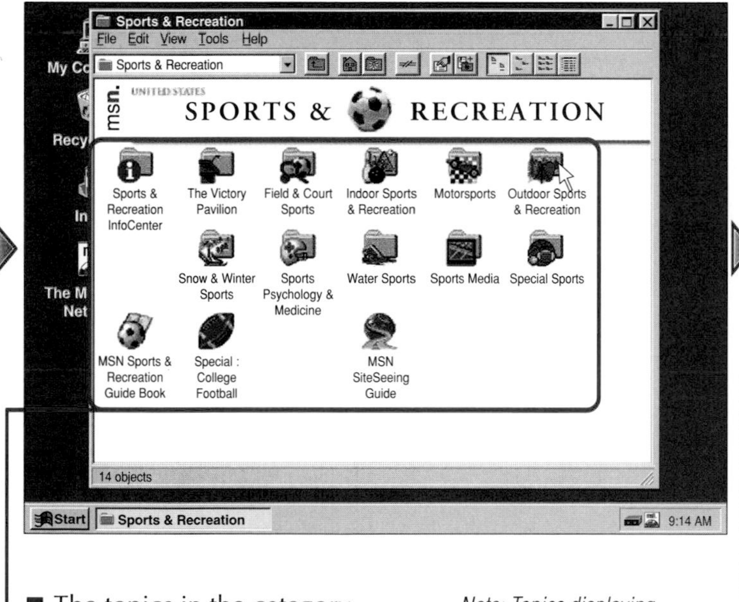

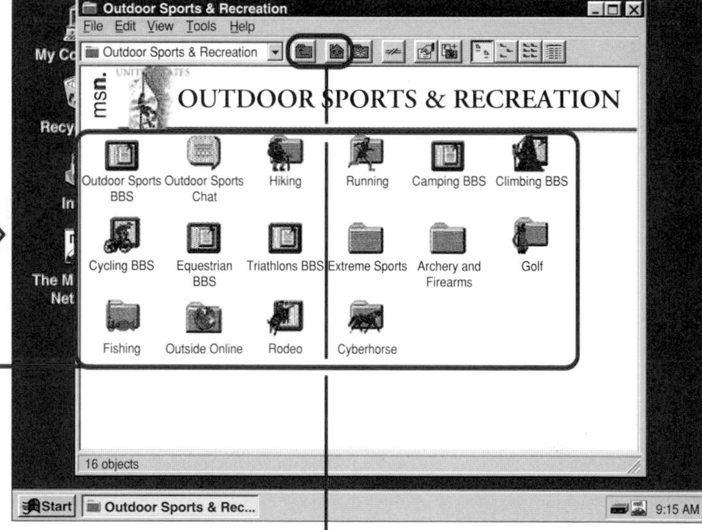

■ The topics in the category appear.

3 To select a topic of interest, move the mouse over the topic (example: **Outdoor Sports & Recreation**) and then quickly press the left button twice.

Note: Topics displaying a folder ( ) contain subtopics.

■ The subtopics of the topic appear.

4 Repeat step 3 until an item of interest appears.

■ To return to a previous window, move the mouse over one of the following options and then press the left button.

- Returns to previous window.
- Returns to **The Microsoft Network** main window.

JOIN A CHAT ROOM

You can have conversations with other MSN members by simply typing back and forth.

JOIN A CHAT ROOM

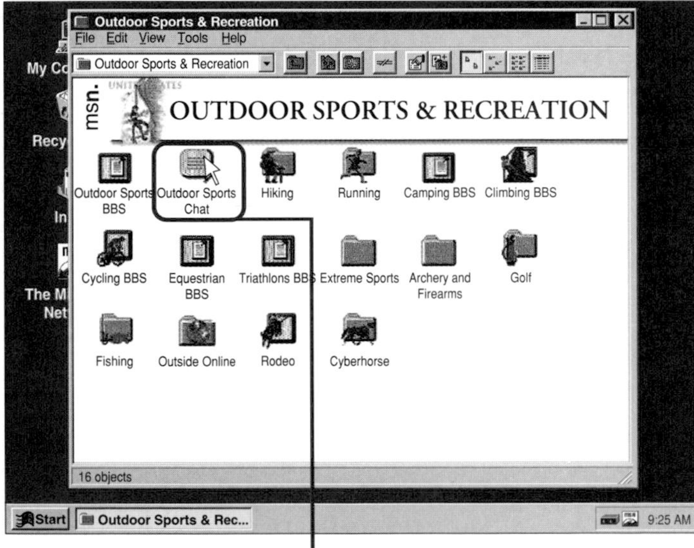

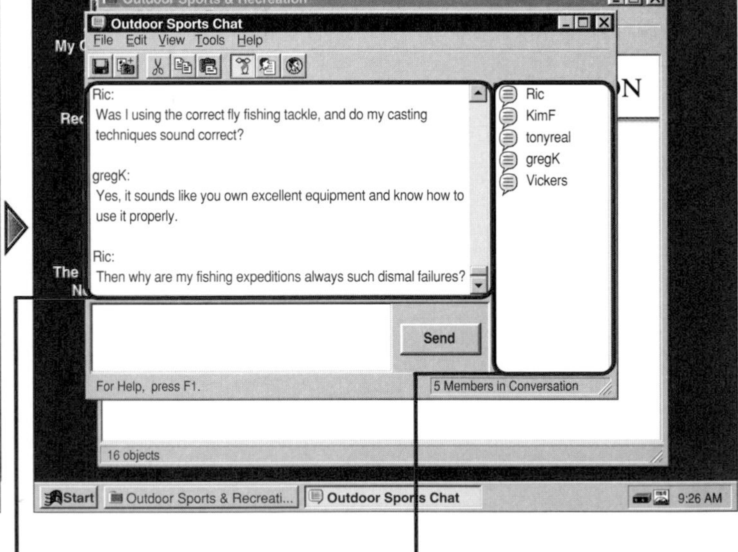

1 Browse through the categories until you find a chat room of interest.

Note: To browse through categories, refer to page 138.

■ A chat room usually displays a special symbol (💬) and has the word **Chat** in the title.

2 Move the mouse over the chat room you want to join and then quickly press the left button twice.

■ A chat window appears.

■ This area displays the current conversation.

■ This area displays all the participants in the conversation.

Tip ***Chat World*** *is a main MSN category devoted entirely to chatting.*

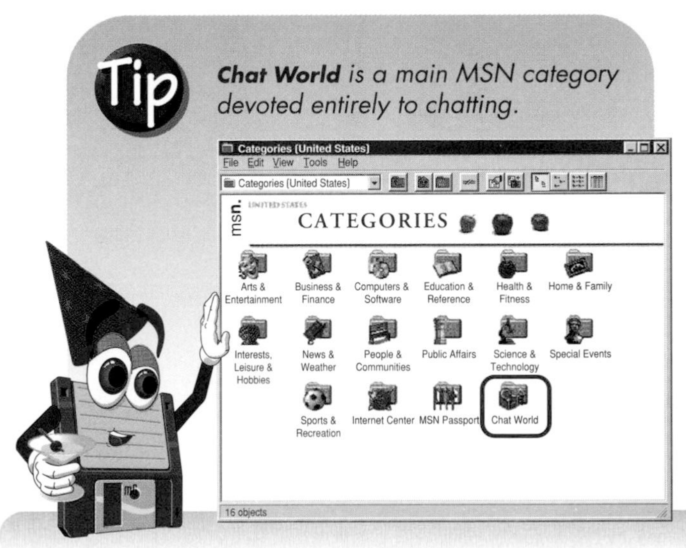

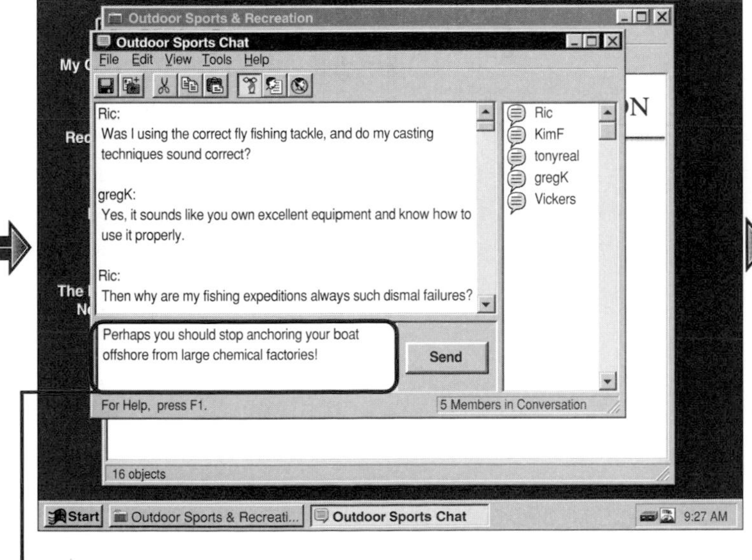

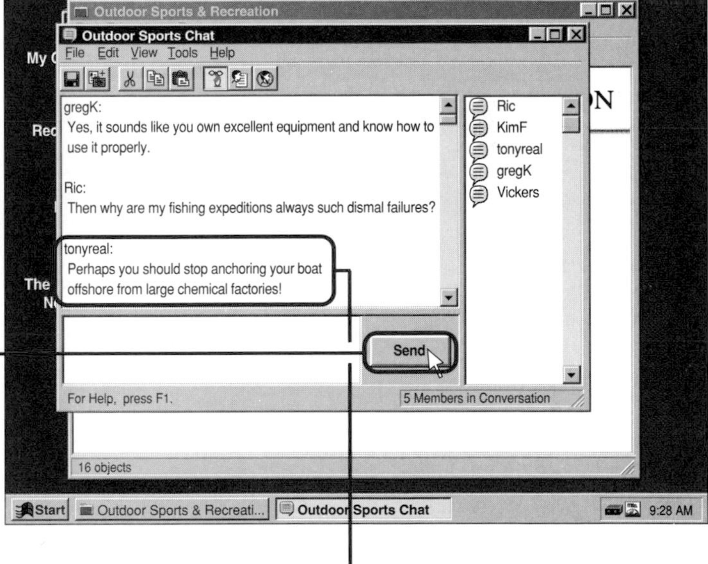

3 To participate in the conversation, move the mouse over this area and then press the left button. Then type a message.

■ If you want to create a line break in your message, press and hold down **Ctrl** on your keyboard and then press **Enter**.

4 To send your message, move the mouse over **Send** and then press the left button.

■ In time, the message you typed appears for all to see.

DISPLAY BULLETIN BOARD MESSAGES

The Microsoft Network offers hundreds of bulletin boards where people with similar interests exchange ideas, ask questions and share information.

DISPLAY BULLETIN BOARD MESSAGES

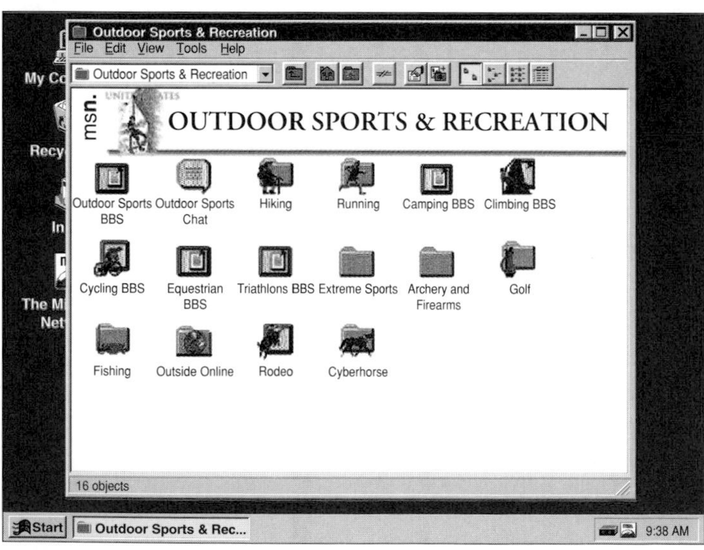

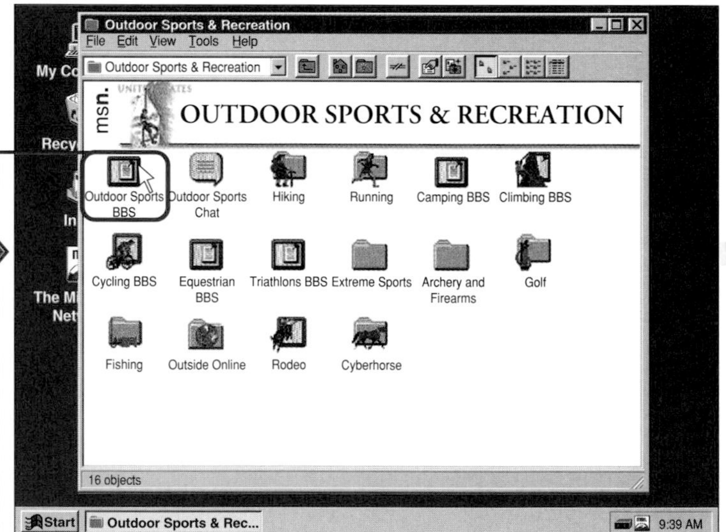

1 Browse through the categories until you find a bulletin board of interest.

Note: To browse through categories, refer to page 138.

■ A bulletin board usually displays a special symbol ( ) and has the letters **BBS** in the title.

2 Move the mouse over the bulletin board of interest and then quickly press the left button twice.

Tip ***Here are some of the bulletin boards available on The Microsoft Network.***

Arts & Crafts
Colleges and Universities
Jokes
Medicine
Mutual Funds
Outdoor Sports
Parenting in the 90's
Pets
Real Estate
Religion
Virtual Reality
Wine

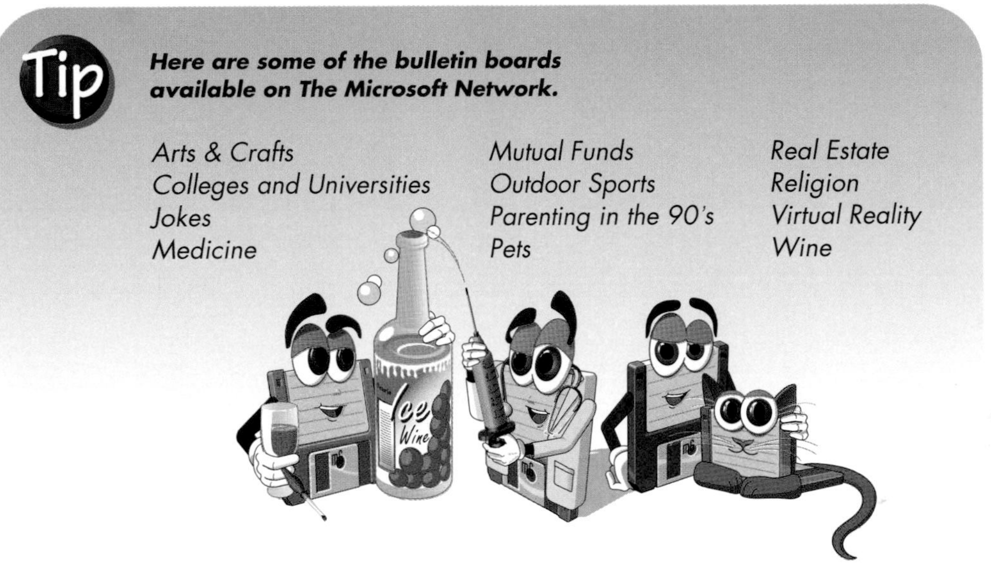

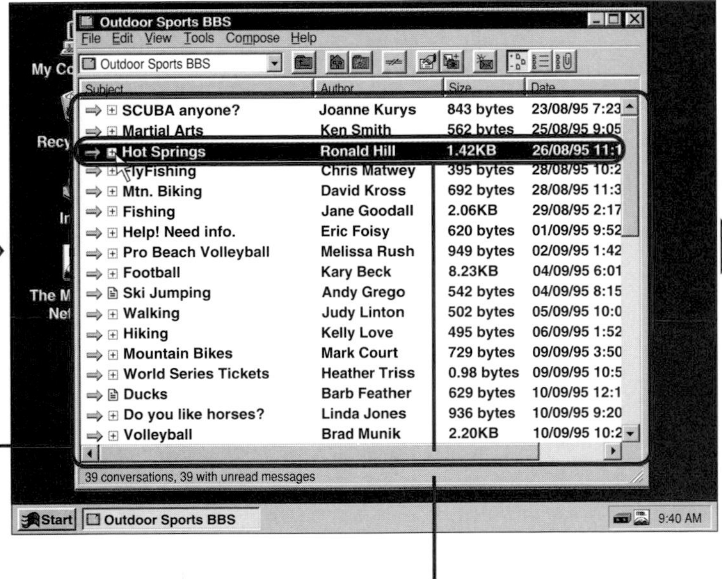

■ A list of messages in the bulletin board appears.

■ A message that has replies displays a plus sign (⊞). A message that has no replies displays a file symbol (🗎).

3 To view the replies to a message, move the mouse over the plus sign (⊞) beside the message and then press the left button.

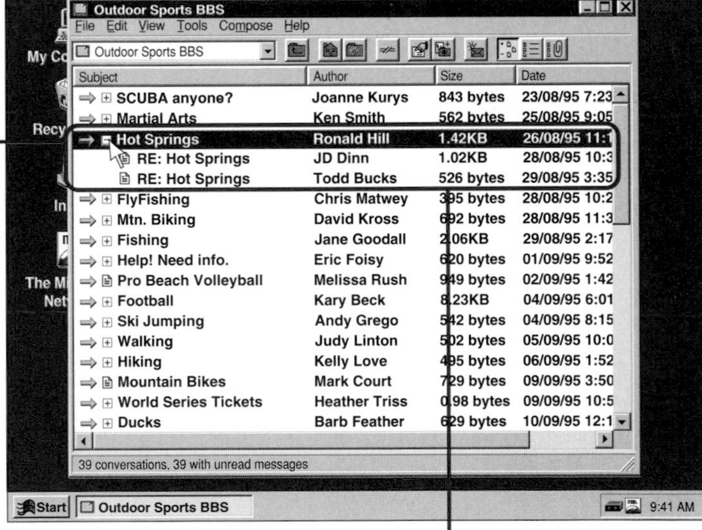

■ The replies to the message appear. The replies are indented below the original message.

■ The plus sign (⊞) changes to a minus sign (⊟) to indicate the replies are now displayed.

■ To once again hide the replies, move the mouse over the minus sign (⊟) and then press the left button.

READ MESSAGES

You can read messages to learn the opinions and ideas of other MSN members.

READ MESSAGES

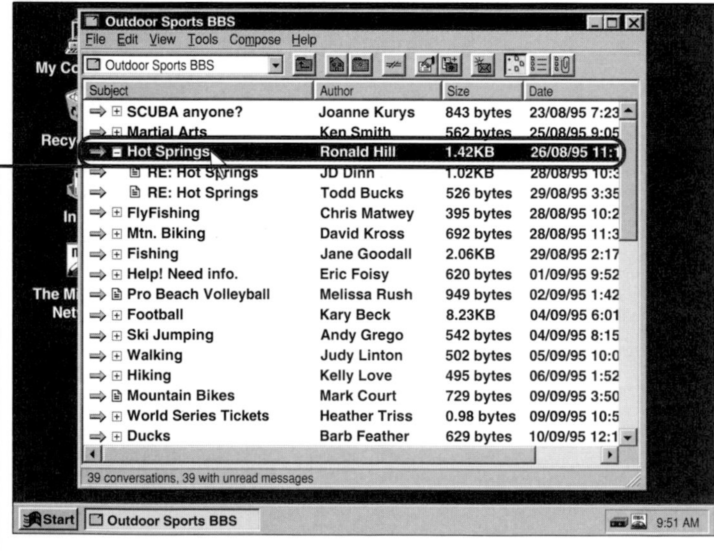

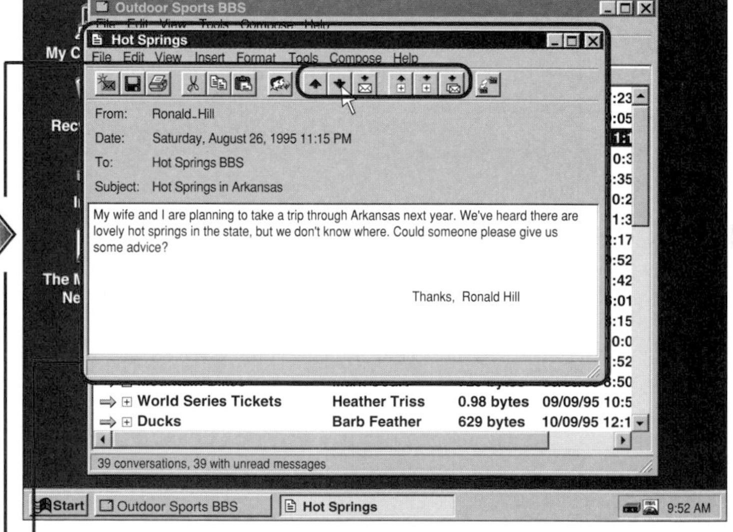

1 Move the mouse over the message of interest and then quickly press the left button twice.

- The message appears.

2 To display another message, move the mouse over one of the following options and then press the left button.

- Previous message
- Next message
- Next unread message
- Previous conversation
- Next conversation
- Next unread conversation

Tip
The Microsoft Network organizes bulletin board messages into conversations.
A conversation is a series of messages on a particular subject. A conversation includes the original message and all replies to the message.
NEW DOG
I just bought a new dog & can't decide what to name him. Any suggestions?
Re: NEW DOG
What about "Muffin"?
Re: NEW DOG
I think "Fluffy" is a great name for a dog.
Re: NEW DOG
I like the name "Bunny".

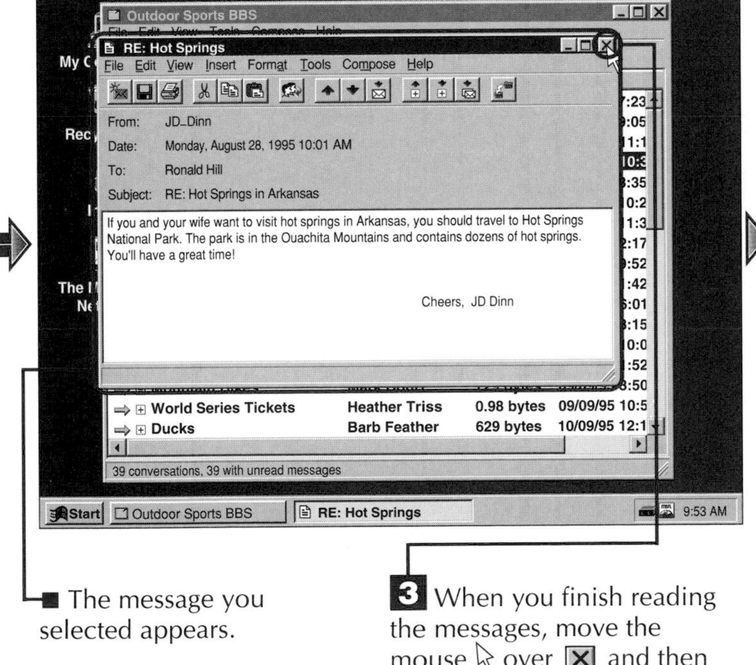

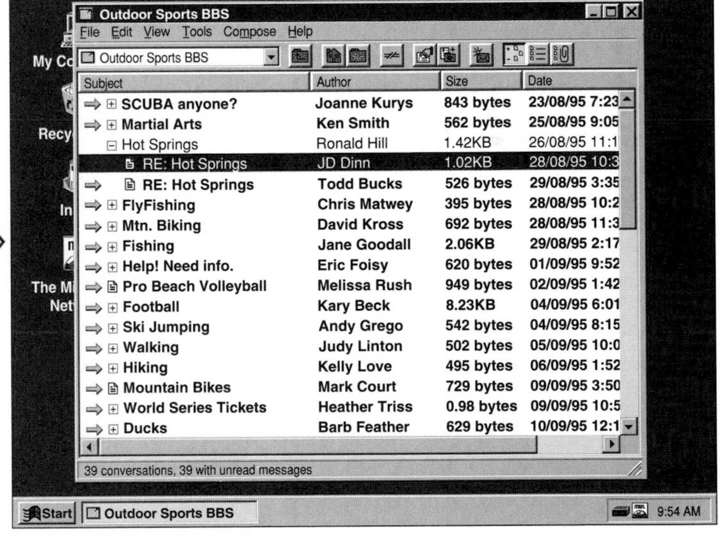

■ The message you selected appears.

3 When you finish reading the messages, move the mouse over ☒ and then press the left button.

■ Messages you have read appear in regular type. Messages you have not read appear in **bold type**.

REPLY TO A MESSAGE

You can reply to a message to answer a question, express an opinion or supply additional information.
Reply

REPLY TO A MESSAGE

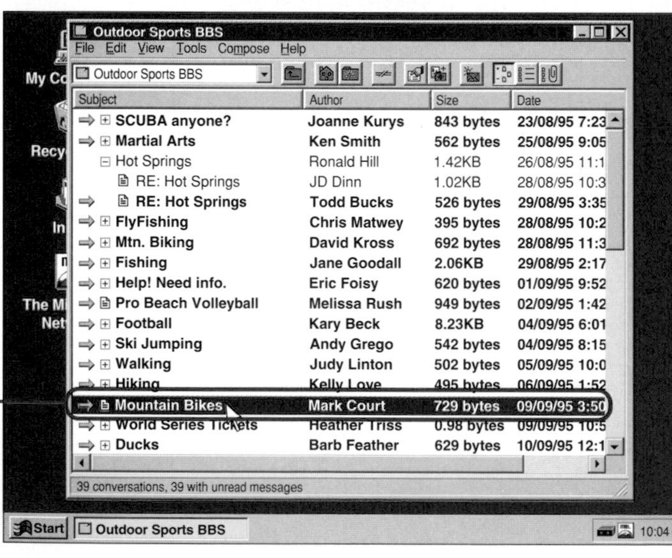

1 To open the message you want to reply to, move the mouse over the message and then quickly press the left button twice.

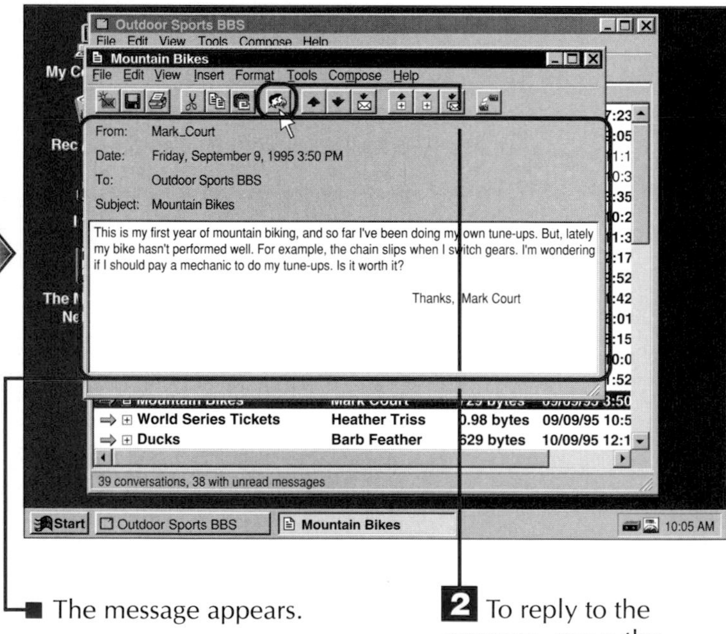

■ The message appears.

2 To reply to the message, move the mouse over the reply button and then press the left button.

Reply to a message only when you have something important to say. Replying "Me too" or "I agree" is not very informative.

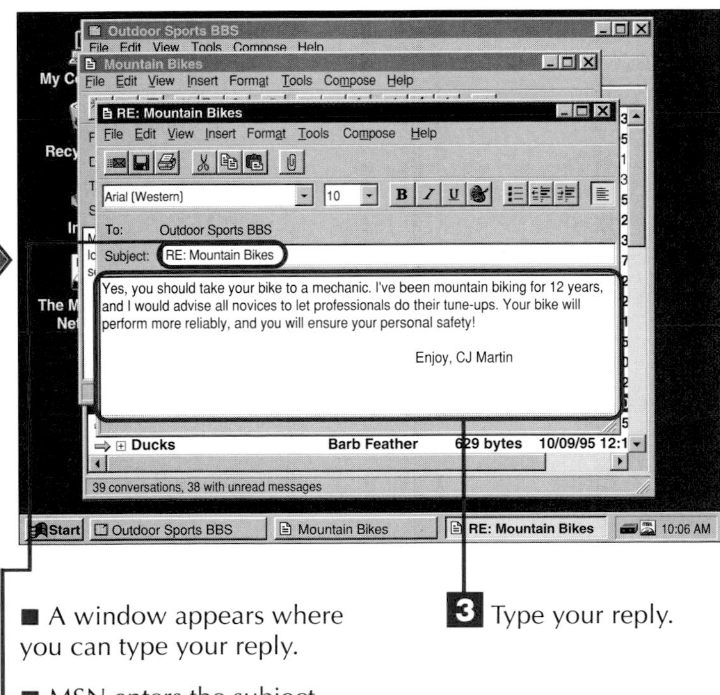

■ A window appears where you can type your reply.

■ MSN enters the subject for you.

3 Type your reply.

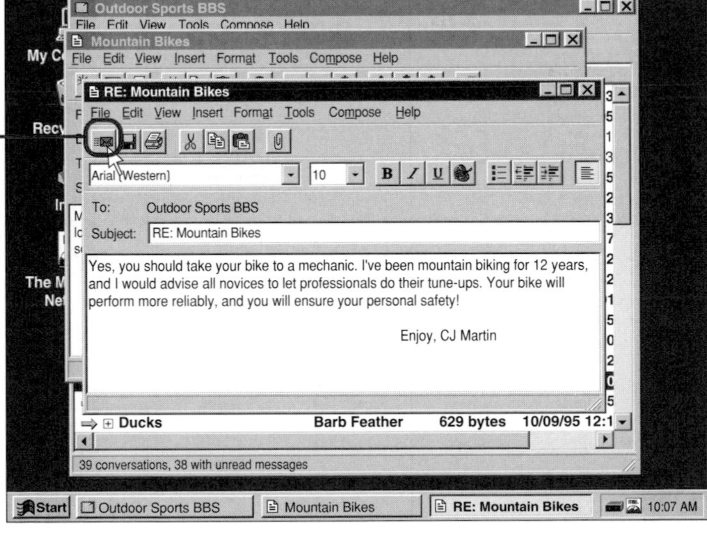

4 To send the message, move the mouse over [send icon] and then press the left button.

CREATE A NEW MESSAGE

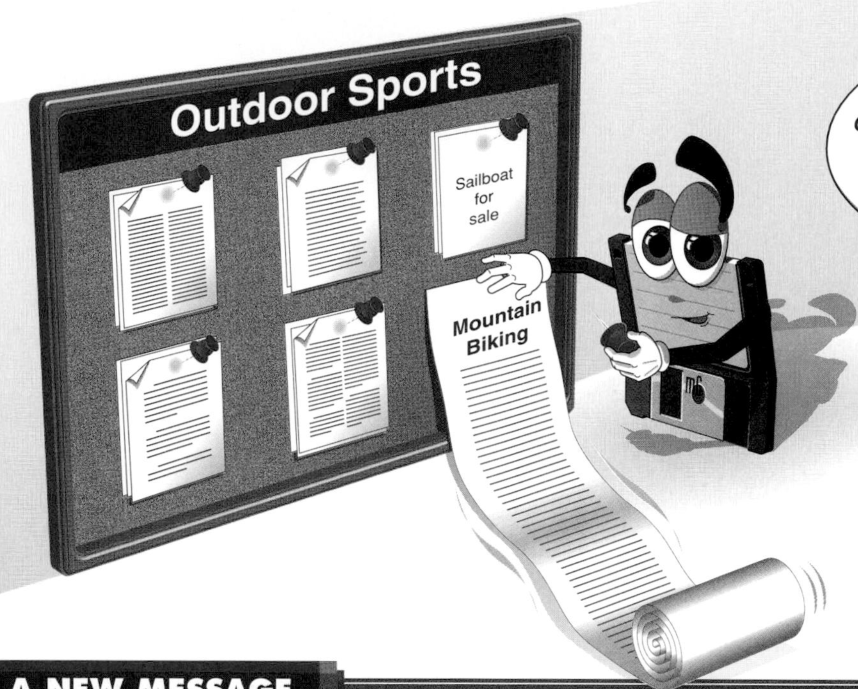

CREATE A NEW MESSAGE

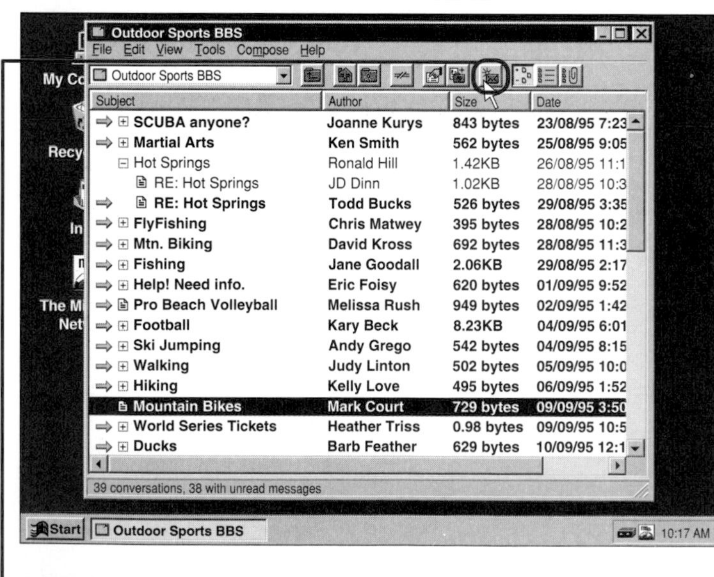

1 Move the mouse over the icon and then press the left button.

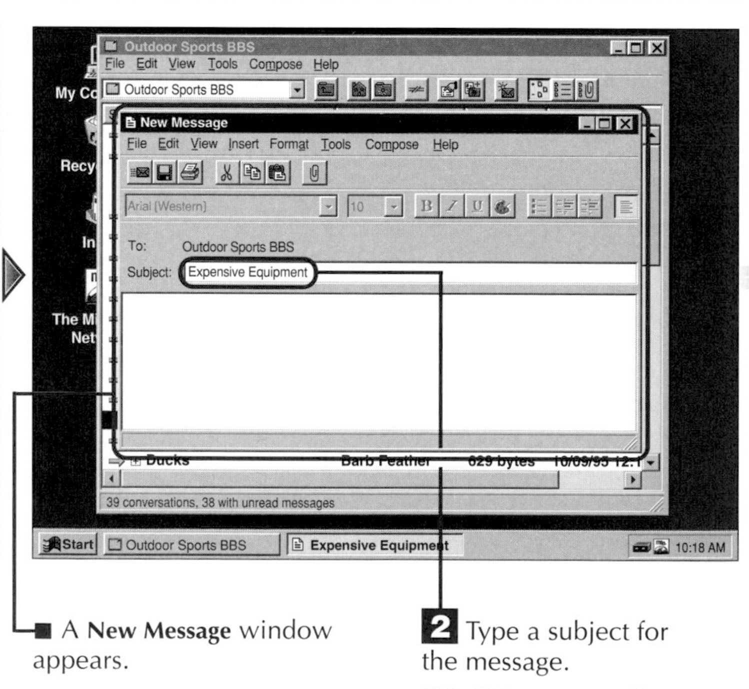

■ A **New Message** window appears.

2 Type a subject for the message.

Note: Make sure your subject is descriptive and brief.

Tip
You can use special characters, called smileys, to express emotions in messages. These characters represent human faces if you turn them sideways.
Crying :'-)
Wink ;-)
Grin :-D
Yelling :-O
Smile :-)

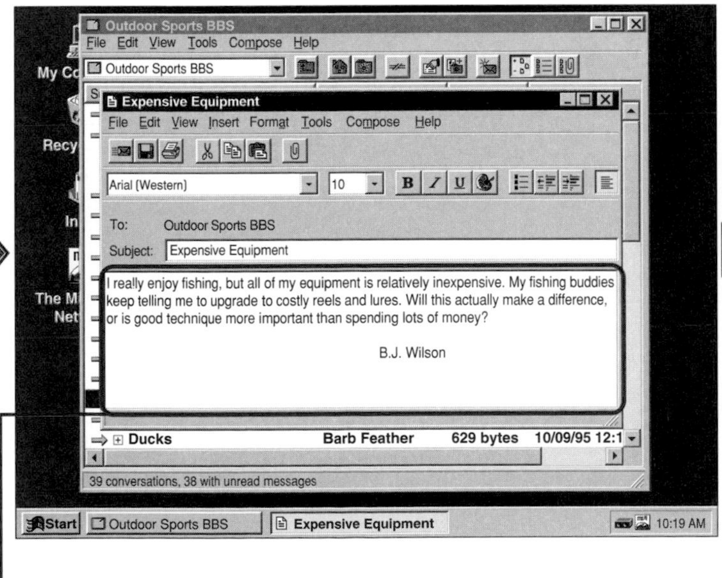

3 To create your message, move the mouse I over this area and then press the left button. Then type your message.

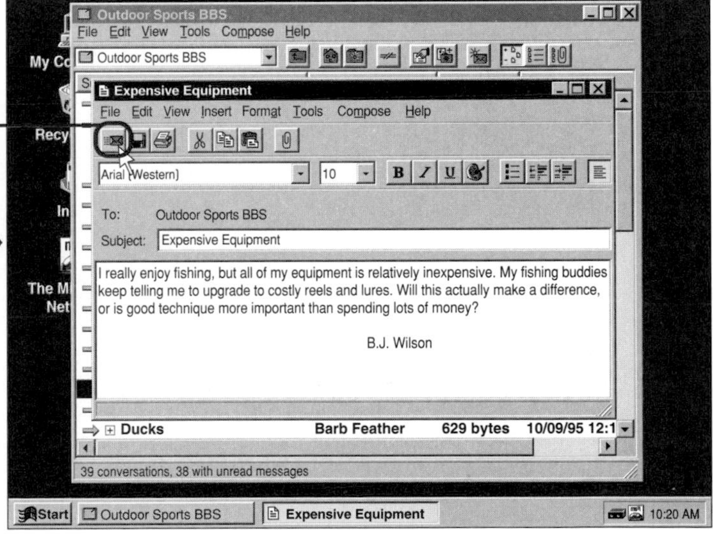

4 To send the message, move the mouse over [send icon] and then press the left button.

ADD AN ITEM TO FAVORITE PLACES

You can place all your favorite items in one location. This lets you quickly access information that interests you.

ADD AN ITEM TO FAVORITE PLACES

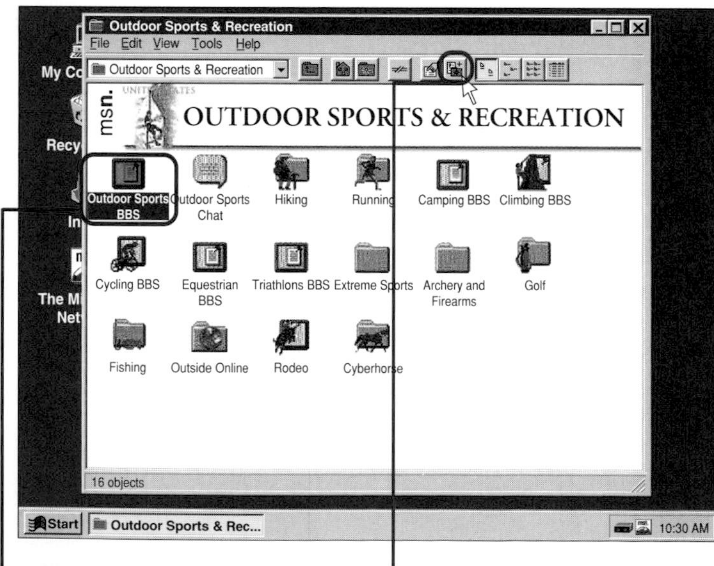

1 Move the mouse over the item you want to add to Favorite Places and then press the left button.

2 To add the item, move the mouse over and then press the left button.

*Note: If the Favorite Places button ( ) is not available, refer to the **Tip** on page 139 to display the toolbar.*

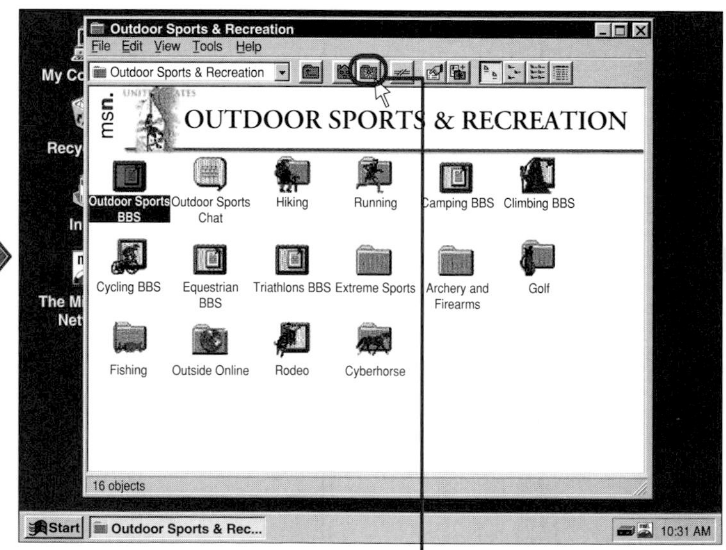

You can display all your favorite places at any time.

1 Move the mouse over and then press the left button.

SIGN OUT OF THE MSN

You should disconnect from The Microsoft Network when you no longer want to use the information and services it provides.
MSN TODAY
E - MAIL
FAVORITE
PLACES

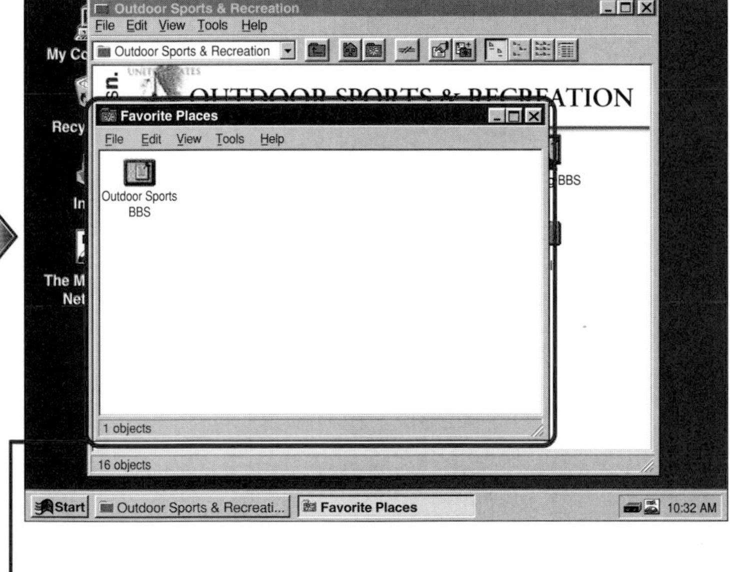

■ The **Favorite Places** window appears, displaying the items you added.

SIGN OUT

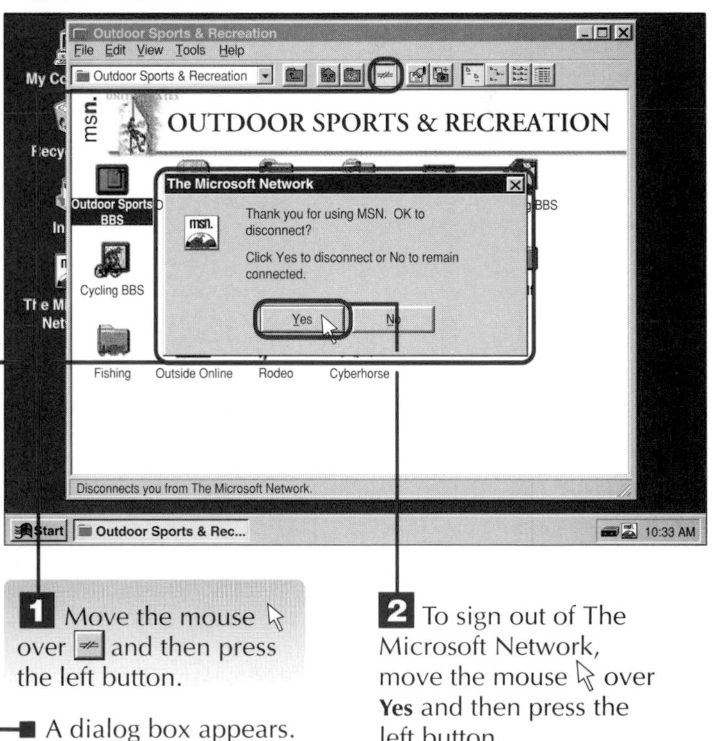

1 Move the mouse over and then press the left button.

■ A dialog box appears.

2 To sign out of The Microsoft Network, move the mouse over **Yes** and then press the left button.

My Computer
New Briefcase
Recycle Bin
Inbox
The Microsoft Network
Start
New Briefcase
9:04 AM
PUSH
POWER
RESET
disc
PHONES
VOL
BUSY
EJECT

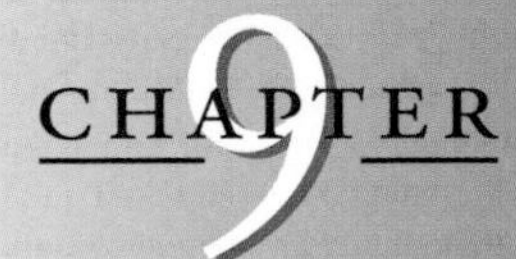

CHAPTER 9

BRIEFCASE

- *Create a Briefcase*
- *Work with Briefcase Files*
- *Update Briefcase Files*

In this chapter you will learn how to use Briefcase to work with files while you are away from the office.
MicroFLOPPY
Double Sided

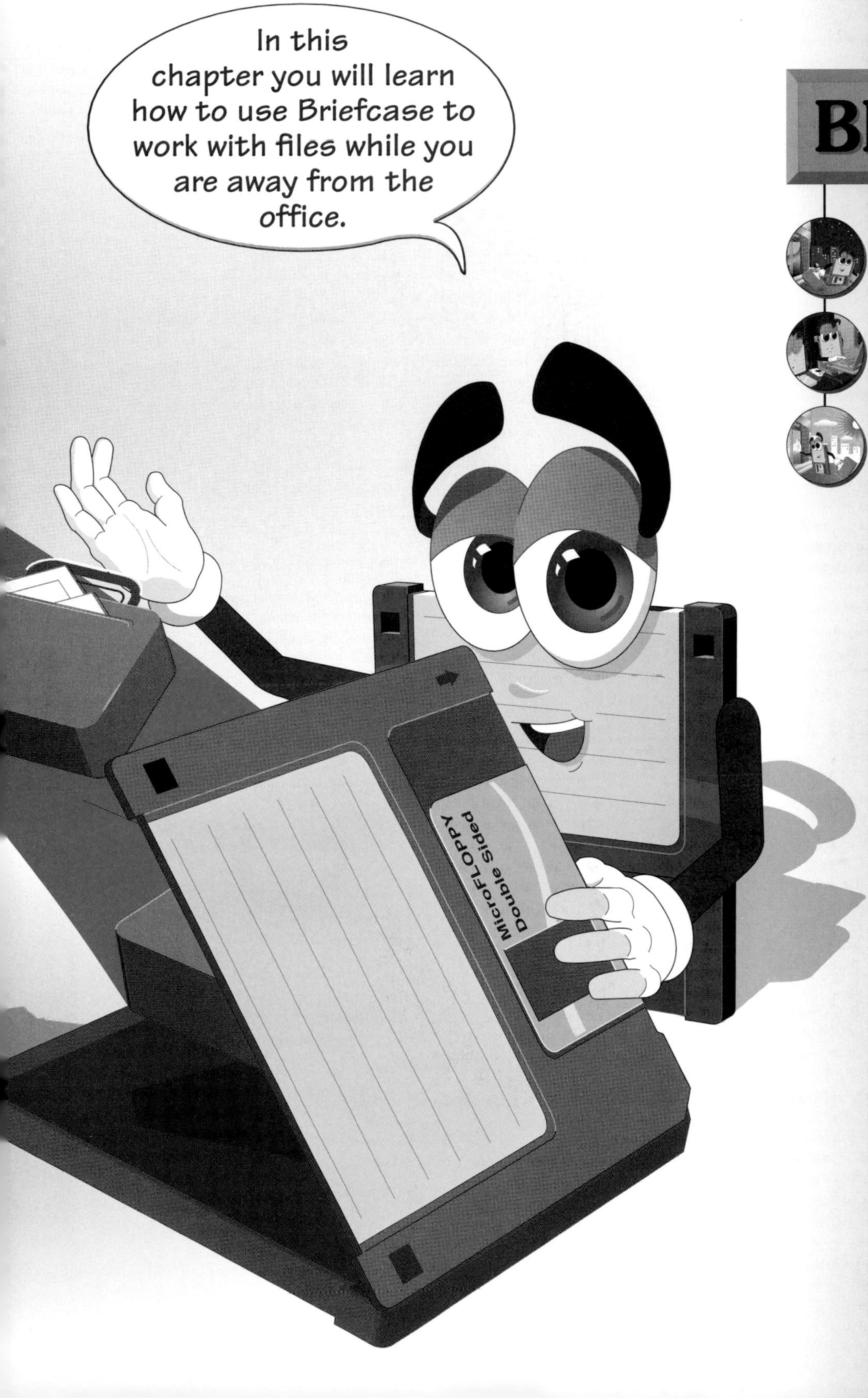

CREATE A BRIEFCASE

ABC INC.
Briefcase lets you work with files while you are away from the office. When you return, Briefcase will update all the files you changed.

CREATE A BRIEFCASE

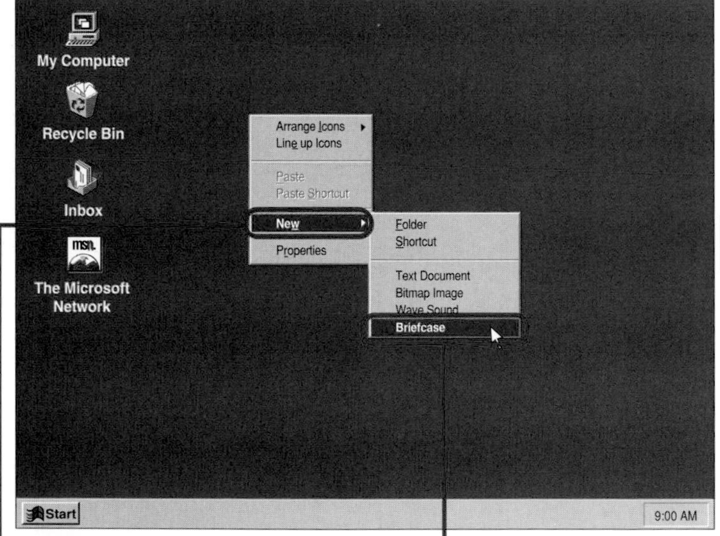

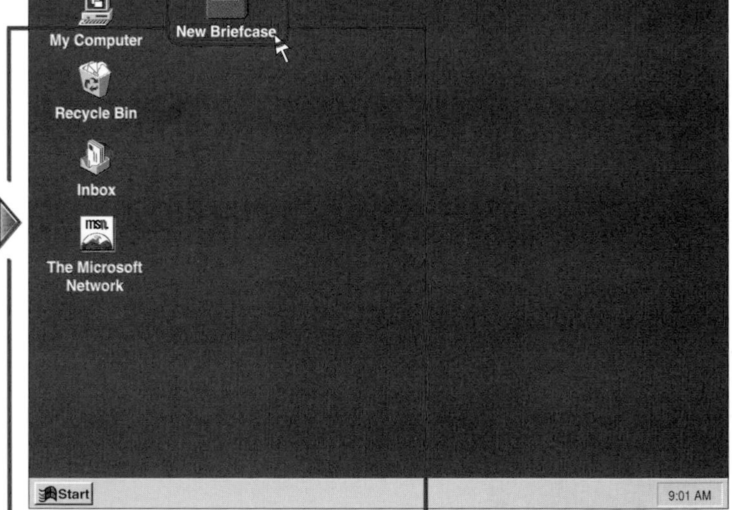

1 Move the mouse over a blank area on your desktop and then press the **right** button. A menu appears.

2 Move the mouse over **New**.

3 Move the mouse over **Briefcase** and then press the left button.

*Note: If **Briefcase** is not available, you must add the Windows component, which is found in the Accessories category. To do so, refer to page 96.*

■ A new briefcase appears.

Note: You can rename the briefcase as you would any file.

4 To view the contents of the briefcase, move the mouse over the briefcase and then quickly press the left button twice.

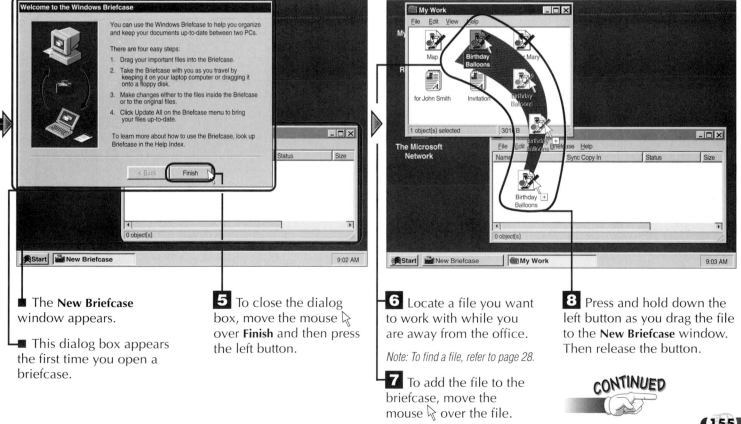

Tip
While traveling, you can use Briefcase to work with office files on a portable computer.
When at home, you can use Briefcase to work with office files on your home computer.

■ The **New Briefcase** window appears.

■ This dialog box appears the first time you open a briefcase.

5 To close the dialog box, move the mouse over **Finish** and then press the left button.

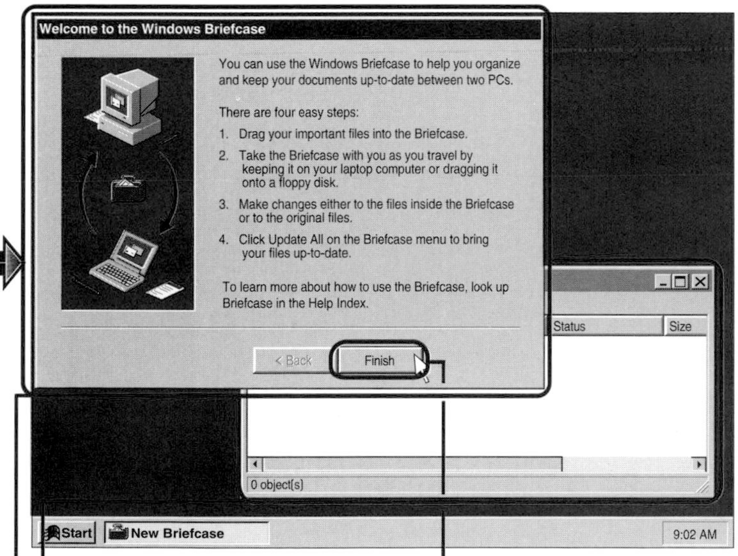

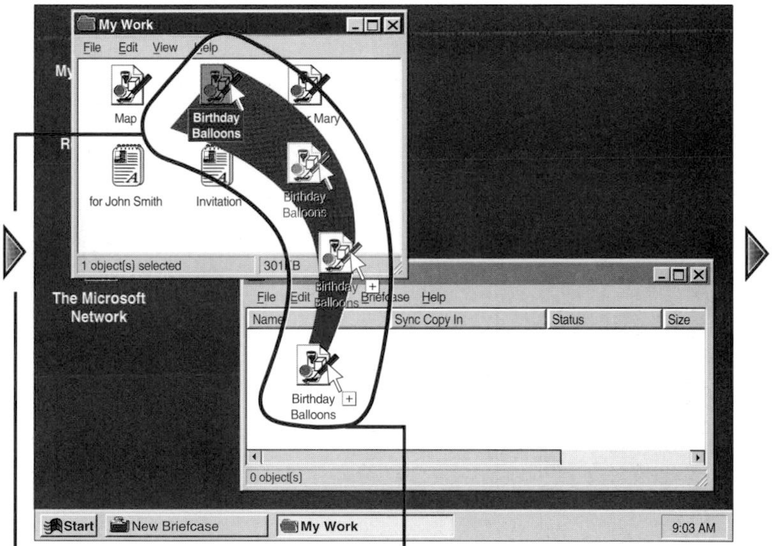

6 Locate a file you want to work with while you are away from the office.

Note: To find a file, refer to page 28.

7 To add the file to the briefcase, move the mouse over the file.

8 Press and hold down the left button as you drag the file to the **New Briefcase** window. Then release the button.

CONTINUED

CREATE A BRIEFCASE

You can move a briefcase you created to a floppy disk. A floppy disk lets you transfer the briefcase files to your home or portable computer.

CREATE A BRIEFCASE (CONTINUED)

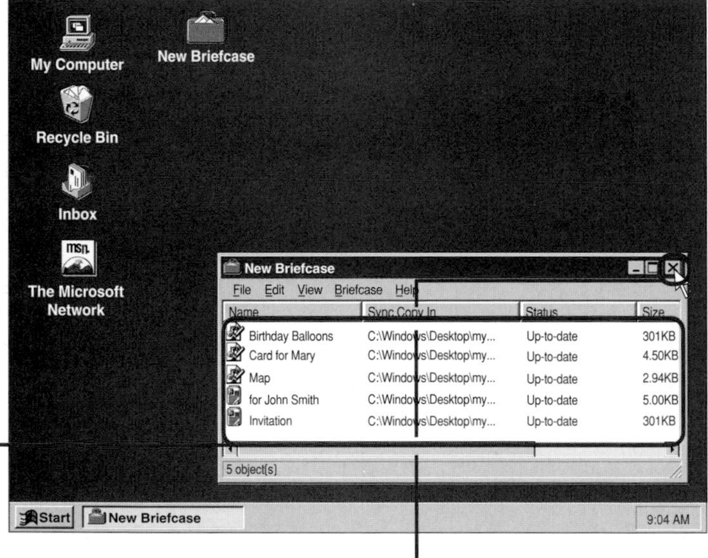

9 Repeat steps 6 to 8 on page 155 for each file you want to work with while you are away from the office.

10 To close the **New Briefcase** window, move the mouse over ☒ and then press the left button.

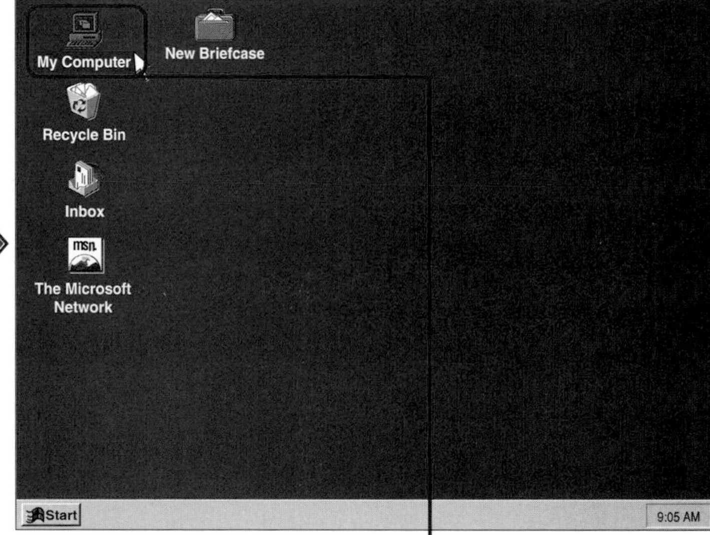

11 To place the briefcase on a floppy disk, insert a disk into a drive.

12 Move the mouse over **My Computer** and then quickly press the left button twice.

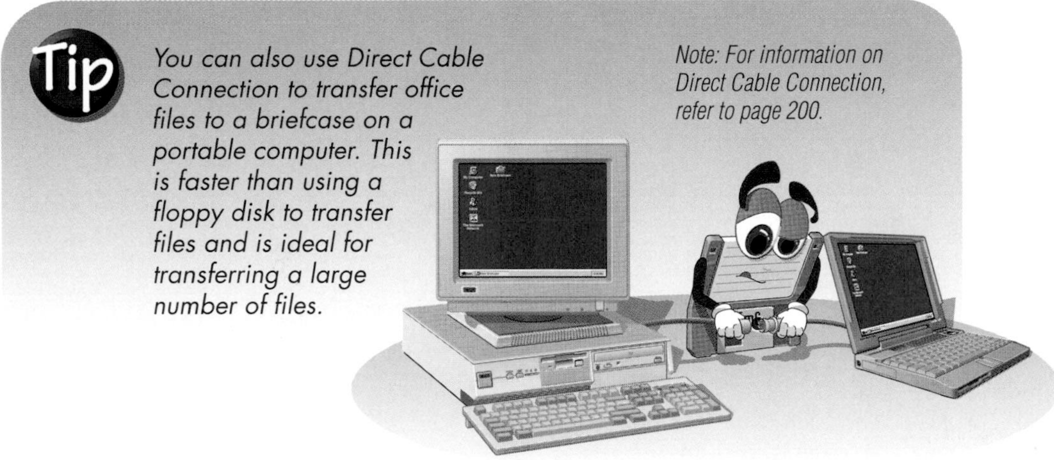

Tip You can also use Direct Cable Connection to transfer office files to a briefcase on a portable computer. This is faster than using a floppy disk to transfer files and is ideal for transferring a large number of files.

Note: For information on Direct Cable Connection, refer to page 200.

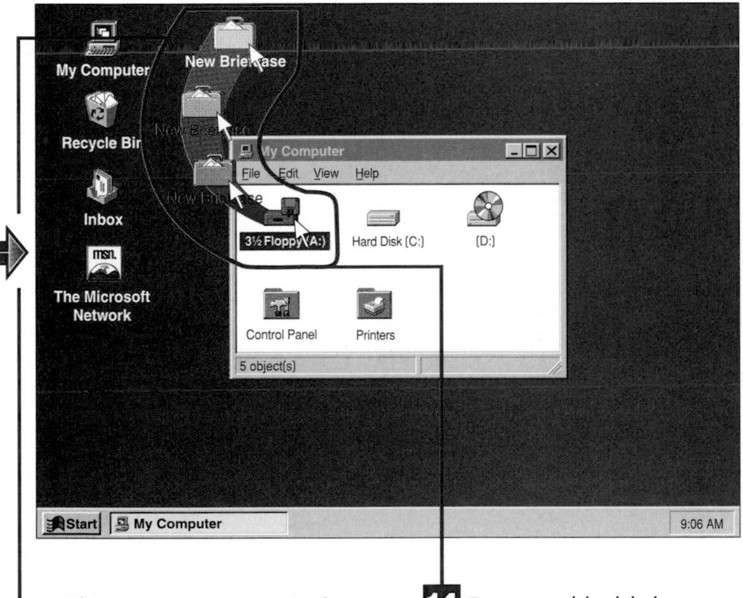

■ The **My Computer** window appears.

13 To place the briefcase on the floppy disk, move the mouse over the briefcase.

14 Press and hold down the left button as you move the briefcase to the drive containing the disk. Then release the button.

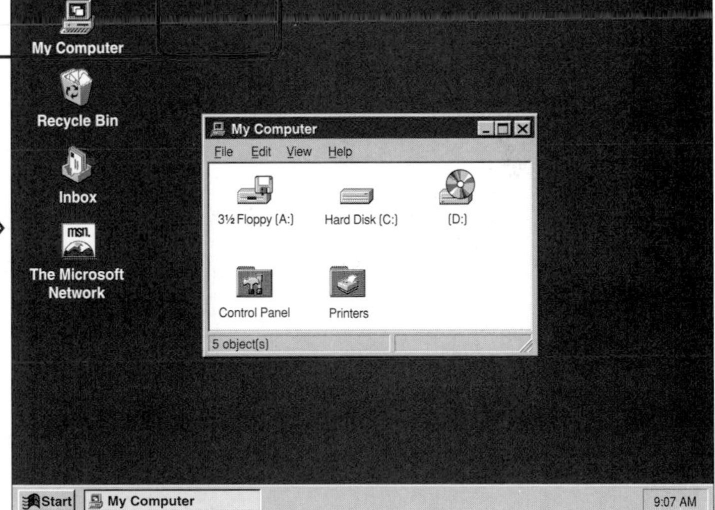

■ The floppy disk now contains the briefcase.

■ The briefcase disappears from your screen.

15 Remove the floppy disk from the drive. You can now use the floppy disk to transfer the files to your home or portable computer.

Note: To work with briefcase files, refer to page 158.

WORK WITH BRIEFCASE FILES

When traveling or at home, you can work with briefcase files as you would any other files on your computer.

WORK WITH BRIEFCASE FILES

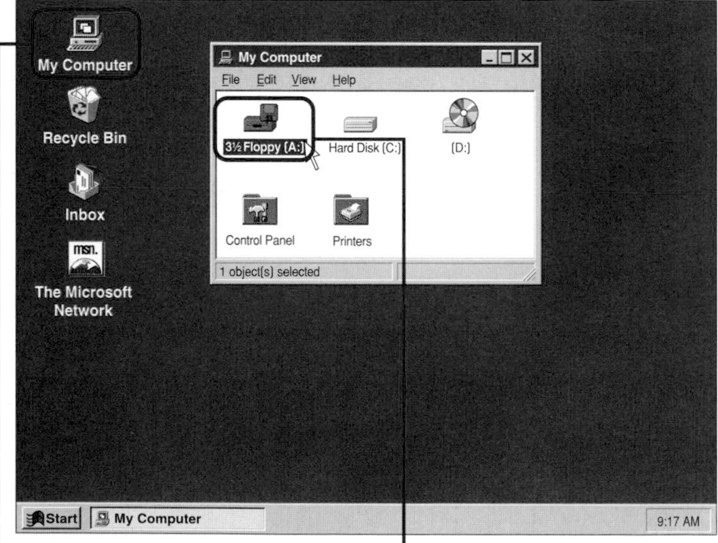

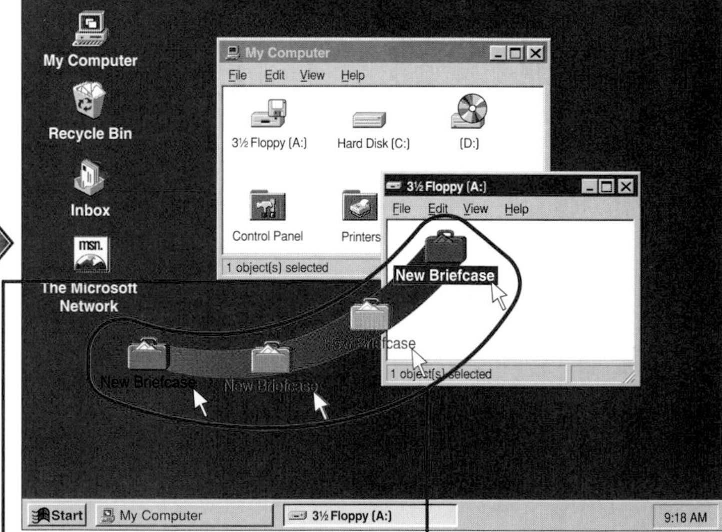

1 On your home or portable computer, insert the floppy disk containing the briefcase.

2 Move the mouse over **My Computer** and then quickly press the left button twice.

■ The **My Computer** window appears.

3 Move the mouse over the drive containing the floppy disk and then quickly press the left button twice.

■ The contents of the floppy disk appear.

4 To move the briefcase from the floppy disk to your desktop, move the mouse over the briefcase.

5 Press and hold down the left button as you move the briefcase to a blank area on the desktop. Then release the button.

IMPORTANT

Do not rename the files in the briefcase or the original files on your office computer. If you do, Briefcase will not update the files.

6 To view the contents of the briefcase, move the mouse over the briefcase and then quickly press the left button twice.

■ The contents of the briefcase appear. You can now work with files in the briefcase as you would any file.

7 When you finish working with the files, move the mouse over ☒ and then press the left button to close the briefcase window.

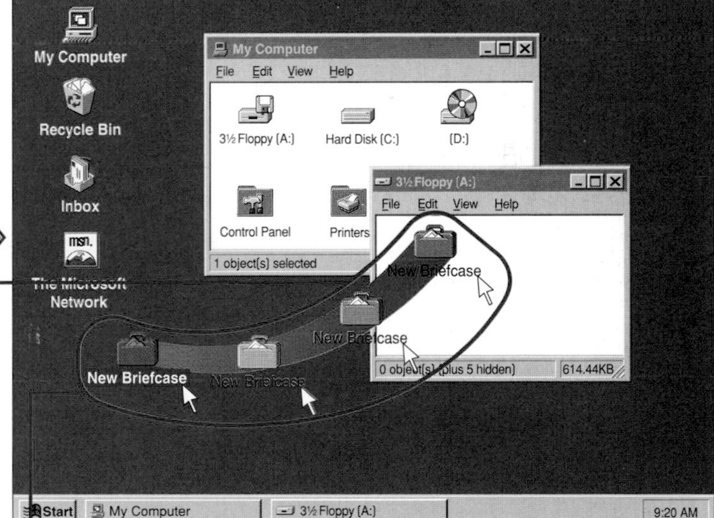

8 To return the briefcase to the floppy disk, move the mouse over the briefcase.

9 Press and hold down the left button as you move the briefcase to the floppy disk window. Then release the button.

10 Remove the floppy disk from the drive. You can now use the floppy disk to return the files to your office computer.

Note: To update the files you changed, refer to page 160.

UPDATE BRIEFCASE FILES

ABC INC.
When you return to the office, you can quickly update the files you changed.

UPDATE BRIEFCASE FILES

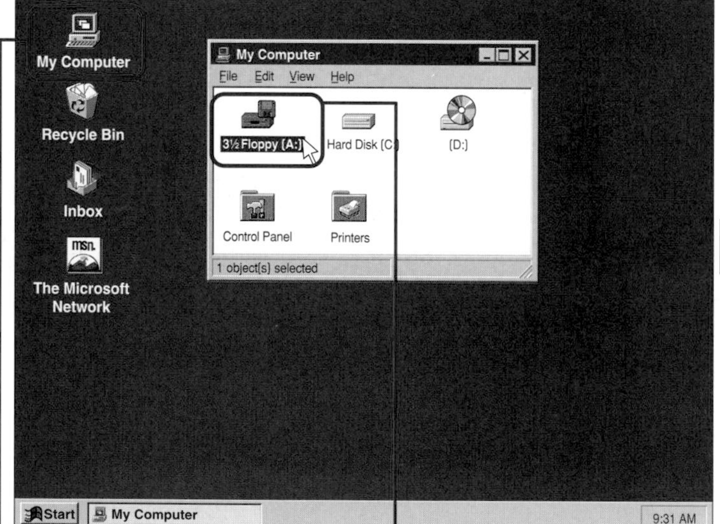

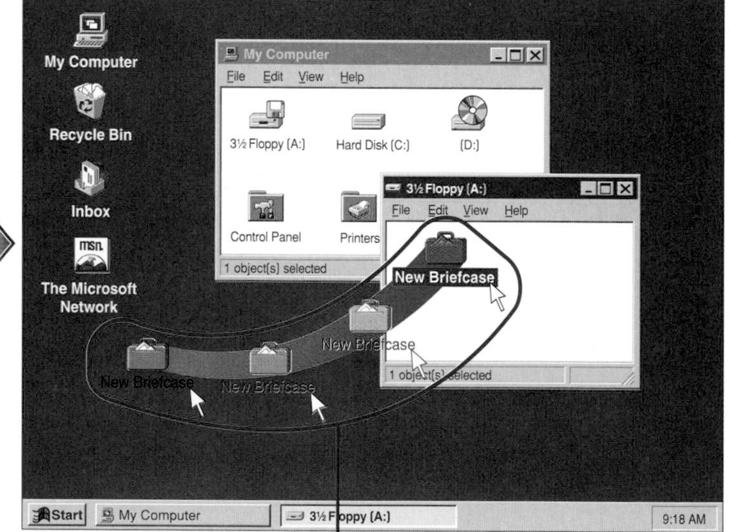

1 Insert the floppy disk containing the briefcase into your office computer.

2 Move the mouse over **My Computer** and then quickly press the left button twice.

■ The **My Computer** window appears.

3 Move the mouse over the drive containing the floppy disk and then quickly press the left button twice.

■ The contents of the floppy disk appear.

4 To move the briefcase from the floppy disk to your desktop, move the mouse over the briefcase.

5 Press and hold down the left button as you move the briefcase to a blank area on the desktop. Then release the button.

Tip *Windows compares the files in the briefcase to the files on your office computer to decide which files need to be updated.*

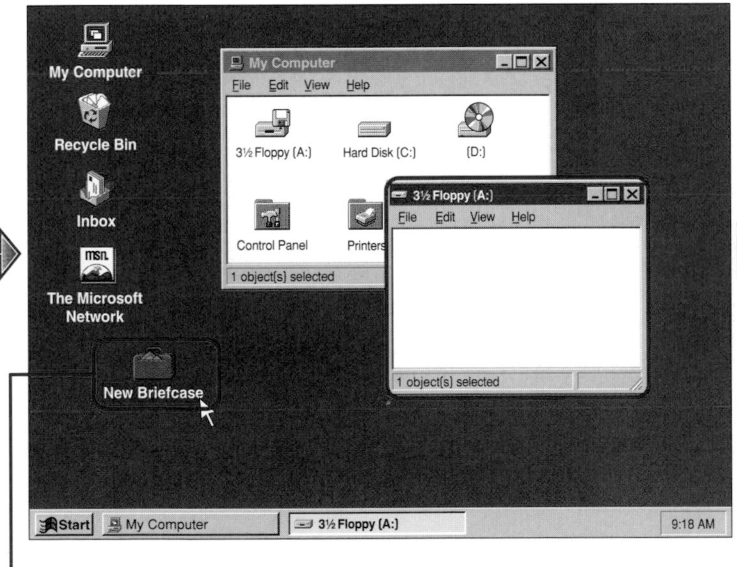

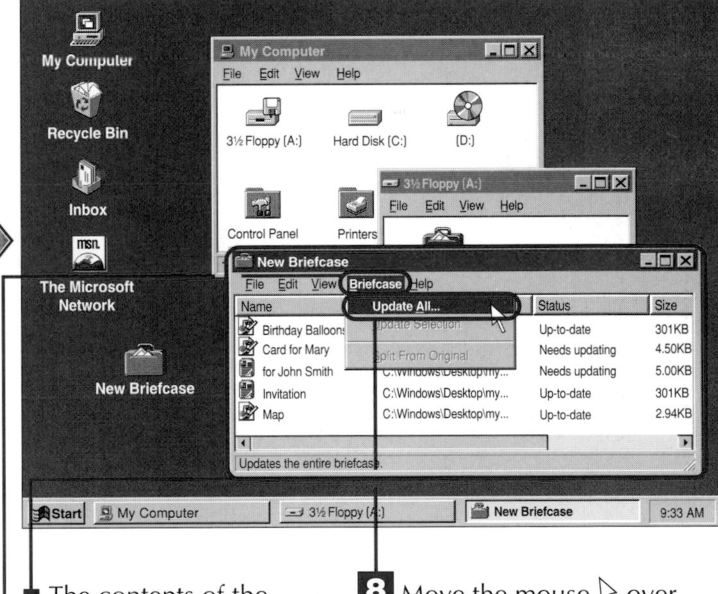

6 To view the contents of the briefcase, move the mouse over the briefcase and then quickly press the left button twice.

■ The contents of the briefcase appear.

7 Move the mouse over **Briefcase** and then press the left button.

8 Move the mouse over **Update All** and then press the left button.

■ The **Update New Briefcase** dialog box appears.

CONTINUED

UPDATE BRIEFCASE FILES

Windows tells you exactly which files need to be updated.

UPDATE BRIEFCASE FILES (CONTINUED)

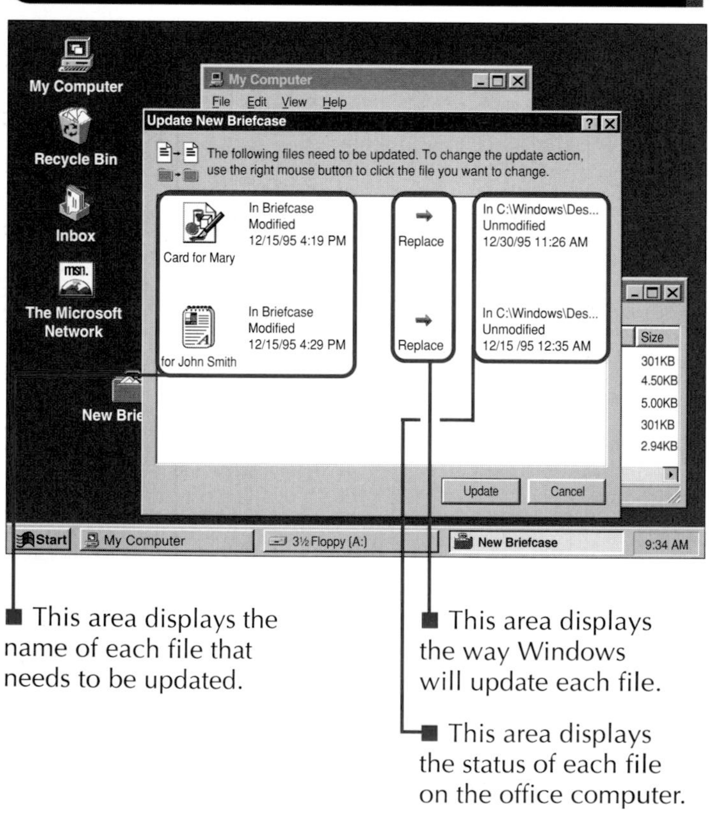

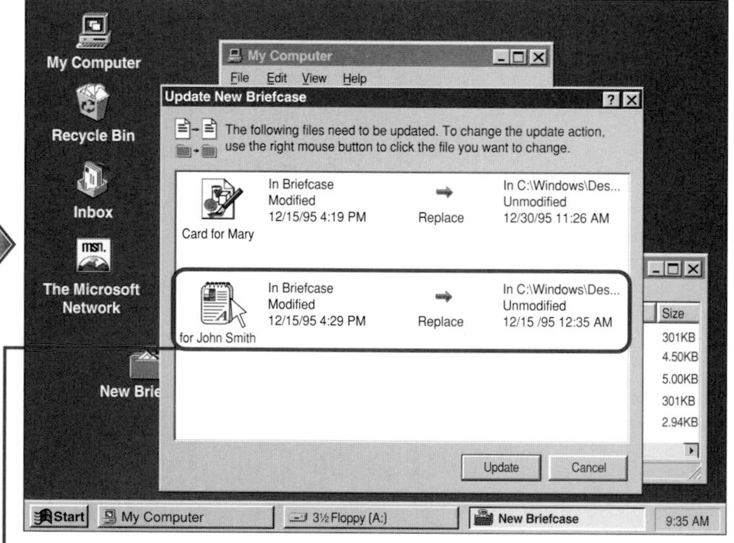

■ This area displays the name of each file that needs to be updated.

■ This area displays the way Windows will update each file.

■ This area displays the status of each file on the office computer.

9 To change the way Windows will update a file, move the mouse ⇖ over the file and then press the **right** button. A menu appears.

You can create a new briefcase every time you want to work away from the office. Delete an old briefcase as you would delete any file.

Note: Deleting a briefcase does not remove the original files from your computer.

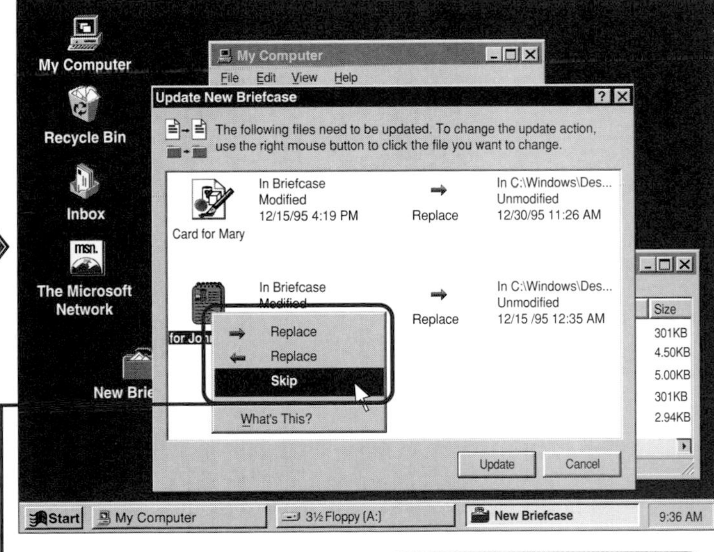

10 Move the mouse over the way you want Windows to update the file and then press the left button.

➡ Replace
Replace office file with briefcase file.

⬅ Replace
Replace briefcase file with office file.

Skip
Do not update the file.

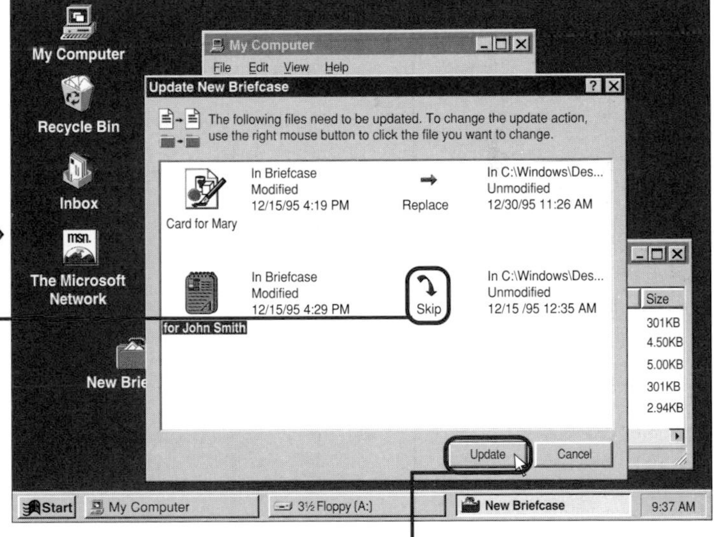

■ This area displays the way Windows will now update the file.

11 To change the way Windows updates other files, repeat steps **9** and **10** for each file.

12 To update the files, move the mouse over **Update** and then press the left button.

In this chapter you will learn how to use a network to share and access information and equipment.

CHAPTER 10

NETWORKS

Introduction to Networks

Turn on Sharing

Name Your Computer

Share Information

Share a Printer

Set the Default Printer

Browse Through a Network

Find a Computer

Map a Network Drive

INTRODUCTION TO NETWORKS

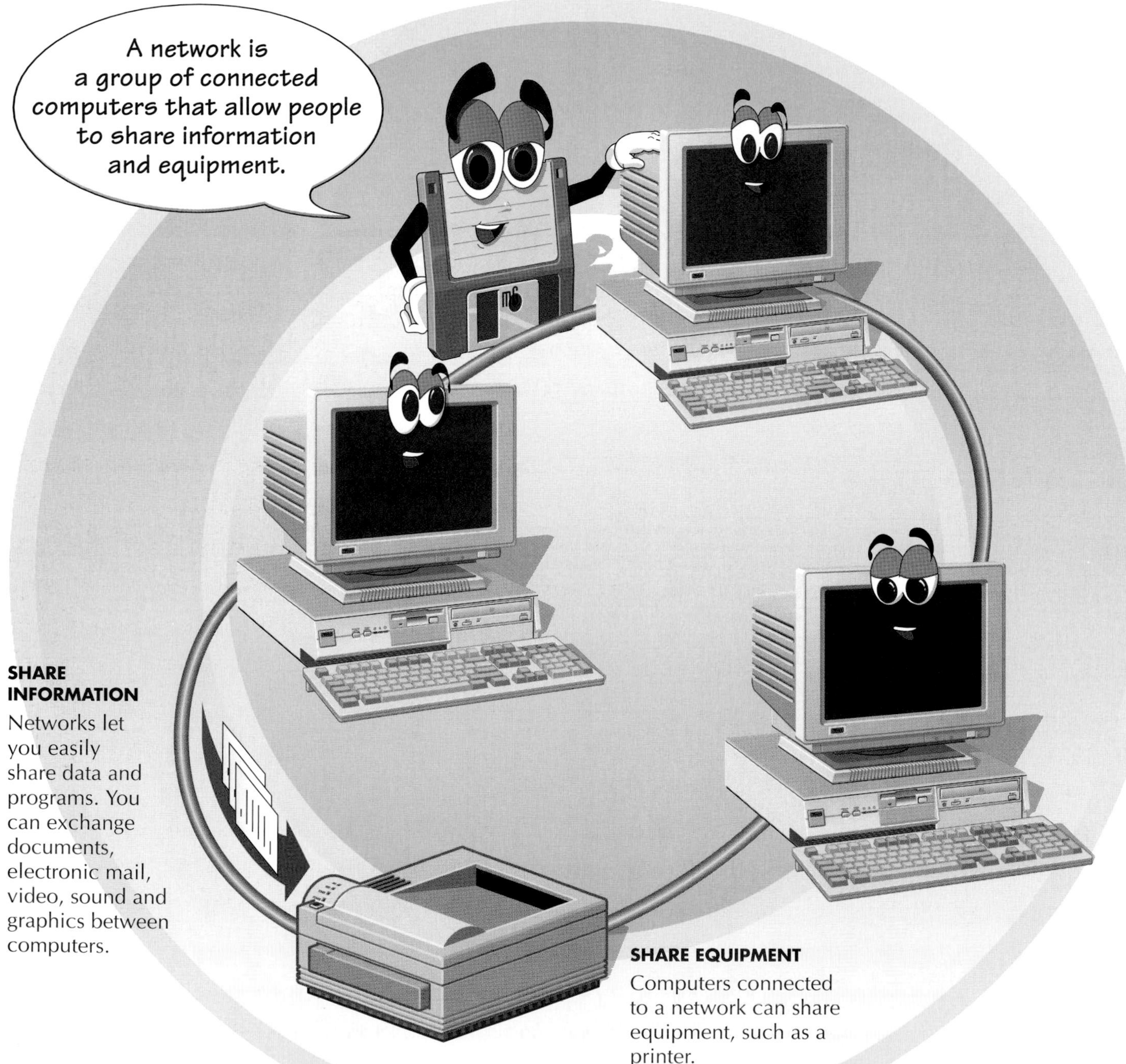

A network is a group of connected computers that allow people to share information and equipment.

SHARE INFORMATION

Networks let you easily share data and programs. You can exchange documents, electronic mail, video, sound and graphics between computers.

SHARE EQUIPMENT

Computers connected to a network can share equipment, such as a printer.

TURN ON SHARING

Before you can share information or a printer with individuals on a network, you must set up your computer to share resources.

TURN ON SHARING

1 Move the mouse over **Start** and then press the left button.

2 Move the mouse over **Settings**.

3 Move the mouse over **Control Panel** and then press the left button.

■ The **Control Panel** window appears.

4 Move the mouse over **Network** and then quickly press the left button twice.

CONTINUED

TURN ON SHARING

You can choose to give individuals on a network access to your files and/or printer.

TURN ON SHARING (CONTINUED)

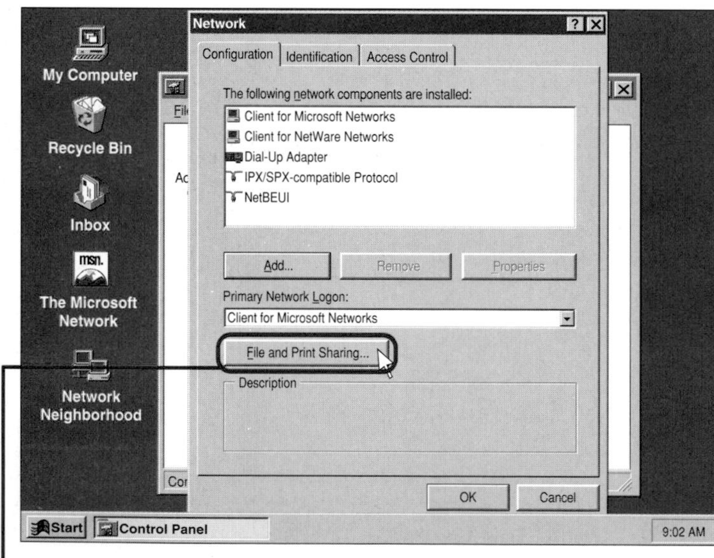

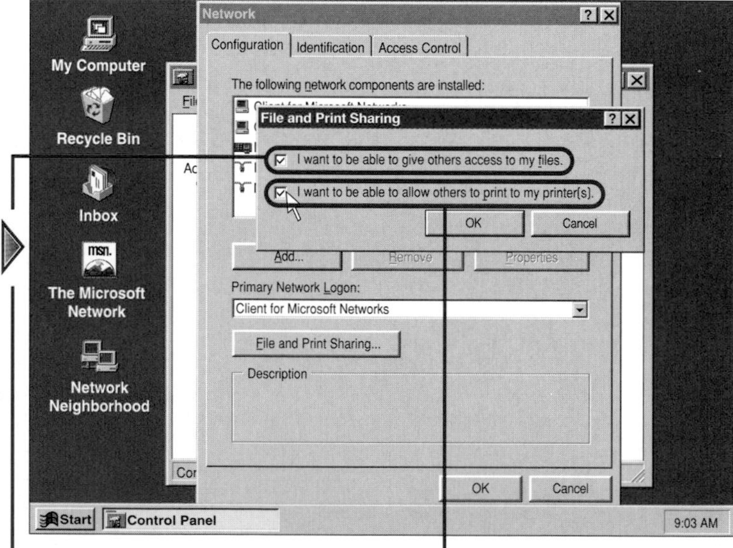

■ The **Network** dialog box appears.

5 Move the mouse ↖ over **File and Print Sharing** and then press the left button.

■ The **File and Print Sharing** dialog box appears.

6 To share your files, move the mouse ↖ over this option and then press the left button (☐ changes to ☑).

7 To share your printer, move the mouse ↖ over this option and then press the left button (☐ changes to ☑).

Once you set up your computer to share information and/or a printer, you must specify exactly what you want to share.

■ *To specify the information you want to share, refer to page 172.*

■ *To specify the printer you want to share, refer to page 176.*

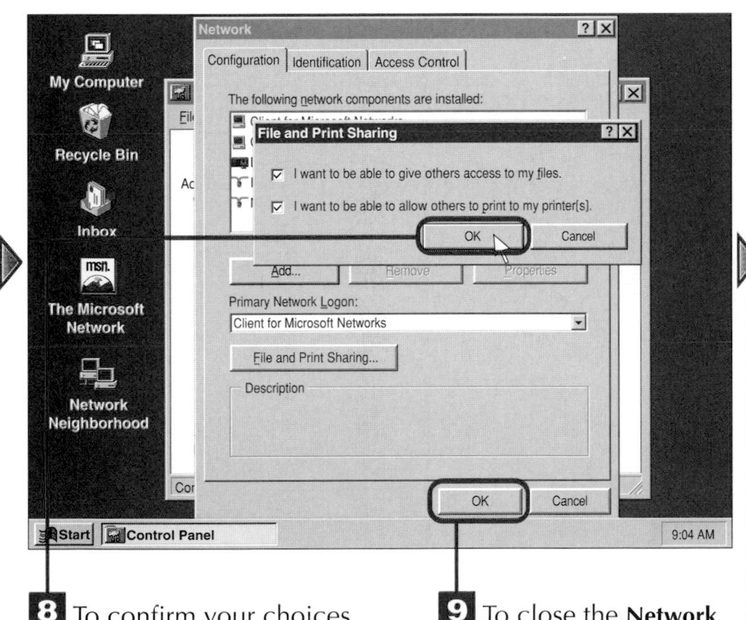

8 To confirm your choices, move the mouse over **OK** and then press the left button.

9 To close the **Network** dialog box, move the mouse over **OK** and then press the left button.

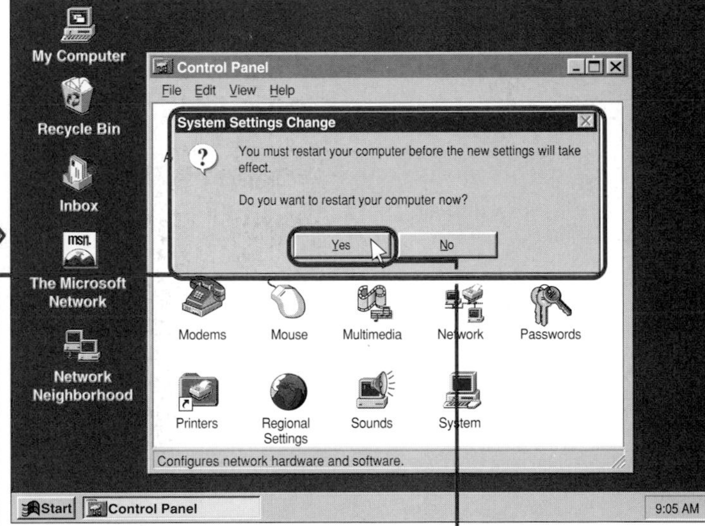

■ The **System Settings Change** dialog box appears, telling you Windows needs to restart your computer before the new settings will take effect.

10 To restart your computer, move the mouse over **Yes** and then press the left button.

NAME YOUR COMPUTER

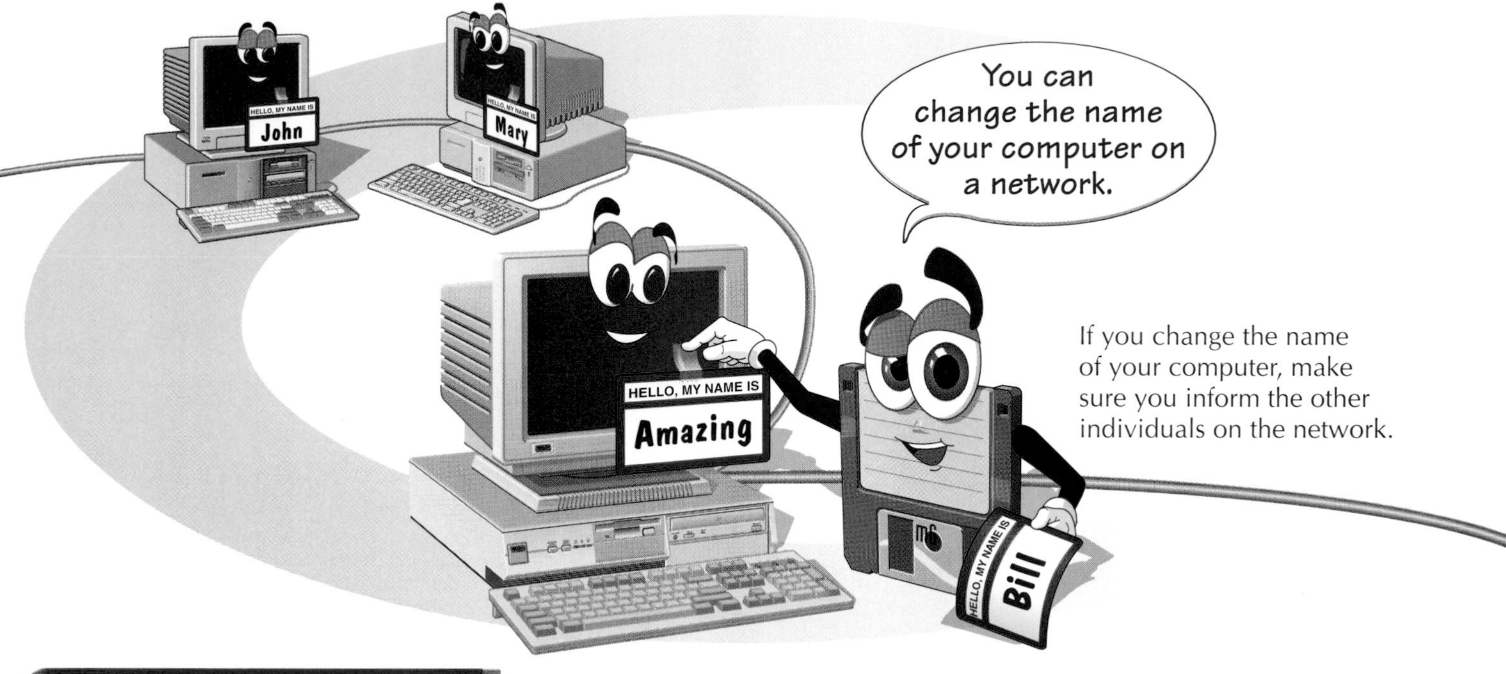

If you change the name of your computer, make sure you inform the other individuals on the network.

NAME YOUR COMPUTER

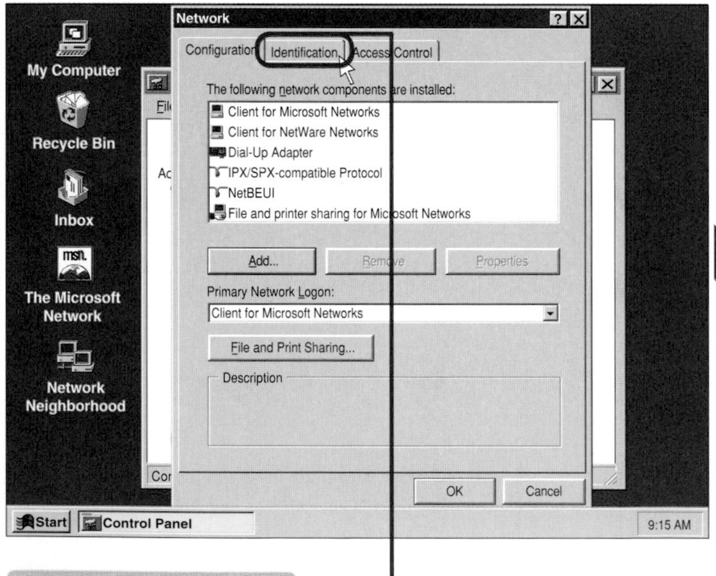

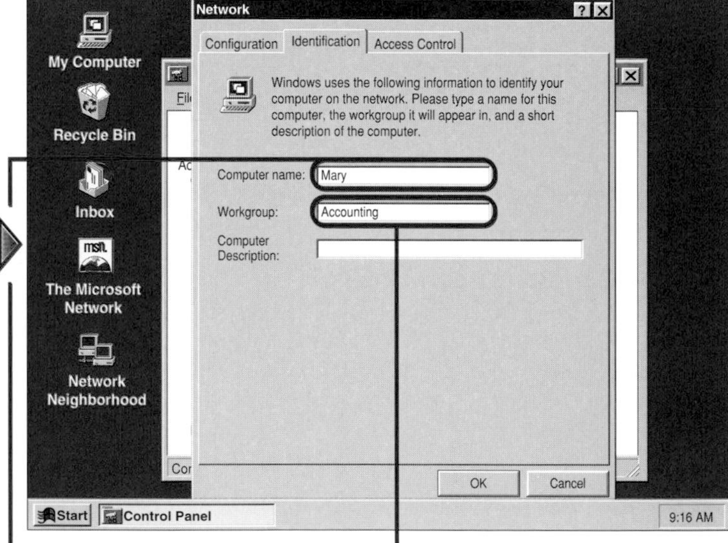

1 To display the **Network** dialog box, perform steps **1** to **4** on page 167.

2 Move the mouse over the **Identification** tab and then press the left button.

3 Type a name for your computer.

■ This area identifies the workgroup your computer belongs to.

*Note: For information on workgroups, refer to the **Tip** on page 171.*

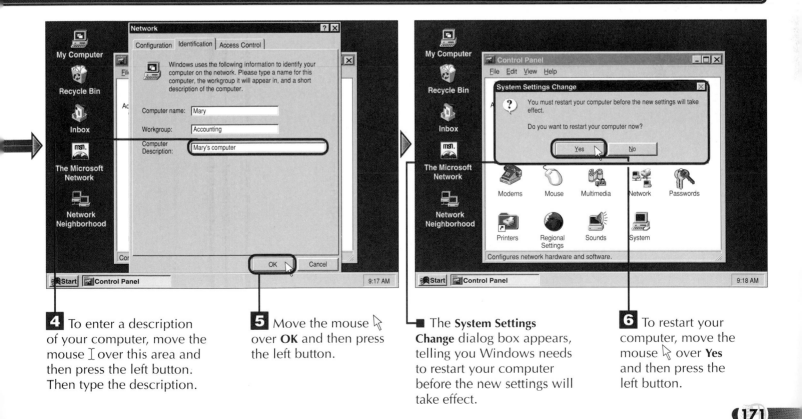

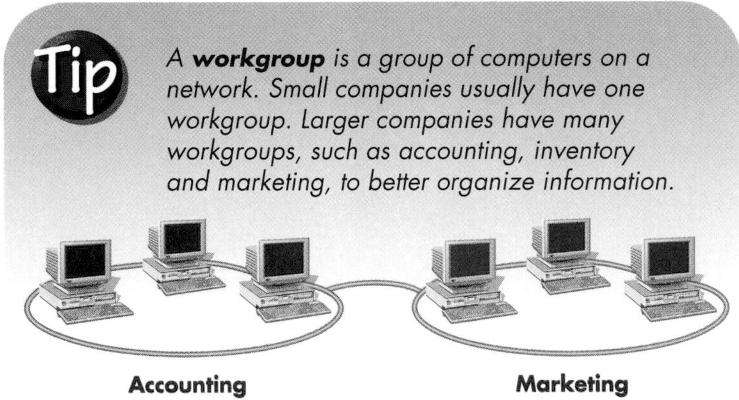

Tip
A **workgroup** is a group of computers on a network. Small companies usually have one workgroup. Larger companies have many workgroups, such as accounting, inventory and marketing, to better organize information.
Accounting
Marketing

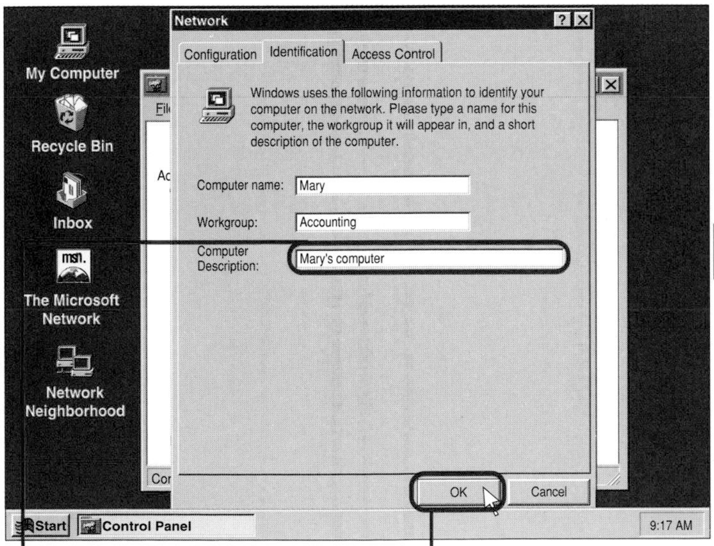

4 To enter a description of your computer, move the mouse I over this area and then press the left button. Then type the description.

5 Move the mouse over **OK** and then press the left button.

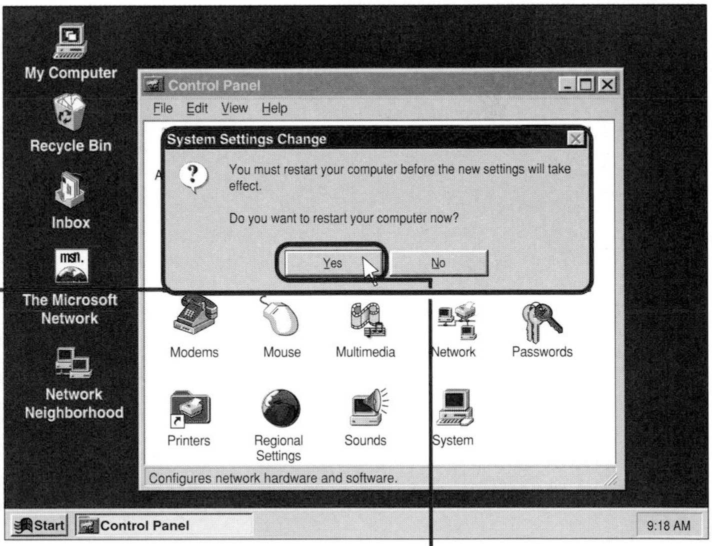

■ The **System Settings Change** dialog box appears, telling you Windows needs to restart your computer before the new settings will take effect.

6 To restart your computer, move the mouse over **Yes** and then press the left button.

SHARE INFORMATION

You can specify exactly what information you want to share with individuals on a network.

SHARE INFORMATION

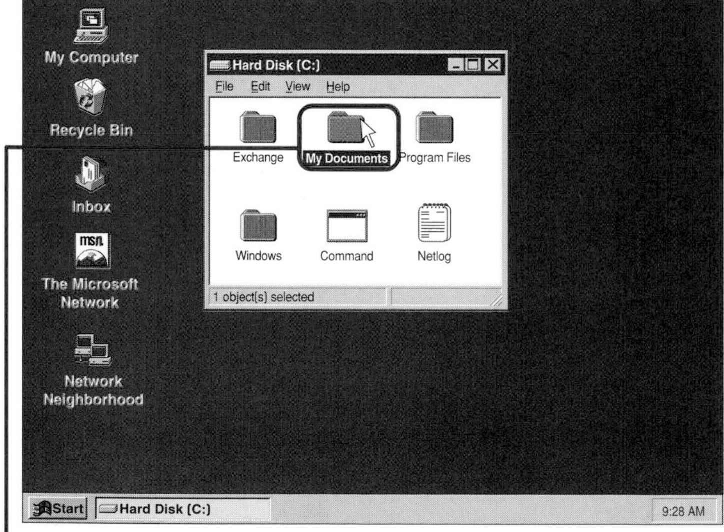

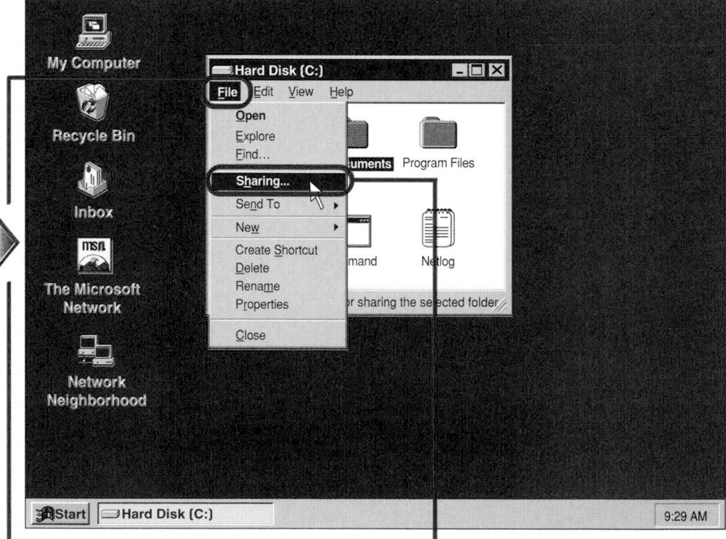

1 Move the mouse over the folder you want to share and then press the left button.

2 Move the mouse over **File** and then press the left button.

3 Move the mouse over **Sharing** and then press the left button.

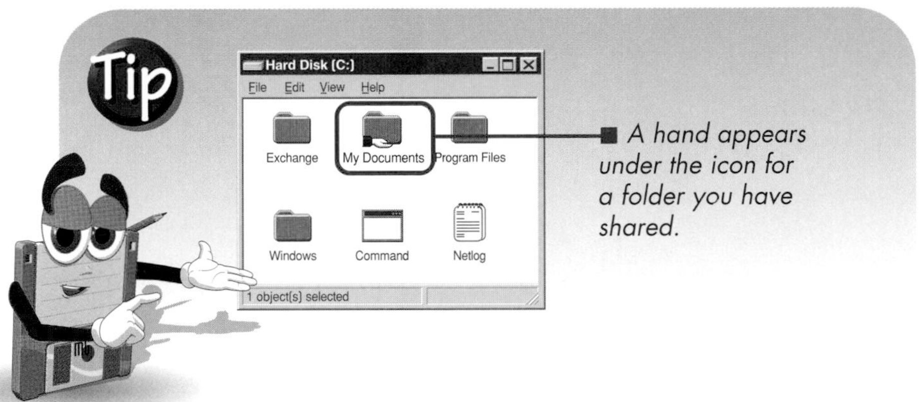

■ *A hand appears under the icon for a folder you have shared.*

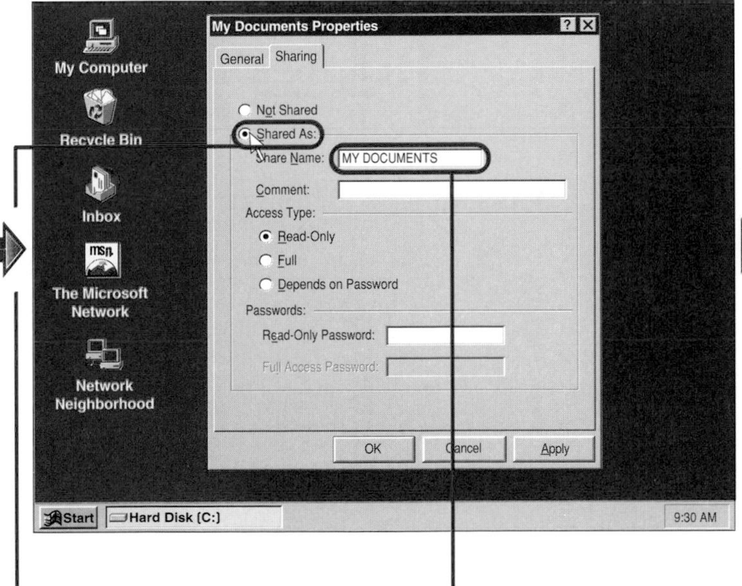

■ The **Properties** dialog box appears.

4 Move the mouse over **Shared As:** and then press the left button (○ changes to ◉).

■ This area displays the name of the folder you selected. Individuals on the network will see this name.

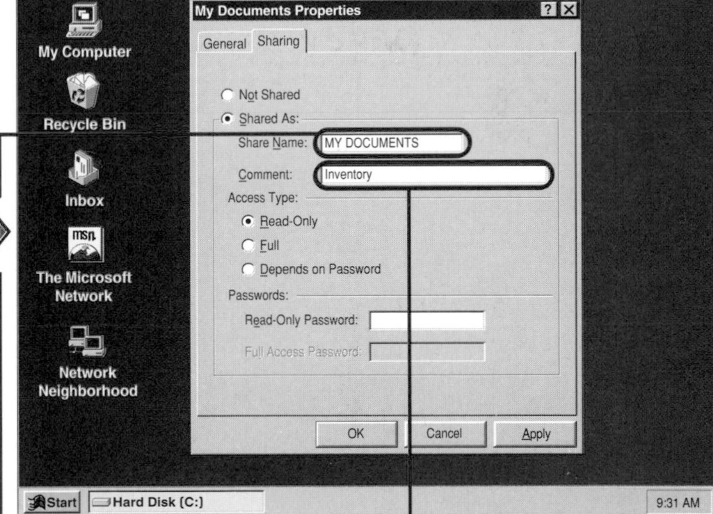

5 If you want to give the folder a different name, move the mouse over this area and then press the left button. Then type a new name.

6 To type a comment about the folder, move the mouse over this area and then press the left button. Then type a comment.

CONTINUED

SHARE INFORMATION

There are three types of access to information that you can give individuals on a network.

SHARE INFORMATION (CONTINUED)

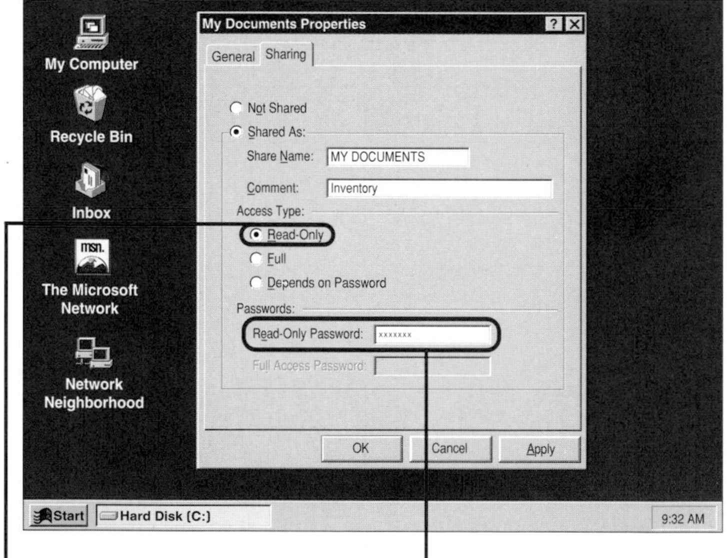

Read-Only

1 To select **Read-Only** access, move the mouse over this area and then press the left button (○ changes to ◉).

2 If you want Windows to request a password before allowing individuals to access the information, press Tab on your keyboard. Then type a password.

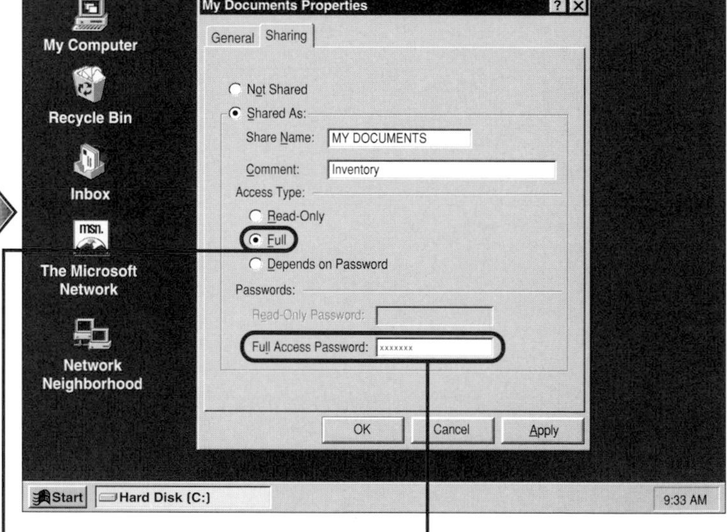

Full

1 To select **Full** access, move the mouse over this area and then press the left button (○ changes to ◉).

2 If you want Windows to request a password before allowing individuals to access the information, press Tab on your keyboard. Then type a password.

Read-Only
All individuals on the network can read, but not change or delete, information.

Full
All individuals on the network can read, change and delete information.

Depends on Password
Some individuals on the network get Read-Only access, while others get Full access. The type of access depends on which password they enter.

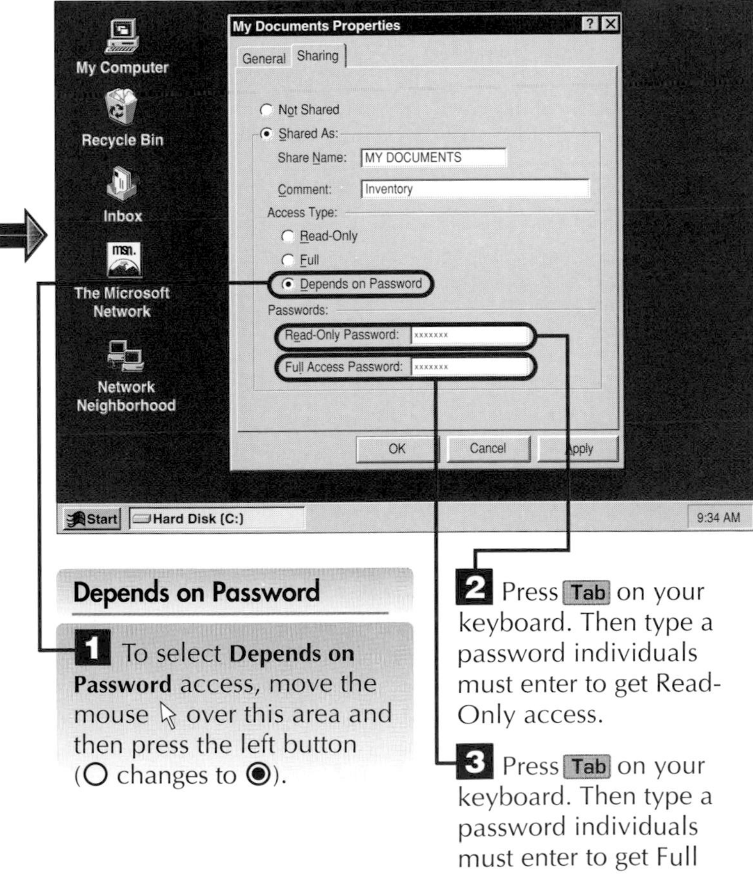

Depends on Password

1 To select **Depends on Password** access, move the mouse over this area and then press the left button (○ changes to ◉).

2 Press Tab on your keyboard. Then type a password individuals must enter to get Read-Only access.

3 Press Tab on your keyboard. Then type a password individuals must enter to get Full access.

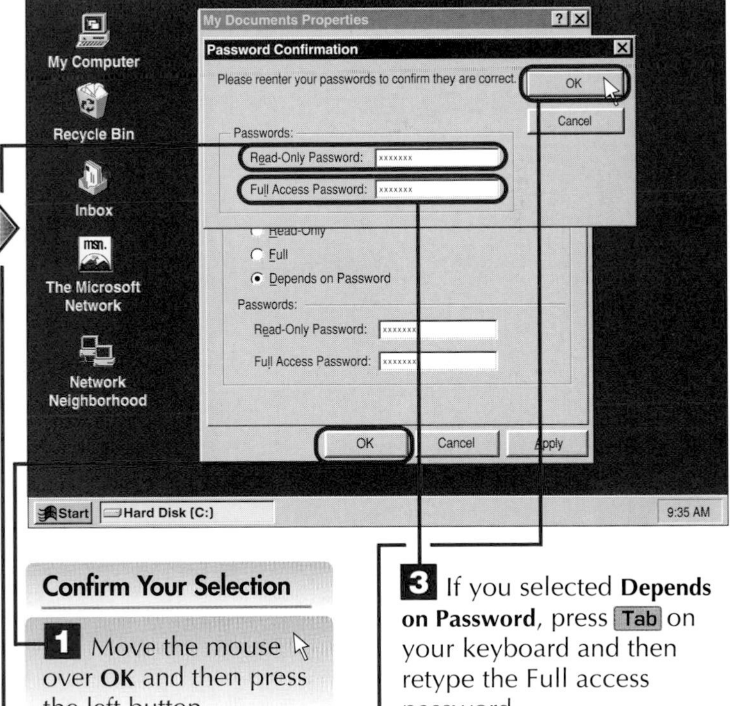

Confirm Your Selection

1 Move the mouse over **OK** and then press the left button.

2 A dialog box appears if you entered a password. To confirm the password, retype the password.

3 If you selected **Depends on Password**, press Tab on your keyboard and then retype the Full access password.

4 Move the mouse over **OK** and then press the left button.

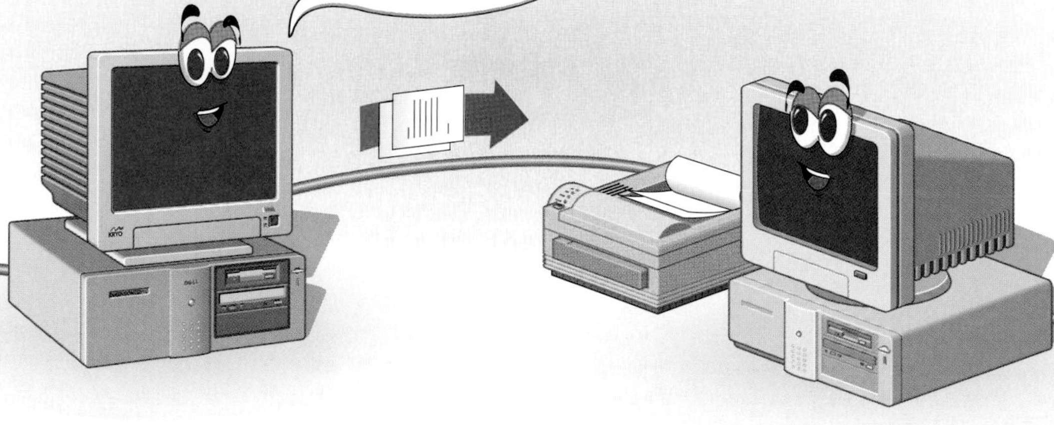

You can share your printer with other individuals on a network.

SHARE A PRINTER

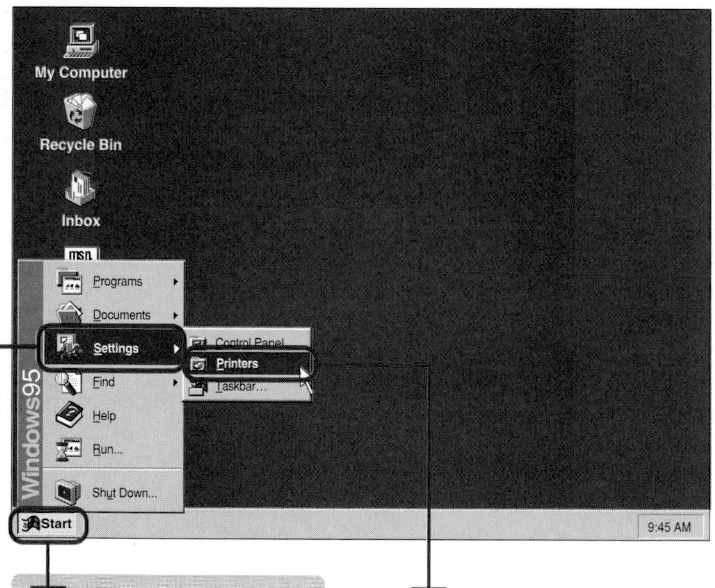

1 Move the mouse over **Start** and then press the left button.

2 Move the mouse over **Settings**.

3 Move the mouse over **Printers** and then press the left button.

■ The **Printers** window appears.

4 Move the mouse over the printer you want to share and then press the left button.

■ *A hand appears under the icon for a printer you have shared.*

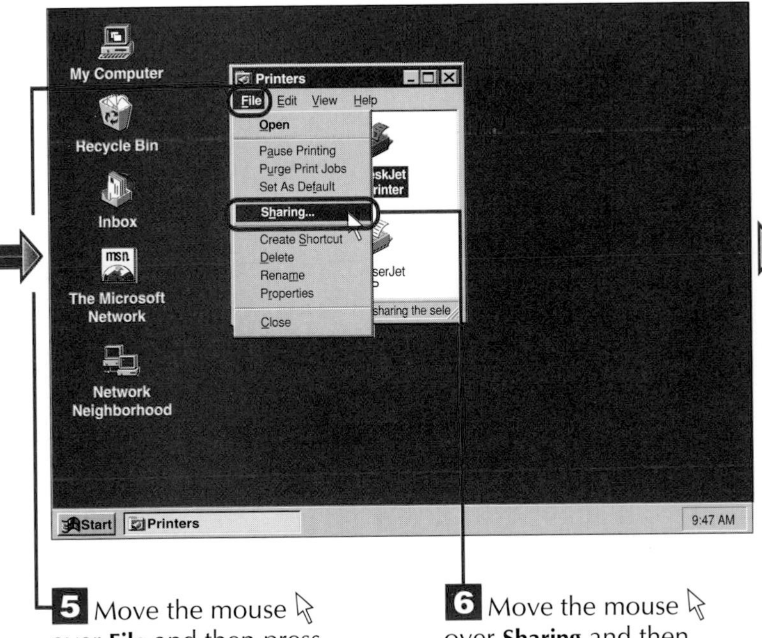

5 Move the mouse over **File** and then press the left button.

6 Move the mouse over **Sharing** and then press the left button.

■ The **Properties** dialog box appears.

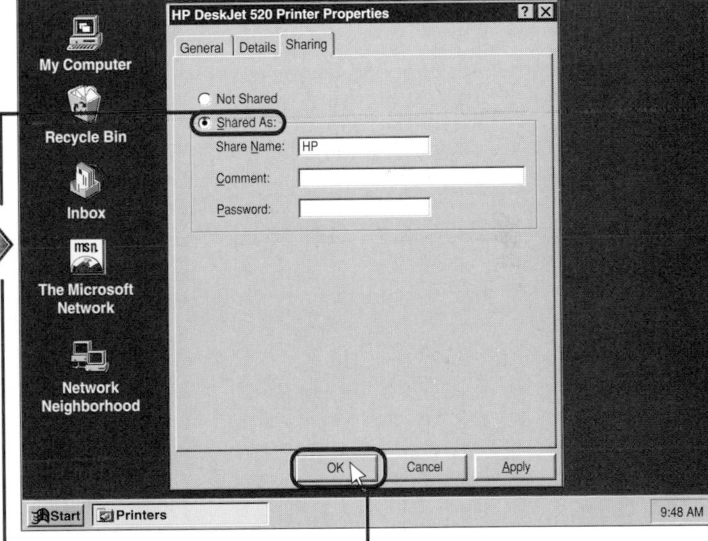

7 Move the mouse over **Shared As:** and then press the left button (○ changes to ◉).

8 Move the mouse over **OK** and then press the left button.

■ Your printer is now available to other computers on the network.

Note: If colleagues want to use your printer, they must install the printer software on their computers. To do so, they must perform the steps starting on page 108.

SET THE DEFAULT PRINTER

If you have access to more than one printer, you can choose one to automatically print your documents.

SET THE DEFAULT PRINTER

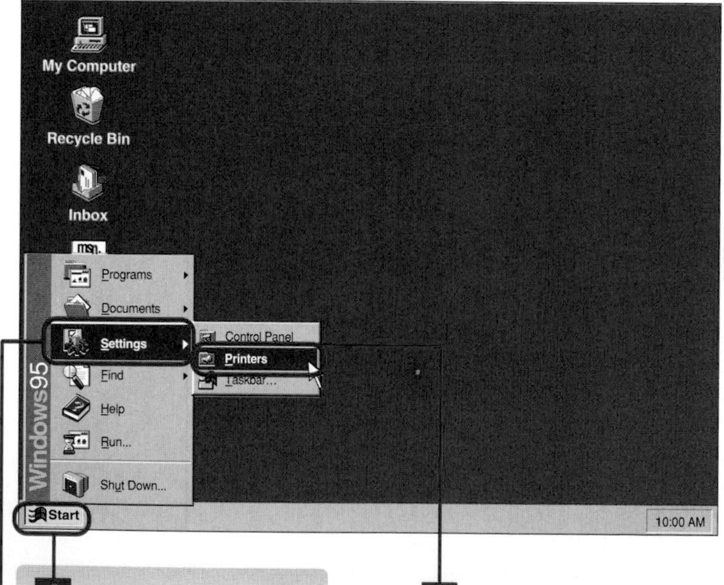

1 Move the mouse over **Start** and then press the left button.

2 Move the mouse over **Settings**.

3 Move the mouse over **Printers** and then press the left button.

■ The **Printers** window appears. It displays the printers you can use to print your documents.

4 Move the mouse over the printer you want to set as your default printer and then press the left button.

Tip
When selecting your default printer, choose the printer you use most often. Unless you specify another printer, your computer will automatically use the default printer.
DEFAULT

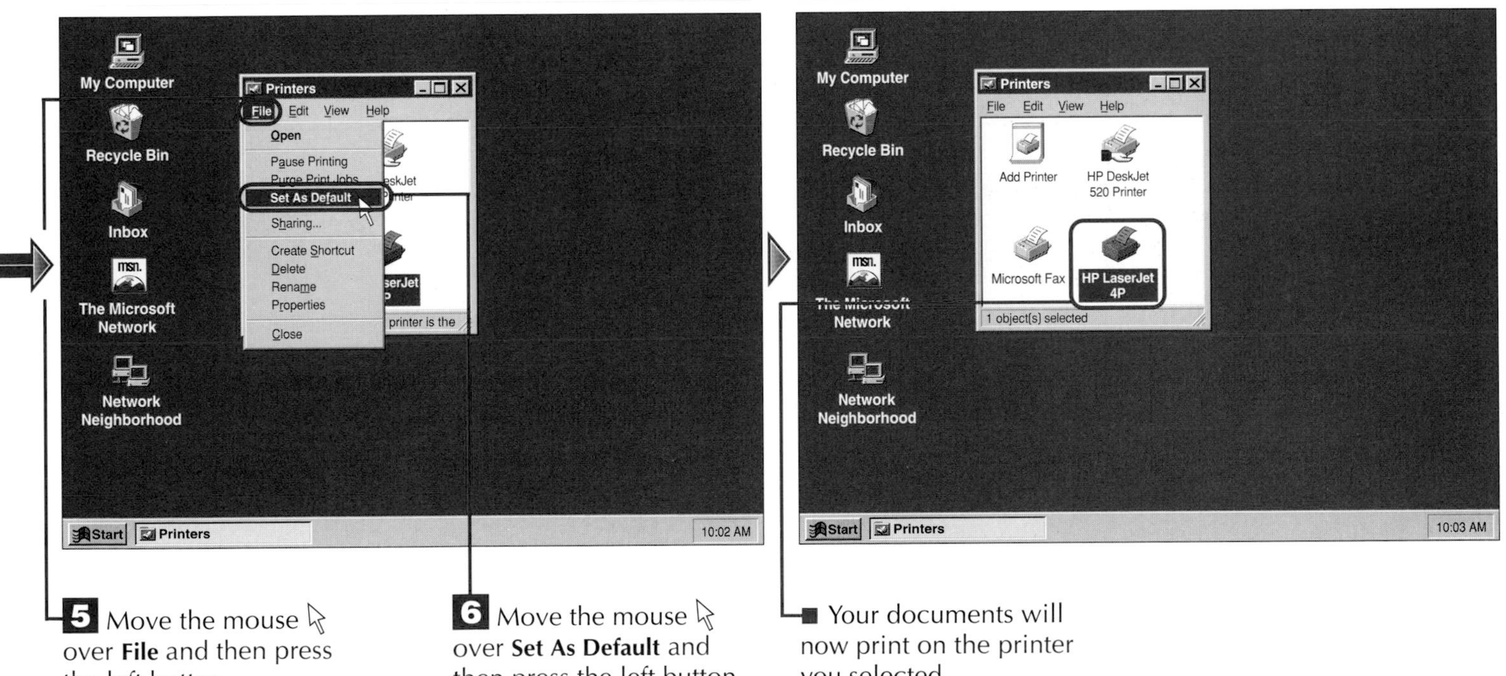

5 Move the mouse over **File** and then press the left button.

6 Move the mouse over **Set As Default** and then press the left button.

■ Your documents will now print on the printer you selected.

BROWSE THROUGH A NETWORK

You can easily browse through the information available on your network.

BROWSE THROUGH A NETWORK

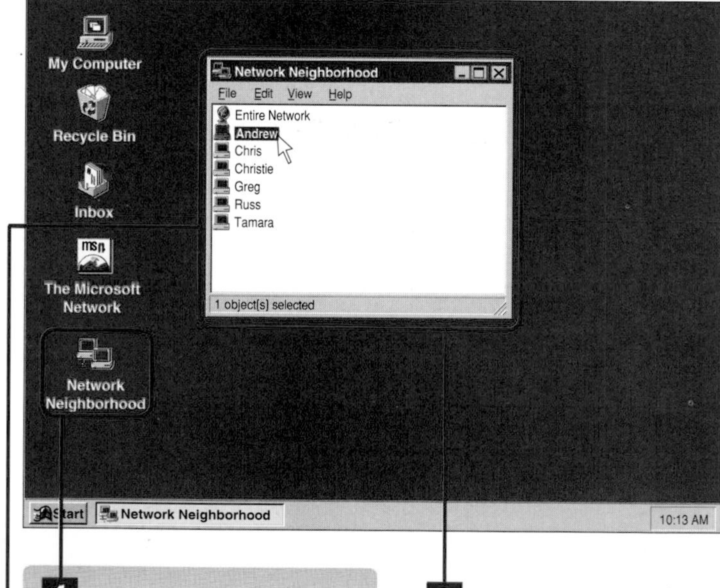

1 Move the mouse over **Network Neighborhood** and then quickly press the left button twice.

■ The **Network Neighborhood** window appears. This window displays all the computers and printers in your workgroup.

2 Move the mouse over the computer containing the files you want to work with and then quickly press the left button twice.

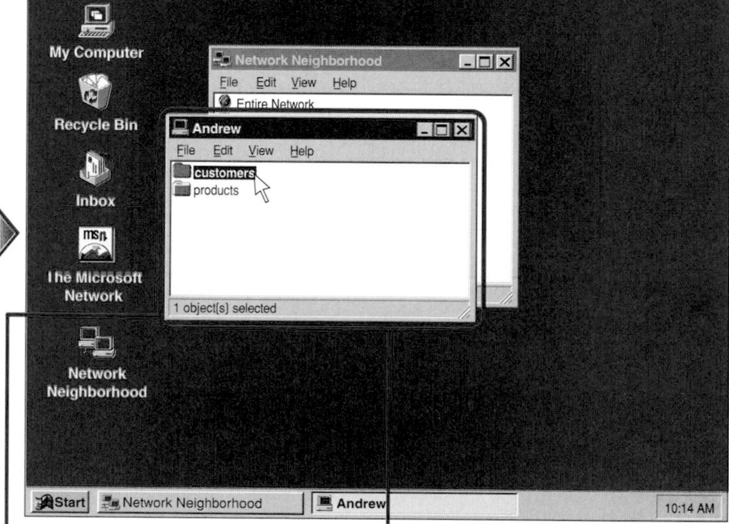

■ A list of the items shared by the computer appears.

3 Move the mouse over the folder containing the information you want to work with and then quickly press the left button twice.

Tip
My Computer
Recycle Bin
Inbox
The Microsoft Network
Network Neighborhood
Start
My Computer lets you browse through the contents of your own computer.
Network Neighborhood lets you browse through the contents of other computers on the network.

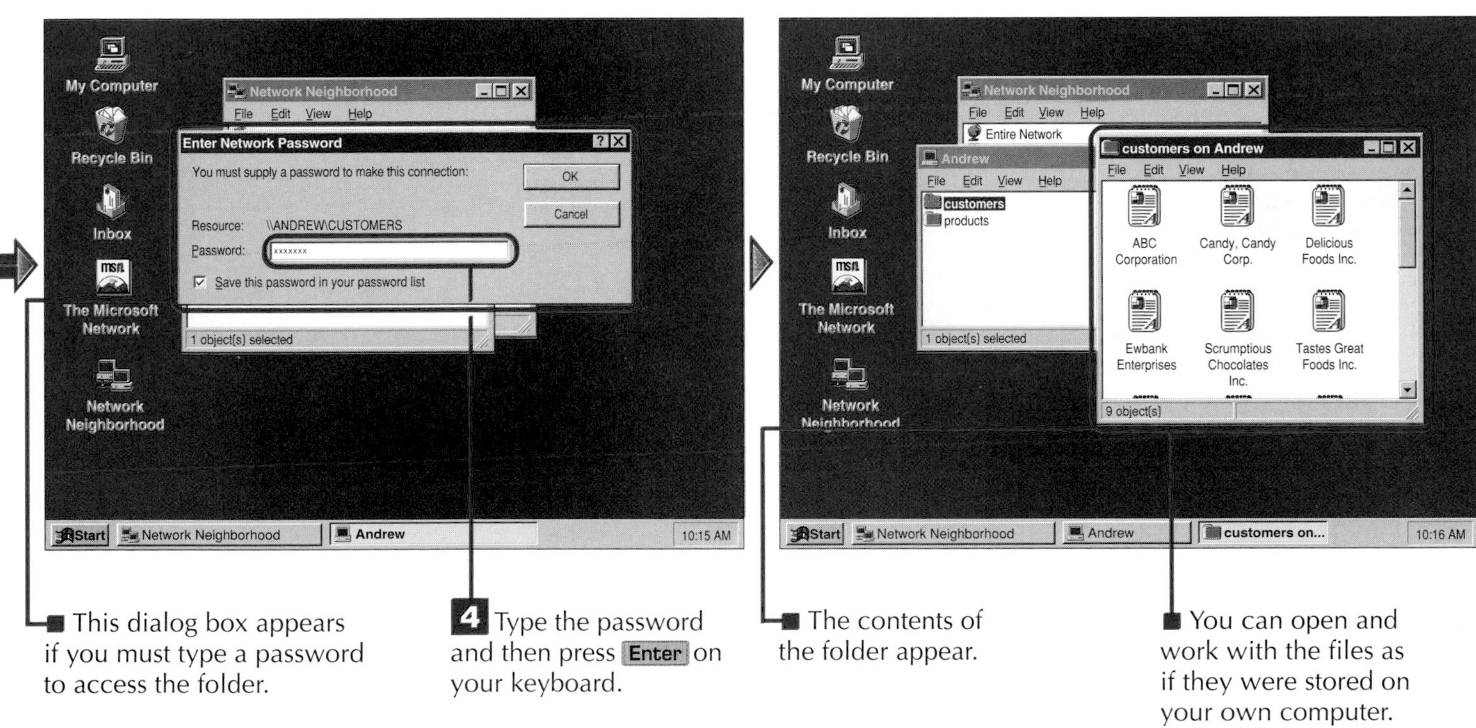

■ This dialog box appears if you must type a password to access the folder.

4 Type the password and then press **Enter** on your keyboard.

■ The contents of the folder appear.

■ You can open and work with the files as if they were stored on your own computer.

FIND A COMPUTER

You can quickly locate a computer on a network. This is especially useful if your network consists of hundreds of computers.

FIND A COMPUTER

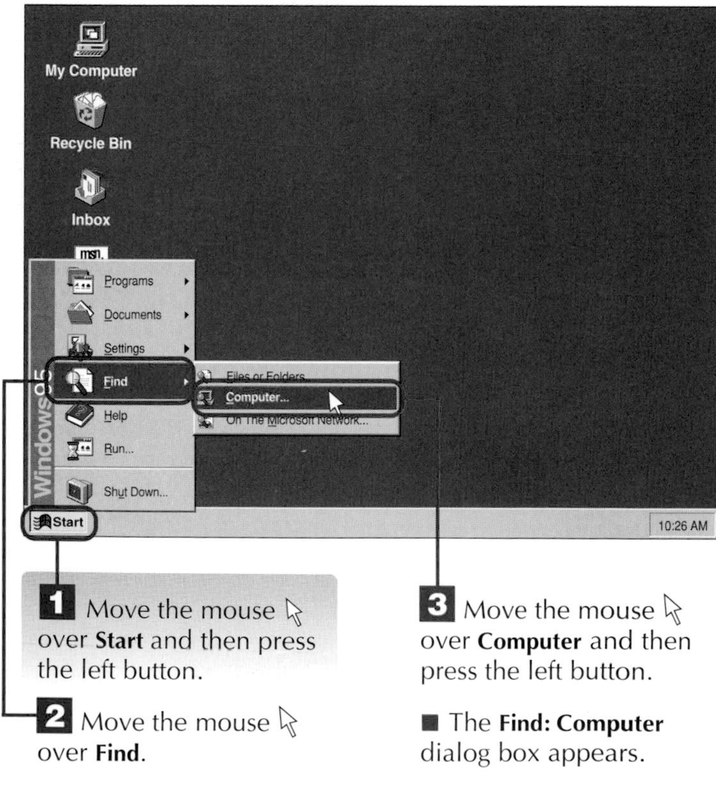

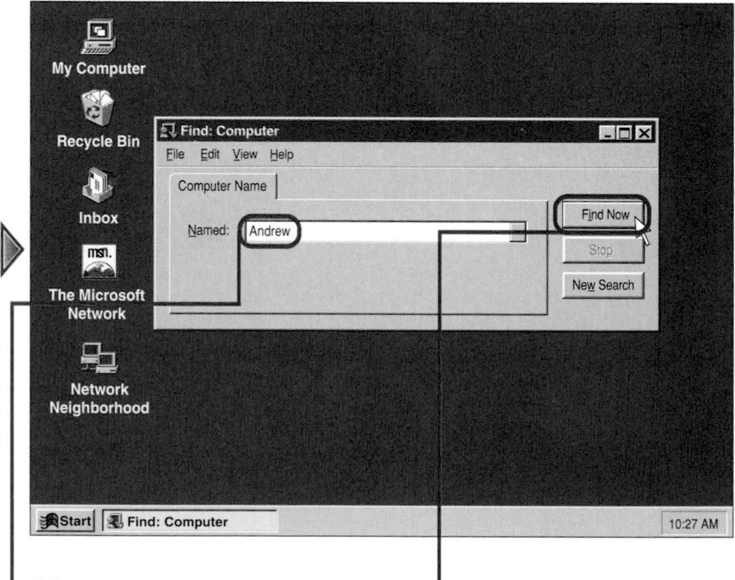

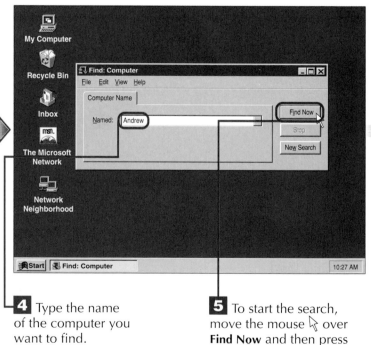

1 Move the mouse over **Start** and then press the left button.

2 Move the mouse over **Find**.

3 Move the mouse over **Computer** and then press the left button.

■ The **Find: Computer** dialog box appears.

4 Type the name of the computer you want to find.

5 To start the search, move the mouse over **Find Now** and then press the left button.

There are three ways to access information on a network.

- *Find the computer that stores the information you want to use, as discussed on page 182.*
- *Browse through the network using Network Neighborhood, as discussed on page 180.*
- *Map a network drive, as discussed on page 184.*

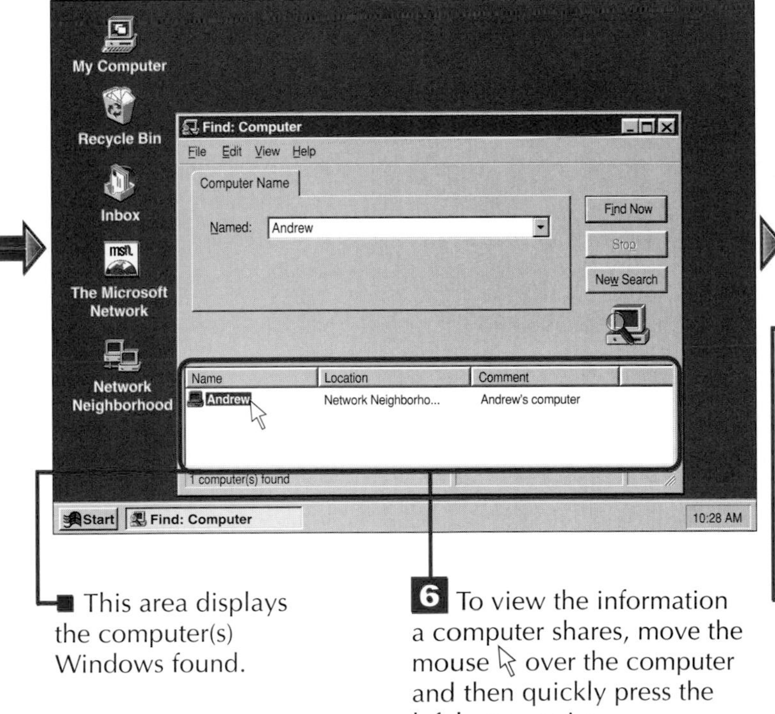

- This area displays the computer(s) Windows found.

6 To view the information a computer shares, move the mouse over the computer and then quickly press the left button twice.

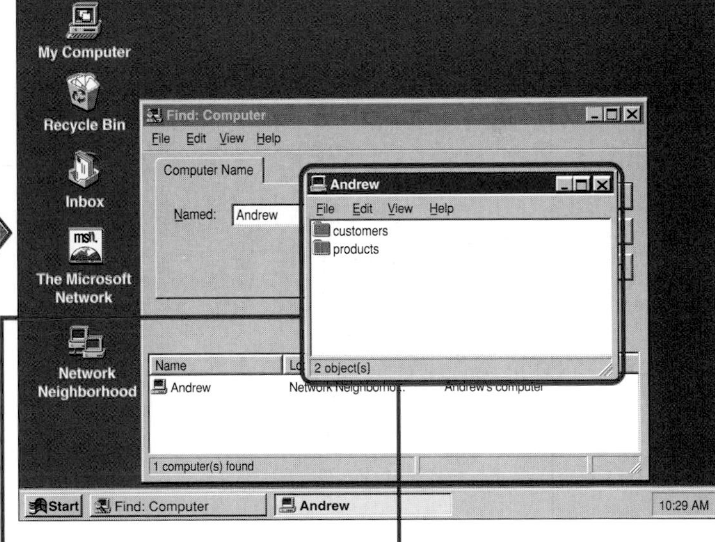

- A list of the items shared by the computer appears.

- You can open and work with the folders and files as if they were stored on your own computer.

Note: You may be asked to type a password to access some shared items.

MAP A NETWORK DRIVE

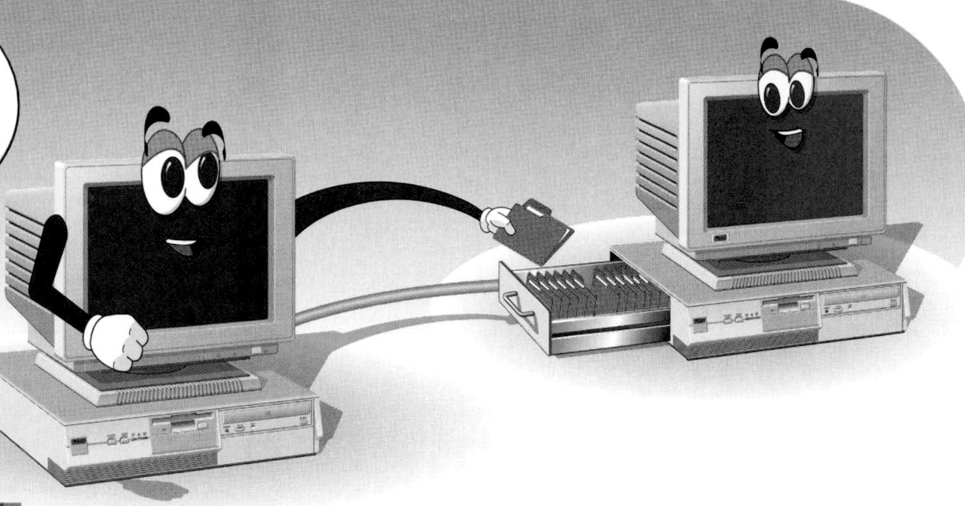

If you frequently use information stored on another computer, you can have Windows provide a quick way to access the information.

MAP A NETWORK DRIVE

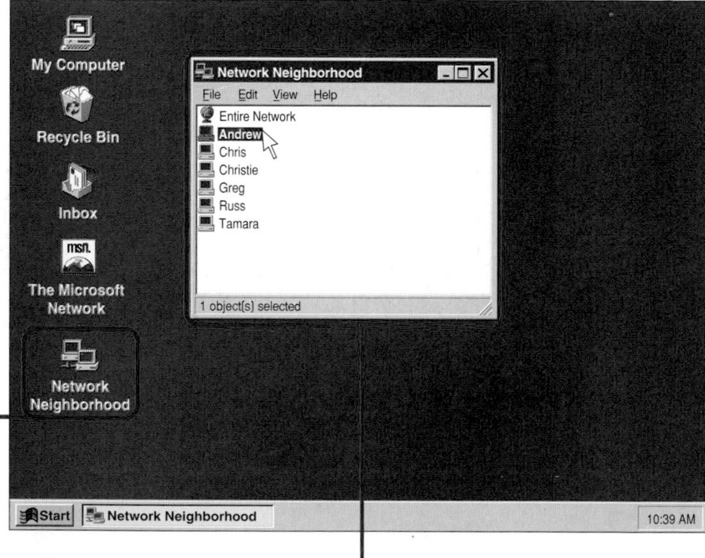

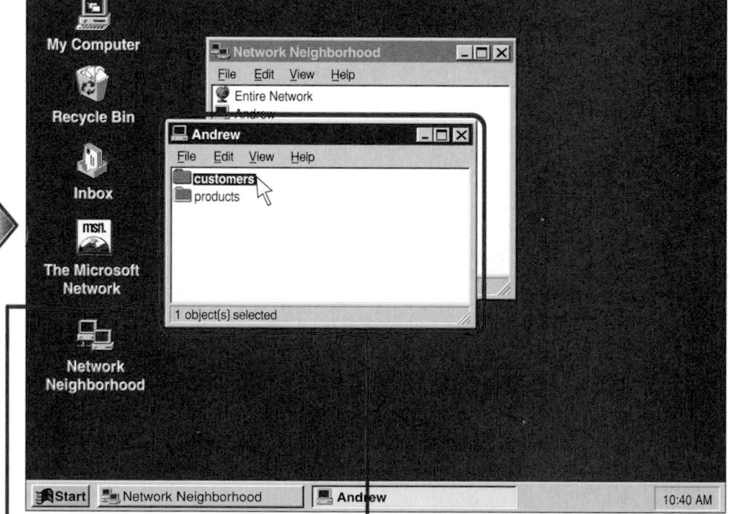

1 Move the mouse over **Network Neighborhood** and then quickly press the left button twice.

■ The **Network Neighborhood** window appears.

2 Move the mouse over the computer containing the information you want to be able to easily access and then quickly press the left button twice.

■ A list of the items shared by the computer appears.

3 Move the mouse over the folder you want to be able to easily access and then press the left button.

Tip

After you map (assign) a drive to a folder, the drive appears in the My Computer window.

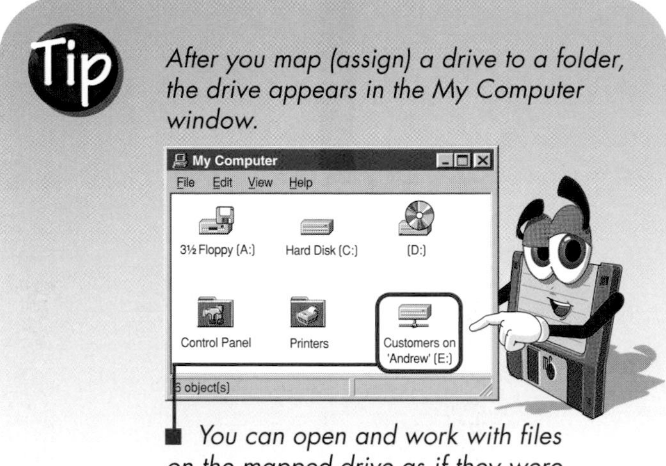

■ *You can open and work with files on the mapped drive as if they were stored on your own computer.*

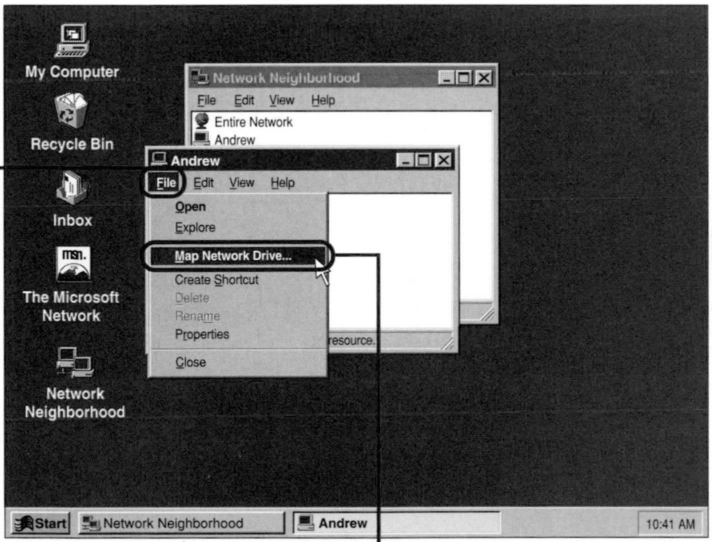

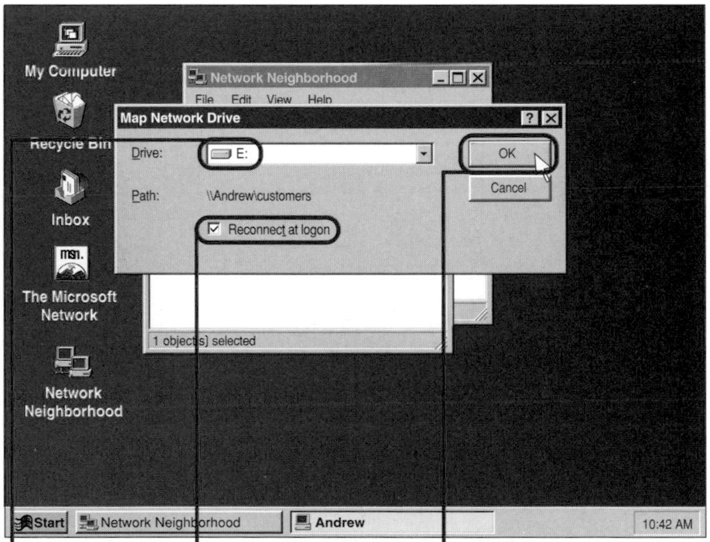

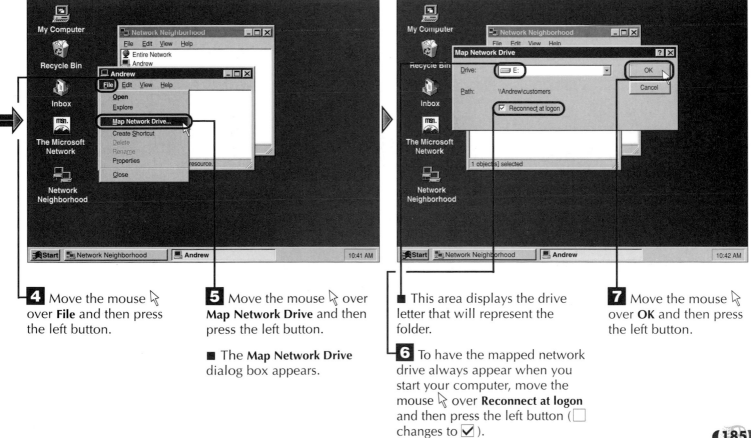

4 Move the mouse over **File** and then press the left button.

5 Move the mouse over **Map Network Drive** and then press the left button.

■ The **Map Network Drive** dialog box appears.

■ This area displays the drive letter that will represent the folder.

6 To have the mapped network drive always appear when you start your computer, move the mouse over **Reconnect at logon** and then press the left button (☐ changes to ☑).

7 Move the mouse over **OK** and then press the left button.

ABC Corp
Maxi

CHAPTER 11

DIAL-UP NETWORKING

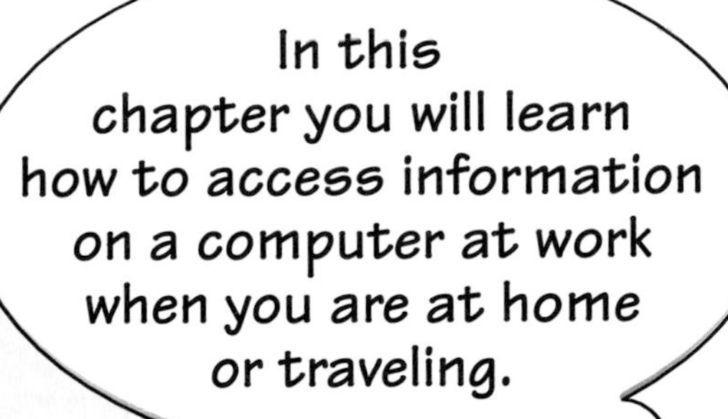
In this chapter you will learn how to access information on a computer at work when you are at home or traveling.

INTRODUCTION TO DIAL-UP NETWORKING

INTRODUCTION

When at home or traveling, you can use Dial-Up Networking to access information on a computer at work.

■ The computer you use to contact the office computer must have a modem.

Note: To install a modem, refer to page 104.

You can work with files stored on the office computer. You can also send and receive messages.

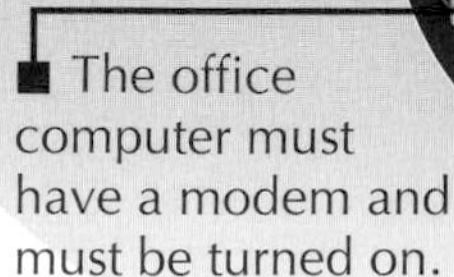

■ The office computer must have a modem and must be turned on.

SET UP OFFICE COMPUTER

Before you can dial in to an office computer, you must set up the computer.

To set up the office computer, you must buy the Microsoft Plus! package, which is available at computer stores.

SET UP OFFICE COMPUTER

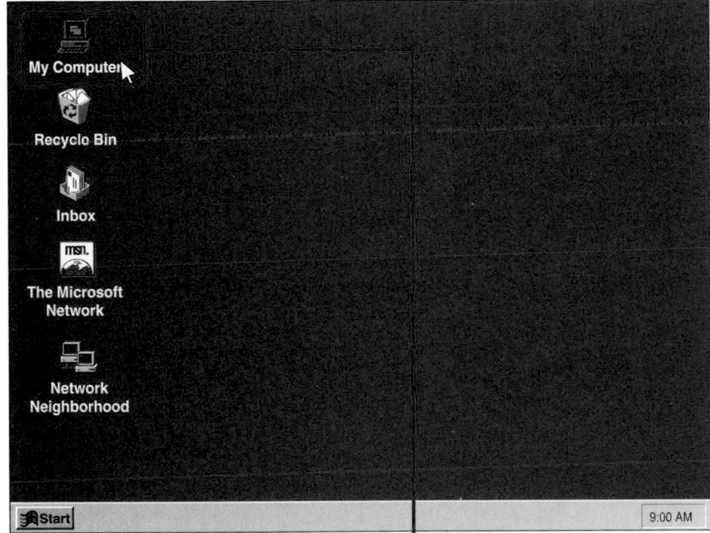

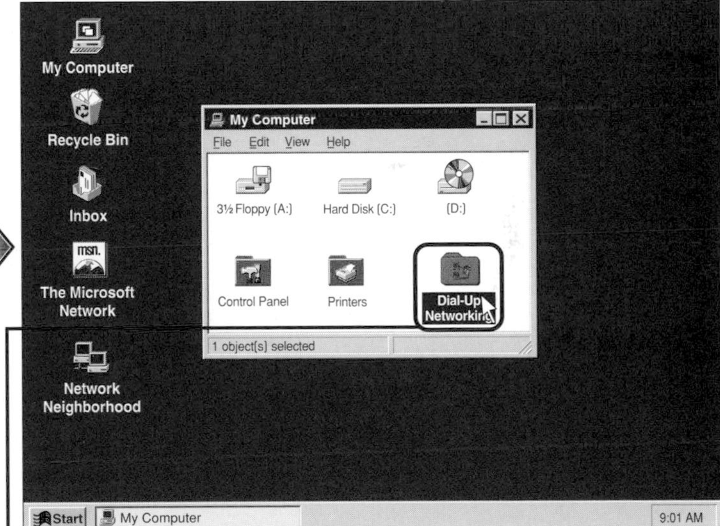

Perform the following steps on the office computer.

1 Move the mouse over **My Computer** and then quickly press the left button twice.

■ The **My Computer** window appears.

2 Move the mouse over **Dial-Up Networking** and then quickly press the left button twice.

*Note: If **Dial-Up Networking** is not available, you must add the Windows component, which is found in the Communications category. To do so, refer to page 96.*

*When you add Dial-Up Networking, you may be asked to provide a computer and workgroup name. For information on workgroups, refer to the **Tip** on page 171.*

SET UP OFFICE COMPUTER

You can assign a password so only those people who know the password can access information stored on the office computer.

SET UP OFFICE COMPUTER (CONTINUED)

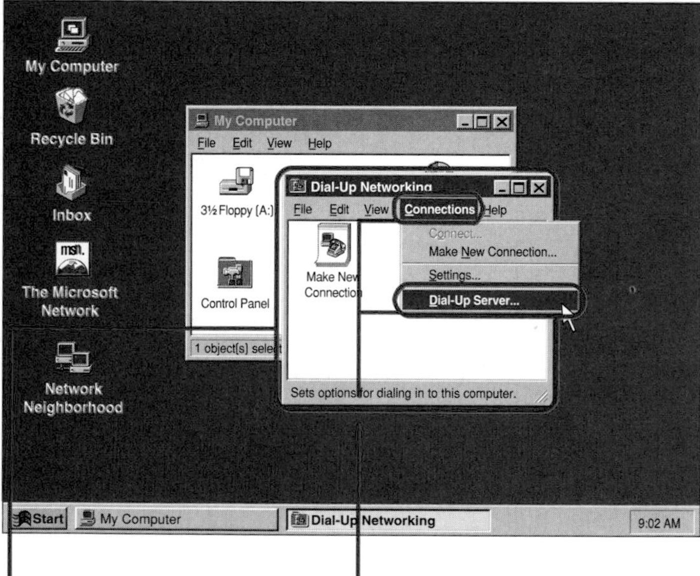

■ The **Dial-Up Networking** window appears.

*Note: If the **Welcome to Dial-Up Networking** or **Make New Connection** dialog box appears, press Esc on your keyboard to close the dialog box.*

3 Move the mouse over **Connections** and then press the left button.

4 Move the mouse over **Dial-Up Server** and then press the left button.

*Note: If **Dial-Up Server** is not available, you must install the Dial-Up Networking Server component from the Microsoft Plus! package.*

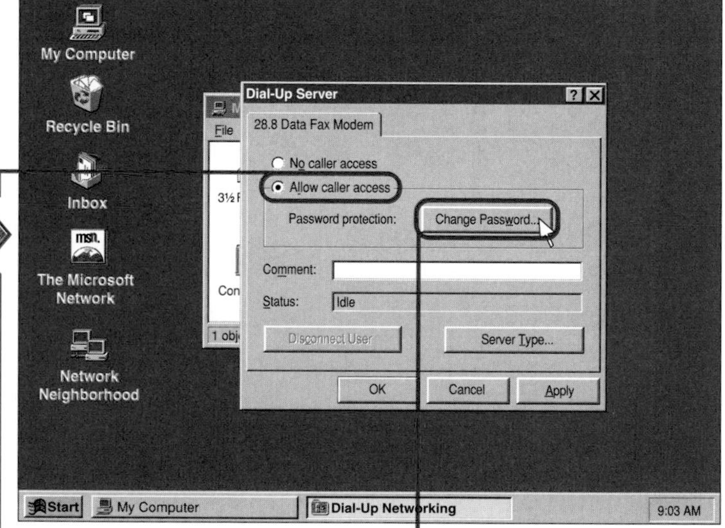

■ The **Dial-Up Server** dialog box appears.

5 Move the mouse over **Allow caller access** and then press the left button (○ changes to ◉).

6 To assign a password, move the mouse over **Change Password** and then press the left button.

IMPORTANT

When you dial in to an office computer, you can only access information shared by the computer.

■ To turn on file and printer sharing on the office computer, refer to page 167.

■ To specify what information you want the office computer to share, refer to page 172.

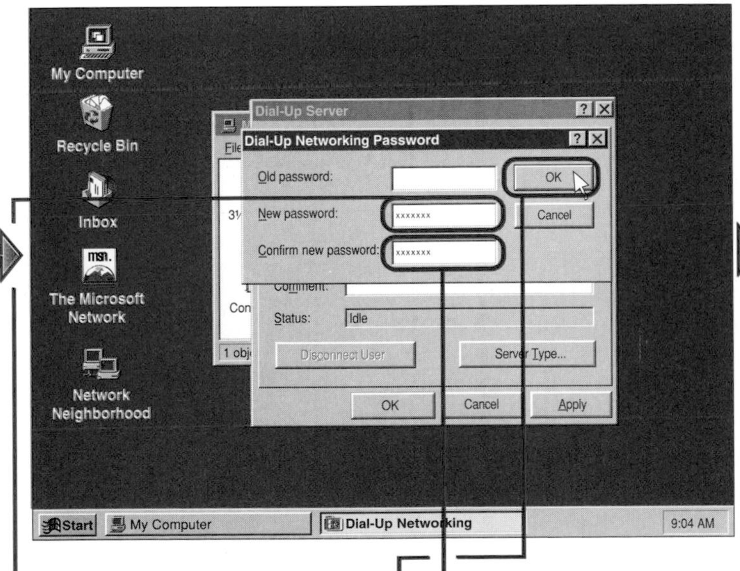

■ A dialog box appears.

7 Move the mouse over this area and then press the left button. Then type a password.

8 Press Tab on your keyboard. Then type the password again.

9 Move the mouse over **OK** and then press the left button.

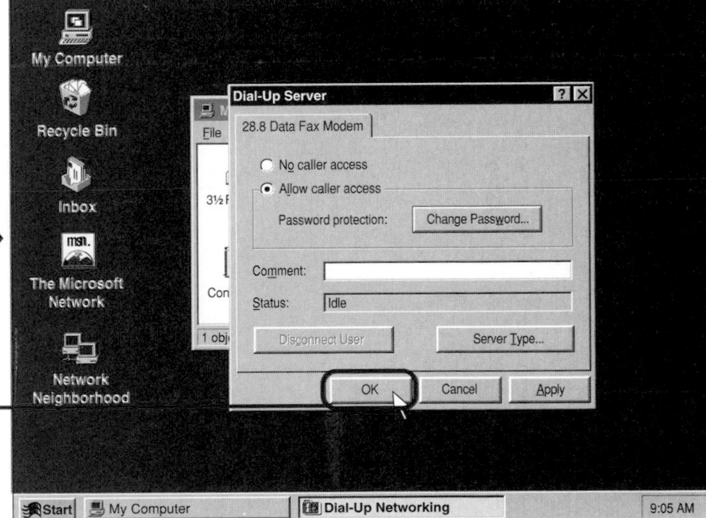

10 Move the mouse over **OK** and then press the left button.

Note: To set up the connection to the office computer, refer to page 192.

SET UP CONNECTION TO OFFICE COMPUTER

SET UP CONNECTION TO OFFICE COMPUTER

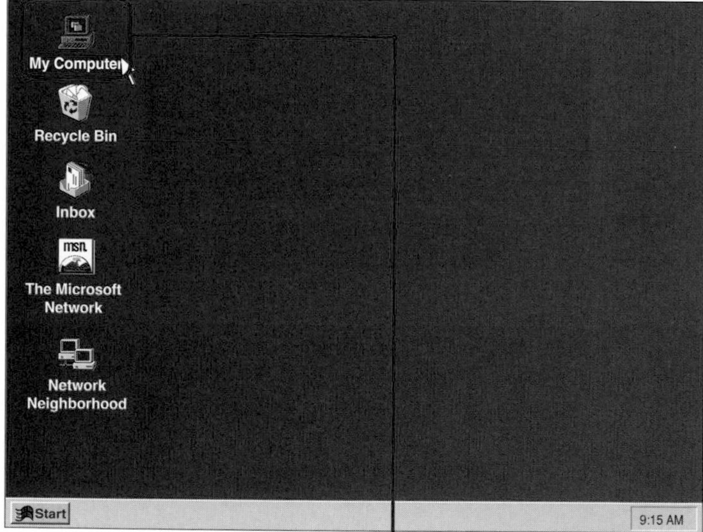

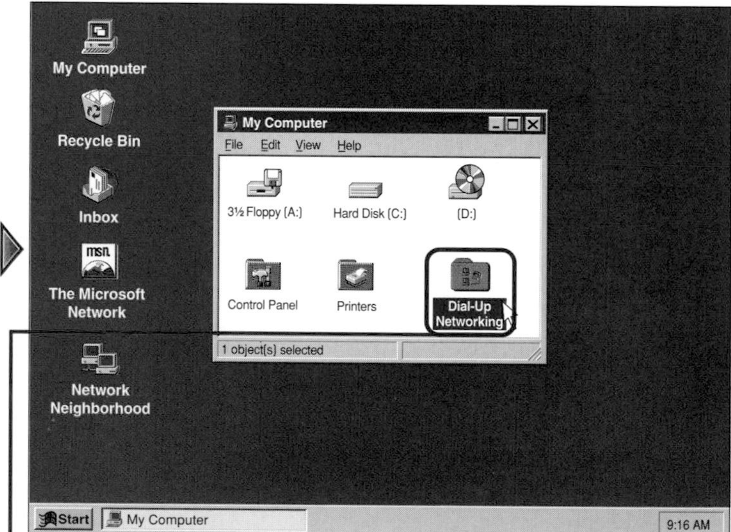

Perform the following steps on your home or portable computer.

1 Move the mouse over **My Computer** and then quickly press the left button twice.

■ The **My Computer** window appears.

2 Move the mouse over **Dial-Up Networking** and then quickly press the left button twice.

*Note: If **Dial-Up Networking** is not available, you must add the Windows component, which is found in the Communications category. To do so, refer to page 96.*

*When you add Dial-Up Networking, you may be asked to provide a computer and workgroup name. For information on workgroups, refer to the **Tip** on page 171.*

IMPORTANT
To use Dial-Up Networking, both the office computer and the computer you use when at home or traveling must have a modem. The office computer must also be turned on.

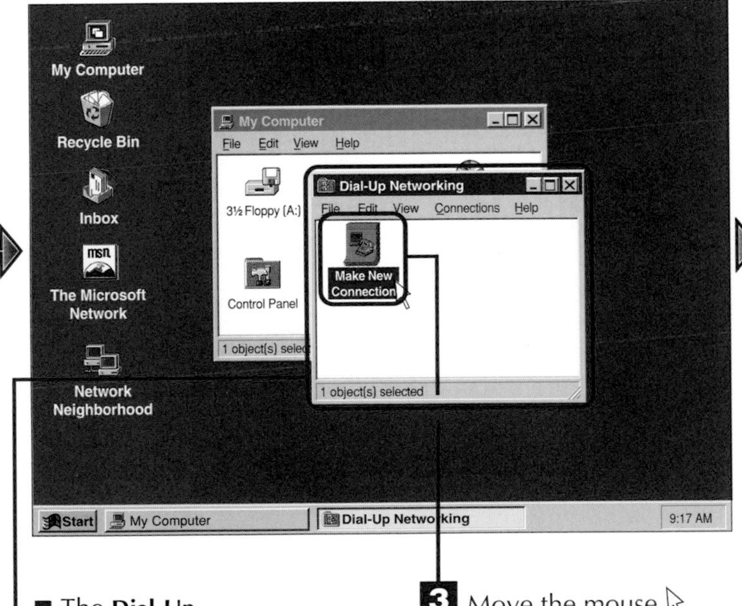

■ The **Dial-Up Networking** window appears.

*Note: If the **Welcome to Dial-Up Networking** dialog box appears, press Esc on your keyboard to close the dialog box. If the **Make New Connection** dialog box appears, skip to step 4.*

3 Move the mouse over **Make New Connection** and then quickly press the left button twice.

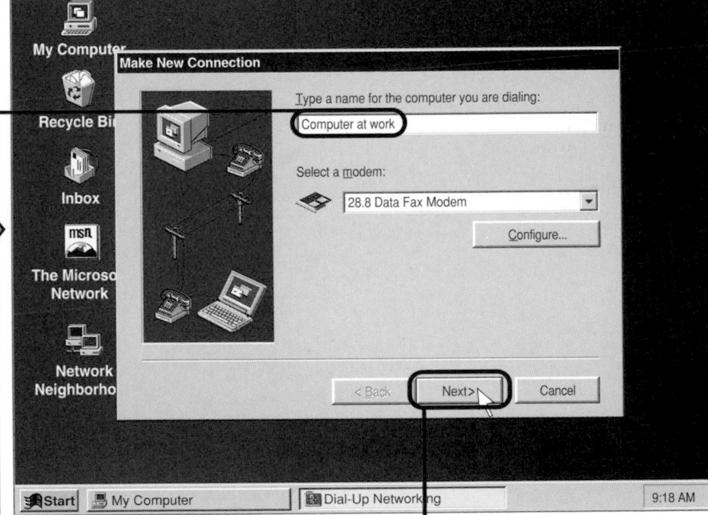

■ The **Make New Connection** dialog box appears.

4 Type a name for the computer you want to contact.

5 Move the mouse over **Next** and then press the left button.

SET UP CONNECTION TO OFFICE COMPUTER

Windows will store the information you enter about the office computer. This will help you quickly connect to the computer later on.

SET UP CONNECTION TO OFFICE COMPUTER (CONTINUED)

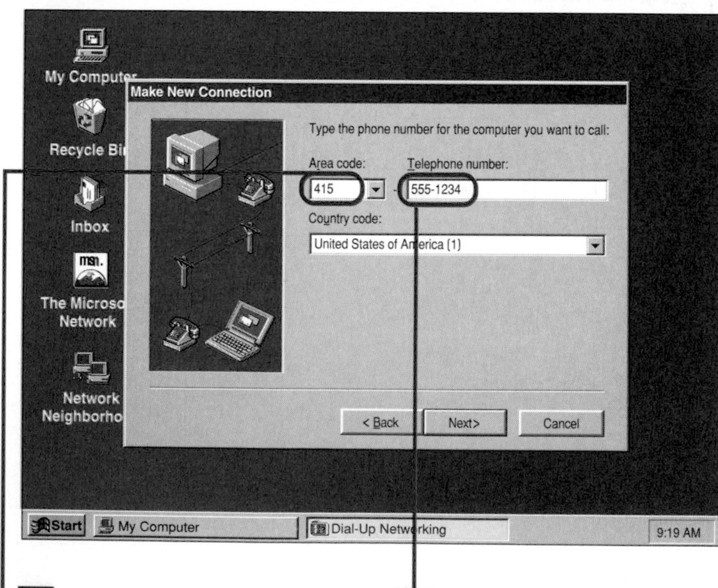

6 Type the area code for the computer you want to contact.

7 Press **Tab** on your keyboard. Then type the telephone number.

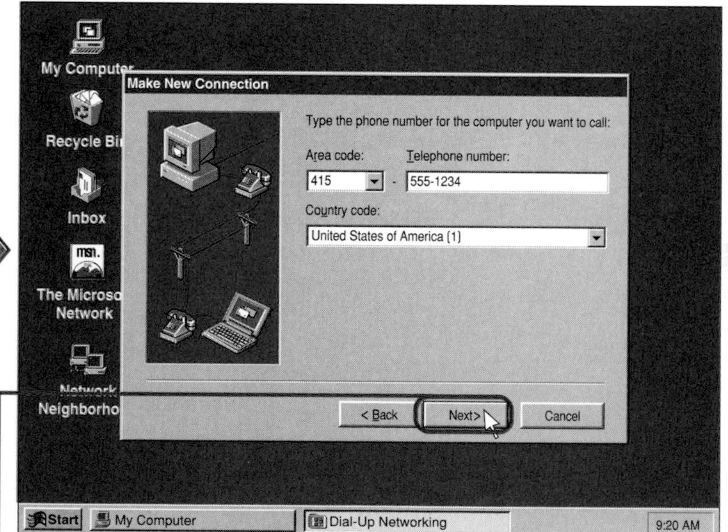

8 Move the mouse over **Next** and then press the left button.

You only need to set up a connection to an office computer once. After the connection is set up, you can dial in to the computer at any time. To do so, refer to page 196.

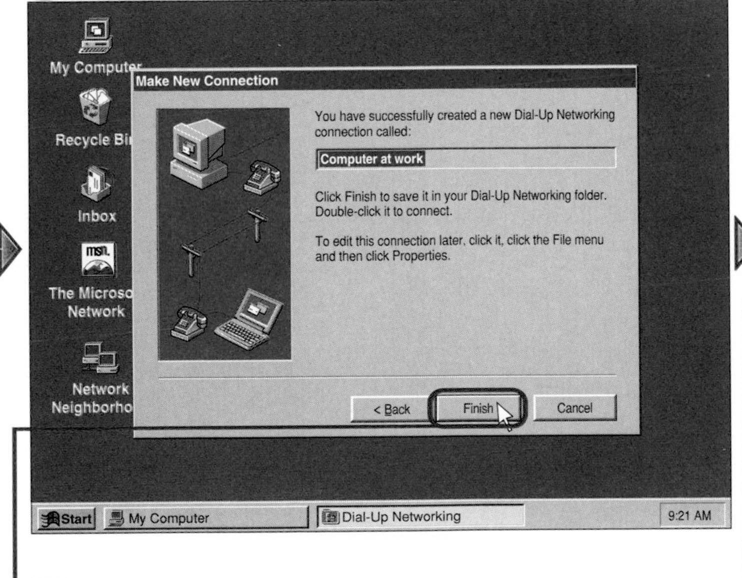

9 Move the mouse over **Finish** and then press the left button.

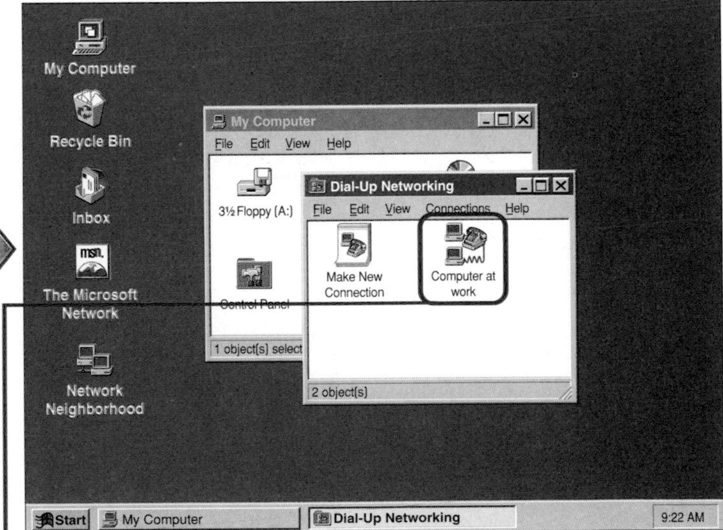

■ An icon appears for the connection you set up.

Note: To use this icon to connect to the office computer, refer to page 196.

DIAL IN TO OFFICE COMPUTER

DIAL IN TO OFFICE COMPUTER

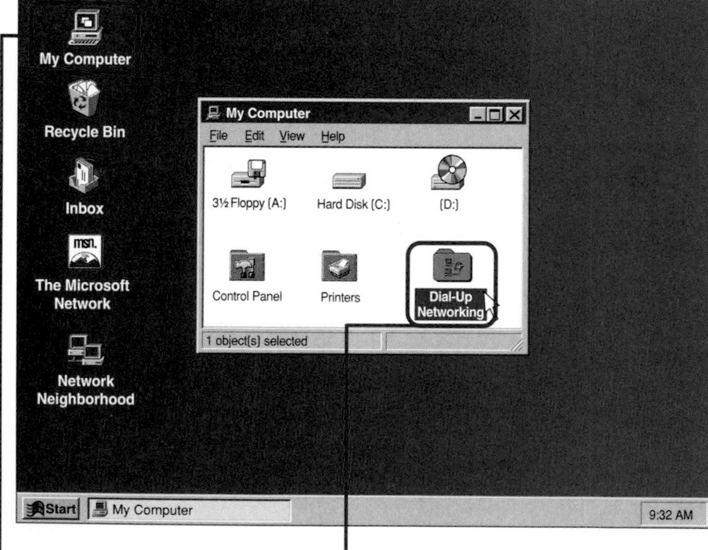

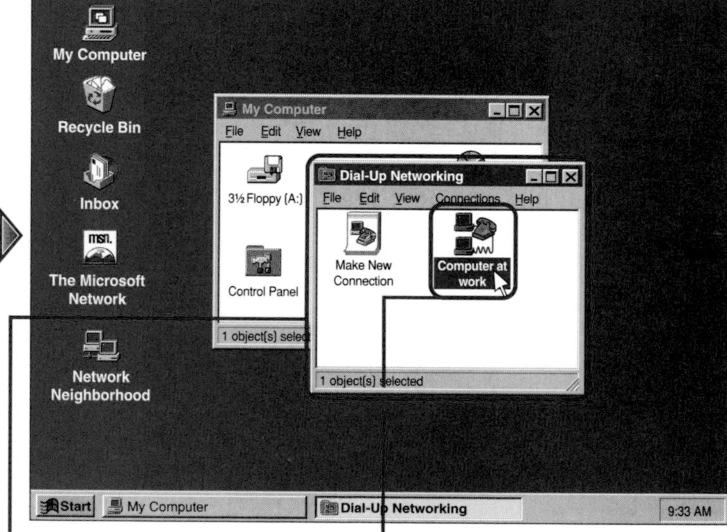

1 Move the mouse over **My Computer** and then quickly press the left button twice.

■ The **My Computer** window appears.

2 Move the mouse over **Dial-Up Networking** and then quickly press the left button twice.

■ The **Dial-Up Networking** window appears, displaying an icon for each connection you have set up.

Note: To set up a connection, refer to page 192.

3 To connect to a computer, move the mouse over the icon for the computer and then quickly press the left button twice.

■ The **Connect To** dialog box appears.

Tip

Connecting to an office computer lets you access information you need while away from the office. You can update files, exchange electronic mail, send faxes and access information on a network as if you were directly connected to the office computer.

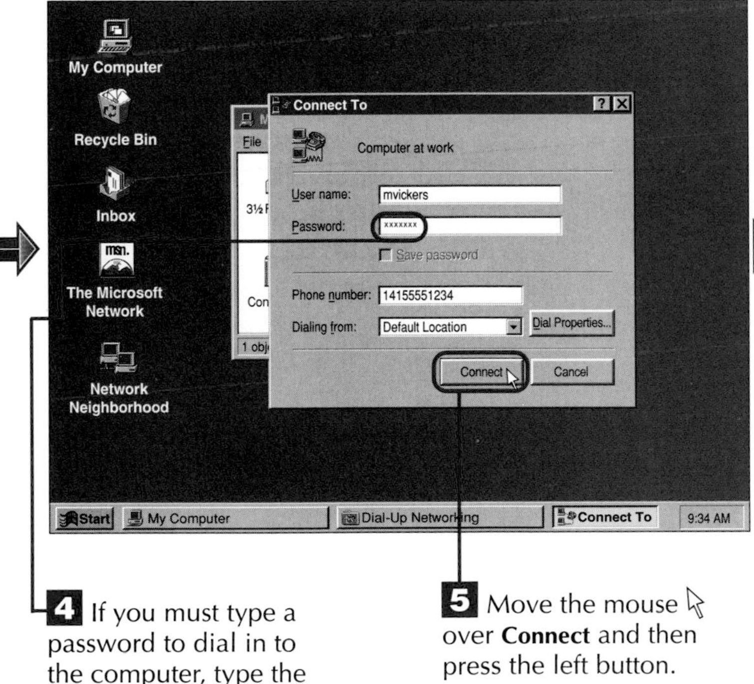

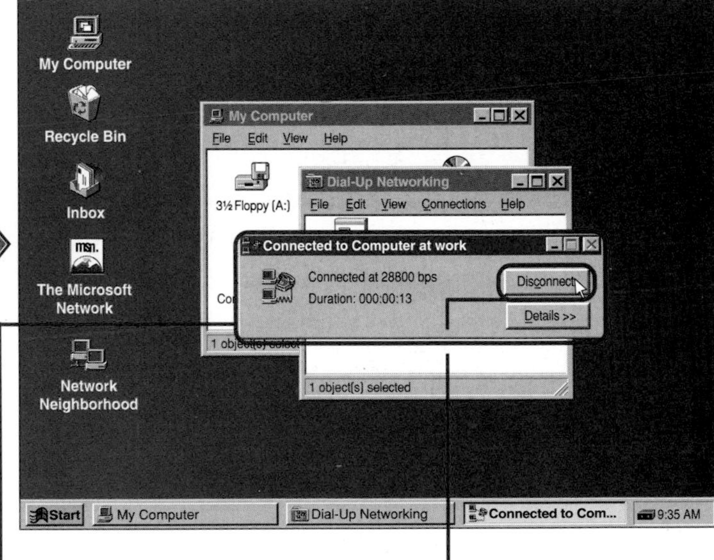

4 If you must type a password to dial in to the computer, type the password.

5 Move the mouse over **Connect** and then press the left button.

■ This dialog box appears when you are successfully connected to the office computer.

■ You can use the Find feature to display the files shared by the office computer. For more information, refer to page 182.

6 To disconnect, move the mouse over **Disconnect** and then press the left button.

In this chapter you will learn how to directly connect two computers to share information.
HOST

CHAPTER 12

DIRECT CABLE CONNECTION

Set Up Direct Cable Connection

Re-Establish Direct Cable Connection

SET UP DIRECT CABLE CONNECTION

You can use a special cable to directly connect two computers to share information.

Guest

The guest is a computer that can access information on the host and the network attached to the host.

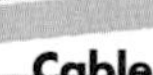

Cable

Make sure you plug the cable into both computers before performing the steps below. You can buy the required cable at most computer stores.

SET UP DIRECT CABLE CONNECTION

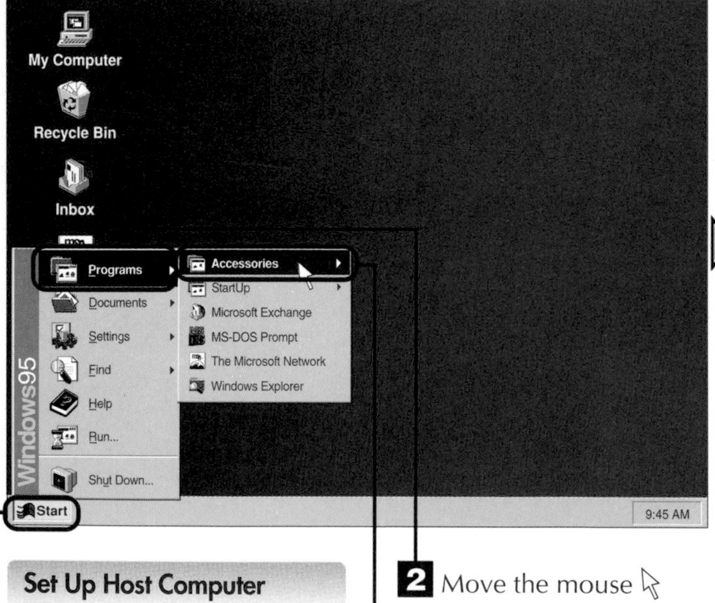

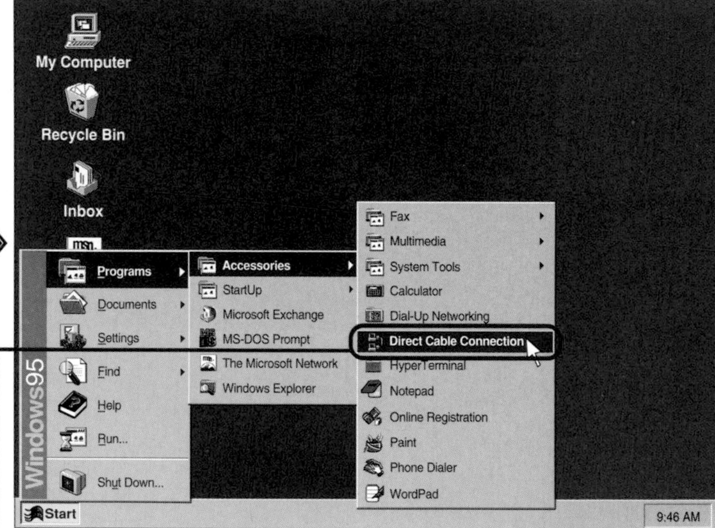

Set Up Host Computer

1 On the host computer, move the mouse over **Start** and then press the left button.

2 Move the mouse over **Programs**.

3 Move the mouse over **Accessories**.

4 Move the mouse over **Direct Cable Connection** and then press the left button.

*Note: If **Direct Cable Connection** is not available, you must add the Windows component, which is found in the Communications category. To do so, refer to page 96.*

*When you add Direct Cable Connection, you may be asked to provide a computer and workgroup name. For information on workgroups, refer to the **Tip** on page 171.*

Host

The host is a computer that provides information. Make sure the host is set up to share the information the guest wants to access.

■ To turn on sharing on the host computer, refer to page 167.

■ To specify what information you want the host computer to share, refer to page 172.

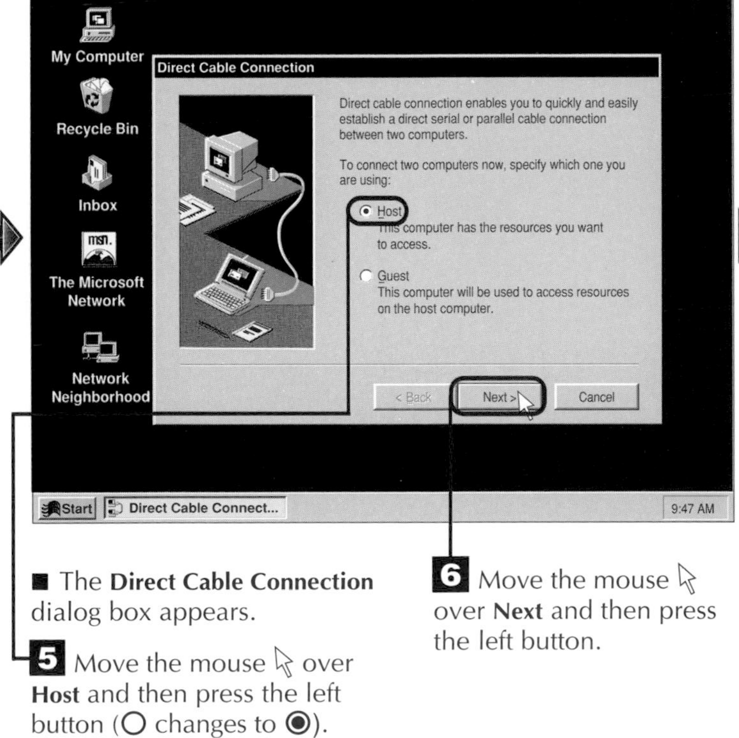

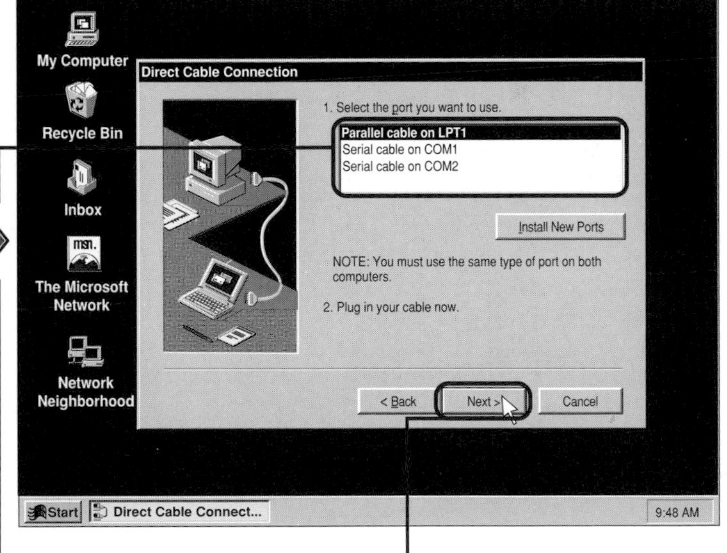

■ The **Direct Cable Connection** dialog box appears.

5 Move the mouse over **Host** and then press the left button (○ changes to ◉).

6 Move the mouse over **Next** and then press the left button.

7 Move the mouse over the port the cable plugs into and then press the left button.

8 Move the mouse over **Next** and then press the left button.

SET UP DIRECT CABLE CONNECTION

You must set up both the host and guest computers before the computers can exchange information.
HOST
GUEST

SET UP DIRECT CABLE CONNECTION (CONTINUED)

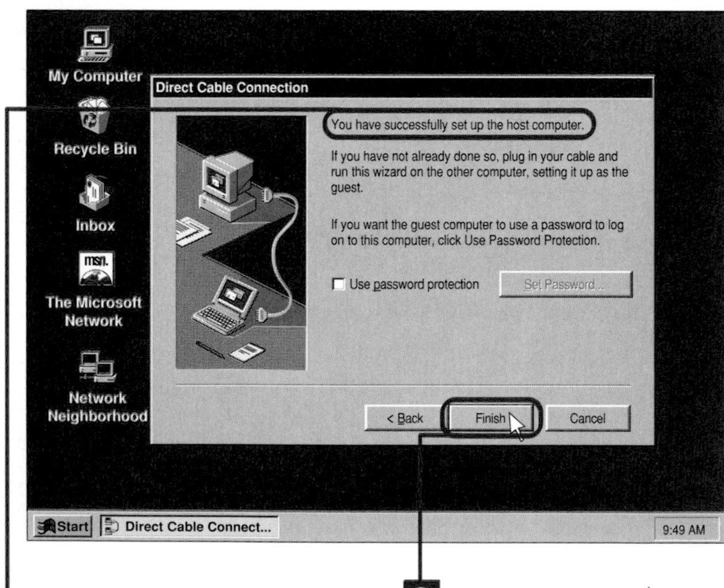

■ This message appears when you finish setting up the host computer.

9 Move the mouse over **Finish** and then press the left button.

■ A dialog box appears, telling you the status of the connection.

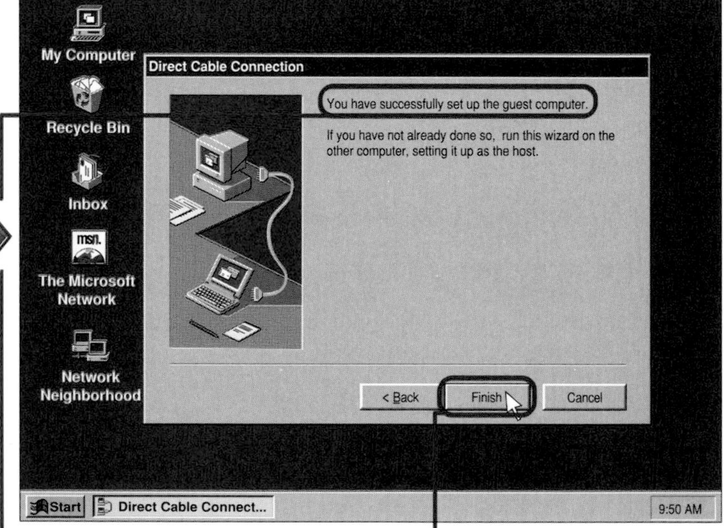

Set Up Guest Computer

1 On the guest computer, perform steps **1** to **8** starting on page 200, selecting **Guest** in step **5**.

■ This message appears when you finish setting up the guest computer.

2 To connect the guest and host computers, move the mouse over **Finish** and then press the left button.

You only need to set up a direct cable connection between two computers once. After you set up a connection, you can easily reconnect the computers at any time. For more information, refer to page 204.

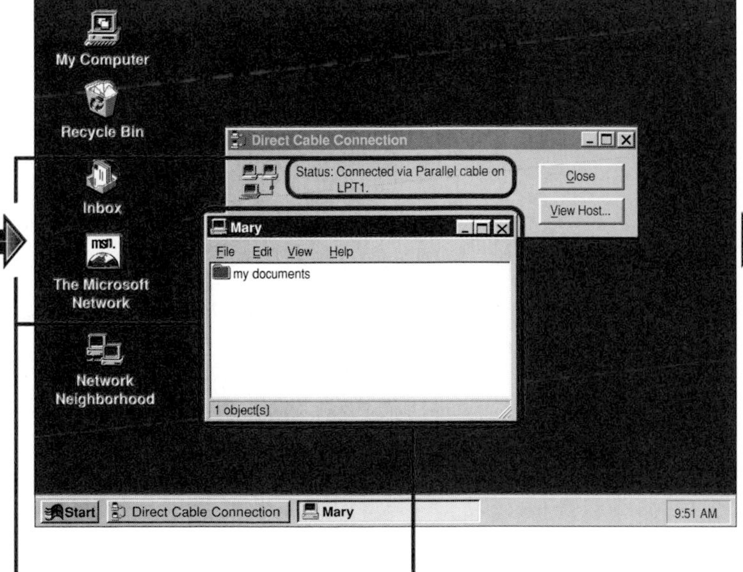

■ This message appears when the computers are successfully connected.

■ A window also appears, displaying the items shared by the host computer.

■ You can open and work with the folders and files in the window as if the information were stored on the guest computer.

Note: To access information on a network connected to a host, you can use the Find feature to find a computer. To do so, refer to page 182.

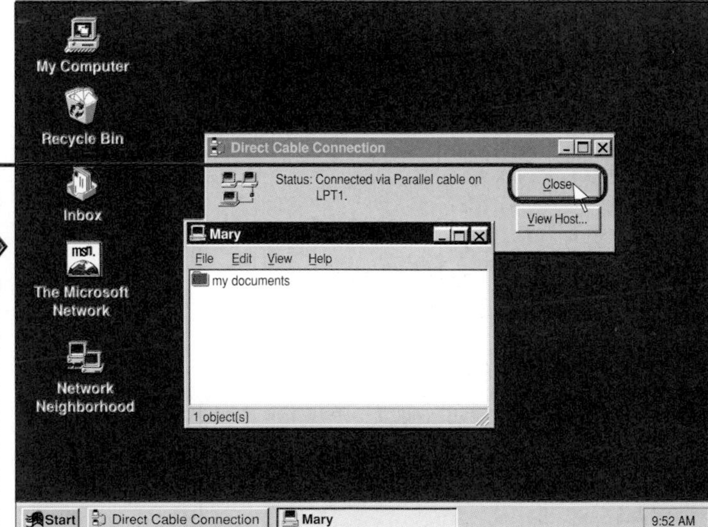

Close the Connection

1 Move the mouse over **Close** and then press the left button.

RE-ESTABLISH DIRECT CABLE CONNECTION

Once you set up a direct cable connection between two computers, you can quickly exchange information at any time.
maranGraphics

RE-ESTABLISH DIRECT CABLE CONNECTION

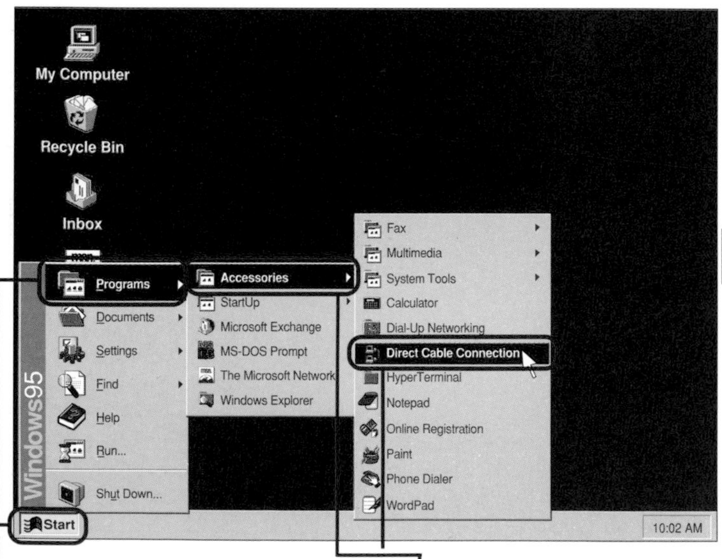

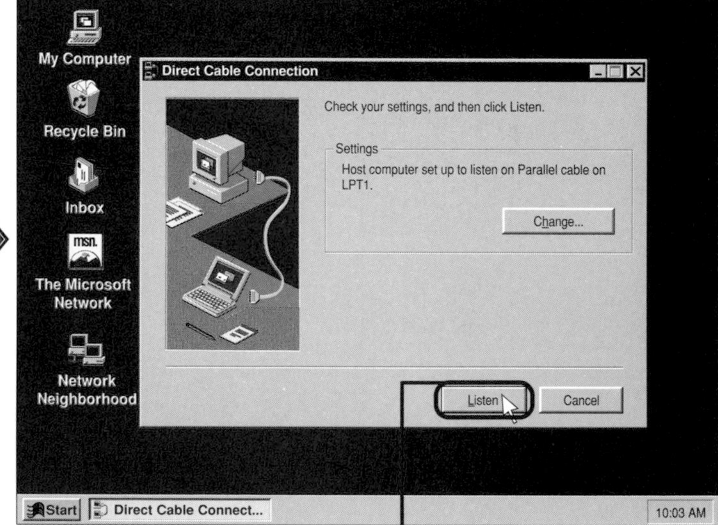

On Host Computer

1 On the host computer, move the mouse over **Start** and then press the left button.

2 Move the mouse over **Programs**.

3 Move the mouse over **Accessories**.

4 Move the mouse over **Direct Cable Connection** and then press the left button.

■ The **Direct Cable Connection** dialog box appears.

5 Move the mouse over **Listen** and then press the left button.

■ A dialog box appears, telling you the status of the connection.

You can use Direct Cable Connection to transfer files from your office computer to a portable computer. This lets you use office files when traveling or at home.

If you want the files to update automatically when you return to the office, use the Briefcase feature.

Note: For information on the Briefcase feature, refer to page 154.

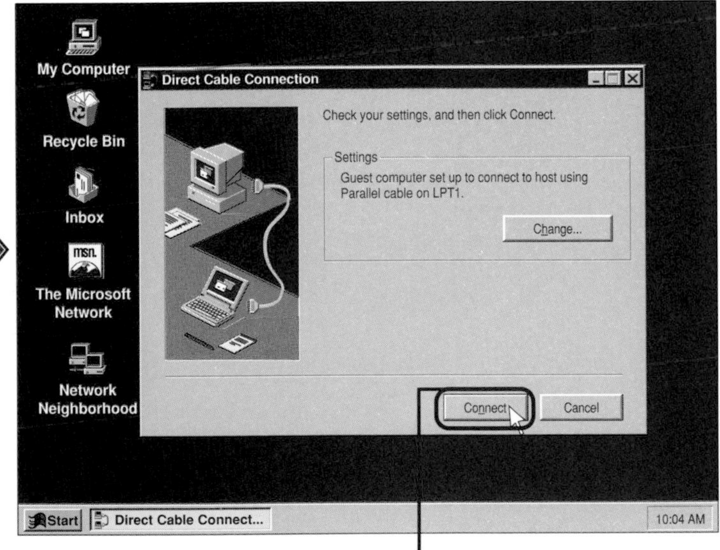

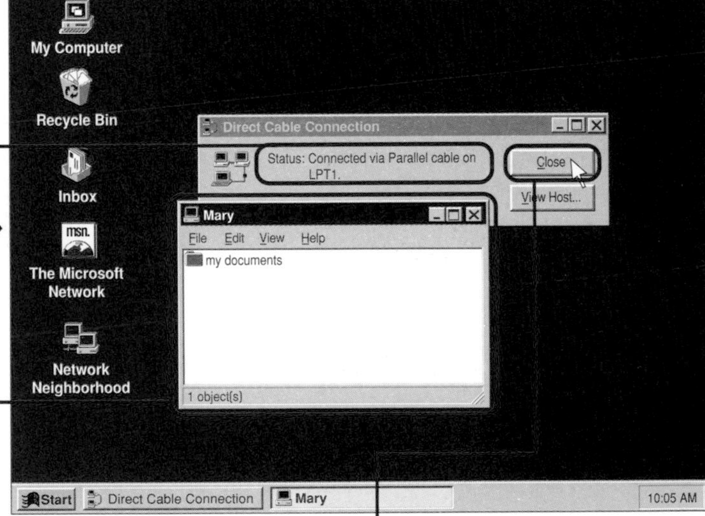

On Guest Computer

1 On the guest computer, perform steps **1** to **4** on page 204.

■ The **Direct Cable Connection** dialog box appears.

2 Move the mouse over **Connect** and then press the left button.

■ This message appears when the computers are successfully connected.

■ A window also appears, displaying the items shared by the host computer. You can open and work with the folders and files in the window as if the information were stored on the guest computer.

Close the Connection

1 Move the mouse over **Close** and then press the left button.

INDEX

D

E

INDEX

INDEX

O

P

R

S

T

V

W

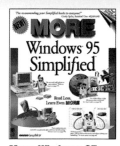

DUMMIES PRESS

The fun & easy way to learn about computers and more!

Windows 3.1 For Dummies,™ 2nd Edition
by Andy Rathbone

ISBN: 1-56884-182-5
$16.95 USA/$22.95 Canada

MORE Windows For Dummies™
by Andy Rathbone

ISBN: 1-56884-048-9
$19.95 USA/$26.95 Canada

DOS For Dummies,® 2nd Edition
by Dan Gookin

ISBN: 1-878058-75-4
$16.95 USA/$22.95 Canada

The Internet For Dummies™
by John Levine & Carol Baroudi

ISBN: 1-56884-024-1
$19.95 USA/$26.95 Canada

Personal Finance For Dummies™
by Eric Tyson

ISBN: 1-56884-150-7
$16.95 USA/$22.95 Canada

PCs For Dummies,™ 2nd Edition
by Dan Gookin & Andy Rathbone

ISBN: 1-56884-078-0
$16.95 USA/$22.95 Canada

Macs For Dummies,™ 2nd Edition
by David Pogue

ISBN: 1-56884-051-9
$19.95 USA/$26.95 Canada

Here's a complete listing of IDG's...*For Dummies* Titles

Title	Author	ISBN #	Price
DATABASE			
Access 2 For Dummies™	by Scott Palmer	ISBN: 1-56884-090-X	$19.95 USA/$26.95 Canada
Access Programming For Dummies™	by Rob Krumm	ISBN: 1-56884-091-8	$19.95 USA/$26.95 Canada
Approach 3 For Windows For Dummies™	by Doug Lowe	ISBN: 1-56884-233-3	$19.99 USA/$26.99 Canada
dBASE For DOS For Dummies™	by Scott Palmer & Michael Stabler	ISBN: 1-56884-188-4	$19.95 USA/$26.95 Canada
dBASE For Windows For Dummies™	by Scott Palmer	ISBN: 1-56884-179-5	$19.95 USA/$26.95 Canada
dBASE 5 For Windows Programming For Dummies™	by Ted Coombs & Jason Coombs	ISBN: 1-56884-215-5	$19.99 USA/$26.99 Canada
FoxPro 2.6 For Windows For Dummies™	by John Kaufeld	ISBN: 1-56884-187-6	$19.95 USA/$26.95 Canada
Paradox 5 For Windows For Dummies™	by John Kaufeld	ISBN: 1-56884-185-X	$19.95 USA/$26.95 Canada
DESKTOP PUBLISHING/ILLUSTRATION/GRAPHICS			
CorelDRAW! 5 For Dummies™	by Deke McClelland	ISBN: 1-56884-157-4	$19.95 USA/$26.95 Canada
CorelDRAW! For Dummies™	by Deke McClelland	ISBN: 1-56884-042-X	$19.95 USA/$26.95 Canada
Harvard Graphics 2 For Windows For Dummies™	by Roger C. Parker	ISBN: 1-56884-092-6	$19.95 USA/$26.95 Canada
PageMaker 5 For Macs For Dummies™	by Galen Gruman & Deke McClelland	ISBN: 1-56884-178-7	$19.95 USA/$26.95 Canada
PageMaker 5 For Windows For Dummies™	by Deke McClelland & Galen Gruman	ISBN: 1-56884-160-4	$19.95 USA/$26.95 Canada
QuarkXPress 3.3 For Dummies™	by Galen Gruman & Barbara Assadi	ISBN: 1-56884-217-1	$19.99 USA/$26.99 Canada
FINANCE/PERSONAL FINANCE/TEST TAKING REFERENCE			
QuickBooks "X" For Dummies™	by Stephen L. Nelson	ISBN: 1-56884-227-9	$19.99 USA/$26.99 Canada
Quicken "X" For DOS For Dummies™, 2nd Edition	by Stephen L. Nelson	ISBN: 1-56884-210-4	$19.95 USA/$26.95 Canada
Quicken "X" For Macs For Dummies™	by Stephen L. Nelson	ISBN: 1-56884-211-2	$19.95 USA/$26.95 Canada
Quicken "X" For Windows For Dummies™, 2nd Edition	by Stephen L. Nelson	ISBN: 1-56884-209-0	$19.95 USA/$26.95 Canada
The SAT I For Dummies™	by Suzee Vlk	ISBN: 1-56884-213-9	$14.99 USA/$20.99 Canada
TurboTax For Windows For Dummies™	by Gail A. Perry, CPA	ISBN: 1-56884-228-7	$19.99 USA/$26.99 Canada
GROUPWARE/INTEGRATED			
Lotus Notes 3.0/3.1 For Dummies™	by Paul Freeland & Stephen Londergan	ISBN: 1-56884-212-0	$19.95 USA/$26.95 Canada
Microsoft Office 4 For Windows For Dummies™	by Roger C. Parker	ISBN: 1-56884-183-3	$19.95 USA/$26.95 Canada
Microsoft Works For Windows 3 For Dummies™	by David C. Kay	ISBN: 1-56884-214-7	$19.99 USA/$26.99 Canada

FOR MORE INFO OR TO ORDER, PLEASE CALL ▸ 800 . 762 . 2974 For volume discounts & special orders please call Tony Real, Special Sales, at 415. 312. 0644

Title	Author	ISBN #	Price
INTERNET/COMMUNICATIONS/NETWORKING			
CompuServe For Dummies™	by Wallace Wang	ISBN: 1-56884-181-7	$19.95 USA/$26.95 Canada
Modems For Dummies™, 2nd Edition	by Tina Rathbone	ISBN: 1-56884-223-6	$19.99 USA/$26.99 Canada
Modems For Dummies™	by Tina Rathbone	ISBN: 1-56884-001-2	$19.95 USA/$26.95 Canada
MORE Internet For Dummies™	by John Levine & Margaret Levine Young	ISBN: 1-56884-164-7	$19.95 USA/$26.95 Canada
NetWare For Dummies™	by Ed Tittel & Deni Connor	ISBN: 1-56884-003-9	$19.95 USA/$26.95 Canada
Networking For Dummies™	by Doug Lowe	ISBN: 1-56884-079-9	$19.95 USA/$26.95 Canada
ProComm Plus 2 For Windows For Dummies™	by Wallace Wang	ISBN: 1-56884-219-8	$19.99 USA/$26.99 Canada
The Internet Help Desk For Dummies™	by John Kaufeld	ISBN: 1-56884-238-4	$16.99 USA/$22.99 Canada
The3 Internet For Dummies™, 2nd Edition	by John Levine & Carol Baroudi	ISBN: 1-56884-222-8	$19.99 USA/$26.99 Canada
The Internet For Macs For Dummies™	by Charles Seiter	ISBN: 1-56884-184-1	$19.95 USA/$26.95 Canada
MACINTOSH			
Mac Programming For Dummies™	by Dan Parks Sydow	ISBN: 1-56884-173-6	$19.95 USA/$26.95 Canada
Macintosh System 7.5 For Dummies™	by Bob LeVitus	ISBN: 1-56884-197-3	$19.95 USA/$26.95 Canada
MORE Macs For Dummies™	by David Pogue	ISBN: 1-56884-087-X	$19.95 USA/$26.95 Canada
PageMaker 5 For Macs For Dummies™	by Galen Gruman & Deke McClelland	ISBN: 1-56884-178-7	$19.95 USA/$26.95 Canada
QuarkXPress 3.3 For Dummies™	by Galen Gruman & Barbara Assadi	ISBN: 1-56884-217-1	$19.99 USA/$26.99 Canada
Upgrading and Fixing Macs For Dummies™	by Kearney Rietmann & Frank Higgins	ISBN: 1-56884-189-2	$19.95 USA/$26.95 Canada
MULTIMEDIA			
Multimedia & CD-ROMs For Dummies™, Interactive Multimedia Value Pack	by Andy Rathbone	ISBN: 1-56884-225-2	$29.95 USA/$39.95 Canada
Multimedia & CD-ROMs For Dummies™	by Andy Rathbone	ISBN: 1-56884-089-6	$19.95 USA/$26.95 Canada
OPERATING SYSTEMS/DOS			
MORE DOS For Dummies™	by Dan Gookin	ISBN: 1-56884-046-2	$19.95 USA/$26.95 Canada
S.O.S. For DOS™	by Katherine Murray	ISBN: 1-56884-043-8	$12.95 USA/$16.95 Canada
OS/2 For Dummies™	by Andy Rathbone	ISBN: 1-878058-76-2	$19.95 USA/$26.95 Canada
UNIX			
UNIX For Dummies™	by John Levine & Margaret Levine Young	ISBN: 1-878058-58-4	$19.95 USA/$26.95 Canada
WINDOWS			
S.O.S. For Windows™	by Katherine Murray	ISBN: 1-56884-045-4	$12.95 USA/$16.95 Canada
Windows "X" For Dummies™, 3rd Edition	by Andy Rathbone	ISBN: 1-56884-240-6	$19.99 USA/$26.99 Canada
PCS/HARDWARE			
Illustrated Computer Dictionary For Dummies™	by Dan Gookin, Wally Wang, & Chris Van Buren	ISBN: 1-56884-004-7	$12.95 USA/$16.95 Canada
Upgrading and Fixing PCs For Dummies™	by Andy Rathbone	ISBN: 1-56884-002-0	$19.95 USA/$26.95 Canada
PRESENTATION/AUTOCAD			
AutoCAD For Dummies™	by Bud Smith	ISBN: 1-56884-191-4	$19.95 USA/$26.95 Canada
PowerPoint 4 For Windows For Dummies™	by Doug Lowe	ISBN: 1-56884-161-2	$16.95 USA/$22.95 Canada
PROGRAMMING			
Borland C++ For Dummies™	by Michael Hyman	ISBN: 1-56884-162-0	$19.95 USA/$26.95 Canada
"Borland's New Language Product" For Dummies™	by Neil Rubenking	ISBN: 1-56884-200-7	$19.95 USA/$26.95 Canada
C For Dummies™	by Dan Gookin	ISBN: 1-878058-78-9	$19.95 USA/$26.95 Canada
C++ For Dummies™	by S. Randy Davis	ISBN: 1-56884-163-9	$19.95 USA/$26.95 Canada
Mac Programming For Dummies™	by Dan Parks Sydow	ISBN: 1-56884-173-6	$19.95 USA/$26.95 Canada
QBasic Programming For Dummies™	by Douglas Hergert	ISBN: 1-56884-093-4	$19.95 USA/$26.95 Canada
Visual Basic "X" For Dummies™, 2nd Edition	by Wallace Wang	ISBN: 1-56884-230-9	$19.99 USA/$26.99 Canada
Visual Basic 3 For Dummies™	by Wallace Wang	ISBN: 1-56884-076-4	$19.95 USA/$26.95 Canada
SPREADSHEET			
1-2-3 For Dummies™	by Greg Harvey	ISBN: 1-878058-60-6	$16.95 USA/$22.95 Canada
1-2-3 For Windows 5 For Dummies™, 2nd Edition	by John Walkenbach	ISBN: 1-56884-216-3	$16.95 USA/$22.95 Canada
1-2-3 For Windows For Dummies™	by John Walkenbach	ISBN: 1-56884-052-7	$16.95 USA/$22.95 Canada
Excel 5 For Macs For Dummies™	by Greg Harvey	ISBN: 1-56884-186-8	$19.95 USA/$26.95 Canada
Excel For Dummies™, 2nd Edition	by Greg Harvey	ISBN: 1-56884-050-0	$16.95 USA/$22.95 Canada
MORE Excel 5 For Windows For Dummies™	by Greg Harvey	ISBN: 1-56884-207-4	$19.95 USA/$26.95 Canada
Quattro Pro 6 For Windows For Dummies™	by John Walkenbach	ISBN: 1-56884-174-4	$19.95 USA/$26.95 Canada
Quattro Pro For DOS For Dummies™	by John Walkenbach	ISBN: 1-56884-023-3	$16.95 USA/$22.95 Canada
UTILITIES			
Norton Utilities 8 For Dummies™	by Beth Slick	ISBN: 1-56884-166-3	$19.95 USA/$26.95 Canada
VCRS/CAMCORDERS			
VCRs & Camcorders For Dummies™	by Andy Rathbone & Gordon McComb	ISBN: 1-56884-229-5	$14.99 USA/$20.99 Canada
WORD PROCESSING			
Ami Pro For Dummies™	by Jim Meade	ISBN: 1-56884-049-7	$19.95 USA/$26.95 Canada
More Word For Windows 6 For Dummies™	by Doug Lowe	ISBN: 1-56884-165-5	$19.95 USA/$26.95 Canada
MORE WordPerfect 6 For Windows For Dummies™	by Margaret Levine Young & David C. Kay	ISBN: 1-56884-206-6	$19.95 USA/$26.95 Canada
MORE WordPerfect 6 For DOS For Dummies™	by Wallace Wang, edited by Dan Gookin	ISBN: 1-56884-047-0	$19.95 USA/$26.95 Canada
S.O.S. For WordPerfect™	by Katherine Murray	ISBN: 1-56884-053-5	$12.95 USA/$16.95 Canada
Word 6 For Macs For Dummies™	by Dan Gookin	ISBN: 1-56884-190-6	$19.95 USA/$26.95 Canada
Word For Windows 6 For Dummies™	by Dan Gookin	ISBN: 1-56884-075-6	$16.95 USA/$22.95 Canada
Word For Windows 2 For Dummies™	by Dan Gookin	ISBN: 1-878058-86-X	$16.95 USA/$22.95 Canada
WordPerfect 6 For Dummies™	by Dan Gookin	ISBN: 1-878058-77-0	$16.95 USA/$22.95 Canada
WordPerfect For Dummies™	by Dan Gookin	ISBN: 1-878058-52-5	$16.95 USA/$22.95 Canada
WordPerfect For Windows For Dummies™	by Margaret Levine Young & David C. Kay	ISBN: 1-56884-032-2	$16.95 USA/$22.95 Canada

ORDER FORM

TRADE & INDIVIDUAL ORDERS
Phone: **(800) 762-2974**
or **(317) 895-5200**
(8 a.m.–6 p.m., CST, weekdays)
FAX : **(317) 895-5298**

EDUCATIONAL ORDERS & DISCOUNTS
Phone: **(800) 434-2086**
(8:30 a.m.–5:00 p.m., CST, weekdays)
FAX : **(817) 251-8174**

CORPORATE ORDERS FOR 3-D VISUAL™ SERIES
Phone: **(800) 469-6616** *ext.* **206**
(8 a.m.–5 p.m., EST, weekdays)
FAX : **(905) 890-9434**

Qty	ISBN	Title	Price	Total

Shipping & Handling Charges

	Description	First book	Each add'l. book	Total
Domestic	Normal	$4.50	$1.50	$
	Two Day Air	$8.50	$2.50	$
	Overnight	$18.00	$3.00	$
International	Surface	$8.00	$8.00	$
	Airmail	$16.00	$16.00	$
	DHL Air	$17.00	$17.00	$

Subtotal ________

CA residents add applicable sales tax ________

IN, MA and MD residents add 5% sales tax ________

IL residents add 6.25% sales tax ________

RI residents add 7% sales tax ________

TX residents add 8.25% sales tax ________

Shipping ________

Total ________

Ship to:

Name ________

Address ________

Company ________

City/State/Zip ________

Daytime Phone ________

Payment: □ Check to IDG Books (US Funds Only)
□ Visa □ Mastercard □ American Express

Card # ________ Exp. ________ Signature ________